Tecumseh

John
Richardson

Matthew Elliott

Roger Hale Sheaffe

Augustus John Foster

The Invasion
of Canada

Books by Pierre Berton

THE ROYAL FAMILY
THE MYSTERIOUS NORTH
KLONDIKE
JUST ADD WATER AND STIR
ADVENTURES OF A COLUMNIST
FAST, FAST, FAST RELIEF
THE BIG SELL
THE COMFORTABLE PEW
THE COOL, CRAZY, COMMITTED WORLD OF THE SIXTIES
THE SMUG MINORITY
THE NATIONAL DREAM
THE LAST SPIKE
DRIFTING HOME
HOLLYWOOD'S CANADA
MY COUNTRY
THE DIONNE YEARS
THE WILD FRONTIER
THE INVASION OF CANADA

PICTURE BOOKS
THE NEW CITY (with Henri Rossier)
REMEMBER YESTERDAY
THE GREAT RAILWAY

ANTHOLOGIES
GREAT CANADIANS
PIERRE & JANET BERTON'S CANADIAN FOOD GUIDE
HISTORIC HEADLINES

FOR YOUNGER READERS
THE GOLDEN TRAIL
THE SECRET WORLD OF OG

The Invasion of Canada

VOLUME ONE: 1812-1813

by PIERRE BERTON

An Atlantic Monthly Press Book
LITTLE, BROWN AND COMPANY   BOSTON

LIBRARY OF CONGRESS CATALOG CARD NO. 80-82299

FIRST AMERICAN EDITION

Endpapers by Tom McNeely
Maps by Geoffrey Matthews

ATLANTIC-LITTLE, BROWN BOOKS
ARE PUBLISHED BY
LITTLE, BROWN AND COMPANY
IN ASSOCIATION WITH
THE ATLANTIC MONTHLY PRESS

Printed and bound in Canada
by
T. H. Best Printing Company Limited

The conquest of Canada is in our power. I trust I shall not be deemed presumptive when I state that I verily believe that the militia of Kentucky are alone competent to place Montreal and Upper Canada at your feet.

Henry Clay, to the United States Senate, February 22, 1810.

CONTENTS

Maps

Maps by Geoffrey Matthews

Cast of Characters

PRELUDE TO INVASION

British and Canadians

Sir James Craig, Governor General of Canada, 1807–11.

Sir George Prevost, Governor General of the Canadas and commander of the forces, 1811–15.

Francis Gore, Lieutenant-Governor of Upper Canada, 1806–17. On leave in England, 1811–15.

Major-General Isaac Brock, Administrator of Upper Canada and commander of the forces in Upper Canada, 1810–12.

William Claus, Deputy Superintendent, Indian Department, Upper Canada, 1806–26.

Matthew Elliott, Superintendent of Indian Affairs at Amherstburg, 1796–97; 1808–14.

Robert Dickson (known as *Mascotapah*, the Red-Haired Man), fur trader. Led Menominee, Winnebago, and Sioux in attack on Michilimackinac.

Augustus Foster, British Minister Plenipotentiary to America, 1811–12.

Americans

Thomas Jefferson, President, 1801–9.

James Madison, President, 1809–17.

William Eustis, Secretary of War, 1809–12.

William Henry Harrison, Governor, Indiana Territory, 1800–1813. Commander of the Army of the Northwest from September, 1812.

William Hull, Governor, Michigan Territory, 1805–12. Commander of the Army of the Northwest, April–August, 1812.

Henry Dearborn, Secretary of War, 1801–9. Senior major-general, U.S. Army, 1812–13.

Henry Clay, Speaker of the House of Representatives, November, 1811. Leader of the War Hawks.

Indian Leaders

The Prophet. Born Laulewausika; later Tenskwatawa.

Tecumseh, the Prophet's older brother, leader of the Indian Confederacy.

THE DETROIT FRONTIER

Isaac Brock's Command: Summer, 1812

Thomas Bligh St. George, Lieutenant-Colonel; commanding officer, Fort Amherstburg.

Henry Procter, Lieutenant-Colonel; succeeded St. George as commanding officer, Fort Amherstburg.

J.B. Glegg, Major; Brock's military aide.

John Macdonell, Lieutenant-Colonel; Brock's provincial aide, Acting Attorney-General of Upper Canada.

Adam Muir, Major, 41st Regiment.

William Hull's Command: Summer, 1812

Duncan McArthur, Colonel, 1st Regiment, Ohio Volunteers.

James Findlay, Colonel, 2nd Regiment, Ohio Volunteers.

Lewis Cass, Colonel, 3rd Regiment, Ohio Volunteers.

James Miller, Lieutenant-Colonel, 4th U.S. Infantry (regular army).

Henry Procter's Command: Winter, 1812–13

Ebenezer Reynolds, Major, Essex Militia.

Roundhead, Wyandot chief.

William Henry Harrison's Command: Winter, 1812–13

James Winchester, Brigadier-General; commander, left wing, Army of the Northwest.

John Allen, Lieutenant-Colonel, 1st Kentucky Rifles.

William Lewis, Lieutenant-Colonel, 5th Regiment, Kentucky Volunteers.

Samuel Wells, Lieutenant-Colonel, 17th U.S. Infantry (regular army).

THE NIAGARA FRONTIER

Isaac Brock's Command: Fall, 1812

Christopher Myers, Lieutenant-Colonel; commanding officer, Fort George.

Roger Hale Sheaffe, Major-General; second-in-command to Brock. Commanded British forces on Brock's death.

Thomas Evans, Brigade Major, Fort George.

John Dennis, Captain, 49th Regiment; commander of flank company defending Queenston.

John Williams, Captain, 49th Regiment.

James Crooks, Captain, 1st Lincoln Militia.

William Holcroft, Captain, Royal Artillery.

Frederic Rolette, Lieutenant, Provincial Marine.

Robert Irvine, Second-Lieutenant, Provincial Marine.

John Brant, Mohawk chief.

John Norton, Captain, Indian Department; leader of Mohawks.

Henry Dearborn's Command: Fall, 1812

Stephen Van Rensselaer, Major-General, New York state militia; senior commander on the Niagara frontier.

Solomon Van Rensselaer, Lieutenant-Colonel; cousin and aide-de-camp to Stephen Van Rensselaer.

John Lovett, Major; aide to Stephen and Solomon Van Rensselaer. In charge of artillery at Fort Grey at Battle of Queenston Heights.

William Wadsworth, Brigadier-General, Upper New York State militia.

Alexander Smyth, Brigadier-General, regular army, Niagara frontier. Replaced Stephen Van Rensselaer following Battle of Queenston Heights.

John Chrystie, Lieutenant-Colonel, 13th U.S. Infantry (regular army).

John Fenwick, Lieutenant-Colonel, U.S. Light Artillery.

John E. Wool, Captain, 13th U.S. Infantry.

Winfield Scott, Lieutenant-Colonel, 2nd U.S. Artillery.

Peter B. Porter, Quartermaster General, Upper New York State. Member of the War Hawk faction in Congress.

Jesse D. Elliott, Lieutenant, U.S. Navy.

The Strategic Significance of Michilimackinac

PREVIEW: Porter Hanks's War

MICHILIMACKINAC ISLAND, MICHIGAN TERRITORY, *U.S.A. The small hours of a soft July morning in 1812.*

The lake is silent, save for the whisper of waves lapping the shoreline. In the starlight, the island's cliffs stand out darkly against the surrounding flatland. In the fort above the village at the southern tip the American commander, Lieutenant Porter Hanks, lies asleep, ignorant of a war that will tragically affect his future. Napoleon has entered Russia; Wellington is pushing toward Madrid; and in Washington, the die has been cast for invasion. But history has passed Hanks by. It is nine months since he has heard from Washington; for all he knows of the civilized world he might as well be on the moon.

The civilized world ends at the Detroit River, some 350 miles to the southeast as the canoe travels. Mackinac Island is its outpost, a minor Gibraltar lying in the narrows between Lakes Huron and Michigan. Whoever controls it controls the routes to the fur country – the domain of the Nor'Westers beyond Superior and the no man's land of the upper Missouri and Mississippi. It is a prize worth fighting for.

Hanks slumbers on, oblivious of a quiet bustling in the village directly below – of low knockings, whispers, small children's plaints quickly hushed, rustlings, soft footsteps, the creak of cartwheels on grass – slumbers fitfully, his dreams troubled by a growing uneasiness, until the drum roll of reveille wakes him. He suspects something is going to happen. He has been seven years a soldier, knows trouble when he sees it, has watched it paddling by him for a week. An extraordinary number of Indians have been passing the fort, apparently on their way to the British garrison at St. Joseph's Island, forty-five miles to the northeast, just beyond the border. Why? The answers are strangely evasive. The Ottawa and Chippewa chiefs, once so friendly, have turned suspiciously cool. On the British side, it is said, the tribes have gathered by the hundreds from distant frontiers: Sioux from the upper Mississippi, Winnebago from the Wisconsin country, Menominee from the shores of Green Bay.

Hanks peers over the palisades of the fort and gazes down on the village below, a crescent of whitewashed houses, following the curve of a pebbled beach. He sees at once that something is wrong. For the village is not sleeping; it is dead. No curl of smoke rises above the cedar-bark roofs;

no human cry echoes across the waters of the lake; no movement ruffles the weeds that edge the roadway.

What is going on? Hanks dispatches his second-in-command, Lieutenant Archibald Darragh, to find out. But he does not need to wait for Darragh's report. Clambering up the slope comes his only other commissioned officer, the surgeon's mate, Sylvester Day, who prefers to live in the village. Dr. Day's breathless report is blunt: British redcoats and Indians have landed at the opposite end of the island. All the villagers have been collected quietly and, for their own safety, herded into an old distillery under the bluff at the west end of town. Three of the most prominent citizens are under guard as hostages.

Hanks reacts instantly to this news: musters his men, stocks his blockhouses with ammunition, charges his field pieces, follows the book. He must know that he is merely playing soldier, for he has fewer than sixty effective troops under his command — men rendered stale by their frontier exile. Presently he becomes aware of a British six-pounder on the forested bluff above, pointing directly into his bastion. Through the spring foliage he can see the flash of British scarlet and — the ultimate horror — the dark forms of their native allies. A single word forms in his mind, a truly terrible word for anyone with frontier experience: massacre — *visions of mutilated bodies, decapitated children, disembowelled housewives, scalps bloodying the pickets.*

Hanks can fight to the last man and become a posthumous hero. If it were merely the aging troops of Fort St. Joseph that faced him, he might be prepared to do just that. But to the last woman? To the last child? Against an enemy whose savagery is said to be without limits?

A white flag flutters before him. Under its protection a British truce party marches into the fort, accompanied by the three civilian hostages. The parley is brief and to the point. Hanks must surrender. The accompanying phrase "or else" hangs unspoken in the air. The hostages urge him to accept, but it is doubtful whether he needs their counsel. He agrees to everything; the fort and the island will become British. The Americans must take the oath of allegiance to the King or leave. His troops are to be paroled to their homes. Until exchanged they can take no further part in the war.

The war? What war? The date is July 17. A full month has passed since the United States declared war on Great Britain, but this is the first Hanks has heard of it. An invasion force has already crossed the Detroit River into Canada and skirmished with the British, but nobody in Washington, it seems, has grasped the urgency of a speedy warning to the western flank of the American frontier. It is entirely characteristic of this senseless and tragic conflict that it should have its beginnings in this topsy-turvy fashion, with the invaders invaded in a trackless wilderness hundreds of miles from the nerve centres of command.

For its dereliction the American government will pay dear. This blood-less battle is also one of the most significant. The news of the capture of Michilimackinac Island will touch off a chain of events that will frustrate the Americans in their attempt to seize British North America, an enter-prise that most of them believe to be, in Thomas Jefferson's much-quoted phrase, "a mere matter of marching."

OVERVIEW
The War of 1812

THE INVASION OF CANADA, which began in the early summer of 1812 and petered out in the late fall of 1814, was part of a larger conflict that has come to be known in North America as the War of 1812. That war was the by-product of a larger struggle, which saw Napoleonic France pitted for almost a decade against most of Europe. It is this complexity, a war within a war within a war, like a nest of Chinese boxes, that has caused so much confusion. The watershed date "1812" has different connotations for different people. And, as in Alice's famous caucus race, everybody seems to have won *something*, though there were no prizes. The Russians, for instance, began to win their own War of 1812 against Napoleon in the very week in which the British and Canadians were repulsing the invading Americans at Queenston Heights. The Americans won the last battle of their War of 1812 in the first week of 1815 – a victory diminished by the fact that peace had been negotiated fifteen days before. The British, who beat Napoleon, could also boast that they "won" the North American war because the Treaty of Ghent, which settled the matter, had nothing to say about the points at issue and merely maintained the *status quo*.

This work deals with the war that Canada won, or to put it more precisely *did not lose*, by successfully repulsing the armies that tried to invade and conquer British North America. The war was fought almost entirely in Upper Canada, whose settlers, most of them Americans, did not invite the war, did not care about the issues, and did not want to fight. They were the victims of a clash between two major powers who, by the accident of geography, found it convenient to settle their differences by doing violence to the body of another. The invasion of Canada was not the first time that two armies have bloodied neutral ground over issues that did not concern the inhabitants; nor has it been the last.

Of all the wars fought by the English-speaking peoples, this was one of the strangest – a war entered into blindly and fought (also blindly) by men out of touch not only with reality but also with their own forces. Washington was separated from the fighting frontier by hundreds of miles of forest, rock, and swamp. The ultimate British authority was an ocean away and the nominal authority a fortnight distant from the real command. Orders could take days, weeks, even months to reach the troops.

Like some other wars, this one began bloodlessly with expressions of civility on both sides and the conviction that it would be over by Christmas. It did not end that way, for horror breeds hatred, and no war (certainly not this one) can be free of atrocity. Nor was it free of bombast. As in most wars, the leaders on both sides were convinced that their cause was just and that the Deity was firmly in their camp, leading them to victory. Slogans about "freedom" and "slavery," "despotism" and "liberty" were batted back and forth across the border like shuttlecocks. Each side believed, or pretended to believe, that the other was held in thrall by a pernicious form of government.

At the outset, it was a gentlemen's war. Officers on opposing sides met for parleys under flags of truce, offered hospitality, exchanged cordialities, murmured the hope that hostilities would quickly end. Belligerents addressed one another in flowery terms. The same men who declared they would never be slaves of the enemy had "the honour to be y'r humble and obedient servant." When Isaac Brock fell at Queenston, the men responsible for his death joined in the general grief. Roger Sheaffe, his successor, expressed in writing his great regret for the wounds suffered by an opposing commander – wounds that put him out of action and helped Sheaffe win the day. "If there be anything at my command that your side of the river cannot furnish, which would be either useful or agreeable...I beg you will be so good as to have me apprised of it," he wrote to the enemy. When the first word of the declaration of war reached the British post at Fort George on the Niagara frontier, its officers were entertaining their American opposite numbers at dinner. They insisted that the meal continue as if hostilities had not commenced, then, with much handshaking and expressions of regret, accompanied their guests to their boats. Within a few weeks, the former dinner companions were ripping through one another's homes and fortifications with red-hot cannonballs.

For a war of thirty months' duration, the casualties were not heavy. In those same years many a European battle counted far more dead and wounded in a single day. But for those who did fall, it was a truly terrible war, fought under appalling conditions far from civilization and medical aid. Those victims who were torn to pieces by cannonballs, their brains often spattering their comrades, might be considered lucky. The wounded endured agonies, banged about in open carts, exposed to blizzards or driving rain, hauled for miles over rutted tracks to the surgeon's table where, with a musket ball clamped between their teeth and when possible a tot of rum warming their bellies, they suffered the horrors of a hasty amputation.

As the war progressed, it grew more vicious. There was savagery on both sides by white frontiersmen as well as Indians, who scalped the fallen sometimes when they were still alive. Men were roasted in flaming buildings, chopped to pieces by tomahawks, sliced open by bayonets, drowned, frozen, or felled by sickness, which took more lives on both sides than all the battles combined. There were times when a third of an army was too ill to fight. The diseases were given vague names like "ague" and "swamp fever," which might mean influenza, pneumonia, malaria, typhus, dysentery, or simply that the combatants were too cold, too weary, or too dispirited to march or even stand. And no wonder: on both sides the armies, especially the citizen soldiers of the militia, were ill equipped for war. Men were forced to trudge through ankle-deep snow and to wade freezing rivers without shoes; to sleep in the open without blankets; to face the Canadian winter lacking mitts and greatcoats, their clothes in tatters, their hands and feet bound in rags, tormented by frostbite in January and insects in June. The military may have seen the war coming, but the politicians were not prepared to pay its price.

At the planning level, the war was marked by incredible bungling. As in so many wars, but especially in this one, the day was often won not by the most brilliant commander, for there were few brilliant commanders, but by the least incompetent. On the American side, where civilian leaders were mixed in with regular army officers, the commands were marked by petty jealousies, vicious infighting, bitter rivalries. On certain memorable occasions, high-ranking officers supposedly fighting the British preferred to fight each other with pistols at dawn. Old soldiers were chosen for command simply because they *were* old soldiers; they acted like sports heroes long past their prime, weary of the contest, sustained only by the glamour of the past, struggling as much against the ambitions of younger aspirants as against the enemy. Some were chosen capriciously. One general was given an important command solely for political reasons – to get him out of the way.

On the Canadian side, where "democracy" was a wicked word and the army was run autocratically by British professionals, there was little of this. Many of these men, however, were cast-offs from Europe. The officers gained their commissions through purchase, not competence. With certain exceptions, the cream of the British Army was with Wellington, fighting Napoleon's forces on the Iberian Peninsula. Aging veterans made up part of the garrison forces in Canada. Boys of fourteen and fifteen fought with the militia. Lacklustre leadership, incompetent planning, timidity and vacillation were too often the concomitants of command on both sides of the border.

The militia on both sides was a rabble. Hastily summoned and hastily trained when trained at all, they fought sometimes reluctantly, sometimes with gallantry. On the Canadian side these citizen soldiers were drilled about three days in a month. They were called up when needed, placed away from the centre of the line, on the flanks (when the line existed at all), and, after an engagement, sent back to their homes and farms until needed once more. The more patriotic signed up for the duration and became seasoned warriors. The American army was a confusion of regular soldiers, state militia, and federal volunteers recruited from the militia for terms of service that ranged from one month to a year or more.

On both sides men thought nothing of leaving the scene of battle to thresh their grain at harvest time. For most of the men who fought it, then, it was a part-time war. Some refused to fight. In spite of the harsh discipline, men on both sides mutinied. Soldiers were shot for desertion, forced to ride bent saplings, to stand barefoot on sharpened stakes, branded, or flogged almost to death. Neither threats nor pleas could stop thousands of American militiamen from refusing to fight on foreign soil. To the dismay of their commanders, these amateur soldiers took democracy at its face value, electing their own officers and, on occasion, dismissing them. In Upper Canada treason worked its slow poison, even invading the legislature. Farmers were hanged for abetting the enemy; tribunes of the people took refuge on foreign soil to raise squads of traitors; dark suspicions, often unfounded, seeped down the concession roads, causing neighbour to denounce neighbour.

The war, like other wars, brought disaster to thousands and prosperity to thousands more. Prices rose; profits boomed. The border might be in flames, its people at each other's throats, but that did not prevent merchants on both sides from crossing over in the interests of commerce. Americans on the eastern shore of Lake Champlain fed the British troops fighting on the western side. Montreal middlemen grew rich supplying the needs of New England. Pork, beef, and grain from Vermont and other states found their way into the commissariats of Upper Canada. Before the invasion came to an end, two out of every three soldiers fighting for the safety and honour of Canada were subsisting on beef brought in by enemy contractors.

In the Atlantic provinces and the neighbouring New England states, the war scarcely existed. On July 3, 1812, the Lieutenant-Governor of Nova Scotia issued a proclamation announcing that his province and New Brunswick would abstain from predatory warfare against their neighbours and that trade would continue "without Molestation." Between Maine and New Brunswick it was more than business as usual; it was frolic as usual. The border town of St. Stephen, realizing that its American neighbour, Calais, could not obtain fireworks for its Independence Day celebration, obligingly helped out with a gift of gun powder.

But on the fighting frontier it was civil war. There is a story that the man who fired the first cannonball across the river during the battle of Detroit killed his best friend on the American side – a legend, possibly, but perfectly plausible. Almost everyone had a friend or a relative on the other side of the border. Sheaffe, the British general, had a sister Margaret in Boston. William Hull, the defender of Detroit, had a brother Isaac living on the Thames. The border was irrelevant; people crossed it as they would a street. Many owned land or had business interests on the other side. One of these was John Askin of Sandwich, Upper Canada, the venerable fur trader and patriarch (various members of whose extensive family will appear from time to time in these pages). During the war, Askin continued to correspond with his friend and kinsman Elijah Brush, the militia commander at Detroit, who was married to Askin's daughter Adelaide. When the Americans invaded Sandwich and Askin was forced to flee, Brush obligingly detailed some of his men to harvest Askin's crops. When Detroit fell, Brush consigned his personal papers, money, and members of his family to Askin's care. None of this prevented Askin's sons, nephews, and grandsons from taking up arms and killing Americans.

They did so reluctantly, for this was a war that almost nobody wanted. The British, who had been embroiled with Napoleon for seven years, certainly did not want it, did not believe it would occur, and in a clumsy, last-minute effort tried to prevent it. The Canadian settlers, struggling to master a forbidding if fertile wilderness, did not want it either; at best it was an interruption, at worst a tragedy. The majority, whenever possible, did their best to stay out of it. Nor did the mass of the American people want to go to war; a great many, especially in the New England states, sat it out; others fought half-heartedly. Congress, in the words of a Kentucky editor, was "driven, goaded, dragged, forced, kicked" into the conflict by a small, eloquent group that Thomas Jefferson dubbed the War Hawks.

America went to war as a last resort because her leaders felt that the nation's honour had been besmirched to a point where any other action would be unthinkable. In their zeal to conquer Napoleon, the British pushed the Americans too far and dismissed their former colonists with an indifference that bordered on contempt, thus repeating the errors of 1776. In that sense, the War of 1812 was a continuation of the American Revolution.

It began with Napoleon, for without Napoleon there would have been no war. (The President, James Madison, remarked after the fact that had he known Napoleon would be defeated his country would have stayed out of it.) Great Britain, fighting for her life against France, was bent on all-out maritime warfare. If a neutral America, reaping the economic benefits, was bruised a little on the high seas, well, that was unfortunate but necessary. America, in British eyes, was a weak, inconsequential nation that could be pushed around with impunity. In the words of the London *Courier*, "two fifty gun ships would be able to burn, sink and destroy the whole American navy."

This attitude was expressed first in the British policy of boarding American ships and impressing American seamen for service in the Royal Navy on the grounds that they were deserters from British service. At least three thousand and perhaps as many as seven thousand fell victim to this practice, which infuriated the country and was one of the two chief causes of the war.

The other was the equally galling Orders in Council, the last enacted in November, 1807, as an act of reprisal against the French. With cool disdain for the rights of neutrals as well as for American sea power, the British warned that they would seize on the open ocean any ship that dared sail directly for a Napoleonic port. By 1812 they had captured almost four hundred American vessels, some within sight of the U.S. coast, and played havoc with the American export trade.

There were other irritants, especially in the more volatile southern and western states, where a serious economic depression was blamed, not without reason, on the British blockade. The slump hit the Mississippi Valley in 1808, shortly after Britain proclaimed the Orders in Council. Prices collapsed. Cotton and tobacco could no longer be exported. This, combined with the growing Indian threat to the frontier settlements, was used to bolster the arguments of those seeking an excuse for war. In Kentucky especially – the most hawkish of states – and in Ohio and the territories, it was widely believed that British agents were goading the various tribes to revolt. There was talk of teaching the Indians a lesson, even driving the British out of North America, thereby breaking the fur monopoly, opening the land to settlement, and strengthening the Union. Certain western expansionists also saw the coming war as one of liberation. It was widely believed that most Canadians wanted to become Americans. If they did not, well, that was their destiny.

In the summer of 1812, with three American armies threatening the border strongpoints – Amherstburg, Queenston, Montreal, and Kingston – the early fall of Upper Canada and the subsequent collapse of Quebec seemed certain. In British North America there were some three hundred thousand souls, in the Union to the south, almost eight million. In Upper Canada, three out of five settlers were newly arrived Americans, people of uncertain loyalties, lured from New York, Pennsylvania, and Connecticut by the promise of cheap land. They

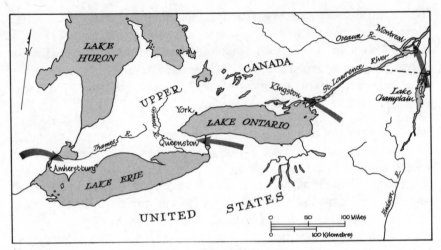

American Invasion Strategy, Summer, 1812

scarcely thought of themselves as British, though they were forced into a token oath of allegiance, and they certainly did not call themselves Canadian. (That word was reserved for their French-speaking neighbours, many of whom lived on American soil in the vicinity of Detroit.) Surely these people would not oppose an invasion by their compatriots!

Nor, on the face of it, would they. There is little evidence of any surge of national pride rippling across the grain fields, swamps, and forests of Upper Canada in the early days of the war; quite the opposite. The main emotion was not patriotism but fear: fear of the invaders who could and did loot the farms to feed themselves; fear of the British regulars, whose task it was to stiffen the backbones of the reluctant citizen soldiers; fear of the Indians; fear of losing a harvest, a homestead, and above all a life. Many of the militia had to be goaded into fighting, while large numbers of settlers expressed pro-American sympathies, sometimes openly, more often privately. It is possible, even probable, that without the war the province would eventually have become another state in the Union. The Americans could have had it by osmosis. But the war intervened.

How was it that a tiny population, badly divided, with little claim to any national sentiment, was able to ward off continued attack by a powerful neighbour with vastly greater resources? There are at least three considerations.

First, the British presence. The regulars were few in number but well disciplined. Raw troops were no match for them. And, thanks to Isaac Brock's prescience, the country was better prepared for war than its enemy.

Second, American ineptness, especially in the war's first, crucial year. The United States was not a military nation. Her leaders were antiquated or inexperienced, her soldiers untrained, her government unready for conflict, her state militia reluctant to fight on foreign soil.

Third, and by no means least, the alliance between the Indians and the British, which led to decisive victories in the campaigns of 1812.

History has tended to gloss over the contributions made by the various tribes – and especially by the polyglot army under the leadership of the Shawnee war chief Tecumseh – in the first year of the war. Yet without the presence of the Indians at crucial turning points in the conflict, much of Upper Canada would surely have been in the hands of the Americans by the spring of 1813, if not sooner. British regulars alone could not have stemmed the tide. To shore up the thinly held garrisons the Indians were essential.

They were often a nuisance. Mercurial and unreliable, indifferent to the so-called civilized rules of warfare, difficult, even impossible to control, they came and went as they pleased, consuming vast quantities of scarce provisions. But as guerrillas they were superb. Their very presence was enough to terrify the Americans into submission.

For this, the United States had itself to blame. Jeffersonian policy, stripped of its honeyed verbiage, was to cheat the Indians out of their hunting-grounds. This thinly disguised thievery alienated the tribes in the Northwest, produced the phenomenon of the Shawnee Prophet, led to the inspired leadership of Tecumseh, and eventually drove thousands of native Americans into the arms of the British, leaving America's left flank dangerously exposed in the war that followed.

The only group of Americans who truly thirsted for war, apart from the handful of congressmen known as War Hawks, were Tecumseh's followers. In revenging themselves on the hated Long Knives they hoped to regain the lands from which they had been driven. It was a wistful fantasy, doomed to failure. One of the several ironies of this foolish and unnecessary war is that the warriors who helped save Canada gained nothing except a few American scalps.

The role of the Indians and that of the British regulars was played down in the years following the war. For more than a century it was common cant that the diverse population of Upper Canada – immigrants, settlers, ex-Americans, Loyalists, Britons, Scots, and Irish – closed ranks to defeat the enemy. This belief still lingers, though there is little evidence to support it. Certainly the old Loyalists and their sons rushed to the colours, and in the capital of York the British aristocracy (whose leading ornament was the Reverend Doctor John Strachan) glowed with patriotic fervour. But the mass of the people were at best apathetic and at worst disaffected. Some five hundred of the latter have been officially identified – men and women who either fled to the other side or supported the enemy by word or deed. Who can guess how many more kept prudently silent or worked in secret for the invaders? The reluctance of the militia to do battle when the war went badly suggests that the number was not small.

Traditionally, a common enemy unites a people in a common cause, especially when family farms are overrun, crops despoiled, homesteads gutted, livestock dispersed. But again there is little evidence of a united front against the enemy on the part of the people who suffered these disasters; it is doubtful if they were any angrier at the Americans than at the British and Indians, who actually caused a third of the devastation. The total bill for war losses came to almost a million dollars at a time when a private soldier's daily pay was twenty-five cents. Compensation was not paid until 1824 and never paid in full. None of that helped make the cause universally popular.

Yet, in an odd way, the war did help to change Upper Canada from a loose aggregation of village states into something approaching a political entity. The war, or more properly the *myth* of the war, gave the rootless new settlers a sense of community. In the end, the myth became the reality. In the long run it did not matter who fought or who did not, who supported the cause or who disdained it. As the years went by and memories dimmed, as old scars healed and old grudges evaporated, as aging veterans reminisced and new leaders hyperbolized, the settlers began to believe that they had repelled the invader almost single-handed. For the first time, Upper Canadians shared a common tradition.

It was a tradition founded to a considerable extent on a rejection of American values – a rejection encouraged and enforced by the same pro-British ruling elite who fed the myth of the people's war and who made sure that the province (and eventually all of Canada) would embark on a course markedly different from that of the people to the south. They were, after all, "the enemy," and to be pro-American in post-war Upper Canada was to be considered vaguely traitorous. This attitude affected everything – politics, education, civil liberties, folkways, architecture. It affects us to this day, even those who do not think of themselves as Upper Canadian.

Thus the war that was supposed to attach the British North American colonies to the United States accomplished exactly the opposite. It ensured that Canada would never become a part of the Union to the south. Because of it, an alternative form of democracy grew out of the British colonial oligarchy in the northern half of the continent. The Canadian "way" – so difficult to define except in terms of negatives – has its roots in the invasion of 1812–14, the last American invasion of Canada. There can never be another.

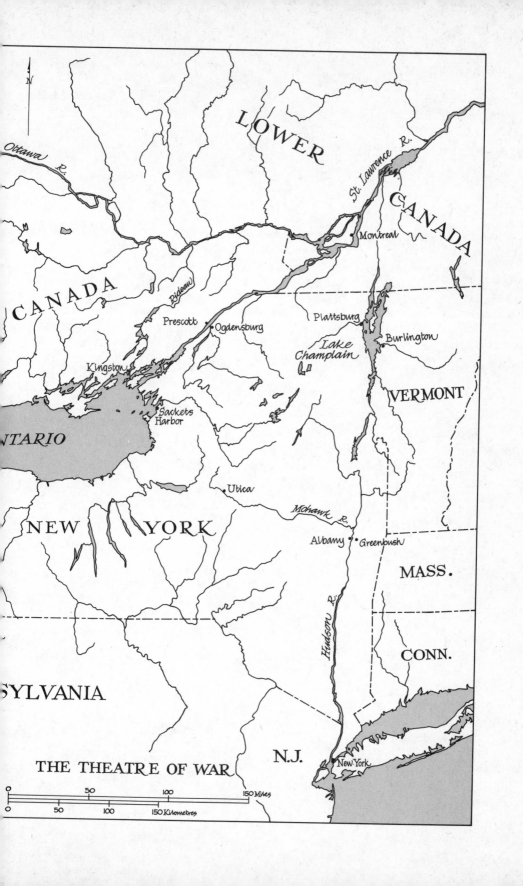

THE THEATRE OF WAR

I

PRELUDE TO INVASION:
1807–1811
The Road to Tippecanoe

See our western brothers bleed!
British gold has done the deed.
Child and Mother, Son and Sire,
Beneath the tomahawk expire.

> – *On the Battle of Tippecanoe,*
> National Intelligencer, *July 11, 1812.*

ABOARD THE BRITISH FRIGATE *Melampus*, lying off Hampton Roads, Chesapeake Bay, Virginia, February, 1807.

The decks are clear of officers, for an entertainment is in progress. Music. Laughter. The tinkling of glass and silver. Leaning over the rail is an oddly assorted trio of impressed American seamen. One, William Ware, is an Indian from Pipe Creek, Maryland, a one-time wagoner who had served aboard the U.S. frigate *Chesapeake* until he was impressed, fifteen months ago, by a British boarding party in the Bay of Biscay. Another, Daniel Martin, is a Negro from Westport, Massachusetts, impressed at the same time as Ware. The third is a white man, John Strachan, also from Maryland, pressed on board *Melampus* off Cape Finisterre in 1805.

For two years Strachan has been waiting for a chance to escape, and now it has come. Because of the festivities, every boat except the captain's gig has been hoisted in. There is no chance of pursuit. Strachan and his companions leap into the gig and cast off. Somebody hails them: where do they think they're going? They shout back that they are going ashore, and as they pull for land, a hail of musket balls rains upon them. Unharmed, they reach Lowell's Point, haul the boat onto the beach, carefully place the oars on the seats, give three hearty cheers, and dash away to freedom.

It is short lived. At Hampton Roads, the three sign up for service in the American navy aboard *Chesapeake* and soon find themselves at the centre of the "*Chesapeake* incident," which brings America to the very brink of war with Britain.

The date is June 22, 1807. The American frigate is a few hours out of Hampton Roads, bound for the Mediterranean. As she passes a British squadron anchored in American waters, a fifty-gun man-of-war, *Leopard*, the flagship of Vice-Admiral George Berkeley, detaches itself and slips off in pursuit. James Barron, *Chesapeake*'s captain, knows exactly what is happening: the British dander is up; the captain of *Melampus* wants his men back. On the streets and quays of Hampton Roads, where British and American sailors and officers mingle, the presence of known deserters has not gone unnoticed. The Royal Navy has been especially infuriated by one Jenkin Ratford, a British deserter intemperate enough to shout gibes and insults at his former officers. In vain the British have asked for Ratford; the Americans have refused to give him up. Nor will they return the three men who stole the captain's gig from *Melampus*. Now, all four men have thumbed their noses at the British and are safely aboard *Chesapeake*, which is heading out to sea, its lower decks apparently crowded with other British deserters, all well known to the captain but concealed under assumed names. This is too much for Vice-Admiral Berkeley. Off goes an order to every British vessel to stop *Chesapeake* at sea and take the deserters by force. As it happens, Berkeley's own flagship is the one that will essay the task.

Stopped by *Leopard*, Captain Barron cannot believe the British will attack and so makes no attempt to clear *Chesapeake*'s decks for action. A young lieutenant comes aboard, demands the return of the four men – the only ones he can identify since the *Melampus* deserters have not taken false names and Ratford, who is now called Wilson, is easily recognizable from his earlier intemperate encounters. Barron, who has all four hidden below, feigns ignorance. After some fruitless talk, the Englishman leaves. *Leopard*'s captain continues the discussion through a loud hailer. When Barron refuses his demands, *Leopard* fires a shot across *Chesapeake*'s bow. No reply.

It is too late now for the British to back down. *Leopard* opens fire with her port guns, and a ten-minute cannonade follows. Twenty-one cannonballs tear into *Chesapeake*'s starboard hull. Another shatters her mizzen-mast. Her mainmast topples, her sails are shredded, shrouds cut away, spars splintered. By the time Barron strikes his colours, three of his men are dead and eighteen, including himself, are wounded. The British board the battered frigate but refuse to accept it as a prize. All they want are the three deserters from *Melampus* and the wretched Ratford, whom they will proceed to hang at Halifax to their own great satisfaction and the fury of the American public.

The Americans are in a ferment. The man on the street finds it intolerable that British boarding parties can seize sailors from American ships on the pretext that they are Royal Navy deserters, then force them to serve in the hell hole of a British man-of-war. There is some doubt that the *Melampus* trio *were* impressed (the British insist they volunteered, and certainly two are thoroughgoing rogues), but that evidence is kept secret. To the Americans it is a flagrant attack on national sovereignty. In the words of John Quincy Adams, "No nation can be Independent which suffers her Citizens to be stolen from her at the discretion of the Naval or military officers of another."

But to Britain, impressment is a necessity. Her navy has trebled in size since the war with France began. She cannot man her ships with volunteers. Worse, thousands of British sailors are deserting to American merchantmen, lured by better conditions and better pay — four times as much. Who can blame the British for recapturing bona fide deserters in time of war? Certainly not the British public; they applaud it.

But who is a bona fide deserter? Americans and British speak the same language, look alike, dress alike. British boarding parties, hungry for men, do not always bother with the niceties. They grab whom they can. No one knows how many American seamen have been pressed into British service (the figures run between three and seven thousand), but it takes only a few publicized cases to enrage the American public. Even when a case of mistaken identity is proved and admitted, months elapse before the seaman is returned. Service in the British Navy is like a prison sentence or worse, for as Samuel Johnson once remarked, "no man will be a sailor who has contrivance enough to get himself into jail; for being in a ship is being in jail, with the chance of being drowned." Some American seamen have been known to cut off their hands to avoid impressment; some who refuse to serve are flogged unmercifully by the British; and a few, including the three escapees from *Melampus*, are prepared to risk death to get away.

Their recapture from *Chesapeake* touches off an international incident. Riots break out in New York, where a mob does its best to dismantle a British ship. The British consul is forced to seek police protection while an English diplomat on a tour of the Union finds it prudent to assume an incognito. Public meetings throughout the land denounce the perfidious British. In Quebec, Lieutenant-Colonel Isaac

Brock notes that "every American newspaper teems with violent and hostile resolutions against England, and associations are forming in every town for the ostensible purpose of attacking these Provinces."

The future general is right: the country is emotionally ready for war, more so, in fact, than it will be in 1812. But its leaders are not ready. The President, Thomas Jefferson, threatens war but does not mean it – a dangerous posture. "If the English do not give us the satisfaction we demand, we will take Canada which wants to enter the Union," he tells the French minister to Washington. The Frenchman takes these bellicose remarks languidly and reports to Paris that he does not believe that either Jefferson or his foreign secretary, James Madison, wants war. Jefferson bans British warships from American waters, enforces an embargo preventing all ships from sailing out of U.S. ports for foreign destinations, and hopes that these threats will force the British to abandon impressment. But the British do not yield and the embargo is a failure. The public's ardour for war cools quickly. The crisis passes.

But there is one group of Americans whose ardour does not cool. In the oak and hickory forests of Ohio, in the cornfields along the Maumee and the Wabash, on the banks of the Au Glaize and on the Tippecanoe in Indiana Territory, there is a quickening of the blood, a stirring of old and painful memories of the defeat at Fallen Timbers and the surrender of hunting grounds at Greenville. The war fever, filtering through to the tribes of the Old Northwest, revives the dying hopes of the native Americans for a new conflict in which they will fight side by side with the British against the Long Knives. The Northwest has been at peace since General Anthony Wayne's decisive victory in 1794. But the *Chesapeake* incident acts as a catalyst to animate the tribes and shatter the calm that has prevailed north of the Ohio for more than a decade.

Among the British, the incident produces two oddly contrary reactions. On the one hand it convinces them that America will continue to bluff rather than fight, a conclusion that will lead to calamitous results in 1812. On the other hand they are encouraged to strengthen their defences in Canada against possible invasion. This is Isaac Brock's doing. "It is impossible to view the late hostile measures of the American government towards England, without considering a rupture between the two countries as probable to happen," the young lieutenant-colonel writes, and as the crisis smoulders, he goes on to press for a better trained and expanded militia and for repairs to the

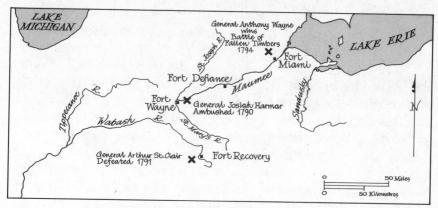

American-Indian Battles, 1790–1794

fortress of Quebec. He does not easily get his way, but from this time on the prospect of an American invasion is never far from that determined and agile mind. When and if the Americans come, Isaac Brock intends to be ready.

•

VINCENNES, INDIANA TERRITORY, August 17, 1807. William Henry Harrison is delivering his gubernatorial message to the legislature.

"The blood rises to my cheek," he cries, "when I reflect on the humiliating, the disgraceful scene, of the crew of an American ship of war mustered on its own deck by a British lieutenant for the purpose of selecting the innocent victims of their own tyranny!"

Harrison's cheeks are sallow, but the blood must rise to them with fair frequency. It rises again as he contemplates the malefactions of British Indian agents, who he is convinced are goading the Indians to violence and murder on the frontier, "for who does not know that the tomahawk and scalping knife of the savage are always employed as instruments of British vengeance. At this moment, fellow citizens, as I sincerely believe, their agents are organizing a combination amongst the Indians within our limits, for the purpose of assassination and murder...."

By British agents Harrison means certain members of the British Indian Department in Upper Canada, especially Thomas McKee, Simon Girty (the "White Indian"), and, worst of all, Matthew

Elliott, the Pennsylvania Irishman who defected to the British during the Revolutionary War and led Indian ambushes that wiped out American detachments. The American frontiersmen will not soon forget that Elliott and Girty watched while the Delaware slowly tortured and burned to death Colonel William Crawford, after wiping out most of his men. So great is the hatred of Elliott in Detroit, it is said, that he hesitates to cross the river from his palatial home in Amherstburg for fear of being tarred and feathered. He has been one of the key members of the British Indian Department; no white man has so much influence with the tribes, especially the Shawnee. At the moment he is under a cloud, dismissed for financial irregularities. Nonetheless he remains a force and will soon be back in the good graces of the British.

But the Governor of Indiana cannot get it into his head that it is not so much British conniving that has caused the Indians to rise up sporadically in defence of their lands as his own policies and those of his political superiors in Washington. Harrison is not a mean or wicked man. His sense of justice is outraged when white juries refuse to convict one of their own for killing a native. The Governor's problem is that he wants to turn the Indians into farmers in order to deprive them of their hunting-grounds. That is official government policy, laid down by Thomas Jefferson, who is not a mean or wicked man either but who, in a private letter to Harrison outlining that policy, sounds very much like a hypocrite:

"Our system is to live in perpetual peace with the Indians, to cultivate an affectionate attachment from them by everything just and liberal which we can do for them within the bounds of reason...."

So far so good, despite the qualification. But then:

"When they withdraw themselves to the culture of a small piece of land, they will perceive how useless to them are the extensive forests, and will be willing to pare them off...in exchange for necessaries for their farms and families. To promote this...we shall push our trading houses, and be glad to see the good and influential individuals among them in debt, because we observe that when these debts go beyond what the individuals can pay, they become willing to lop them off by a cession of lands...."

To this machiavellian scheme Jefferson appends a chilling warning. Should any tribe refuse the proffered hand and take up the hatchet, he says, it will be driven across the Mississippi and the whole of its lands confiscated.

It all fits neatly with Harrison's own ambitions, which include statehood for Indiana. To become a state the territory needs a population of at least sixty thousand, and there are fewer than half that number living in small settlements connected by trails cut through the jungle of the forest. To attract more people, Harrison requires the lure of cheap land. The Indians have the land. The Governor must secure it for the settlers, one way or another.

The blood rises to Harrison's cheek once more when he recalls how he has been bested by that one-eyed savage known as the Shawnee Prophet. The Prophet has sprung from nowhere and in two years has become more notorious than any other Indian. He seems to have invented a new religion, one tenet of which is the heresy, to the whites, that all Indian lands are held in common and cannot be divided, sold, or bartered away. The ritual includes much mumbo-jumbo – shaking, jerking, and dancing about (derived perhaps from the white sect known as the Shakers, who have helped spark a religious revival on the frontier). It is not confined to any particular tribe – indeed, it has split some tribes – but appears to attract the younger braves who are acting in defiance of their elders. To Harrison, this so-called Prophet is an imposter and a fool who "speaks not the words of the Great Spirit but those of the devil and of the British agents." Harrison sees British agents everywhere, in every wigwam, behind every bush, plotting and conniving.

Yet even Harrison must concede that the Prophet is not quite a fool, for on one memorable occasion he has fooled Harrison, who thought to discredit him by demanding that he produce a miracle.

"Who is this pretended prophet who dares to speak in the name of the Great Creator?" the Governor asked, in a message to the Delaware. "Examine him.... Demand of him some proof...some miracles.... If he is really a prophet, ask him to cause the sun to stand still, the moon to alter its course, the rivers to cease to flow.... No longer be imposed on by the arts of an imposter...."

To which the Prophet replied, blandly, that he would accept the challenge and cause the sun to darken. He even named the date and the time – 11:32 in the forenoon of June 16, 1806.

The story is told and retold. How the Prophet sent word to Indians for leagues around to assemble on June 16; how the day dawned clear; and how, an hour before the appointed time, the Prophet, gowned in flowing robes, stepped from his wigwam into the circle of onlookers and at exactly 11:32 pointed his finger at the sun.

Slowly the sky darkens; the dark shadow of the moon crosses the solar face; a murmur rises from the assembly. The Prophet waits, then calls out to the Great Spirit to remove his hand from the source of all light. The call is heeded. Pandemonium!

It is too much. Harrison, the soldier-scholar-statesman, outsmarted by an aborigine who managed to learn in advance the date of a solar eclipse! The long, moody features grow moodier. He will continue to call the Prophet a fool, but he knows that he is up against a force beyond his power to control. "This business must be stopped," he tells the head men of the Shawnee. "I will no longer suffer it." But he will have to suffer it, for the chiefs themselves cannot control the Prophet; he has put some of them in fear of their lives. When several of the older Delaware chiefs refused to go along with the new religion, the Prophet had them murdered. His messengers have carried his words to all tribes within a radius of six hundred miles, and the message is always the same: follow me; rid yourself of your old leaders; and (this is Harrison's real concern) don't give up the land.

The Prophet's land policy collides with Harrison's ambition. The tall slender governor with the sombre face and the brooding eyes is no frontier bumpkin or upstart party hack of limited vision. He looks like a scholar and is one. With his long nose and gaunt features he could, in different guise, be mistaken for a Roman priest or an Italian noble in a Renaissance painting. He is slightly out of place here in the wilderness, for he was reared in luxury on a Virginia plantation, trained in Greek and Latin, and has a passion for military history, whose lessons he hopes to absorb.

He has always been a little out of place. He might have made a good doctor, but his medical studies were cut short by a fall in the family fortunes. In the army, where young officers were drinking themselves into early graves, the temperate ensign buried himself in his books. He will not let himself be seen out of control, through drink or through any other vice, for he has the Harrison name to uphold: his father was one of the signers of the Declaration of Independence.

He was a good soldier – he might, someone once said, have been another Washington. He fought with the "mad general," Anthony Wayne, at the Battle of Fallen Timbers, the epic victory over the Indians that won twenty-five thousand square miles of territory for the white men. Now, a soldier no more but with a soldier's bearing and a soldier's outlook, he is, at thirty-nine, a rising politician, living like an aristocrat in the backwoods in his vast brick mansion – the first in the territory – on the outskirts of Vincennes. He calls it Grouseland; with its hand-carved mantels and doors, its four great chimneys, its thirteen rooms and its circular staircase, it has made him proud but property poor.

His problems are only beginning. He has heard from Billy Wells, the Indian commissioner and interpreter at Fort Wayne, that eighty Indians under the Prophet's leadership have gathered at Greenville. Wells, an old frontiersman married to the sister of Little Turtle, the Miami chief, sends a messenger to Greenville to deal with the Prophet and ask him and his supporters to come to Fort Wayne for a parley. The answer is given, not by the Prophet but by his elder brother, a handsome war chief with flashing hazel eyes. It is astonishingly blunt:

"Go back and tell Captain Wells that my fire is kindled on the spot appointed by the Great Spirit above, and if he has anything to communicate to me, *he* must come *here*; and I will expect him in six days from this time."

This is not the way Indians talk to white men. This is the way white men talk to Indians. For the first time an Indian has sent back a message that is stinging in its style and insulting in its content.

William Henry Harrison will hear from the Prophet's brother again and again in the years to come, for he is one of the most extraordinary native North Americans of whom history has record.

His name is Tecumseh, and six years later in the second year of the war, he and Harrison will meet face to face in mortal combat.

●

WASHINGTON, D.C., August, 1807. Augustus John Foster, aide to the British minister to the United States, has just dispatched a letter to his mother bewailing his "sad disappointment" over the *Chesapeake* affair. It is not the incident itself that disturbs him – like every upper-class Englishman, he is convinced that the Royal Navy acted correctly – but the cruel turn of fate that has forced him to remain in the United States, "a land of swamps and pawnbrokers," and especially in Washington, "a sink of imagination."

Foster, who has spent four years at the British legation, cannot wait to shake Washington's red gumbo from his boots, but the country is in such an uproar that he cannot leave while there is the slightest danger of a rupture between the two nations. Personally, he dismisses the chance of war, cannot conceive that anyone in this ridiculous capital village would have the temerity to challenge the British lion. Still, as he has informed his mother, the Americans keep themselves in a constant ferment: "anything enflames them." He must remain at his post until tempers calm down.

He is an apple-cheeked young aristocrat of twenty-seven with the typical upper-class Englishman's view of Americans. To describe them, in his letters home, he beggars the lexicon of every defamatory epithet. Americans are "consummate rascals," "ragamuffins and adventurers," "the scum of every nation on earth."

"Corruption, Immorality, Irreligion, and, above all, self-interest, have corroded the very pillars on which their Liberty rests."

Clearly, Foster was not bred for America. His father was a Member of Parliament. His mother, an earl's daughter, lives with the Duke and Duchess of Devonshire in an amiable *ménage à trois*. His aunt is married to the Earl of Liverpool. After the London of Mrs. Siddons and Lord Byron, of Turner and Gainsborough, the tiny capital of seven thousand souls must indeed seem a sinkhole. Just seven years old, it has become the butt of jokes – a wretched community of bogs and gullies, broken tree stumps, piles of brushwood and refuse, ponds, potholes, and endless gluelike mud, which mires the carriages on Pennsylvania Avenue and makes sensible communication all but impossible. Paving is non-existent; the streets are mere ruts. Wells are the only source of water; there is no public supply. Petty thieves and burglars abound. Pigs and cattle wander the paths that pass for avenues. The climate is intolerable, the swamps malarial.

Above this morass, each on its separate hillock, rise, incongruously, two jerry-built Greek temples yet unfinished: the Capitol and the Executive Mansion. The columns in the former are so weak they crack under the weight of the visitors' gallery; the latter is still unplastered, its timber already rotting. The roofs of both are so badly constructed that they leak embarrassingly in every rainstorm. Even the politicians hate Washington. Some, if they had their way, would move the seat of government to Philadelphia.

Foster cannot stomach the politicians. Why, there are scarcely five congressmen who look like gentlemen! He treats them all with an amused disdain, which the more perceptive must find maddening. But then, one legislator has actually urinated in his fireplace! Foster relishes that tale. And then there was the business of the caviar that he had his *maitre d'* prepare from Potomac sturgeon. On serving it to his

44

congressional guests, he found them spitting it out by the mouthful, having mistaken it for black raspberry jam. Is this what democracy has wrought? "The excess of democratic ferment in this people is conspicuously evinced by the dregs having got to the top," he reports to Whitehall. It is unthinkable that these grotesque politicians would dare declare war on his country!

Whitehall agrees. The outcry over the *Chesapeake* incident subsides, and by mid-October Foster feels able to escape from the country in which he believes he has sacrificed the four best years of his life. He would not return, he declares, were he to be paid ten thousand pounds a year. But return he will in 1811, a Yankeephobe, singularly blind to the impending war, the wrong man in the wrong place at the wrong time.

Foster's smug views are typical. He is scarcely back in London, reporting the state of affairs in Washington, when the British make a second move to enrage the Americans. Having called Jefferson's bluff, they proceed to tighten their blockade of the French ports. Spencer Perceval's government issues new Orders in Council forbidding neutral ships on pain of seizure to trade with Europe except through Britain. Any vessel that tries to enter any port controlled by Napoleon without first touching at Britain (and paying the required duties and taxes) will be treated as an enemy.

The British are clearly prepared to go beyond the accepted rules for dealing with non-belligerents. They will, if necessary, seize American shipping in the open seas as well as within territorial limits. In no other way can they hope to throttle the French.

In American eyes this is an intolerable return to colonial days. Using the excuse of war, the British are attempting to monopolize the commerce of the world – or so the Americans believe. The Orders represent a clear threat to the fledgling nation. Has the War of Independence been for nothing?

It is clear from Britain's maritime policy that she holds the new union in contempt. To Englishmen, Americans are all uncouth frontiersmen with little breeding and no culture, "less popular and less esteemed among us than the base and bigotted Portuguese, or the ferocious and ignorant Russians," in the words of the *Edinburgh Review*. The British ruling class believes, with Foster, that the Americans will not fight, and, believing that, thinks nothing of goading the former colonists to fury. "America," declares Lord Sidmouth, the Lord Privy Seal, "is no longer a bugbear; there is no terror in her threats."

For the moment, the policy works. In this yeasty winter of 1808 – the year of Goethe's *Faust* and Beethoven's Fifth Symphony – America will not go to war over the Orders in Council or the *Chesapeake* affair. The country is badly divided. The Federalist opposition centred largely in the New England states is staunchly opposed to any violent solution. Yet the country's honour has been slighted, her morale badly bruised, and there are some in the Congress who cannot forget the insult and will not let their colleagues forget. They are Republicans, mainly from the southwestern interior and the frontier states. Soon they will be known as the War Hawks, and the time is coming when they will prevail.

●

FORT AMHERSTBURG, UPPER CANADA, July 11, 1808. One thousand Indian warriors and one hundred chiefs are gathered on the Canadian side of the Detroit River to hear the Lieutenant-Governor of Upper Canada, Francis Gore, cautiously and delicately extend the hand of British friendship. A genial figure, he is in his fortieth year, the smooth face gone slightly to flesh, the cheeks pink from good living. He is careful to play down the possibility of war; that might excite his listeners to premature violence – the last thing the British want. But if war should come, the Indians will be needed.

"I am sure, my Children, that it is quite unnecessary for me to call to your remembrance the faithful assurance with which the King, your Father, has so uniformly complied with all his Engagements and Promises made to your Forefathers and yourselves in former times. . . .

"Nothing is required of you in return for your Great Father's benevolence and religious regard to his promises, but a renewal and faithful observance of the engagements made by your ancestors and yourselves. . . .

"I will not offend you by entertaining the smallest doubt of your readiness on all occasions, when called upon to prove your affectionate attachment to the King, your Great Father. . . .

"I came not to invite you to take up the Hatchet, but I wish to put you on your guard against any attempt that may be made by any enemy whatever to disturb the peace of your Country. . . ."

It is the *Chesapeake* affair that has brought the Lieutenant-Governor to Amherstburg – that and the whisper of a threat from Napoleon that the French may once again take an interest in North America. Since the end of the Revolution, the British have tended to neglect the Indians. Now it is time to mend fences. But the task is complicated: how to regain the affection of the natives, take advantage of their antagonism to the Americans, subtly include them in plans for the defence of Canada, yet at the same time give Washington no cause to believe that British agents are stirring up the tribes to attack? The council at Amherstburg, to which Gore comes late, has been going on for ten days. The public manifestations of friendship and goodwill are innocuous. But who knows what is said to the Indians in private?

Gore cannot even be sure that his listeners will be given an accurate account of what he is saying, for he speaks in English, his remarks interpreted by the superintendent-general of the British Indian Department, William Claus, and his deputy, Matthew Elliott. Elliott has just been reinstated in the key post of Amherstburg, and when the Lieutenant-Governor announces his restoration to favour there are grunts of approval from his audience. In their ritual reply, the Wyandot, senior to all the tribes, express pleasure: "We can place confidence in and rely on him as a man of experience."

It is through Elliott that the government's new Indian policy will be channelled. And he will interpret Whitehall's directives in his own way, according to his prejudices. These are well known: he is pro-Indian, especially pro-Shawnee, and violently anti-American. If war comes it is in Elliott's personal interest that the British win, and not merely for reasons of patriotism. Word has reached him that if the Yankees capture Fort Amherstburg, they intend to kill him and two of his colleagues.

On and off, he has been a member of the Indian Department since the days of the Revolution when he fought with the Shawnee against the Americans. (It remains a secret to the day of his death that he once acted as an emissary for the Americans to try to keep the Shawnee neutral before hostilities began.) Even while out of favour he has acted unofficially for the department, for he is part of that clique, like a band of brothers who follow their own conventions—men who have spent long years with the tribes, who speak the languages fluently, who have lived with Indian women, fathered Indian children, attended Indian councils, fought when necessary on the Indian side. It is a family compact: son often follows father in the service, and the sons are sometimes of mixed blood.

It is toward the Shawnee, especially, that the officers of the Indian Department lean—"that contemptible tribe...always more insolent and troublesome than any other," in the words of Elliott's nemesis, Captain Hector McLean. It was McLean's observation, in 1799, that "the whole of the Officers of the Department are indeed in some way connected with this tribe either by Marriage or Concubinage." That is certainly true of Elliott, who has fathered two sons by a Shawnee woman and often taken Shawnee chieftains as guests under his roof.

Captain McLean was the cause of Elliott's dismissal, under a cloud, in 1798. The scandal revolved around the traditional British practice of dispensing annual "presents" to the tribes – food, dry goods, tools, weapons. McLean, then in command at the fort, was convinced that Elliott was adding to his departmental pittance by diverting a generous portion of government largess to his own use. How else could he stock his extensive farm with cattle and feed and clothe some fifty servants and slaves? Trapping the slippery Elliott became a minor obsession with McLean. His chance came in the winter of 1797 when he was able to prove that the agent had requisitioned supplies for 534 Indians in a settlement whose total population was only 160. On this evidence Elliott was dismissed.

But now, in 1808, the government, set on a new and more aggressive course, finds it cannot do without him. Elliott's successor, Thomas McKee, son of his old comrade Alexander McKee, is a hopeless drunkard who cannot be depended upon to preside over delicate negotiations. Even before his official reappointment, Elliott has been working for the government without McKee's knowledge, dispatched on a secret mission to sound out the major chiefs in private: to impress upon them "with Delicacy and caution" that England expects their aid in the event of war and to remind them that the Americans are out to steal their lands. And who better than Elliott to invite the Prophet to attend the Amherstburg council? He, of all the Indian agents, knows the family most intimately; his chief clerk is married to the Prophet's sister. So here he is, back in charge again, his honour restored by Gore's convenient fiction that the charges against him were never proved.

A strange creature, this Elliott, Gore must feel – rather ugly and more than a little haughty, swarthy, with small features and a pug nose – a black Donegal Irishman transplanted early into the American wilderness, a rough diamond who has experienced everything, shrunk from nothing. There are Americans who believe that he and Alexander McKee took more scalps after General Arthur St. Clair's disastrous defeat by Little Turtle in 1791 than did the Indians. He cannot read or write; it is an effort for him to put his signature to a document; a clerk accompanies him everywhere to handle his extensive business. He has been a justice of the peace and is now a member of the legislature of Upper Canada, the richest farmer in the region. Though he is in his seventieth year, he will be quite prepared to lead his troops into battle in the war to come.

Elliott had expected the Prophet to travel to Amherstburg for the council, but the Prophet does not appear. In his stead comes his older brother, Tecumthe or Tecumseh, of whom the British have little if any knowledge. Of all the chieftains present at Amherstburg, only this tall catlike Shawnee is in favour of war with the Americans, as Gore, in his letter to his superior, Sir James Craig, the Governor General of the two Canadas, makes clear:

"The Prophet's brother, who is stated to me to be his principal support and who appears to be a very shrewd intelligent man, was at Amherstburg while I was there. He told Colonel Claus and Captain Elliott that they were endeavouring to collect the different Nations to form one settlement on the Wabash about 300 miles South West of Amherstburg in order to preserve their country from all encroachment. That their intention at present is not to take part in the quarrels of White People: that if the Americans encroach upon them they are resolved to strike – but he added that if their father the King should be in earnest and appear in sufficient force they would hold fast by him."

Tecumseh makes it clear that he does not fully trust the British. The Indians have long memories. They have not forgotten how, when Mad Anthony Wayne defeated them at Fallen Timbers in 1794, the British closed the gates of nearby Fort Miami, and he now reminds Elliott of the number of chiefs who fell as a result. Tecumseh is ready to fight beside the British, but on his own terms. If they are preparing to use him for their own ends (as they are) he is also planning to use them for his.

•

FORT WAYNE ON THE MAUMEE RIVER, September 22, 1809. William Henry Harrison has ridden deep into Indian territory to bargain for land. He is hungry for it. At Vincennes he has felt himself cramped, hemmed in, frustrated in his ambition. The country to the south of the capital is sunken and wet; the sere prairie to the northwest will not be fit for settlement for many years. But just

Harrison's Purchase

beyond the Indiana border, twenty-one miles to the north along the eastern bank of the Wabash, lie three million acres of farm land, the hunting-grounds of the tribes. Harrison means to have it all, has already secured the agreement of the President, James Madison, Jefferson's successor, who makes one stipulation only: get it as cheaply as possible.

The Governor has travelled on horseback for 350 miles on one of those tireless peregrinations for which he is so well fitted, temperamentally as well as physically. He has summoned the chiefs of the affected tribes – the Miami, Delaware, Eel, Potawatomi – to a great council here at Fort Wayne. But he has not summoned the Shawnee, for they are nomads and, in Harrison's view, have no claim to the land.

The council fire is lit. Eleven hundred tribesmen, squatting in a vast circle, listen as Harrison speaks against the murmur of the Maumee. Four sworn interpreters translate his message: the European war has ruined the price of furs, therefore the tribes must adopt a new way of life. The government will buy their lands, pay for them with a permanent annuity. With that income they can purchase domestic animals and become farmers. The Indians, says Harrison, wrongly blame their own poverty and the scarcity of game on the encroachment of white settlers – but that is not the true cause of their misfortunes. The British are to blame! It is they who have urged the wanton destruction of game animals for furs alone.

The chiefs listen, retire, drink Harrison's whiskey, wrangle among themselves. The Potawatomi, who are the poorest and most wretched of the tribes, want to sell; the Delaware waver. But the Miami are inflexible. The British have urged them to hold the lands until they are surveyed and can be sold at the going price of two dollars an acre. Harrison is offering a mere fraction of that sum. Why should they take less?

To counter this recalcitrance, Harrison summons all his histrionic abilities and at the next council fire on the twenty-fifth presents himself in the guise of a patient but much-injured father, betrayed by his own offspring:

"My Children: My Heart is oppressed. If I could have believed that I should have experienced half of the mortification and disappointment which I now feel, I would have entreated your Father the President to have chosen some other Representative to have made known his wishes to you. The proposition which I have made you, I fondly hoped would have been acceptable to all. . . . Is there some evil spirit amongst us?" This evil spirit, Harrison makes clear, is British.

The speech rolls on. Ironically, Harrison is urging tribal solidarity – Tecumseh's crusade – though for very different reasons. War with Great Britain is never far from his mind. The solidarity he proposes must include, also, the white Americans. ("The people upon the other side of the big water would desire nothing better than to set us once more to cut each other's throats.")

He ends with a remarkable pledge:

"This is the first request your new Father has ever made you. It will be the last, he wants no more of your land. Agree to the proposition which I now make you and send on some of your wise men to take him by the hand. He will set your Heart at ease. He will tell you that he will never make another proposition to you to sell your lands."

The palaver lasts for five more days, and in the end Harrison persuades the Miami to give up the idea that the land is worth two dollars an acre. "Their tenaciousness in adhering to this idea," he comments, "is quite astonishing and it required no little pains to get them to abandon it." And, he might have added, no little whiskey. A drunken frolic follows, in which one of the Miami braves is mortally wounded.

Harrison is jubilant. "The compensation given for this cession of lands. . .is as low as it could possibly be made," he writes to Washington. ". . .I think. . .upon the whole that the bargain is a better one for the United States than any that has been made by me for lands south of the Wabash." As soon as the treaty is ratified and a sales office opened "there will be several hundred families along this Tract."

Well may Harrison savour his triumph. The annuities paid the Indians for relinquishing the land are minuscule: the Miami, who get the most, will receive a total of only seven hundred dollars a year. To pay all the annuities forever the government will not have to set aside more than fifty thousand dollars. At two dollars an acre – the price the settlers will pay – the land is potentially worth six million dollars. Thanks to Harrison the government has made an enormous paper profit. No wonder, when his third term of office ends, a grateful legislature recommends him for a fourth, praising his "integrity, patriotism and firm attachment to the general government."

There remains one small cloud on the horizon: Harrison has ignored the Shawnee. By spring the cloud looms larger. The Prophet and his brother Tecumseh, furious with the old chieftains, refuse to concede that any land cession is valid unless approved by all the tribes. The Great Spirit, so the Prophet says, has directed him to collect all the Indians at the mouth of the Tippecanoe, where it joins the Wabash, whereupon one thousand tribesmen forsake their elders and flock to the new settlement, appropriately named Prophet's Town. With the Indians in ferment, Harrison does not dare put surveyors on the newly purchased land. Settlement comes to a standstill. Families flee the frontier. More will leave "unless the rascally prophet is driven from his present position or a fort built somewhere on the Wabash about the upper boundary of the late purchase."

It is not easy to cow the Prophet into submission. Some of the old chiefs have tried, but "this scoundrel does not appear however to be intimidated." In fact, the old chiefs are in fear of their lives. Harrison, determined to threaten his adversary with a show of force, sends for a detachment of regular troops. There is much bustling about with the local militia in Vincennes – constant musterings, parades and reviews – which serves only to increase the panic of the white settlers. Finally, Harrison dispatches his interpreter, James Barron, with a letter intended to convince the Prophet of the folly of taking up arms against the United States:

"Our bluecoats are more numerous than you can count, and our hunting shirts are like leaves of the forests or the grains of sand on the Wabash. Do not think that the red coats can protect you, they are not able to protect themselves, they do not think of going to war with us, if they did in a few moons you would see our flags wave on all the Forts of Canada."

Barron is lucky to escape with his life. The Prophet receives him, surrounded by Indians of different tribes, gazes upon him in silence and contempt for several minutes, then spits out his defiance:

"...You...are a spy. There is your grave. Look on it!" And points to the spot on which the interpreter is standing.

At this moment, there emerges from the Indian lodges a tall figure in fringed deerskin who takes the frightened Barron under his wing and asks him to state his business. Barron reads Harrison's message, which concludes with a canny invitation: if the Shawnee can prove title to the ceded lands then, of course, they will be returned to the tribe. It is a hollow promise, for there is no title as white men understand the term. But Harrison's message invites the Prophet to come to visit him: if his claim is just, the Governor will personally escort him to the President.

But it is not the Prophet who will lead the delegation to Vincennes. A new warrior is assuming leadership – the tall Indian who again that night saves Barron's life from a group of squaws sent to tomahawk him. Harrison has not yet met him, would not know him to see him, is only now becoming aware of his presence. Someone who has encountered him has described him to the governor "as a bold, active, sensible man, daring in the extreme and capable of any undertaking." He is the Prophet's brother, whom Harrison now sees as "the Moses of the family, really the efficient man" – Tecumseh, the Leaping Panther.

●

VINCENNES, INDIANA TERRITORY, August 16, 1810. Governor Harrison is seated in an armchair on his estate of Grouseland in the shade of a canopy on the southwest side of the great brick mansion that has all but beggared him. To pay the bills for its construction he has been forced to give up four hundred acres of prime land; but then, some might say, he wants the Shawnee (for whom he is waiting) to give up much more.

The Shawnee have kept him waiting for some days and the Governor is growing impatient. He has made much of this assembly, inviting the town's leading citizens and their ladies, territorial officers and supreme court justices, all arranged like chess pieces on the lawn, in the canopy's shade, guarded by a platoon of soldiers.

If Harrison is nervous, his long features do not reveal it. He operates under a strict maxim – never show fear in front of an

Indian. This particular Indian, however, has become uncommonly difficult. Harrison had asked him to come to Vincennes with a small escort, but Tecumseh, who does not take instructions from white men, arrived with more than three hundred armed and painted warriors. That was Saturday. Harrison wanted to start the council on Monday, but Tecumseh would not be hurried. Suspecting treachery, he sent his spies and informers to work through the community, warning of possible trouble. Now it is Thursday; he is coming at last, accompanied by thirty warriors, their faces smeared with vermilion war paint, all armed with tomahawks and clubs.

Tecumseh advances under the curious scrutiny of the dignitaries — a handsome figure, tall for his tribe (at least five foot ten), with an oval rather than an angular face, his complexion light copper, his nose handsome and straight, his mouth "beautifully formed like that of Napoleon." Everyone who has met him notices his eyes, which are a clear, bright hazel under dark brows, and his teeth, which are white and even. He is naked to the waist, his head shaved save for a scalp lock. He walks with a brisk elastic step in spite of a bent leg fractured and imperfectly set after a youthful fall from a pony. There are some who think him the finest specimen of a man they have ever seen, but no authentic likeness exists on paper or canvas, for Tecumseh refuses to have his portrait painted by a white man.

He halts, looks over the assemblage, sees the soldiers, feigns anger, pretends to suspect treachery. He will not go near the canopy, not because he fears the soldiers but because he wishes to place himself on an equal footing with his adversary. He intends to speak as in a council circle, which puts every man on the same level.

The game continues. Harrison's interpreter, Barron, explains that it will be a nuisance to rearrange the seats. Tecumseh disagrees; only the whites need seats, the Indians are accustomed to sitting on the ground: "Houses are made for white men to hold councils in. Indians hold theirs in the open air."

"Your father requests you sit by his side," says Barron, indicating the Governor.

Tecumseh raises an arm, points to the sky.

"*My* father! The Great Spirit is my father! The earth is my mother — and on her bosom I will recline." And so sits cross-legged on the ground, surrounded by his warriors.

The problem is that Tecumseh refuses to act like a Harrison Indian. Nor does he act like a white man. He is unique and knows it. On his endless missions to other tribes, in his dogged attempt to forge an Indian confederacy, it is necessary for him to say only "I am Tecumseh." That is enough to explain his purpose.

This attitude disconcerts Harrison. In his reports to Washington he tries to shrug off Tecumseh: his speeches here at the great council, he says, are "insolent and his pretensions arrogant." Yet he is forced to take him seriously. The talks drag on for days; but when the Shawnee war chief speaks, the Governor listens, for this half-naked man in the deerskin leggings is one of the greatest orators of his time.

His reputation has preceded him. He is known as a consummate performer who can rouse his audience to tears, laughter, fury, action. Even those who cannot understand his words are said to be held by the power of his voice. White men who have heard him speak at past councils have struggled to describe his style: in 1806 at a council at Springfield, Ohio, "the effect of his bitter, burning words...was so great on his companions that the whole three hundred warriors could hardly refrain from springing from their seats. Their eyes flashed, and even the most aged, many of whom were smoking, evinced the greatest excitement. The orator appeared in all the power of a fiery and impassioned speaker and actor. Each moment it seemed as though, under the influence of his overpowering eloquence, they would abruptly leave the council and defiantly return to their homes."

Like his physical presence, Tecumseh's oratory is, alas, filtered through the memories of eyewitnesses. Even the best interpreters cannot keep up with his flights of imagery, while the worst garble his eloquence. Occasionally, in the printed record—admittedly imperfect—one hears faintly the echoes of that clear, rich voice, calling across the decades:

"It is true I am Shawnee. My forefathers were warriors. Their son is a warrior. From them I take only my existence. From my tribe I take nothing. I am the maker of my own fortune. And oh! that I might make that of my red people, and of my country, as great as the conceptions of my mind, when I think of the Spirit that rules the universe....

"The way, and the only way, to check and stop this evil, is, for all the red men to unite in claiming a common and equal right in the land; as it was at first; and should be yet; for it never was divided, but belongs to all, for the use of each. That no part has a right to sell, even to each other, much less to strangers who want all and will not do with less....

"Sell a country! Why not sell the air, the clouds and the great sea, as well as the earth? Did not the Great Spirit make them all for the use of his children?"

In this three-hour speech at the great council of Vincennes, Tecumseh threatens to kill any chief who sells land to the white man:

"I now wish you to listen to me. If you do not it will appear as if you wished me to kill all the chiefs that sold you the land. I tell you so because I am authorized by all the tribes to do so. I am the head of them all. I am a Warrior and all the Warriors will meet together in two or three moons from this. Then I will call for those chiefs that sold you the land and shall know what to do with them. If you do not restore the land you will have a hand in killing them."

But from his opening words it is clear that Tecumseh feels that he is not getting through to Harrison:

"Brother, I wish you to listen to me well—I wish to reply to you more explicitly, as I think you do not clearly understand what I before said to you. I will explain again...."

He is like a patient parent, indulging a small unheeding child. But Harrison will never understand, cannot understand. Land is to him private property, circumscribed by fences and surveyors' pins, tied down by documents, deeds, titles. He wants to be fair, but he cannot comprehend this Indian. The land has been bought from its rightful owners and paid for. It is purely a business matter.

Now it is the Governor's turn to speak. He ridicules the idea of a single Indian nation, dismisses the Shawnee claim to ownership of the disputed lands (the Shawnee, he points out, come from farther south), praises the United States above all other nations for a long record of fair dealing.

The Indians listen patiently, waiting for the translations. Not far away on the grass lies the Potawatomi chief Winemac, in fear of his life at Tecumseh's hands, for he is one of those who has agreed to cede the land. He hides in his buckskins a brace of pistols, a gift from the Governor to guard him from assassination. A sergeant and twelve soldiers, originally detailed to guard the assembly, have moved off a distance to escape the searing sun.

The Shawnee translation of Harrison's remarks ends. The Potawatomi translation begins. Suddenly Tecumseh rises and, with violent gestures, starts to shout. Harrison notes, with concern, that Winemac is priming his pistols. John Gibson, the Indiana secretary, who understands the Shawnee tongue, whispers to Lieutenant Jesse Jennings of the 7th Infantry to bring up the guard quickly: "Those fellows mean mischief." Tecumseh's followers leap to their feet, brandishing tomahawks and war clubs. Harrison draws his sword. A Methodist minister runs to the house, seizes a rifle, and prepares to protect the Governor's family. Up runs the twelve-man guard, muskets ready. Harrison motions them to hold their fire, demands to know what Tecumseh is saying. The answer is blunt: the Governor is a liar; everything he has said is false; the United States has cheated the Indians. The angry Harrison banishes Tecumseh and his followers from Grouseland. They leave in a fury, but the following day, his anger spent, Tecumseh apologizes.

What is the meaning of this singular incident? Had Tecumseh planned a massacre, as some believe, only to be faced down by Harrison and his troops? That is unlikely. It is more probable that, hearing the translation of Harrison's words, he briefly lost his remarkable self-possession. It is also possible that it was a carefully staged part of a plan to convince Harrison of Tecumseh's strength and leadership.

Harrison, mollified by the apology, visits Tecumseh at his camp on the outskirts of Vincennes and finds the Shawnee in a totally different mood. The menacing savage has been transformed into a skittish adversary. The two sit together on a bench, Tecumseh talking all the while and edging closer to the governor, who is forced to move over. Tecumseh continues to talk, continues to crowd Harrison, who presently finds himself on the very end of the bench. Harrison at length protests. The Shawnee laughs: how would he like to be pushed right off, as the Indians have been pushed off their lands by white encroachment?

But beneath this burlesque Harrison recognizes a firmness of purpose that makes him apprehensive. As the council proceeds Tecumseh makes it clear that he intends to prevent, by force if necessary, the lands ceded at Fort Wayne from falling into the hands of the whites. His final words are unequivocal:

"I want the present boundary line to continue. Should you cross it I assure you it will be productive of bad consequences."

Harrison has no choice but to halt the surveys of the disputed territory. He will not get his two dollars an acre until the power of the Shawnee brothers is broken forever.

•

WHO ARE THESE SHAWNEE BROTHERS? Harrison may well ask himself. Where have they sprung from? What was it that produced from one Indian tribe and from the same parents the two most compelling native leaders of their time? What has made them rise above their own fellows, their own kin, so that their names are familiar to all the tribes from Michilimackinac to the borders of Florida?

The two do not even look like brothers. If Tecumseh is grudgingly admired, the Prophet is universally despised. To the white romantics one is a "good" Indian, the other "bad" – the noble savage and the rogue native, neat stereotypes in the bosom of a single family. Part of the contrast is physical. Tecumseh is almost too handsome to be true; his younger brother is ugly, awkward, and one-eyed, a handkerchief masking the empty socket, mutilated in childhood by a split arrow. One is a mystic, mercurial and unpredictable, the other a clear-eyed military genius. Yet the two are indivisible, their personalities and philosophies interlocking like pieces of an ivory puzzle.

In looking forward to a new future for the tribes, the brothers are gazing back upon an idyllic past when the vast hunting-grounds were open to all. The idea of land held in common springs directly from the Shawnee experience and must have been held by others before them. Always partially nomadic, the Shawnee were deprived of any share of the profits from lands sold to white men in Kentucky. The sedentary Iroquois pocketed the cash while the advancing pressure of settlement forced the Shawnee northward and westward always onto lands occupied by other tribes. For years now they have been hunting over the disputed territory east of the Wabash, but in Harrison's conventional view they do not "own" it because the Miami were there first. Tecumseh's own wanderings underline the Shawnee dilemma. He has no fixed home but has moved northward from settlement to settlement, from Kentucky to Indiana to Ohio to Prophet's Town on the Tippecanoe. Men with such a history must feel the land belongs to all.

Unlike the Prophet, Tecumseh is a warrior. The major influence in his life was his older brother, Cheeseekau, fourteen years his senior and clearly a replacement for his father, who died when Tecumseh was an infant. Cheeseekau taught him to hunt with bow and arrow (nurturing in him a contempt for firearms, which frighten away deer), to fight with a tomahawk, and to develop his scorn and hatred of the white man, especially white Americans. From the age of fifteen,

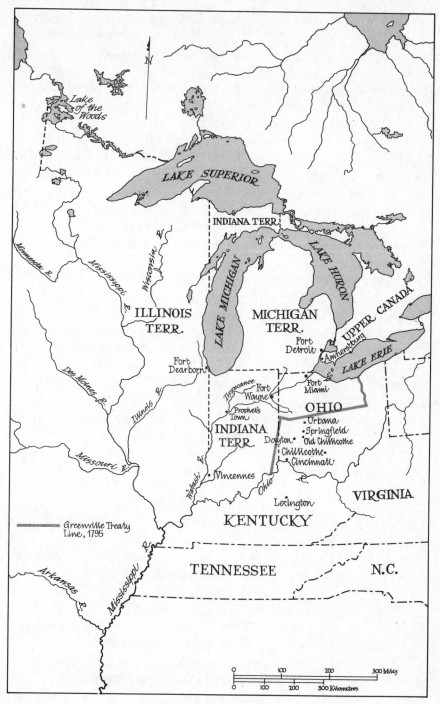

Tecumseh's Frontier

when he survived his first skirmish at his brother's side against the Kentucky volunteers, he has done battle with American frontiersmen and American soldiers. He has fought in every major engagement, rising to band leader after Cheeseekau's death in the Cherokee war in 1792 and emerging unscathed two years later at the disastrous Battle of Fallen Timbers, when another brother fell to an American musket ball.

Yet his closest companion for fifteen years was a white youth, Stephen Ruddell, who has become a Methodist missionary to the Shawnee. Captured by the tribe during the Revolution and adopted into a Shawnee family, young Ruddell was present on the famous occasion when, at sixteen, Tecumseh impassively watching a white prisoner being consumed by the slow fire of the stake, rose up and in a speech that foreshadowed later eloquence swore he would never again allow such horror in his presence.

It is this mixture of savagery and compassion that baffles men like Harrison. In battle, stripped naked save for a breech cloth, his face daubed with ochre, his tomahawk stained with blood, Tecumseh is demonic. Yet Ruddell remembers that from his boyhood he was "remarkable...for the dignity and rectitude of his deportment." He does not like to take prisoners in battle, but when he does he treats them with humanity. Nor will he allow the killing of women and children.

Like his younger brother, he has managed to conquer alcohol, not as the result of the mystical experience that transformed the Prophet from an idler and a wastrel into a native messiah but as a simple act of will. Alcohol befuddled his ambition, interfered with the clarity of his vision.

For similar reasons he has managed to free himself from the tyranny of sex. To him, women are inferior creatures; he treats them with courtesy but will not hunt in their company. And like alcohol, they may divert him from his purpose. As a young man he realized his own attraction to the tribal beauties but was determined not to be ensnared. "The handsome are now anxious for me," he told a white acquaintance, "and I am determined to disappoint them."

His first wife, Manete, whom he married at twenty-eight, was a mixed blood, considerably older than he and certainly no beauty. From her as from all his other women he demanded affection and absolute obedience. The day of reckoning came when he asked her to make him a pouch to hold his war paint. She told him she did not know how and offered to find a friend who did. It was the end of the marriage. Tecumseh snatched back the materials, declared that he would save her the trouble, gave her some presents, and banished her forever.

Another wife – the Shawnee are allowed as many as they wish – received a similar rebuff. Tecumseh had killed a turkey and invited friends to dine; he was discomfited to find a few feathers clinging to the fowl when his wife served it. After his guests had gone, he handed her a bundle of clothing and ordered her to leave. Tears, entreaties, promises to do better next time all failed to move him. "I am ashamed of you," said Tecumseh. "We must separate." He did not see her again.

One woman, it is said, intrigued him above all others: Rebecca Galloway, a white girl of sixteen, the daughter of a literate frontiersman at Old Chillicothe, Ohio. She spoke his language, taught him English, introduced him to the Bible, Alexander the Great, Shakespeare's plays (his favourite was *Hamlet*). The passionate Shawnee fell in love; he brought her gifts (a silver comb, a birchbark canoe, furs, venison), called her Star of the Lake, asked for her hand in marriage offering thirty silver brooches as a lure. She was agreeable but made one condition: he must give up the Indian life, adopt white customs and dress. Tecumseh struggled with this dilemma, but his decision was foreordained. He could not bring himself to adopt a course that would cost him the respect of his people. Reluctantly they parted, never to meet again.

Now he is determinedly single. His last wife, White Wing, a Shawnee woman whom he married in 1802, parted from him in 1807. There would be no more women in Tecumseh's life. He is wedded irrevocably to an ideal.

He dreams Pontiac's ancient dream of an Indian confederacy stretching from Florida to Lake Erie – a confederacy strong enough to resist white pressure. To that end he is prepared to travel astonishing distances preaching to the tribes – to the Kickapoo, Wea, Creek, Wyandot, Sauk, Fox, Potawatomi, Miami, Choctaw, Osage and other Indian bands who, like Balkan communities, argue and squabble among themselves, to their own misfortune and the white man's benefit. The nucleus of this alliance already exists at the mouth of the Tippecanoe where the disaffected members of half a dozen tribes have flocked in response to the mystic summons of Tecumseh's younger brother.

The Prophet's background is as remarkable as Tecumseh's, though quite different. Born after his father's death, he was raised by a sister who clearly favoured his older brother. While Tecumseh was dazzling his fellow tribesmen with his skill as a hunter and, later, his prowess as a warrior, the future Prophet, born Laulewausika, was a layabout. He seemed to be a man with no future, no ambition. Then, with the suddenness of a rocket's flare, he changed, overcome by a sense of sin. There was talk of a trance, a visit to the Great Spirit, a vision in which he saw a forked road before him – misery in one direction, happiness in the other. What brought about this miraculous transformation that caused him to be as one reborn? There are only hints, but it is believed in Vincennes that the Shaker preachers, who were influential in the area (their new home only a few miles distant), had their effect. The new name that he adopted to symbolize his reform, Tenskwatawa, is translated as "I am the door," a phrase used by Jesus, and much of his preaching, which began in 1805, resembles fundamentalist Christianity. He urges his followers to give up strong liquor (as he himself did instantly), to stop beating their wives, to cease intertribal warfare, to renounce crimes of theft.

But there is something more, which suggests that the Prophet is in the mainstream of a mystical movement going back to the Delaware prophet who, in 1762, laid the basis for Pontiac's confederacy. The same movement will go forward to future prophets including the most influential of all, Wovoka of the Paiutes, who in the late eighties will spread the ritual of the Ghost Dance across the nation.

These native messiahs invariably appear during the death struggles of a threatened culture; their authority is supernatural, their message nostalgic: their people are to return to the old customs and rid themselves of the white man's ways. Tenskwatawa, the Open Door, preaches that his followers must revert to the clothing, the implements, the weapons, the foods that were in use before the Europeans reached North America. Implicit in this philosophy is a rejection of the white man. Harrison has been told, specifically, by two Indian messengers that the Prophet preaches that "the Great Spirit will in a few years destroy every white man in America."

Tecumseh has been fighting white Americans since 1783; how much has he contributed to the Prophet's thoughts? Harrison cannot know, but it is clear to him that at some time in the first decade of the century the two brothers, who like, respect, and listen to one another, have come together in their thinking. The Prophet's followers become

Tecumseh's followers; onto the Prophet's religion is grafted the politics of the older brother. It is a dangerous combination; Harrison cannot suffer it much longer, especially with the Indians leaning toward the British. The time is ripe for a preventive war.

●

FORT AMHERSTBURG, UPPER CANADA, November 15, 1810. Matthew Elliott sits in the council circle on the parade ground overlooking the wooded islands in the Detroit River and contemplates his dilemma. With him are the officers of the 100th Regiment, his clerk, George Ironsides (married to one of Tecumseh's sisters), James Girty, an Indian Department interpreter, and some two hundred Potawatomi, Ottawa, Winnebago, Sauk, and Fox. They have come to hear Tecumseh speak, and it is Tecumseh's words that illustrate Elliott's dilemma. The Indian Department has plainly done its work too well.

The Shawnee war chief has in his hands a great belt of wampum — thousands of small coloured shells sewn together — given to his predecessors by the British after the defeat of the French, a talisman, sacred in Indian eyes, symbolizing a treaty of friendship between the British and the natives.

"Father," says Tecumseh, "I have come here with the intention of informing you that we have not forgot (we can never forget) what passed between you English Men and our Ancestors — And also to let you know our present determination. . . .

"Father we have a belt to show you, which was given to our Kings when you laid the French on their back. Here it is, Father; on one end is your hand, on the other, that of the Red people. . .and in the middle the hearts of both. This belt, Father, our great Chiefs have been sitting upon ever since, keeping it concealed. . . . Now the Warriors have taken all the Chiefs and turned their faces toward you, never again to look towards the Americans; and we the Warriors now manage the affairs of our Nation; and we sit at or near the Borders where the Contest will begin.

"Father — It is only five Years ago that I discovered this Belt and took it from under our Kings. You Father have nourished us, and raised us up from Childhood we are now Men, and think ourselves capable of defending our Country, in which cause you have given us active assistance and always advice — We now are determined to defend it ourselves, and after raising you on your feet leave you behind, but expecting you will push towards us what may be necessary to supply our Wants...."

The belt is passed around so that all may examine it. It shows two hands, dark against a white background (the Indian hand darker than the British) outstretched in friendship. As the belt moves round the circle, Tecumseh declares that his followers will never quit their father or let go his hand.

The translation is awkward, but the meaning is clear. The younger warriors who follow the Prophet and his brother have overridden the advice of their elders and are bent on war with the Americans; they want the British to help them. Elliott, it seems, has been too successful in implementing the government's Indian policy. His instructions were to win the tribes over to the British side. Well, he has done that. The difficulty is that in turning the Indians against the Americans and toward the British, he and his colleagues have brought the country to the brink of an Indian war.

Elliott is in a delicate position and knows it. If war should come, the Indians have been told, Elliott will be its messenger. The previous July he had told a Miami chief: "My son, keep your eyes fixed on me; my tomahawk is up now; be you ready but do not strike until I give the signal." The Indians are more than ready. Patience is not among their virtues; how does one keep them keyed up to fight, yet hold them back from action for months, perhaps years? For Elliott, it is an impossible task.

He is an old man, into his seventies, trying to act like a young man. This year he has taken his first legal wife, an Irish girl, Sarah Donovan, half a century his junior. No doubt she sees him as a father, for she married him shortly after the death of her own father, a schoolmaster. But it is no token relationship; she will bear him two sons.

He is wealthy enough to retire, has been for a generation. He is by far the richest farmer in the area, though farmer is scarcely the word for Elliott, who runs three thousand acres as a plantation with a staff of overseers, clerks, and several score slaves, both Indian and Negro. Some of the latter go back thirty years to his raids in Kentucky with Alexander McKee and the Girty brothers. The Indians have made Elliott a fortune. Some of the land on which his handsome home rests was bought directly from the Wyandot and Ottawa tribes in contravention of British government policy (but winked at by his superiors, who have so often winked at his activities).

64

His mansion, with its neat lawn, ornamented by tree clumps running down to the river, is furnished as few homes are. He has enough flatware and plate to serve one hundred people. His wife has at least fifty dresses and thirteen pairs of kid gloves. He himself owns eleven hats. There are no banks in the Canadas; one's wealth is stored in the attic. In one trunk, Elliott keeps nine hundred pounds' worth of silver plate.

It does not occur to the old man that he can retire. This is his life; he knows no other. He is close to exhaustion, but the job must be done. He dictates a note to his superior, Superintendent William Claus. Restraint is necessary, of course, he agrees, but – a little wistfully – would it not be proper to keep up "the present spirit of resistance"? Claus sends the note to Gore at York, who passes it on to the ailing governor general, Sir James Craig, at Quebec, who chews over it for months.

Craig is faced with the same dilemma; his own policy has brought about this problem. A distressing possibility confronts him: what if the Indians should attack prematurely and the British be blamed? His conscience tweaks him, and on November 25 he writes to the British chargé d'affaires in Washington asking him to warn the American secretary of state that he suspects the Indians are planning to attack the American frontier. That surreptitious message forms one of the strands in the skein of events that will lead to a bloody dénouement the following year at Prophet's Town on the Tippecanoe.

As the Governor General attempts to conciliate the Americans at the possible expense of the Indians, his underlings at Amherstburg have been attempting to conciliate the Indians at the possible expense of the Americans. For the traditional dispensation of presents includes a generous supply of hatchets, guns, and ammunition, ostensibly for hunting game but equally serviceable in the kind of frontier skirmish that is already arousing Yankee dander. Within a year the discovery of some of these weapons will fuel the growing American demand for war.

The ceremony follows a time-honoured ritual. Each chief hands Matthew Elliott a small bundle of cedar sticks to the number of his tribe, cut in three lengths to represent men, women, and children. With these, Elliott's clerks determine how the gifts are to be dispersed. Now the presents are brought from the storehouse and heaped around a series of stakes, each of which bears the name of a tribe. Elliott makes a brief speech, calls the chiefs forward, points to the mounds of gifts – bales of blankets and calico cloth, great rolls of tobacco, stacks of combs, scissors, mirrors, needles, copper pots, iron kettles – and weapons. On a signal the young men dart forward, carry the presents to the waiting canoes. Within three minutes the lawn is empty.

This lavish distribution disturbs the new commander of the British forces in Upper Canada, Brigadier-General Isaac Brock. How, he asks Governor General Craig, can the Indians be expected to believe the British are strictly neutral "after giving such manifest indications of a contrary sentiment by the liberal quantity of military stores with which they were dismissed"? Brock is critical of Elliott – "an exceedingly good man and highly respected by the Indians; but having in his youth lived a great deal with them, he has naturally imbibed their feelings and prejudices, and partaking in the wrongs they continually suffer, this sympathy made him neglect the considerations of prudence, which ought to have regulated his conduct." In short, Elliott can help to start an Indian war.

Sir James Craig agrees. He insists that Elliott and his colleagues "use all their influence to dissuade the Indians from their projected plan of hostility, giving them clearly to understand that they must not expect assistance from us."

Many months pass before Elliott is aware of this policy. Sir James is mortally ill with dropsy, his limbs horribly swollen, his energies sapped. Weeks go by before he is able to reply to Elliott's request to maintain "the present spirit of resistance." More weeks drag on before Elliott receives them. The regular mail service from Quebec extends no farther than Kingston and goes only once a fortnight. In the rest of Upper Canada post offices are almost unknown. Letters to York and Amherstburg often travel by way of the United States. It is March, 1811, before Elliott receives Craig's statement of neutrality and the Indians have long since gone to their hunting camps, out of Elliott's reach. He will not be in touch again for months. British policy has done an about-face on paper, but the Indians, goaded to the point of revolt by Harrison's land hunger, are not aware of it. Events are starting to assume a momentum of their own.

•

VINCENNES, INDIANA TERRITORY, July 30, 1811. Once again in the shade of an arbour on his estate of Grouseland, William Henry Harrison faces his Shawnee adversary in a great council. The stalemate continues over the disputed lands which, with Tecumseh's threat still hanging over the territory, remain unsurveyed. The Governor is convinced that Tecumseh has come to Vincennes to strike a blow for the Indian cause – that here on Harrison's home ground he intends to murder all the neutral chiefs and, if necessary, the Governor himself. He has ignored Harrison's request to come with a small party; three hundred warriors have arrived on the outskirts of Vincennes by land and water.

The town is in a panic; already in the back country some roving bands of Indians have been slaughtering white families encroaching on their territory. Harrison has responded with a show of force. On the day of Tecumseh's arrival, July 27, he pointedly reviews some seven hundred militiamen. He places three infantry companies on duty, moving them about in such a way that the Indians will believe there are five. He shifts his dragoons about the town at night on foot and horseback in order to place Tecumseh's followers in a state of "astonishment and Terror."

Tecumseh strides into the council with 170 warriors, all armed with knives, tomahawks, bows and arrows. Harrison meets him guarded by a force of seventy dragoons. Each man carries a sabre; each has two pistols stuck in his belt. In this warlike atmosphere the council begins, only to be interrupted by a violent downpour.

Harrison is impatient to end it. He is tired of palaver; a plan of action is forming in his mind. If the Indians want war he intends to give it to them, whether Washington condones it or not. He refuses to negotiate further over the new purchase; that, he tells Tecumseh, is up to the President. But if Tecumseh really wants peace, as he claims, then let him turn over to Harrison the Potawatomi braves in his camp who murdered four white men the previous fall.

Tecumseh speaks. His response, even Harrison admits, is artful. He affects to be surprised that the white men should be alarmed at his plans. All he wants to do is to follow the American example and unite the Indian tribes in the same way that the white men united the various states of the Union. The Indians did not complain of *that* union; why should the white men complain when the Indians want to accomplish the same thing? As for the murderers, they are not in his camp, and anyway, should they not be forgiven? He himself has set an example of forgiveness by refusing to take revenge on those who have murdered his people.

Again he makes it clear that he will not allow surveyors to split up the newly purchased territories for sale to white settlers. Harrison responds bluntly: the moon will fall to earth before the President will suffer his people to be murdered, and he would put his warriors in petticoats before he would give up the land fairly acquired from its rightful owners.

There now occurs an oddly chilling incident that illustrates Tecumseh's remarkable self-possession as well as his power over his followers. A Potawatomi leader known as the Deaf Chief because of impaired hearing wishes to challenge Tecumseh's protestations of peace. A friend informs him that as a result Tecumseh has given orders that he is to be killed. The Deaf Chief, undismayed, puts on his war paint, seizes a rifle, tomahawk, war club, and scalping knife, and descends on Tecumseh's camp to find the Shawnee engaged in conversation with Barron, the interpreter. The Deaf Chief rails at him, calls him a coward and an assassin, and then cries out, "Here am I now. Come and kill me!" Tecumseh makes no answer, continues to talk with Barron. The Deaf Chief heaps more insults on him. "You dare not face a warrior!" he screams. Tecumseh, unmoved, keeps up his quiet conversation. The Deaf Chief raves on, calling Tecumseh a slave of the British redcoats. No response; it is as if the Deaf Chief did not exist. At last, exhausted and out of invective, he departs. But that is the last anyone in Vincennes sees of the Deaf Chief, alive or dead.

Tecumseh's zeal and his influence over his people win Harrison's admiration, even as the Governor plans to destroy him:

"The implicit obedience and respect which the followers of Tecumseh pay to him is really astonishing and more than any other circumstance bespeaks him one of those uncommon geniuses, which spring up occasionally to produce revolutions and overturn the established order of things. If it were not for the vicinity of the United States, he would perhaps be the founder of an Empire that would rival in glory that of Mexico or Peru. No difficulties deter him. His activity and industry supply the want of letters. For four years he has been in constant motion. You see him today on the Wabash and in a short time you hear of him on the shores of Lake Erie, or Michigan, or the banks of the Mississippi and wherever he goes he makes an impression favourable to his purpose."

These words are written on August 7, 1811. Harrison can afford to be generous in his estimation of his adversary, for Tecumseh has removed himself from the area. He is off on a six-month tour of the southern United States to try to persuade the tribes—Creek, Choctaw, Osage, and others—to join his confederacy. For the moment he poses no threat, and in his absence Harrison sees his chance. "I hope," he writes to Eustis, the Secretary of War, "...before his return that that part of the fabrick, which he considered complete will be demolished and even its foundations rooted up." Now that the brothers are separated it will be easier to tempt the Prophet into battle. As the Deaf Chief discovered, Tecumseh cannot be provoked unless he wishes to be. But "the Prophet is imprudent and audacious...deficient in talents and firmness."

The plan that has been forming in Harrison's mind has become a fixation. The confederacy is growing; the British are undoubtedly behind it. It must be smashed before Tecumseh returns, smashed on the enemy's home ground, at Prophet's Town on the banks of the Tippecanoe. Harrison cannot submit to further stalemate. He will march in September.

●

THE BATTLE OF TIPPECANOE is not the glorious victory that Harrison, down through the years, will proclaim. It is not even a battle, more a minor skirmish, and indecisive, for Harrison, in spite of his claims, loses far more men than the Indians. Overblown in the history books, this brief fracas has two significant results: it is the chief means by which Harrison will propel himself into the White House (his followers chanting the slogan "Tippecanoe and Tyler Too"); and, for the Indians, it will be the final incident that provokes them to follow Tecumseh to Canada, there to fight on the British side in the War of 1812.

Tippecanoe is unnecessary. It is fought only because Harrison needs it to further his own ambitions. For while the Governor is writing to Washington branding the Prophet as an aggressor ("I can assure you Sir that there is not an Indian...that does not know and acknowledge when asked that he is determined to attack us and wonder at our forbearance"), Tecumseh is warning his brother that he must on no account be goaded into battle.

Harrison means to goad him, but Washington, in the person of Dr. Eustis, the Secretary of War, equivocates. "I have been particularly instructed by the President," the Secretary writes, "to communicate to your excellency his earnest desire that peace may, if possible, be preserved among the Indians, and that to this end every proper measure be adopted. By this it is not intended...that the banditti under the prophet should not be attacked and vanquished, provided such a measure should be rendered absolutely necessary."

69

That is good enough for Harrison. He shores up his position with a series of letters making it clear that such measures *are* absolutely necessary. As soon as Tecumseh is safely out of the way, he informs Eustis that he intends in September to move up to the upper line of the New Purchase (the territory ceded at Fort Wayne) with two companies of regulars, fourteen or fifteen companies of militia, and two troops of dragoons, the latter consisting of about one hundred men. Harrison makes it seem that this is purely a precautionary measure. But "should circumstances render it necessary to break up the Prophet's establishment by force," well then, he adds – preparing Eustis for the inevitable – he can easily get more men to fight, as well as plenty of mounted volunteers from Kentucky, where Indian fighting is a glorious tradition.

The volunteers, in fact, flock to Vincennes. The best known is Joseph Daviess, one of Kentucky's most eloquent lawyers, a brilliant orator, a popular hero, and a mild eccentric, notorious both for his prosecution of Aaron Burr and for his addiction to colourful and often startling costumes. He has a habit of appearing in court wearing a coonskin cap and deerskin leggings and carrying a hunting rifle. In one memorable appearance before the Supreme Court in Washington (the first for any western lawyer) he turned up in ripped corduroy trousers, a threadbare overcoat, and a pair of dilapidated and muddy shoes, and proceeded to down a quantity of bread and cheese while his opponent tried to marshall his case. Now he is hot to do battle in any capacity under the leadership of his hero, Harrison.

"I make free to tell you," he declares, "that I have imagined there were two men in the west who had military talents: And you sir, were the first of the two.... I go as a volunteer, leaving to you sir, to dispose of me as you choose...." He arrives along with some sixty others from his state – former army men and Indian fighters – a commanding figure, thirty-seven years old, resplendent in the uniform of the Kentucky mounted volunteers, the plumes in his hat accentuating his six-foot stature. To one eyewitness, it seems "nothing could be more magnificent. He was the very model of a cavalry officer.... With his tall, muscular form and face of strong masculine beauty, he would have been the pride of any army, and the thunderbolt of a battlefield."

Harrison and the Indians are moving at cross purposes. On September 25, the Prophet sends off runners from his village on the Tippecanoe with a message of peace for Harrison. At ten o'clock the following morning, the Governor dispatches his troops on his "demon-

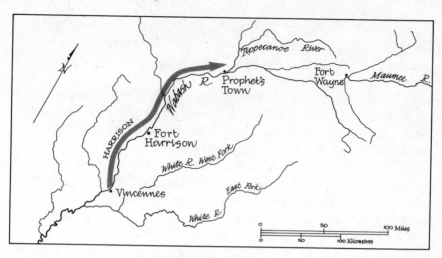

The Wabash

stration of force." They move up the Wabash in shallow flatboats, the regulars in brass-buttoned tailcoats and stove-pipe hats, the citizen soldiers of the militia in deerskin jackets and bearskin caps. When they reach the disputed territory, they build a blockhouse – Fort Harrison – the eloquent Daviess, now a major, chosen to smash a bottle over the new logs. There is much sickness, especially among the regulars, unused to frontier conditions, forced to wade up the Wabash in their skin-tight pantaloons. Shortly, however, the force is augmented by another two hundred and fifty regular soldiers of the 4th U.S. Infantry. On October 28 Harrison leaves the new fort and pushes on toward Prophet's Town at the head of one thousand men – a commanding figure in a fringed calico shirt and a beaver hat into which he has jauntily stuck an ostrich feather.

He moves cautiously, expecting Indians behind every tree, suspicious of ambush. Nothing. At two-thirty on the afternoon of November 6, some dozen miles from his objective, he reaches a small wood, halts, draws up his force in battle order, sends scouts forward. There are Indians just ahead, flitting through the trees, but they will not speak to the interpreters.

Back comes Major Daviess, eager for battle, urging an immediate attack against the insolent savages. Why is Harrison vacillating? Have the troops come this far for nothing? The Governor hesitates, mindful of Washington's order that he must try for a peaceful settlement; then, with his men murmuring their eagerness, moves on, yielding "to what appeared to be the general wish." It matters to no one that Prophet's Town is on land that has never been ceded to the United States.

Three Indians approach. Harrison recognizes one: Chief White Horse, principal counsellor to the Prophet. They are conciliatory. They have been trying to reach Harrison, but the messengers have been looking for him on the south side of the river; Harrison has taken the north bank. He assures them that all he seeks is a proper camping ground and they agree to parley on the morrow.

As the town comes into view, Harrison raises his field glass and through it observes the inhabitants running about in apparent terror and confusion behind a breastwork of logs. After some reconnoitring he camps his army about a mile to the northwest among the leafless oaks on a triangle of ground a few feet above the marshy prairie. Here, in the chill of the night, the men slumber, or try to (some have no blankets), in the warmth of huge fires, their loaded guns beside them, bayonets fixed, their coats covering the musket locks to keep them dry. Harrison has dug no trenches, erected no stakes because, he claims later, he has not enough axes.

What are the Indians thinking and planning? No one knows or will ever know, for most of the accounts of the battle come from white men. Those Indian accounts that do exist are second hand and contradictory, filtered through white reports.

Some things are fairly certain: the Indians, not trusting Harrison, expect him to attack and are determined to strike first; the battle, when it comes, is started accidentally when neither side is prepared; and of the several tribes represented at Prophet's Town it is the Winnebago and the Potawatomi and not the Shawnee who are the fiercest in wanting to disobey Tecumseh's orders not to fight.

It is four o'clock, the night still dark and overcast, a light rain rustling the bushes. On the left flank, directly in front of Captain Robert Barton's infantry company, a shivering picket, Private William Brigham, on his knees, his musket on charge, nervously tries to pierce the gloom. He cannot see farther than three feet. Suddenly — footsteps. Brigham raises his musket and almost shoots his fellow picket, William Brown, who has imprudently left his own post in a state of near terror, certain that Indians are lurking in the bushes ahead. His instinct is to flee at once.

"Brigham," he whispers, "let us fire and run. . ."

But Brigham fears a false alarm.

Suddenly something swishes past them. An arrow? Terrified, they turn and dash back toward the camp. Beside them a rifle barks.

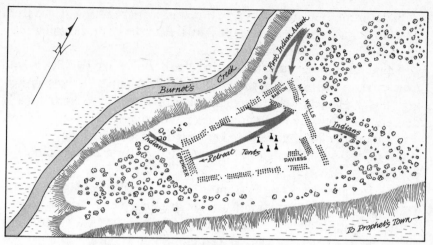

The Battle of Tippecanoe

Another sentry, Stephen Mars, has fired at something moving in the gloom and also dashed toward safety.

In Tent No. 1, Sergeant Montgomery Orr springs awake. Somebody has just rushed past, touching the corner of his tent. He jogs his corporal, David Thompson, awake. Something strikes the tent. Thompson leaps up, seizes his gun as four shots ring out accompanied by a high screaming and yelling. The corporal tumbles back upon the sergeant.

"Corporal Thompson, for God's sake don't give back!" cries Orr, then realizes he is talking to a dead man. He plunges out of the tent, gets a confused impression of a melee – soldiers and Indians firing at each other, Captain Barton trying vainly to form up his men.

Harrison is pulling on his boots when he hears a cacophony of yells and a burst of musketry. One of his officers and two of his men have already been tomahawked and scalped. He calls for his terrified black servant, George, to bring up his favourite mount – a pale grey mare. The boy cannot find her, so Harrison borrows another officer's horse – a black one – and rides into confusion. His men, perfect silhouettes in front of the fires, are falling about him. On the left, Barton's company is already badly mauled. Another has broken. When one of his colonels, mounted on a pale grey mare similar to his missing animal, tumbles to the ground, dead from an Indian musket ball, Harrison realizes that the Indians have mistaken the dead man for himself. An aide rides out on a similar horse; Harrison shoos him back for a black one.

Harrison moves swiftly to reinforce his shattered flank, rides from point to point trying to control the battle. After it is over he will write a careful account, describing the action as if it were a set piece, reconstructing all the movements, making them sound like parade-ground manoeuvres. But at this moment, with the blackened Indians shrieking, the musket fire deafening, the steam rising from fires quickly doused, the clouds of black gun smoke adding to the general overcast, it is impossible for anyone to tell exactly what is happening.

As in every battle, there are moments of horror and moments of heroism.

The Indians are acting in a most un-Indian-like fashion, responding with considerable discipline to signals made by the rattling of deer horns, firing a volley, retreating out of range to reload, advancing again. As Harrison approaches Captain Spier Spencer's company of Kentuckians, known as Yellow Jackets, on the right flank, he can hear the veteran Spencer crying, "Close up, men! Steady! Hold the line!" The Indians have mounted a third attack, so fierce that the balls are shredding the bark from the trees. One strikes Spencer in the head. He continues to shout. Another tears into his thigh, and then another. He calls out for help, and two men rush over, raise him up just as another ball penetrates his body, killing him.

Harrison rides up, sees young John Tipton sighting down a barrel.

"Where's your captain?"

"Dead, sir!"

"Your first-lieutenant?"

"Dead, sir!"

"Your second-lieutenant?"

"Dead, sir!"

"Your ensign?"

"Here, sir!"

Harrison searches about for reinforcements, sees Robb's militia company faltering, rallies them in support of the Yellow Jackets, braces the flank with a company of regulars. A close friend, Thomas Randolph, falls, mortally wounded. Harrison dismounts, bends over his friend, asks if there is anything he can do. Nothing, gasps Randolph, except to look after his child. Harrison keeps that promise.

The impetuous Major Daviess, in charge of the dragoons, is chafing at the rear. He wants to roar into action, but Harrison is holding him back:

"Tell Major Daviess to be patient, he will have an honourable station before the battle is over."

Daviess cannot stand the inaction; he presses Harrison again, gets the same reply, continues to nag. At last the Governor gives in:

"Tell Major Daviess he has heard my opinion twice; he may now use his own discretion."

Daviess has spotted Indians lurking behind some scattered logs seventy-five yards away. Gathering a force of twenty men, he prepares to charge the foe. He has dressed with his customary panache – an unmistakable target, six feet tall, in a white blanket coat that stands out starkly in the gloom. As he leads his men toward the enemy, three balls pierce his body. "I am a dead man," cries Jo Daviess. His followers carry him to the cover of a sycamore tree as the Indians vanish. He has not long to live. "Unfortunately, the Major's gallantry determined him to execute the order with a smaller force than was sufficient," Harrison comments, a little dryly, in his report of the action.

By the time Daviess falls, the entire line is engaged. Daybreak is at hand. As the Indians begin to falter, Harrison determines on a charge from the flanks. This is the climax of the battle. The level of sound is almost unbearable – an ear-splitting mixture of savage yells, shrieks of despair, roar of musketry, agonizing screams, victorious shouts, dying cries mingling in a continuous terrifying uproar that will ring in the ears of the survivors long after the last wound is healed.

Harrison's charge succeeds. The Indians, out of ammunition and arrows, retire across the marshy prairie where horses cannot follow. The Americans shout cries of triumph, utter prayers of thanks, bind up their wounds, scalp all the dead Indians, kill one who is wounded.

Two days later, they sweep through Prophet's Town, empty save for one aged squaw, on a mission of revenge and plunder. They destroy everything including all the beans and corn that they themselves cannot eat – some three thousand bushels stored up for the winter. In the houses they find British weapons, presents dispensed at Amherstburg the previous year; it confirms their suspicion that British agents have been provoking the Indians to attack (though American weapons distributed by the war department as part of the annuity payments to the tribes are also found). Then they burn all the houses and sheds and take their leave. Thus ends the Battle of Tippecanoe, which has often been called the first battle in the War of 1812.

Harrison has lost almost one-fifth of his force. Thirty-seven white corpses lie sprawled on the battlefield. One hundred and fifty men have been wounded of whom twenty-five will die of their injuries, including the luckless sentry Brigham. No one can be sure how many Indians took part in the skirmish. Nobody knows how many died. Harrison, like most military commanders, overestimates the enemy's losses, declares that the Prophet's casualties run into the hundreds. This is wishful thinking; only thirty-six Indian corpses are found.

The battered army limps back to Vincennes. As soon as Harrison is gone, the Indians, who have retreated across the Wabash, return to the ruins of their village. Although a Kickapoo chief reports to the British that "the Prophet and his people do not appear as a vanquished army," Harrison, intent on beating out some flames of dissent from Kentucky (where Daviess's death is mourned and Harrison's strategy and motives scrutinized), has already launched the long propaganda battle that will convince his countrymen that Tippecanoe was a glorious victory.

What has it accomplished? Its purpose was to teach the Indians a lesson they would never forget, to break Tecumseh's confederacy and the Prophet's power, and to stop the sporadic raids on frontier settlements. But the raids increase in fury. Settlers and soldiers are ambushed. Whole families are wiped out, scalped, mutilated. Farmers abandon their fields and cabins; neighbours club together to build blockhouses; some flee the territory. At Grouseland, Harrison constructs an underground escape tunnel, ships his wife and eight children off to safety in Kentucky, buffers the principal homes of Vincennes with log parapets. Instead of terrifying the Indians, Tippecanoe has stirred them to fury. In March, 1812, both Governor Howard of Missouri Territory and General William Clark, the explorer and superintendent of Indian Affairs, voice the opinion that a formidable combination of Indians are on the warpath, that a bloody war must ensue is almost certain, and that the Prophet is regaining his influence.

Tecumseh returns that same month to Prophet's Town. Later he speaks of his experience:

"I stood upon the ashes of my own home, where my own wigwam had sent up its fires to the Great Spirit, and there I summoned the spirits of the braves who had fallen in their vain attempts to protect their homes from the grasping invader, and as I snuffed up the smell of their blood from the ground I swore once more eternal hatred – the hatred of an avenger."

His mission to the south has failed. The Sauk and Osage tribesmen will not follow him. But his northern confederacy is not shattered as

Harrison keeps repeating (and repeating it, is believed). Tecumseh sends runners to the tribes; twelve respond, each sending two leading chiefs and two war chiefs. By May, Tecumseh has six hundred men under his command, making bows and arrows (for they no longer have guns). In Washington, war fever rises on the tales of frontier violence and the legend of Tippecanoe. Tecumseh waits, holds his men back for the right moment. For a while he will pretend neutrality, but when the moment comes, he will lead his confederacy across the border to fight beside the British against the common enemy.

2

PRELUDE TO INVASION:
1812
Marching As to War

We're abused and insulted, our country's degraded
Our rights are infringed both by land and by sea;
Let us rouse up indignant, when those rights are invaded,
And announce to the world, "We're united and free!"

— Anon., circa 1812.

LITTLE YORK, the muddy capital of Upper Canada, February 27, 1812; Brock, in his study, preparing a secret memorandum to that spectacular frontier creature whom the Dakota Sioux call *Mascotapah*, the Red-Haired Man.

His real name is Robert Dickson, and though born a Scot in Dumfriesshire, he is as close to being an Indian as any white can be. His wife is To-to-win, sister to Chief Red Thunder. His domain covers the watershed of the upper Mississippi, some of the finest fur country on the continent, a land of rolling plains, riven by trough-like valleys and speckled with blue lakes, the veinwork of streams teeming with beaver, marten, and otter, the prairie dark with buffalo. He is out there now, somewhere – nobody knows quite where – a white man living like an Indian, exercising all the power of a Sioux chieftain. Brock must find him before the war begins, for Brock is planning the defence of Upper Canada – carefully, meticulously – and the Red-Haired Man is essential to that plan.

Isaac Brock has been preparing for war for five years, ever since the *Chesapeake* affair when, as colonel in charge of the defences of Lower Canada, he forced a grudging administration into allowing him to repair and strengthen the crumbling fortress of Quebec. Now he has power. He is not only a major-general in charge of all the forces in Upper Canada, he is also, in the absence of Francis Gore, the province's administrator, which in colonial terms makes him close to being a dictator, though not close enough for Brock's peace of mind. His years in Canada have been a series of frustrations: frustrations with the civil authorities, whom he views as a nuisance and who prevent him from getting his own way; frustrations with his superior, the new governor general Sir George Prevost, who keeps him on a tight leash lest he do something precipitate and give the Americans cause for war; frustrations with the militia, who are untrained, untidy, undisciplined, and unwilling; frustrations with the civilian population, who seem blithely unaware of the imminence of war; frustrations over money, for he is in debt through no real fault of his own; frustrations, one suspects, over women, for he loves their company but has never been able to bring himself to marry; and finally, frustrations over his posting.

More than anything else, Brock yearns to be with Wellington on the Peninsula, where there is opportunity for active service and its concomitants, glory and promotion. He does not care for Canada, especially this wretched backwater of York with its tiny clique of pseudo-aristocrats, its haggling legislature, and its untutored rabble. In Quebec at least there was sophistication of a sort, and Brock is no rustic: a gourmet, a lover of fine wines, an omnivorous reader, a spirited dancer at society balls, he longs for a larger community.

For all his days in Canada he has been trying to escape his colonial prison. The irony is that this very month the Prince Regent, through Governor General Prevost, has given him leave to depart. Now he cannot go. Duty, with Brock, takes precedence over personal whim. The gentlemen who form the Prince Regent's government may not believe that war is coming, but General Isaac Brock believes it, and "being now placed in a high ostensible situation, and the state of public affairs with the American government indicating a strong presumption of an approaching rupture between the two countries, I beg leave to be allowed to remain in my present command." *Etc. Etc.* Or is it, possibly, more than a strict sense of duty that holds Brock in Canada? Expecting war, does he not also welcome it? May he not now hope to encounter in the colonies what he has longed for on the continent? Glory, honour, adventure all beckon; all these – even death.

His colleagues, friends, subordinates, and adversaries are scarcely aware of the General's inner turmoil. Though his features are not always expressionless – he was once seen to shed a tear at the execution of a soldier – he keeps his frustrations to himself. He is a remarkably handsome man with a fair complexion, a broad forehead, clear eyes of grey blue (one with a slight cast), and sparkling white teeth. His portraits tend to make him look a little feminine – the almond eyes, the sensitive nostrils, the girlish lips—but his bearing belies it; his is a massive figure, big-boned and powerful, almost six feet three in height. He has now, at forty-two, a slight tendency to portliness, and the flush of middle age is on his cheeks; but he is, in his own words, "hard as nails."

He is popular with almost everybody, especially the soldiers who serve him—a courteous, affable officer who makes friends easily and can charm with a smile. But there is also an aloofness about him, induced perhaps by the loneliness of command; on those rare occasions when he does take somebody into his confidence it is likely to be a junior officer of the volunteer army rather than one of his immediate subordinates.

He has no use for democracy. It is an American word, as treasonous in his lexicon as communism will be to a later generation of military authoritarians. Even the modest spoonful of self-determination allowed the settlers of Upper Canada annoys him. He has gone before the legislature this very month to ask that the civilians, who train part time in the militia, be forced to take an oath of allegiance. The militia in his view contains "many doubtful characters." In addition, he wants to suspend the age-old right of habeas corpus. The House of Assembly turns him down on both counts, a decision that, to Brock, smacks of disloyalty: "The great influence which the numerous settlers from the United States possess over the decisions of the lower house is truly alarming, and ought immediately, by every practical means, [to] be diminished." To Brock, the foundations of the colonial superstructure are threatened by treacherous foreign democrats, boring from within, but he cannot convince the Assembly of that.

So he turns to military matters and the secret message to the Red-Haired Man. As a good military commander, Brock has put himself in the boots of his opposite numbers. He is confident that he knows what the Americans will do.

Through their hunger for land they have managed to alienate almost all the tribes on their northwestern frontier. The Indians, then, are the key to American intentions. In other circumstances, it would make sense to hit Canada in the midriff, at Kingston and Montreal, cutting off the supply routes to the upper province, which then must surely fall. But Brock knows that this militarily attractive option is no option at all as long as America's left flank is in flames. The Indians must be subdued, and for that enterprise a very considerable force will be required, drawn principally, Brock believes, from Ohio, whose people are "an enterprising, hardy race, and uncommonly expert on horseback with the rifle." To meet this threat he has already dispatched two hundred regulars to reinforce the garrison at Fort Amherstburg, across from the American military base at Detroit. These will not be enough to counter any American thrust across the Detroit River, but Brock hopes that their presence will stiffen the resolve of the militia, and more important, convince the Indians that Britain means business. For it is on the Indians that the security of Upper Canada depends. If he can rouse the Indians, the United States will be forced to concentrate much of its limited military strength on the northwestern frontier, thereby weakening any proposed thrust along the traditional invasion routes toward Montreal and the St. Lawrence Valley.

Brock views the Indians as a means to an end. His attitude toward them changes with the context. They are "a much injured people" (a slap at American Indian policy), but they are also a "fickle race" (when some insist on remaining neutral). To Brock, as to most white men, Indians are Indians. (It is as if Wellington lumped Lapps with Magyars and Poles with Scots.) He makes little distinction between the tribes; Sioux and Shawnee, Wyandot and Kickapoo are all the same to him—savages, difficult to deal with, inconstant but damned useful to have on your side. Brock means to have as many oddly assorted Indians on his side as he can muster, and that is the substance of his secret communication with the Red-Haired Man.

The Indians, in Brock's assessment, will fight the Americans only if they are convinced the British are winning. If he can seize the island of Mackinac in the far west at the outset of the war, he believes the Indians will take heart. Some will undoubtedly help him attack Detroit (for Brock believes the best defence is offence), and if Detroit falls, more Indians will join the British—perhaps even the Mohawks of the Six Nations, who have been distressingly neutral. The main American invasion, Brock believes, will come at the Niagara border along the neck of land between Lake Ontario and Lake Erie. Anything else will be a diversion.

To put his domino theory into practice, at the outset Brock needs Indians to subdue by their presence, if not their arrows, the defenders of Michilimackinac. He expects the Red-Haired Man to supply them. The secret letter is deliberately couched in euphemisms, and even Brock's immediate superior, the cautious Governor General Prevost, is not aware of it:

CONFIDENTIAL COMMUNICATION TRANSMITTED TO MR. ROBERT DICKSON RESIDING WITH THE INDIANS NEAR THE MISSOURI

Sir,

As it is probable that war may result from the present *state of affairs*, it is very desirable to ascertain the degree of cooperation that you and *your friends* might be able to furnish, in case of such an Emergency taking place. You will be pleased to report with all practicable expedition upon the following matters.

1st. The number of your friends, that might be depended upon.

2. Their disposition toward us.

3. Would they assemble, and march under your orders.

4. State the succours you require, and the most eligible mode, for their conveyance.

5. Can *Equipment* be procured in your *Country*.

6. An immediate direct communication with you, is very much wished for.

7. Can you point out in what manner, that object may be accomplished.

8. Send without loss of time a few *faithful* and *Confidential* Agents – Selected from *your friends*.

9. Will you individually approach the Detroit frontier next spring.

If so, state time and place where *we* may meet. *Memo.* Avoid mentioning names, in your *written communications*.

Almost five months will pass before Brock receives an answer to this memorandum. And when on July 14, at Fort George at the mouth of the Niagara River, an Indian runner finally arrives with a reply from Robert Dickson, it will already be outdated by events. Long before that, the Red-Haired Man and his friends, anticipating Brock, will have departed for the British post at St. Joseph's to prepare for the invasion of the unsuspecting island of Mackinac.

•

WASHINGTON, D.C., March 20, 1812. Spring has come to the capital after an unseasonably cold winter. It is, as one newspaper points out, excellent weather for campaigning; the roads are no longer rivers of mud and slush. Why are the troops not moving north?

At the British legation on Pennsylvania Avenue this bright afternoon, a young officer arrives with dispatches from the British foreign secretary. They tell a familiar tale. In the face of French intransigence, the British government cannot – will not – repeal the Orders in Council that are at the heart of the dispute between the two nations. Lord Wellesley has felt that decision important enough to justify chartering a special ship to rush word of it across the Atlantic.

The Minister Plenipotentiary to America, who must now carry this news to the President, is the same Augustus John Foster who once swore he would not return to Washington for ten thousand pounds a year. Nevertheless, he is back, and no longer in a junior post. His absence from the London social scene since the spring of 1811 has lost him his intended – a priggish young woman named Annabella Milbanke, who will later conclude a loveless and disastrous marriage with Lord Byron. But how could any ambitious young diplomat refuse such a promotion?

How, for that matter, could His Majesty's government have selected Foster to be its eyes, ears, and tongue at this most critical of times? To the clear indications of approaching war Foster's eyes are uncommonly blind, his ears remarkably deaf, and, in his dispatches, his tongue lamentably silent. At thirty-three, with his round, boyish face, he is, to quote one politician, "a pretty young gentleman...better calculated for a ballroom or a drawing room, than for a foreign minister."

He spends a good deal of time in ballrooms, drawing rooms, and at dinner tables, entertains as many as two hundred guests at a time and lavishly overspends his expense account (perhaps to counteract the impression conveyed by his juvenile looks, for which, as he complains to his mother, the new Duchess of Devonshire, he is "greatly abused"). He seems to know everybody, rubs shoulders with all the major participants in the dangerous game being played out in the capital this spring, yet manages to miss the significance of what he sees and hears. He dines with the Speaker of the House, Henry Clay, whom he describes as "very warlike," John C. Calhoun, the fiery young congressman from South Carolina, Peter B. Porter, the belli-cose leader of the House committee on foreign relations, and other members of the ginger group known as War Hawks, but he does not believe that war will come.

The War Hawks are only a handful, yet they effectively control Congress. Five of them room together in the same boarding house, predictably dubbed the War Mess. Clay is their leader, a brilliant, fervent orator who has been Speaker since the opening of the fall session. Poetically handsome, with fair, tousled hair and a quizzical smile, he is no disinterested chairman. He thinks nothing of leaving his neutral post and invading the floor of the House to speak, sometimes for hours. He has seen to it that his cronies chair the key committees, notably the naval committee and the foreign relations committee. The latter – Peter B. Porter's committee – is packed with Clay supporters. Its majority report, brought down in November, 1811, was unequivocal. Since Britain would not budge on the two major issues threatening peace – the Orders in Council and impressment – therefore "we must now tamely submit and quietly submit or we must resist by those means which God has placed within our reach." In short, a call to war.

At dinner with the President in the still unfinished Executive Mansion, Foster encounters another actor in the drama, the dashing Comte Edouard de Crillon, whose extraordinarily thick legs he cannot help remarking. The following day he invites the count to his own table where they discuss the count's estate in Chile. It is all bunkum, as Foster will presently learn: there is no Chilean estate and no Comte de Crillon, either – only a charlatan named Soubiron, a master at masquerade. This imposter has attached himself to a handsome Irish rascal named John Henry, and the two are in the process of palming off a series of letters that Henry has written while in the pay of Sir James Craig, the former governor general of Canada. It develops that Henry, at his own suggestion, was sent by Craig in 1808 as a spy to Federalist New England to see if anyone within the opposition party there might help force a separation from the Union – in short, to seek and make contact with traitors. Henry, being remarkably unsuccessful, was paid a pittance, but the cunning Soubiron believes that copies of the letters, now more than three years old, are worth a minor fortune.

And so, to James Madison, they appear to be. The President is persuaded to squander the entire secret service fund of $50,000 for documents he believes will discomfit the Federalists, lay some of their leaders open to the charge of treason, and embarrass the British.

Madison's coup backfires. Henry has named no names, mentioned no specifics. The President's enemies quickly discover that the Irishman is not the reformed patriot he pretends to be and that the chief executive has looted the treasury for a batch of worthless paper. But the Henry affair, revealing yet another instance of British perfidy, helps to arouse further public feeling already inflamed by Tippecanoe and its aftermath, by a depression in the southwest brought on by the Orders in Council, and by continuing British high-handedness on the seas – more sailors impressed, more ships seized. "If this event does not produce a war, nothing will do so," Augustus Foster comments after Madison tables the letters on March 9. But war does not come, and this helps shore up Federalist convictions (and Foster's) that for all the Republicans' warlike clamour, the government is bluffing, as it had been after the *Chesapeake* affair. Tragically, the congressional doves do not take the War Hawk movement seriously.

Nor does Foster. He is extraordinarily well informed, for he moves in the highest circles, dining regularly with congressmen, senators, and the President himself. He knows that William Hull, Governor of Michigan Territory, has come to town, hoping (Foster believes) to be made Secretary of War in place of the genial but ineffective incumbent, William Eustis. He knows that a former secretary of war, Henry Dearborn, is also in town, trying to decide whether or not to give up his sinecure as collector of customs in Boston and take over command of the expanding army. He must know that Hull, who is another of his dinner guests, is also pondering the offer of an army command in the northwest. The United States, in short, is acting like a nation preparing for war; the President himself, in Foster's words, is "very warlike," but there is no sense of urgency in the reports he sends to Whitehall. He prefers the company of the President's warm-hearted and unwarlike wife, Dolley, who could not attend his January ball marking the Queen's birthday for political reasons but was forced to gaze on the preparations at a distance, from her bedroom window.

Preparations for war are the responsibility of a trio of old hands – all sixtyish – from the Revolution – Hull, Eustis, and Dearborn. Unlike Clay and his Hawks, these ex-soldiers, none of whom has had experience with staff command, can scarcely be said to be champing at the bit. Hull and Dearborn cannot even make up their minds whether to shoulder the responsibility of leadership. Eustis, a one-time surgeon's assistant, is genial, courteous, and a staunch party man but generally held to be incompetent – an executive unable to divorce himself from detail. Congress has refused to create two assistant secretaries, and so the entire war department of the United States consists of Eustis and eight clerks.

Governor Hull has been invited to the capital to discuss the defence of the northwestern frontier. Brock's assessment has been dead on: the Indians have dictated Washington's strategy; with Tecumseh's followers causing chaos in Indiana and Michigan territories, the United States has no option but to secure its western flank.

Washington believes in Hull. He has a reputation for sound judgement, personal courage, decisive command. During the Revolution he fought with distinction, survived nine battles, received the official thanks of Congress. One gets a fleeting picture of a gallant young field officer in his mid-twenties, rallying his troops on horseback at Bemis Heights, stemming a retreat in the face of Gentleman Johnny Burgoyne's regulars, or helping Mad Anthony Wayne carry the Stony Point fort at bayonet point (a bullet creasing his hat, another clipping his boot).

The President and the Secretary of War listen carefully to Hull's advice. The Governor points out that the United States must secure Lake Erie by reinforcing the tiny fort at Detroit and building warships to command the water routes in order to allow the swift movement of men and supplies. Hull realizes that the Indians hold the key to defeat or victory. A formidable army at Detroit, denying the lake to British transport, can cut the Indians off from the British and perhaps prevent a general uprising of the tribes. And without the Indians, he is convinced, "the British cannot hold Upper Canada."

Eustis goes along with Hull's plan only to discover that no American captain can be found who will take command on Lake Erie. Besides, it costs money to build ships, and Congress is niggardly with naval funds. Hull and Eustis, caught up in the war fever, persuade themselves that it will be enough to march a considerable force north to strengthen Detroit, cow the Indians into neutrality, and convince the British across the river that the natives are under control. Should war come, Detroit will be the springboard for an invasion that will drive the British out of all the country west of Niagara.

Hull declines the command of the army that will reinforce Detroit; he does not wish to give up his post as governor of Michigan Territory. A substitute is found in Colonel Jacob Kingsbury, an old frontier campaigner, aged fifty-seven, who first accepts but then backs out as the result of an attack of gout — an episode that hints at the paucity of leadership material in the American military establishment. Hull is hurriedly called for and told he can keep the governorship if he will accept a commission as brigadier-general in command of the Army of the Northwest.

Finally, Hull agrees. He is to raise an army of twelve hundred volunteers from the Ohio militia (as Brock has predicted) to be augmented by some four hundred regular troops. With this force he is to cut a road through forest and swamp for two hundred miles from Urbana, Ohio, to Detroit and thus secure the frontier.

Henry Dearborn, after cautiously weighing the lifetime post of customs collector against the less secure appointment of Commander-in-Chief of the American Army, finally settles on the latter and is commissioned major-general. He, too, has a plan. If war comes, the main army will attack Montreal by the historic Champlain water route, thus cutting off all of Upper Canada from reinforcements and supplies. At the same time, three columns will strike at Canada from the border points of Detroit, Niagara, and Sackets Harbor. The attack from Detroit will take care of the Indians. The other two, from opposite ends of Lake Ontario, will serve to slice up the upper province, knocking out the major British fortresses at Niagara and Kingston. Dearborn's headquarters will be at Albany, the nerve centre from which roads veer off to the three eastern invasion points. (Detroit is so remote that Dearborn treats it as a separate command.)

On paper all of this makes sense, but it depends on inspired leadership, swift communications, careful timing, well-trained troops, an efficient war department, and a united, enthusiastic nation. None of these conditions exists.

Dearborn leaves the capital early in April for Boston, where he expects, with misplaced optimism, to raise his citizen army. Given the New England governors' violent opposition to war, it is a forlorn hope. Hull, who departs for the Ohio frontier, will have better luck.

In the capital, the war fever grows in the face of British stubbornness. On April 15, Augustus Foster attends a great dinner given by the New Orleans deputies to mark Louisiana's entry into the Union. He is in the best possible position to assess the temper of the Congress, for most of its members are present along with the cabinet. Foster finds himself sandwiched between – of all people – the two leading War Hawks. Henry Clay, on one side, is as militant as ever. The twenty-six-year-old John Calhoun, on the other, is "a man resolved," his tone cool and decided. It all seems very curious to Foster. He decides that a great many people are afraid of being laughed at if they don't fight and thus arrives, quite unconsciously, at the nub of the matter.

Far to the north, in Quebec City, the new governor general of Canada, Sir George Prevost, has no illusions about the future. He warns the British government that he shortly expects a declaration of war from Madison. Foster cannot yet see it. To him, it is merely "a curious state of things." The party grows too noisy for him, and presently he takes his leave, repairing to the Executive Mansion, there to enjoy the more peaceful company of the engaging Dolley Madison.

•

DAYTON, OHIO, April 6, 1812. Duncan McArthur, one of Wayne's old frontier scouts, now General of the Ohio militia, that "enterprising, hardy race" of which Brock has written, is haranguing his citizen soldiers.

"Fellow citizens and soldiers," cries McArthur, "the period has arrived when the country again calls its heroes to arms...!" Who, he asks, will not volunteer to fight against perfidious England — "that proud and tyrannical nation, whose injustice prior to 1776, aroused the indignation of our fathers to manly resistance?"

"Their souls could no longer endure slavery," says McArthur. "The HEAVEN protected patriots of Columbia obliged the mighty armies of the tyrant to surrender to American valor...."

He warms to his subject, sneers at Britain's "conquered and degraded troops," gibes at "the haughty spirit of that proud and unprincipled nation," calls for vengeance, justice, victory.

What is going on? Is the country in a state of war? The eager volunteers, harking to their leader's braggadocio, must surely believe that the United States and Britain are at each other's throats. Yet war has not been declared. Few Englishmen believe it likely nor does the majority of Americans. Nonetheless, the call has gone out from Washington for volunteers, and Ohio has been asked to fill its quota. For Duncan McArthur, the original war — the War of Independence — has never ended.

"Could the shades of the departed heroes of the revolution who purchased our freedom with their blood, descend from the valiant mansions of peace, would they not call aloud to arms?" he asks. "And where is that friend to his country who would not obey that call?"

Where indeed? McArthur is preaching to the converted. By May, Ohio's quota of twelve hundred volunteers will be over-subscribed. Sixteen hundred militiamen answer the call. These will form the undisciplined core of the Army of the Northwest, which Brigadier-General William Hull, Governor of Michigan, will lead to Detroit.

The new general joins his troops at Dayton, Ohio, after a journey that has left him weak from cold and fever. In spite of his reputation he is a flabby old soldier, tired of war, hesitant of command, suspicious of the militia who he knows are untrained and suspects are untrustworthy. He has asked for three thousand men; Washington finally allows him two thousand. He does not really want to be a general, but he is determined to save his people from the Indians. A Massachusetts man, he has been Governor of Michigan for seven years and now feels he knows it intimately – every trail, every settlement, every white man, woman, and child, and much of the Canadian border country. He is convinced that the Indians, goaded by the British, are particularly hostile to the Michigan settlers. He sees himself as their protector, their father-figure, and he looks like a stereotype father in a popular illustration, the features distinguished if fleshy, the shock of hair dead white. (He is only fifty-eight, but some of his men believe him closer to seventy.) He chews tobacco unceasingly, a habit that muddies the illusion, especially when he is nervous and his jaws work overtime. There is a soft streak in Hull, no asset in a frontier campaign. As a young man he studied for the ministry, only to give it up for the law, but something of the divinity student remains.

On May 25, Hull parades his troops in the company of Governor Meigs of Ohio, a capable politician with the singular Christian name "Return." The volunteers are an unruly lot, noisy, insubordinate, untrained. Hull is appalled. Their arms are unfit for use; the leather covering the cartridge boxes is rotten; many of the men have no blankets and clothing. No armourers have been provided to repair the weapons, no means have been adopted to furnish the missing clothing, no public stores of arms or supplies exist, and the powder in the magazines is useless. Since the triumph of the Revolution, America has not contemplated an offensive war, or even a defensive one.

For these men, dressed in homespun, armed when armed at all with tomahawks and hunting knives, Hull has prepared the same kind of ringing speech, with its echoes of Tippecanoe, that is being heard in the Twelfth Congress:

"On marching through a wilderness memorable for savage barbarity you will remember the causes by which that barbarity has been heretofore excited. In viewing the ground stained with the blood of your fellow citizens, it will be impossible to suppress the feelings of indignation. Passing by the ruins of a fortress erected in our territory by a foreign nation in times of profound peace, and for the express purpose of exciting the savages to hostility, and supplying them with the means of conducting a barbarous war, must remind you of that system of oppression and injustice which that nation has continually practised, and which the spirit of an indignant people can no longer endure."

Hull and his staff set off to review the troops, a fife and drum corps leading the way. The sound of the drums frightens the pony ridden by one of Hull's staff; it turns about, dashes off in the wrong direction. A second, ridden by Hull's son and aide, Abraham, follows. Soon the General finds his own mount out of control. It gallops after the others, tossing its rider about unmercifully. Encumbered by his ceremonial sword, Hull cannot control the horse; his feet slip out of the stirrups, he loses his balance, his hat flies off, and he is forced to cling to the animal's mane in a most unsoldierly fashion until it slows to a walk. At last the staff regroups, confers, decides not to pass down the ranks in review but rather to have the troops march past. It is not a propitious beginning.

The volunteers have been formed into three regiments. Jeffersonian democracy, which abhors anything resembling a caste system, decrees that they elect their own officers, an arrangement that reinforces Great Britain's contempt for America's amateur army. McArthur is voted colonel of the 1st Regiment of Ohio Volunteers, and it is remarked that he "looks more like a go-ahead soldier than any of his brother officers." A go-ahead soldier on the Ohio frontier, especially an elected one, differs markedly from a go-ahead soldier in Wellington's army. To a later English visitor, McArthur is "dirty and butcher-like, very unlike a soldier in appearance, seeming half-savage and dressed like a backwoodsman; generally considered being only fit for hard knocks and Indian warfare" (which is, of course, exactly the kind of contest that is facing him).

In the volunteer army, officers must act like politicians. More often than not they *are* politicians. McArthur has been a member of the Ohio legislature. The 2nd Regiment of Ohio Volunteers elects a former mayor of Cincinnati, James Findlay, as its colonel. The 3rd votes for Lewis Cass, a stocky, coarse-featured lawyer of flaming ambition who is U.S. marshal for the state. Almost from the outset Hull has his troubles with these three. Cass has little use for him. "Instead of having an able energetic commander, we have a weak old man," he writes to a friend. Hull, on his part, is contemptuous of the militia, whom he found unreliable during the Revolution. Imagine *electing* officers to command!

"Elected officers," he believes, "can never be calculated upon as great disciplinarians. In every station the elected will be unwilling to incur the displeasure of the electors; indeed he will often be found to court their favour by a familiarity and condescension which are totally incompatible with military discipline. The man that votes his officer his commission, instead of being implicitly obedient, as every soldier ought to be, will be disposed to question and consider the propriety of the officer's conduct before he acts. . . ."

Another problem faces Hull. The three militia commanders are full colonels. But James Miller, who will lead the regulars, is only a half-colonel. When Miller protests the injustice of this – if anything, he should outrank the amateurs – Cass, Findlay, and McArthur threaten to quit and disband their regiments unless their rank is maintained. There is nothing that Hull or his superiors in Washington can do about this small-boy petulance. The militia colonels continue to outrank Miller.

The army starts the march north on June 1. A few days later at the frontier community of Urbana, the last outpost of civilization, Hull's suspicions about the militia are reinforced. From this point to Detroit the troops face two hundred miles of wilderness with no pathway, not even an Indian trail to follow. The volunteers turn ugly. They had been promised an advance of fifty dollars each for a year's clothing but have received only sixteen. One unpopular officer is ridden out of camp on a rail, and when the orders come to march, scores refuse to move. Into camp, at this impasse, marches Miller's 4th Infantry Regiment of regulars. These veterans of Tippecanoe prod the wavering volunteers into action, and the troops move out, with McArthur's regiment in the lead, hacking a way through jungle and forest. The following day, three mutinous ringleaders are court-martialled and sentenced to have their heads half shaved and their hands tied and to be marched round the lines with the label "Tory" between their shoulders – a punishment the prisoners consider worse than the death-sentence.

Hull's force is as much a mob as an army. The volunteers mock the General's son Abraham, who, mounted upon a spirited horse, in full uniform and blind drunk, toppled into the Mad River in front of the entire assembly.

"Who got drunk and fell in the Mad River?" somebody calls from the ranks, to which a distant companion answers, "Captain Hull!" and a third echoes, "That's true!"

Hull's March to Detroit

The jests are needed, for the rain falls incessantly. The newly built road becomes a swamp; wagons are mired and have to be hoisted out by brute strength. The troops keep up their spirits on corn liquor supplied by friendly settlers.

Then, at the brand-new blockhouse on the Scioto named Fort McArthur, a bizarre episode dries up the supply of moonshine. A guard named Peter Vassar lies slumped under a tree, befuddled by drink. He hears a sudden noise, seizes his musket, makes sure it is charged, takes deliberate aim, and shoots another sentry, Joseph England, through the left breast, just missing his heart. Vassar is court-martialled and given a grotesque sentence: both ears are cropped and each cheek branded with the letter M. McArthur issues an order restraining settlers from selling liquor to his men without his written permission. The ban does not extend to his officers.

Thus dispirited, the troops plunge through the pelting rain into the no man's land of the Black Swamp, a labyrinth of deadfalls and ghostly trees behind whose trunks Tecumseh's unseen spies keep watch. A fog of insects clogs the soldiers' nostrils and bloats their faces; a gruel of mud and water rots their boots and swells their ankles. They cannot rest at day's end until they hack out a log breast-work against Indian attack. Strung out for two miles day after day, the human serpent finally wriggles to a halt, blocked by rising water and unbridgeable streams. Hull camps his men in ankle-deep mud, builds a blockhouse, names it Fort Necessity, and there, from necessity, the sodden army waits until the floods ebb. Yet Hull is not cast down. He has more than two thousand rank and file under his command and believes his force superior to any that may oppose it.

Finally the troops move on to the head of navigation on a branch of the Maumee River (also known as the Miami of the Lakes). And here a letter catches up with Hull. It is from Eustis, the Secretary of War, urging him to advance with all possible haste to Detroit, there to await further orders. The letter is dated June 18, but it must have been penned on the morning of that day because it fails to include the one piece of information that is essential to prevent a major blunder: in the afternoon of June 18, the United States has officially declared war on Great Britain.

●

IN WASHINGTON, while Hull's army trudges through the swamps of Ohio and Robert Dickson's Indians head for St. Joseph's Island, Henry Clay and his War Hawks are in full cry. In their eyes, Augustus Foster will write, long after the fact, war is "as necessary to America as a duel is to a young naval officer to prevent his being bullied and elbowed in society."

Spurred on by hawkish rhetoric, Washington has been playing a dangerous game of "I dare you" with Westminster. Most Republicans in the Twelfth Congress are opposed to war, but they do not balk at voting for increased military appropriations or an expanded militia. They are confident that Great Britain, faced with the threat of a nuisance war in North America and heavily committed to the struggle against Napoleonic France, will back down at the last moment, cancel the damaging Orders in Council, and abandon the maddening practice of impressment.

But the British do not back down, believing in their turn that the Americans are bluffing, a premise encouraged by Foster's myopia. By the time this fact sinks in, those who have gone along with the War Hawks in Congress cannot in honour vote against what John C. Calhoun calls "the second struggle for our liberty."

By midwinter, Clay and his followers had all but made up their minds that in the face of British intransigence, the only honourable course was war. Their strategy was to make retreat impossible, even for the most dovish Republicans. They will act as the catalyst that, in June, leads to declaration.

Unlike the aging veterans, pondering possible strategies for possible invasion, these are young, vigorous men between the ages of twenty-nine and thirty-six, lawyers all, with an eloquence exceeded only by verbosity. They have been raised on tales of the Revolution told by elders who have forgotten much of the horror but remember all of the glory. They are men of the old frontier, from Kentucky, Tennessee, South Carolina, and the outer edges of New Hampshire and New York – the kind of men who believe in the need to avenge any insult, imagined or real, who know what it means to fight for the land, and who are convinced that the only good Indian is a dead one.

Tippecanoe has given them new impetus. In speech after fiery speech they use every device to convince their colleagues and the country that war – or at least the threat of war – is both necessary and attractive: if Britain can be brought to her senses through an attack on Canada, America's export trade will again flourish, the depression will end, the Indians will be put forever in their place, and the troublesome Canadian border will be done away with. These are debating points. The essence of the Hawks' position is contained in the words of Felix Grundy, the young Tennessee criminal lawyer with the piercing blue eyes who cries that America must "by force redress the violated rights and honor of an injured and insulted people."

There is more than an echo here of Tecumseh and the young braves who have deserted their own elders to follow him down the path of revenge and glory. The leaders of the two war parties are not dissimilar. Both are handsome men, tall and lithe, with flashing eyes and vibrant personalities. Both dress stylishly and with purpose: Clay shows his patriotism by wearing Kentucky homespun instead of British broadcloth; Tecumseh dresses in unadorned deerskin for similar reasons. Each is courageous, quick to take offence; Clay bears the scar of a duel on his thigh, the result of an acrimonious debate in the Kentucky legislature. In an age of oratory, these two who have never met and never will meet are the most eloquent of all. One white witness who heard Tecumseh at the Springfield, Ohio, council in 1806 declares that it was not until he heard Henry Clay speak that he felt he was again in the presence of an orator of the Shawnee's rank. Each man is the acknowledged spokesman of his small group of followers, a group in each case whose influence is far out of proportion to its numbers. And both are convinced that war is the only solution to the slights and grievances which have angered and humiliated them. The British are to Clay what the Americans are to Tecumseh.

Like Tecumseh, Clay is a master of persuasion. In the fall, when the Congress met, few of its members had made up their minds. By June, the majority has become convinced that war is the only answer. John Smilie of Pennsylvania speaks for the formerly uncommitted when he declares: "If we now recede we shall be a reproach to all nations." Inch by inch Smilie has been nudged into a hawkish position, voting a little grudgingly for the various military proposals that have pushed the nation closer to war, but believing almost to the end that commercial retaliation is the answer. James Madison, too, is prepared by spring to go along with war, even though, like his predecessor Jefferson, he has struggled against the idea of involvement in a European conflict. He is a small man, benign of temperament, soft-voiced, distant in his relationships, a scholar, modest and moderate, who owns a single black suit and once lost an election for refusing to supply free whiskey to the voters. His outward composure is sometimes mistaken for weakness; the Federalists think him a pawn of Henry Clay. He is not. Though he dislikes the idea of war, he too comes to believe that his country has no other course. Apart from other considerations, submission would badly damage the Republican Party. Party politics and party unity are important considerations. He is prepared to accept the results of a vote in Congress.

Ironically, during these same weeks the British are preparing to back down. Reports from America are conflicting; Augustus Foster, who is supposed to man their listening post in the capital, continues to believe that the Americans are bluffing; but the oratory in the war congress and Sir George Prevost's warning from Quebec convinces many in Parliament that war is actually possible. Britain responds by dispatching three battalions of regulars to Canada and begins to consider the possibility of a repeal of the Orders in Council. By June, Foster too has changed his mind and reports that the Yankees mean what they say.

The British government, which has been bumbling along, holding a series of sedate hearings into the Orders in Council, now starts to move with uncharacteristic speed. Unfortunately, political affairs have been thrown into disarray by an unprecedented act, the assassination of the Prime Minister, Spencer Perceval, in the lobby of the House of Commons. It is June 16 before the formal motion to repeal the Orders is announced. The move comes too late. There is no Atlantic cable to alert the men of Washington. On June 18, the United States proclaims that a state of war exists between herself and Great Britain. When the news reaches the War Mess on New Jersey Avenue, Calhoun flings his arms about Clay's neck and the two, joined by their fellow Hawks, caper about the table in an approximation of a Shawnee war dance. But would Clay be so boisterous if he could foresee the tragedy that will be visited on his family in less than a year on the frozen banks of the River Raisin?

The news that America is at war brings a more mixed reaction across the nation. The tolling of church bells mingles with the firing of cannon and rockets; flags fly at half-mast while drums beat out the call for recruits; there are parades, cheers, hisses and boos, riots and illuminations depending on the mood of the people, which is divided on both regional and political lines. Five days later, the British motion to repeal the Orders becomes law and the chief reason for the conflict is removed.

At this point, General Hull's army of twenty-two hundred men is in sight of Detroit and within striking distance of the lightly held British fort across the river at Amherstburg. If Hull can capture the fort and disperse his enemies, the route lies open to the capital at York on Toronto Bay. The object is to seize Canada, not necessarily as a permanent prize (although that is in the minds of some) but to hold her hostage to force concessions from the British. Canada, after all, is the only portion of the empire that is open to American attack. Only later in the war, when American defeats are supplanted by American victories, will Madison and his foreign secretary, James Monroe, consider clinging to the conquered nation as part of the Union.

It is a long-held and almost universal belief that Canada is entirely vulnerable, an easy prey to American attack. The campaign, it is thought, will last a few weeks only. The freshman War Hawk, Calhoun, has already declared that "in four weeks from the time that a declaration of war is heard on our frontier the whole of Upper and a part of Lower Canada will be in our possession." Clay's words to the Senate in 1810 are recalled: "...the conquest of Canada is in our power...." Felix Grundy, Clay's fellow boarder at the War Mess, declares: "We shall drive the British from our continent," and adds, charitably, that he is "willing to receive the Canadians as adopted brethren."

The general optimism is reflected in the words of Jefferson himself, who writes to a friend at the outset of war that "upon the whole I have known no war entered into under more favourable circumstances... we...shall strip her [Great Britain] of all her possessions on this continent." The Hawk press reflects these sentiments. In the words of the Kentucky *Gazette*, "Upper and Lower Canada to the very gates of Quebec will fall into the possession of the Yankees the moment the war is started, without much bloodshed, for almost the whole of Upper Canada and a great part of the Lower Province is inhabited by Americans."

At first glance it *does* seem a mere matter of marching. The United States has ten times the military potential of Canada. Congress has authorized a regular force of thirty-five thousand men to serve for five years and undertaken a military call-up of one hundred thousand. But the country is so badly divided that by June only about four thousand regulars have been recruited, bringing the total force to ten thousand, almost half of them untrained recruits and only half available for service in the north. As for the militia, nobody can be sure how many are available or whether they can legally be forced to fight on foreign soil. Like the generals who lead them, few have experience of war.

Even at that, the American forces outnumber the British. In all of British North America there are only forty-five hundred troops, thinly distributed. In Upper Canada a mere fifteen hundred regulars are available to receive the main thrust of the American attack. But as in most wars, the events to follow will be determined not so much by the quality of the men as by the quality of the leadership. The Americans pin their hopes on Hull and Dearborn. Canada is more fortunate. She has Tecumseh, the Leaping Panther, and she also has that impulsive but consummate professional, Major-General Isaac Brock.

3

MICHILIMACKINAC
The Bloodless Victory

...unless Detroit and Michilimackinac be both in our possession at the commencement of hostilities, not only Amherstburg but most probably the whole country, must be evacuated as far as Kingston.

– Isaac Brock, February, 1812.

THE WISCONSIN–FOX PORTAGE, ILLINOIS TERRI-
TORY, June 18, 1812.

On the very day that war is declared, Brock's courier catches up at
last with the Red-Haired Man, Robert Dickson. The courier's name
is Francis Rheaume; he and a companion have logged two thousand
miles scouring the plains and valleys seeking their man. At Fort
Dearborn (Chicago), their quest was almost aborted when the American military commander, Captain Nathan Heald, sniffing treachery,
had them arrested and searched. Heald found nothing; the two men
had hidden Brock's letters in the soles of their moccasins. So here they
are at last, after three months of travel, standing on the height of land
(and also on Brock's letters) where the water in the little streams
trickles in two directions – some toward the Gulf of Mexico, the rest
north to the Great Lakes.

Dickson reads Brock's message, scrawls an immediate reply. He
has, he writes, between two hundred and fifty and three hundred of
his "friends" available and would have more but for a hard winter
with "an unparalleled scarcity of provisions." His friends are ready to
march. He will lead them immediately to the British post at St.
Joseph's Island and expects to arrive on the thirtieth of the month.

With his report, Dickson encloses copies of speeches by three of
the chiefs who will accompany him. They leave no doubt about the
Indians' sympathies: "We live by our English Traders who have
always assisted us, and never more so, than this last year, at the risk of
their lives, and we are at all times ready to listen to them on account of
the friendship they have always shown us."

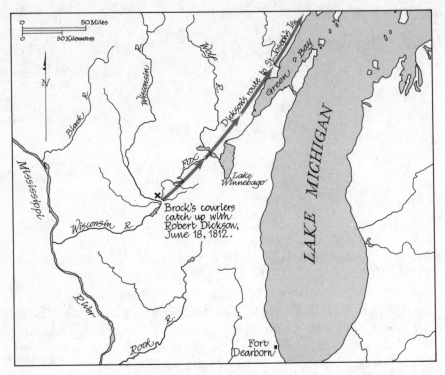

The Wisconsin-Fox Portage

The Prophet's message has also penetrated this lonely land: "We have always found our English father the protector of our women and children, but we have for some time past been amused by the songs of the bad Birds from the lower part of the River – they were not songs of truth, and this day we rejoice again in hearing the voice of our English Father, who never deceives us, and we are certain never will." So speaks Wabasha of the Sioux. The others echo his sentiments.

The Indians will follow Dickson anywhere. Here in this land of chiefs and sub-chiefs he is the real chief – their friend, their protector, and in this last harsh winter their saviour. When he arrived the previous August from St. Joseph's Island with his cargo of winter supplies, he found them starving. A disastrous drought had withered their crops and driven away the game. Dickson beggared himself to save his people, distributing all his provisions – ten thousand dollars' worth – among the tribes. He did this out of patriotism as well as humanity, for he knew that American agents were moving about the country, doing their best to influence the Indians. He assumes American hostility toward Britain, but fortunately, as he tells Brock, he is "possessed of the means of frustrating their intentions."

He is a man of commanding presence, a massive and genial six-footer with a flaming shock of red hair and a ruddy face to match. Everybody likes him, for there is an easy sociability about Dickson, a dignity, a sense of honour and principle. Men of every colour trust him. He is of a different breed from Elliott, McKee, and Girty. Highly literate, he is also humane. He has tried to teach the Indians not to kill and scalp when they can take prisoners; the greatest warriors, Dickson tells his people, are those who save their captives rather than destroy them. The infrequent explorers who cross the empty continent are attracted by Dickson. Zebulon Pike, the young army officer who has given his name to the famous peak, writes of his open, frank manner and his encyclopaedic knowledge of the country. Another, William Powell, reports that the Indians reverence and worship Dickson, who is "generous to a fault."

What is he doing out here in this lonely land? Living often in great squalor, existing for weeks on wild rice, corn, and pemmican or sometimes on nothing but melted snow, going for months without hearing his native tongue, trudging for miles on snowshoes or struggling over long portages with back-breaking loads, he is a man never at rest, like the Cut Head Yanktonais, the roving Sioux with whom he travels, knowing no real home but moving ceaselessly along his string of trading posts like a trapper tending a trapline.

His two brothers, who have also emigrated from Dumfriesshire, prefer the civilized life. One is a rising barrister and future politician at Niagara, the other a well-to-do merchant and militia colonel at Queenston. But Robert Dickson has spent twenty years in Indian country. Why? Certainly not for profit, for he has little money; the fur trade is a risky business. Nor for glory, for there is no glory. For power? He could have more in the white man's world. The answer seems to be that he is here, like so many of his countrymen, for the adventure of the frontier, the risks, the dangers, the excitement, and now, perhaps, because after two decades these are his people and this wild, untravelled country is his home. Who else but Dickson has trekked alone across that immense tract – larger than an American state – that lies west of the Mississippi between the Des Moines and the Missouri? He is a man of extraordinary energy and endurance; nowhere else, perhaps, can he feel fulfilled. In the Canadian Northwest, beyond the Great Lakes and the great bay, there are others like him, living among the Indians, exploring the land. Most are Scotsmen.

Dickson likes the Indians for themselves. He is faithful to his Indian wife, prides himself that he is educating his half-Indian children, is angered by the treatment his people receive from American frontiersmen who see the Indian as a dangerous animal to be exterminated. Added to these grievances against the Americans are the strictures enforced against British traders who still insist on flying the Union Jack over American territory. To evade the recent Non-Importation Act, by which the Americans have tried to prevent British traders from bringing goods into the United States, Dickson has been forced to become a smuggler. So incensed was he over this outrage that he knocked down the customs officer at Michilimackinac who tried to make him pay duty on his trade goods. His patriotism needs no fuelling. He is more than delighted to aid his countrymen.

He loses no time. This very day he dispatches a reply to Brock and sends it to Fort Amherstburg with thirty Menominee warriors. Then, with 130 Sioux, Winnebago, and Menominee, he sets off for St. Joseph's Island at the western entrance to Lake Huron, arriving as promised on the dot of June 30.

St. Joseph's Island, in the words of a young ensign exiled there for satirizing the lieutenant-governor, is "the military Siberia of Upper Canada." It is so remote that its garrison has trouble getting supplies and pay. Quarters are primitive. Rain, snow, and wind pour through the gaps between the blockhouse logs. The troops have shivered all winter for want of greatcoats. They turn out on parade wearing a short covering tailored from blankets intended for the Indians. These blanket coats are not named for St. Joseph's but acquire the phonetic name of the American fortress, forty miles away. As Mackinac or "Mackinaw" coats, created out of necessity, they are destined to become fashionable.

St. Joseph's unpopularity is understandable. Officers almost on arrival begin to think about requesting a transfer. For the troops, the only way out is through desertion. There have been several attempts: in April, 1805, twelve men took off in the garrison's boat; in March, 1810, two privates of the 100th Regiment attempted to escape on foot. Their pursuers found them, one half-dead of cold (he eventually lost both legs), the other a corpse. An investigation uncovered a plan for a mutiny involving a quarter of the garrison.

The fort's commander, Captain Charles Roberts, a twenty-year veteran of the British Army in India and Ceylon, has been in charge since September, 1811. He has, in effect, been pensioned off for garrison duty along with the newly formed 10th Royal Veteran Battalion, a new idea of Brock's for making use of men too old to fight. Brock has been too optimistic about the value of these veterans. In Roberts's words, they are "so debilitated and worn down by unconquerable drunkenness that neither fear of punishment, the love of fame or the honour of their Country can animate them to extraordinary exertions." There are only forty-four of them defending a crumbling blockhouse armed with four ancient and nearly useless six-pound cannon. Roberts himself is experienced, incisive, and eager for action, but he is also mortally ill with a "great debility of the stomach and the bowels."

It is the Indians, then, and the clerks and voyageurs of the North West Company who will form the spearhead of the attack on Michilimackinac. In addition to the members of Dickson's native force, already chafing for action, there are the neighbouring Ottawa and Chippewa tribesmen under John Askin, Jr., a member of the sprawling Askin family, whose patriarch, John, Sr., lives at Sandwich across the river from Detroit. Askin, whose mother is an Ottawa, is interpreter and keeper of the Indian stores at St. Joseph's. His people have blown hot and cold on the subject of war with the Americans. There was a time after the *Chesapeake* incident, when Tecumseh and the Prophet were rallying the tribes, when they were filled with ardour for the old way of life. Sixty, to Askin's astonishment, even refused a gift of rum. But now that ardour has cooled; no one can keep the Indians in a state of animation for long. That is Roberts's problem as the days move on without word from Brock. Dickson's men are becoming restless, but the attack on Mackinac cannot begin without a specific order. If there is going to be a war at all, Roberts wishes it would begin at once.

•

BALTIMORE, MARYLAND, June 18, 1812. John Jacob Astor is hurrying toward Washington, his ample rump rising and falling as he posts his horse. He has come in haste from New York to try to stop the damnfool war. No doubt he feels he has the clout to do just that, but here in Baltimore he learns that he is too late. The war is on – a war that Astor needs as much as he needs a case of smallpox.

He is not a pacifist, merely a businessman. His South West Company straddles the border, the first of the multinational corporations. He has a fortune in trade goods tied up at St. Joseph's on the Canadian side, another fortune in furs at Mackinac on the American side. What will become of these investments? It has apparently not occurred to Astor that the country might actually go to war. As late as February he wrote, in his semi-literate style: "We are happey in the hope of Peace and have not the Smalest Idia of a war with england." He is neither pro-British nor anti-British, merely pro-business, pro-profit. He has been in Canada the past winter, tendering successfully on government bills of specie to support the British army, too preoccupied to sense what is coming. Only at the last moment, as the debates in Congress grow shrill, does he become uneasy and so decides to put his personal prestige on the line and gallop out of New York to reason with the politicians. But now, with war declared, the best he can do is to try to mend his imperilled fortunes.

He determines to get the news as swiftly as possible to his Canadian partners in the South West Company. It does not occur to him that this may be seen as an act approaching treason any more than it occurs to him that his news will travel faster than the official dispatches. The South West Company is owned jointly by Astor and a group of Montreal fur "pedlars," which includes the powerful North West Company. Astor engages in a flurry of letter writing to his agents and partners. Thus the British are apprised of the war before the Americans on the frontier, including General Hull en route to Detroit and Lieutenant Hanks at Michilimackinac, realize it. Brock gets the news on June 26 and immediately dispatches a letter to Roberts at St. Joseph's Island. But a South West Company agent, Toussaint Pothier, based at Amherstburg, has already had a direct communication from Astor. Pothier alerts the garrison, leaps into a canoe, and paddles off at top speed. He beaches his canoe at St. Joseph's on July 3.

Roberts puts his men and Indians on the alert. Lewis Crawford, another South West employee, organizes 140 volunteer voyageurs. A twelve-day interval of frustration follows. Brock's message, which arrives by canoe on July 8, simply advises that the war is on and that Roberts should act accordingly. Roberts requisitions stores and ammunition from the South West Company (the very stores that concern John Jacob Astor, who will, of course, be paid for them), takes over the North West Company's gunboat *Caledonia*, impresses her crew, and sends off a message by express canoe to the North West Company's post at Fort William, asking for reinforcements.

Just as he is preparing to attack Mackinac, a second express message arrives from Brock on July 12. The impetuous general has had his enthusiasm curbed by his more cautious superior, Sir George Prevost. The Governor General is hoping against hope that the reports of war are premature, that the Americans have come to their senses, that a change of heart, a weakness in resolve, an armistice – anything – is possible. He will not prejudice the slightest chance of peace. Brock orders Roberts to hold still, wait for further orders. The perplexed captain knows he cannot hold the Indians for long – cannot, in fact, afford to. By night they chant war songs, by day they devour his dwindling stock of provisions.

Then, on July 15, to Roberts's immense relief, another dispatch arrives from Brock which, though equivocal, allows him to act. The Major-General, with an ear tuned to Sir George's cautionary instructions and an eye fastened on the deteriorating situation on the border, tells Roberts to "adopt the most prudent measures either of offense or defense which circumstances might point out." Roberts resolves to make the most of these ambiguous instructions. The following morning at ten, to the skirl of fife and the roll of drum – banners waving, Indians whooping – his polyglot army embarks upon the glassy waters of the lake.

Off sails *Caledonia* loaded with two brass cannon, her decks bright with the red tunics of the regulars. Behind her follow ten bateaux or "Mackinac boats" crammed with one hundred and eighty voyageurs, brilliant in their sashes, silk kerchiefs, and capotes. Slipping in and out of the flotilla are seventy painted birchbark canoes containing close to three hundred tribesmen – Dickson, in Indian dress, with his fifty feathered Sioux; their one-time enemies, the Chippewa, with coal-black faces, shaved heads, and bodies daubed with pipe clay; two dozen Winnebago, including the celebrated one-eyed chief, Big Canoe; forty Menominee under their head chief, Tomah; and thirty Ottawa led by Amable Chevalier, the half-white trader whom they recognize as leader.

Ahead lies Mackinac Island, shaped like an aboriginal arrowhead, almost entirely surrounded by 150-foot cliffs of soft grey limestone. The British abandoned it grudgingly following the Revolution, realizing its strategic importance, which is far more significant than that of St. Joseph's. Control of Mackinac means control of the western fur trade. No wonder Roberts has no trouble conscripting the Canadian voyageurs!

They are pulling on their oars like madmen, for they must reach their objective well before dawn. Around midnight, about fifteen miles from the island a birchbark canoe is spotted. Its passenger is an old crony from Mackinac, a Pennsylvania fur trader named Michael Dousman. He has been sent by Hanks, the American commander, to try to find out what is taking place north of the border. Dousman, in spite of the fact that he is an American militia commander, is first and foremost a fur trader, an agent of the South West Company, and an old colleague and occasional partner of the leaders of the voyageurs and Indians. He greets Dickson, Pothier, Askin, and Crawford as old friends and cheerfully tells Roberts everything he needs to know: the strength of the American garrison, its armament (or lack of it), and – most important of all – the fact that no one on the island has been told that America is at war.

Dousman's and Roberts's concerns are identical. In the event of a struggle, they want to protect the civilians on the island from the wrath of the Indians. Dousman agrees to wake the village quietly and to herd everybody into the old distillery at the end of town where they can be guarded by a detachment of regulars. He promises not to warn the garrison.

At three that morning, the British land at a small beach facing the only break in the escarpment at the north end of the island. With the help of Dousman's ox team the voyageurs manage to drag the two six-pounders over boulders and through thickets up to the 300-foot crest that overlooks the fort at the southern tip. Meanwhile, Dousman tiptoes from door to door wakening the inhabitants. He silently herds them to safety, then confronts the bewildered Lieutenant Hanks, who has no course but surrender. The first objective in Brock's carefully programmed campaign to frustrate invasion has been taken without firing a shot.

"It is a circumstance I believe without precedent," Roberts reports to Brock. For the Indians' white leaders he has special praise: their influence with the tribes is such that "as soon as they heard the Capitulation was signed they all returned to their Canoes, and not one drop either of Man's or Animal's blood was Spilt...."

Askin is convinced that Hanks's bloodless surrender has prevented an Indian massacre: "It was a fortunate circumstance that the Fort Capitulated without firing a Single Gun, for had they done so, I firmly believe not a Soul of them would have been Saved.... I never saw so determined a Set of people as the Chippawas & Ottawas were. Since

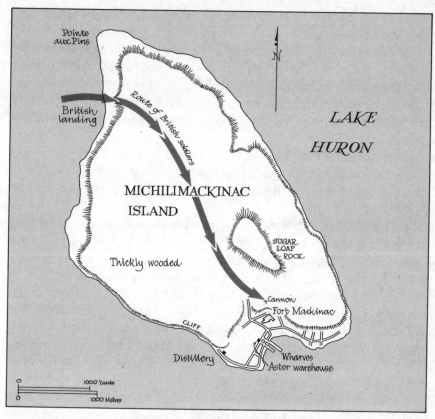

Michilimackinac Island

the Capitulation they have not drunk a single drop of Liquor, nor even killed a fowl belonging to any person (a thing never known before) for they generally destroy every thing they meet with."

Dickson's Indians feel cheated out of a fight and complain to the Red-Haired Man, who keeps them firmly under control, explaining that the Americans cannot be killed once they have surrendered. To mollify them, he turns loose a number of cattle, which the Sacs and Foxes chase about the island until the bellowing animals, their flanks bristling with arrows, hurl themselves into the water.

They are further mollified by a distribution of blankets, provisions, and guns taken from the American commissariat, which also contains tons of pork and flour, a vast quantity of vinegar, soap, candles, and – to the delight of everybody – 357 gallons of high wines and 253 gallons of whiskey, enough to get every man, white and red, so drunk that had an enemy force appeared on the lake, it might easily have recaptured the island.

These spoils are augmented by a trove of government-owned furs, bringing the total value of captured goods to £10,000, all of it to be distributed, according to custom, among the regulars and volunteers who captured the fort. Every private soldier will eventually receive ten pounds sterling as his share of the prize money, officers considerably more.

The message to the Indians is clear: America is a weak nation and there are rewards to be gained in fighting for the British. The fall of Mackinac gives the British the entire control of the tribes of the Old Northwest.

Porter Hanks and his men are sent off to Detroit under parole: they give their word not to take any further part in the war until they are exchanged for British or Canadian soldiers of equivalent rank captured by the Americans – a device used throughout the conflict to obviate the need for large camps of prisoners fed and clothed at the enemy's expense. The Americans who remain on the island are obliged to take an oath of allegiance to the Crown; otherwise they must return to American territory. Most find it easy to switch sides. They have done it before; a good many were originally British until the island changed hands in 1796.

Curiously, one man is allowed to remain without taking the oath. This is Michael Dousman, Hanks's spy and Roberts's prisoner. Dousman is given surprising leeway for an enemy, being permitted to make business trips to Montreal on the promise that he will not travel through U.S. territory. He is required to post a bond for this purpose but has no trouble raising the money from two prominent Montreal merchants.

Dousman's business in Montreal is almost certainly John Jacob Astor's business. All of Astor's furs are now in enemy territory. But the South West Company is still a multinational enterprise, and Astor has friends in high positions in both countries. Through his Montreal partners he manages to get a passport into Canada. In July he is in Montreal making arrangements for his furs to be forwarded from Mackinac Island (which has not yet fallen). These furs are protected in the articles of capitulation; over the next several months, bales of them arrive in Montreal from Mackinac. Astor's political friends in Washington have alerted the customs inspectors at the border points to pass the furs through, war or no war. Over the next year and a half, the bullet-headed fur magnate manages to get his agents into Canada and to bring shipment after shipment of furs out to the New York market. A single consignment is worth $50,000, and there are many such consignments. For John Jacob Astor and the South West Company, the border has little meaning, and the war is not much more than a nuisance.

4

DETROIT
The Disintegration of William Hull

Those Yankee hearts began to ache,
Their blood it did run cold,
To see us marching forward
So courageous and so bold.
Their general sent a flag to us,
For quarter he did call,
Saying, "Stay your hand, brave British boys,
I fear you'll slay us all."

*— From "Come All Ye Bold Canadians,"
a campfire ballad of the War of 1812.*

ABOARD THE SCHOONER *Cuyahoga Packet*, entering Lake Erie, July 2, 1812. William K. Beall, assistant quartermaster general in William Hull's Army of the Northwest, stretches out on deck, admiring the view, ignorant of the fact that his country has been at war for a fortnight and the vessel will shortly be entering enemy waters.

Beall counts himself lucky. He reclines at his ease while the rest of Hull's tattered army trudges doggedly toward Detroit, spurred on by Eustis's order to move "with all possible speed." Thanks to the *Cuyahoga*'s fortuitous presence at the foot of the Maumee rapids, Hull has been able to relieve his exhausted teams. The schooner is loaded with excess military stores – uniforms, band instruments, entrenching tools, personal luggage – and some thirty sick officers and men, together with three women who have somehow managed to keep up with their husbands on the long trek north.

It is a foolhardy undertaking. War is clearly imminent, even though Eustis, the bumbling secretary, gave no hint of it in his instructions to the General. Hull's own officers have pointed out that the *Cuyahoga* must pass under the British guns at Fort Amherstburg, guarding the narrow river boundary, before she can reach Detroit; but their commander, sublimely unaware of his country's declaration, remains confident that she will get there before the army.

The schooner rolls in Erie's swell. The passengers grow queasy, but not William K. Beall. He is enchanted by the vastness of the lake, has never seen anything like it before. He is a prosperous Kentucky plantation owner whose estate on the Ohio River, not far from

Newport, is thirty-six miles square. But this lake! It is hard to conceive of so much fresh water, stretching on beyond the horizon. The only water he has seen since leaving home has flowed sluggishly in the saffron streams veining the dreadful swamps through which the army has just toiled. Beall puts all that out of his mind, basks in the novelty of the heaving deck, opens an appropriate book of poetry – Scott's *Lady of the Lake* – commits three verses to memory, then catnaps as the *Cuyahoga* sails toward the mouth of the Detroit River.

He wakes as the schooner approaches the village of Amherstburg, nestled outside the British fort (which the Americans call Fort Malden). Again he is charmed by what he sees. The little town seems indifferently built, but the countryside is quite lovely – green meadows and sunny wheat fields rippling in the breeze. This southern fringe of orchards is the garden of Upper Canada, but most of the province beyond remains a wilderness, its great forests of pine and oak, maple and basswood broken here and there by small patches of pioneer civilization, like worn spots on a rug. Vast swamps, dark and terrifying, smother the land. Roads are few and in some seasons impassable, being little more than rivers of rutted mud. Sensible travellers move by water, and it is along the margins of the lakes and the banks of the larger rivers that the main communities such as Amherstburg have sprung up. Between these villages lie smaller settlements. Plots of winter wheat, oats, and rye, fields of corn and root vegetables blur the edges of the forest. Here, along the Detroit River, the fruit trees have been bearing for a decade, and cider has become a staple drink. Beall notes that everything appears to wear "the cheering smiles of peace and plenty."

In the distance an Indian canoe contributes to the picturesqueness of the scene. But as the canoe comes closer it is transformed into a Canadian longboat commanded by an officer of the Provincial Marine, Lieutenant Frederic Rolette, with six seamen, armed with cutlasses and pistols, pulling on the oars.

Rolette calls to the *Cuyahoga*'s captain, Luther Chapin, to lower his mainsails. Chapin is open mouthed. He had expected a friendly hail; now he sees six muskets raised against him. Before he can act, Rolette fires his pistol in the air. Chapin struggles with the sail. Beall and his fellow passengers are in confusion. What is happening? Beall orders the captain to hoist the sail again and press on, but Chapin replies that this is not possible.

Rolette now points his pistol directly at young George Gooding, a second-lieutenant in charge of the soldiers and baggage of the U.S. 4th Infantry Regiment. "Dowse your mainsails!" Rolette orders.

Gooding equivocates. "I have no command here, sir," he shouts. Rolette fires directly at the schooner, the ball whistling past Beall's head. The captain pleads for instructions. "Do as you please," answers the rattled Gooding, whose wife is also on deck. As the mainsails tumble, Frederic Rolette boards the packet.

He is astonished to find the decks jammed with American soldiers. They are not aware that the war has started, but Rolette cannot be sure of that. Nor does he know that all but three are ill and that the muskets and ammunition are out of reach in the hold. All he knows is that he is outnumbered five to one.

This does not dismay him, for he is a seasoned seaman, accustomed to act with boldness and decision. At the age of twenty-nine, this French-speaking Quebecker has a naval record any officer might envy. He has fought in the two greatest sea battles of the era – the Nile and Trafalgar – under the finest commander of his time, Horatio Nelson. He has been wounded five times and, before this newest contest is over, will be wounded again. Now, as William Beall approaches to demand his authority for boarding the schooner, Rolette informs him curtly that an express reached Amherstburg the previous night announcing the commencement of hostilities. Then, losing no time, he orders everybody below decks, posts sentries at the hatches and arms chests with orders to shoot any man who approaches them, orders the helmsman to steer the ship under the water battery at Amherstburg and the band to play "God Save the King."

As the schooner docks at the naval yard, the passengers are released under guard to the open deck and all the baggage is removed. Now the British realize the magnitude of their prize. For here are discovered two trunks belonging to General Hull containing documents of extraordinary value. Hull's aide-de-camp – his son Abraham – has foolishly packed the General's personal papers with his baggage. The astonished British discover that they now possess all the details of the army that opposes them: field states, complete returns of the troops, the names and strengths of the regiments, an incomplete draft of Hull's own memorial of March 6 outlining his strategy, and all his correspondence to and from the Secretary of War. It is a find equal to the breaking of an enemy code. The entire package is dispatched to

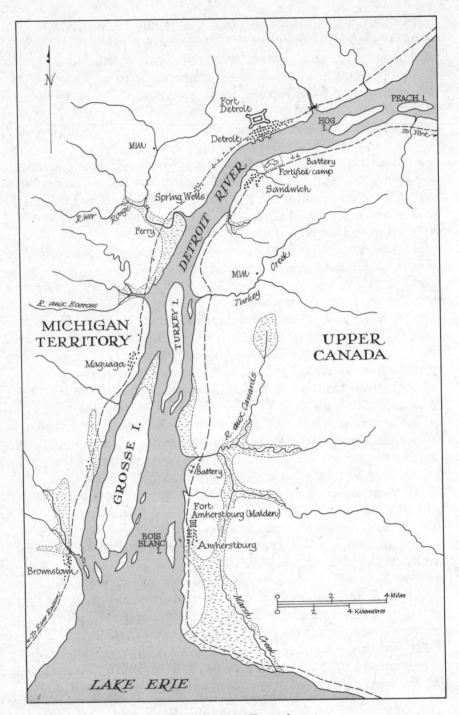

The Detroit Frontier

Brock at York, who immediately grasps its significance and lays his plans.

No one on either side, meanwhile, is quite certain how to behave. Has war actually come? Even the British are reluctant to believe it. William Beall, now a prisoner, doubts it. He is certain that his captors have been wrongly informed, that when Hull demands his return he and his companions will be permitted to go on to Detroit.

The British are polite, even hospitable. Lieutenant Edward Dewar, Beall's opposite number in the quartermaster's department at Fort Amherstburg, urges the Americans not to consider themselves prisoners but merely detainees. It is all very unpleasant, Dewar murmurs; he hopes the report of the war may prove incorrect; he hopes the Americans will be able to spend their time in detention as agreeably as possible; if there is any service he and his fellow officers can render to that end, they will be only too pleased to do so; he only wishes the packet could have passed by without interruption; if authentic information arrives that war has not been declared, they will be released at once. And so on.

George Gooding declares he would like to dine ashore and put up at an inn. Dewar gets permission from his commanding officer, Lieutenant-Colonel Thomas Bligh St. George, but points out the C.O.'s fear that the Indians are much enraged at the Americans and advises them to be on guard against attack. The detainees agree to accept billets aboard another ship, *Thames*, where a guard can be stationed. Meanwhile they must be very careful. At this stage of the war, the British are worried at the horrors their native allies may commit on their new enemies. Dewar tells Beall that he fears that the Indians, in a drunken rage, might enter a tavern and murder all the Americans. To underline the danger he tells how an infuriated Indian had recently stepped up behind a man walking with a British officer and tomahawked him. Don't go out into the streets alone, Dewar warns.

Now, having accepted the parole of Beall and his companions that they will not try to escape, Dewar invites them to his home until their accommodation is prepared. On the wharf, a crowd of Indians look them over. In Beall's eyes some appear to rejoice at their capture, while others terrify him with ferocious frowns. Gooding, who fought at Tippecanoe, recognizes some of his former adversaries. Harrison's bitter seed, broadcast on the banks of the Wabash, is already beginning to sprout.

At Dewar's home there is wine, cider, biscuits. It would be improper, says the Lieutenant, to invite the Americans to dine with him, but he accompanies them to Boyle's Inn and Public House, apologizing in his diffident British fashion for its poor quality but explaining that it is the best in town. Following dinner, the men leave the inn and, accompanied by a British officer, stroll through the streets through crowds of Indians who the nervous Beall feels are glaring directly at him. Every white man, however, bows politely to the strangers and one even invites them into his house and pours them several glasses of wine.

Many of these are Americans, lured to Upper Canada by the prospect of free land and low taxes. They have little interest in politics, less in war. In a province of some sixty thousand, they form a clear but powerless majority, having been shut out of all public office by the elite group of British and Loyalist administrators who control the government. This does not unduly concern them, for they are prospering on their free acreage. Democracy may be virtually non-existent in Upper Canada, but so are taxes, since the province is financed by the British treasury. Beall is intrigued to discover that the master of his floating prison, Captain Martin of the *Thames*, owns a well-stocked farm of three hundred acres but pays an annual levy of exactly $1.06¼.

As for the prospect of war, they dismiss it. During their walk through the village, Lieutenant Dewar remarks to Beall that he will be sorry if the two countries cannot adjust their difficulties without violence. Everyone to whom the American speaks echoes that sentiment.

The women, being non-combatants, are sent to the American side; the men remain aboard the *Thames*. Beall estimates that there are at least five hundred Indians in town. On July 4, as the sounds of Independence Day cannonades echo across the water from Detroit, two hundred Sauk warriors arrive, the largest and best-formed men Beall has ever seen, though in his eyes they are as savage and uncultivated as any other natives.

On the following day, the sound of Hull's bugler blowing reveille reveals that the Army of the Northwest has reached the village of Brownstown, directly across the river, less than a day's march from Detroit. By nightfall, Amherstburg is in a panic. Women and children run crying toward the vessels at the dockside, loading the decks with trunks of valuables. Indians dash about the streets shouting. Consternation and dismay prevail as the call to arms is sounded. The enemy, in short, is within striking distance of the thinly guarded fort, the sole British bastion on the Detroit frontier. If Hull can seize it in one lightning move, his army can sweep up the valley of the Thames and capture most if not all of Upper Canada.

Beall views it all with mixed feelings. A sensitive and compassionate man who is already starting to pine for his wife Melinda, back in Kentucky, he feels "sensibly for those on both sides who might loose [*sic*] their lives." Certainly his British hosts have been decent to the point of chivalry; it is difficult to think of them as the enemy. (Could Beall actually shoot at Dewar if he met him on the field?) On the other hand, he is convinced that his day of deliverance is at hand. Surely General Hull will cross the river, crush all resistance at Amherstburg, free him for further service, and, if the campaign is as decisive as everyone expects, return him swiftly to Melinda's arms!

•

THE CRUCIAL DISPATCH to General Hull, announcing the war, is hidden somewhere in the Cleveland mail. Frustration! Walworth, the postmaster, has written orders to forward it at once by express. But where is it? He can guess what it contains, for the news has already reached Cleveland. A young lawyer, Charles Shaler, stands ready to gallop through swamp and forest to the Rapids of the Maumee and on to Detroit, if need be, once the missing document is found. Nobody, apparently, thinks to send him off at once with a verbal message while others rummage for the official one. Hours pass. Shaler chafes. Then somebody suggests the dispatch might be in the Detroit mail. Reluctantly, the postmaster breaks the law, opens the bags, finds the missing paper.

Off goes Shaler, swimming the unbridged rivers, plunging through the wilderness, vainly seeking a relay steed to replace his gasping horse. Some eighty hours later, on the evening of July 1 (the *Cuyahoga* has already been dispatched) he reaches the rapids, discovers the army has decamped, gallops after it. He reached Hull's force at two the following morning. The General, half-dressed, reads the dispatch, registers alarm, orders Shaler to keep quiet in the presence of others, calls a council of his officers, orders a boat to take after the *Cuyahoga*. It is too late; she cannot be caught. At dawn the army moves on, Shaler riding with the troops. On reaching Detroit, his much-abused horse drops dead of exhaustion.

The army arrives on July 5, after thirty-five days of struggle through Ohio's swampy wilderness. The soldiers find a primitive settlement of twelve hundred straggling on the outskirts of a log fort. Like their neighbours on both sides of the river, most of the people are French speaking, descendants of families that settled the land a century before and whose strip farms with their narrow river frontage betray their Québécois background. In Hull's view they are "miserable farmers," being descended from voyageurs, traders, soldiers, and artisans – people with no agricultural tradition. They raise apples for cider and gigantic pears for pickling but pay little attention to other forms of agriculture, depending principally on hunting, fishing, and trading with the Indians. In short, they cannot provision his troops – and this is Hull's dilemma: his supply line is two hundred miles long, stretching south along the makeshift trace his men have hacked out of the forests. To secure his position, Hull must have two months' provisions. In Chillicothe, the capital, Ohio's energetic governor, Return Meigs, receives the General's plea, raises a company of ninety-five citizen volunteers, and sends them north through Urbana as escort for a brigade of pack horses, loaded with flour and provisions, and a drove of beef cattle. But to reach Hull, this supply train must eventually follow the road that hugs the southwestern shore of Lake Erie and the Detroit River. That will be dangerous because the British control the water.

Hull's more immediate concern is the fate of the baggage captured aboard the *Cuyahoga*. Have the British actually rifled his personal possessions, discovered his official correspondence? He pens a note to Lieutenant-Colonel St. George, the commander at Fort Amherstburg. Dripping with politeness and studiedly casual, it reads more like an interoffice memorandum than a communication between enemies:

Sir,
    Since the arrival of my army at this Encampment...I have been informed that a number of discharges of Artillery and of small arms have been made by some of the Militia of the Territory, from this Shore into Sandwich.
    I regret to have received such information, the proceeding was [un]authorized by me. I am not disposed to make War on Private Property, or to authorise a wanton attack upon unoffending individuals, I would be happy to learn whether you consider private Property a proper objective of seizure and detention, I allude to the Baggage of Officers particularly....

St. George, in his reply to Hull, outdoes the General in verbal niceties:

Sir,

I am honoured with your letter of this days date; I perfectly coincide with you in opinion respecting private property, and any wanton attack upon unoffending individuals, and am happy to find, what I was certain would be the case, that the aggression in question was unauthorized by you.

In respect to the property of officers not on board a vessel at the time of capture I must be judged by the customs of war in like cases, in justice to the captors, and shall always be ready to meet your wishes...when I receive orders...from my government....

Which, translated, simply means: go to hell.

The bearer of Hull's letter, under a flag of truce, is Colonel Cass, whose instructions are to spy out the situation at the British fort. Cass takes a good look, reports that rumour has exaggerated the garrison's strength and also the number of Indians. He believes, and will continue to believe, that Fort Amherstburg can be easily taken.

In spite of the suavity of his correspondence, Thomas Bligh St. George is a badly rattled commander. He is an old campaigner, with forty years of service in the British Army, much of it spent in active warfare on the Mediterranean. But he has been a staff officer for the past decade and clearly has difficulty coping with the present crisis. He commands a lightly garrisoned fort, in need of repair and reinforcement. Across the river an army of two thousand sits poised for invasion. Scrambling about in a fever of preparation he is "so harassed for these five days and nights, I can scarcely write." Brock, who receives this communication, is dismayed to discover that Lieutenant-Colonel St. George has let three days slip by before bothering to inform him that Hull's force has reached Detroit.

Fort Amherstburg is in chaos. Indians are coming and going, eating up the supplies; no one can guess their strength from day to day. The same is true of the militia: St. George has no real idea of how many men he commands or whether he has the resources to supply them. The accounts are in disarray, the returns non-existent. He has not enough officers to organize the militia – many of whom are leaving for home or attempting to leave – or enough arms to supply them. Nor does he know how he can pay them.

The little village of Sandwich lies directly across the river from

Detroit, upriver from Amherstburg. This, St. George knows, will be Hull's invasion point. He stations some militia units at Sandwich but has little hope that they will be effective. To "encourage" them, in St. George's euphemism, he sends along a detachment of regulars. To supply the wants of his confused and amateur army, St. George is obliged to make use of everything that falls in his way. This includes a brigade of eleven bateaux loaded with supplies that the North West Company has dispatched from Montreal to its post at Fort William at the lakehead. St. George seizes the supplies, impresses the seventy voyageurs.

On the docks and in the streets the Indians are engaged in war dances, leaping and capering before the doors of the inhabitants, who give them presents of whiskey. "I have seen the great Tecumseh," William Beall, still captive aboard the *Thames*, writes in his diary. "He is a very plane man, rather above middle-size, stout built, a noble set of features and an admirable eye. He is always accompanied by Six great chiefs, who never go before him. The women and men all fear that in the event of Genl. Hull's crossing and proving successfull, that the Indians being naturally treacherous will turn against them to murder and destroy them."

Tecumseh's followers have shadowed Hull's army all the way through Michigan Territory, warned by their leader to take no overt action until war is declared and he can bring his federation into alliance with Great Britain. Hull has done his best to neutralize him, sending messengers to a council at Fort Wayne, promising protection and friendship if the Indians stay out of the white man's war.

"Neutral indeed!" cries Tecumseh to the assembled tribes. "Who will protect you while the Long Knives are fighting the British and are away from you? Who will protect you from the attack of your ancient enemies, the western tribes, who may become allies of the British?"

Will a policy of neutrality lead to a restoration of the Indian lands, Tecumseh asks, and as he speaks, takes the emissary's peace pipe and breaks it between his fingers. And later:

"Here is a chance presented to us—yes, a chance such as will never occur again—for us Indians of North America to form ourselves into one great combination and cast our lot with the British in this war...."

Tecumseh leaves Fort Wayne with a large party of Shawnee, Kickapoo, Potawatomi, and Delaware to meet Matthew Elliott at Amherstburg. Hull sends another emissary, urges another council at Brownstown, the Wyandot village directly opposite the British fort. Tecumseh refuses:

"I have taken sides with the King, my father, and I will suffer my bones to bleach upon this shore before I will recross that stream to join in any council of neutrality."

Like the Americans, the Wyandot are split into camps of hawks and doves. They are important to Tecumseh's cause because they are the senior tribe, looked up to by all the others. They are Huron, the remnants of the mighty nation destroyed during the French regime. At a great council held on the parade ground at Fort Amherstburg on July 7, one chief, Roundhead, supports Tecumseh. Another, Walk-in-the-Water, advocates neutrality and crosses back into U.S. territory. But Tecumseh has no intention of letting the Wyandot straddle the fence.

Upriver at Detroit, Hull prepares to invade Canada by landing his army at Sandwich. He attempts to move on July 10 but, to his dismay, discovers that hundreds of militiamen, urged on in some cases by their officers, decline to cross the river. They have not committed themselves to fight on foreign soil.

The next day Hull tries again. Two militia companies refuse to enter the boats. One finally gives in to persuasion; the other stands firm. When Hull demands a list of those who refuse to go, the company commander, a Captain Rupes, hands over the names of his entire command. Hull's adjutant harangues the men. Words like "coward" and "traitor" are thrown at them to no avail. Again the crossing is aborted.

The war has yet to develop beyond the comic opera stage. Across the river at Sandwich an equally reluctant body of citizen soldiers—the militia of Kent and Essex counties, only recently called to service—sits and waits. These young farmers have had little if any training, militia service being mainly an excuse for social carousing. They are not eager to fight, especially in midsummer with the winter wheat ripening in the fields. Patriotism has no meaning for most of them; that is the exclusive property of the Loyalists. The majority are passively pro-American, having moved up from New Jersey, New York, and Pennsylvania. Isolated on the scattered farms and absorbed in the wearisome if profitable task of clearing the land and working the soil, they have as yet no sense of a larger community. Few have ever seen a newspaper; they learn of the war tardily, through handbills. Whether or not Upper Canada becomes another American state they do not really care.

Lieutenant-Colonel St. George, who is convinced that these un-willing soldiers—most are not even uniformed—will flee to their homes at the first shot, decides to get them out of the way before the attack is launched. Otherwise, their certain rout would throw his entire force into a state of confusion. The only way he can prevent them from melting away to their farms is to march the lot back to the fort and make the most of them; perhaps their backs can be stiffened by the example of the regulars. Even that is doubtful: from his vantage point in the town of Amherstburg William Beall discovers that many of these former Americans express a desire to join Hull as soon as he crosses into Canada.

At last, on July 12, a bright and lovely Sunday, Hull resolves to make the crossing, even though two hundred of his men continue to stand on their constitutional rights. He fears further mutinies if he keeps his troops inactive, and it is also his fancy that the Canadian settlers will feel themselves liberated from the British yoke once he lands and that they and the Indians will stay out of the war.

Hull's landing is unopposed. Colonel Cass is the first to leap from the lead boat, and thus the first American to set foot on Canadian soil. He immediately unfurls the Stars and Stripes while Hull's staff searches about for a headquarters.

Sandwich is a placid little garden village, almost every house set in a small orchard where peaches, grapes, and apples flourish. The conquering general seizes the most imposing residence – a new brick home, built in the Georgian style the year before, its interior still unfinished, belonging to Lieutenant-Colonel François Bâby, a member of a distinguished pioneer fur-trading family. The Bâbys and the Hulls have been on intimate terms, but when James Bâby, a brother and also a militia colonel, protests (his own home not far away is quickly pillaged), all Hull can say is that *circumstances are changed now*, a phrase which Lieutenant-Colonel Bâby will throw back at him a month later.

Hull has scarcely landed when he insists on issuing a proclamation intended to disperse the militia and cow the inhabitants, many of whom are either terrified of his troops or secretly disposed to his cause. Most have fled, but those who remain welcome the invaders as friends, waving white handkerchiefs and flags from the windows and crying out such phrases as "We like the Americans." At Amherstburg, Beall encounters similar sentiments and confides to his journal that many solicit secret interviews with him, and when these are refused "occasionally and slily say 'Success to the Americans and General Hull', 'Let us alone and we will take Malden [Amherstburg] ourselves', et cetera, and many expressions showing their warmth for us and the Americans and their detestation of the British."

Yet Hull cannot resist issuing a bombastic proclamation that seems designed to set the Canadians on edge. He has it printed, rather imperfectly, in Detroit, borrowing the press of a Roman Catholic priest. It is soon the talk of the countryside:

A PROCLAMATION

INHABITANTS OF CANADA! After thirty years of Peace and prosperity, the United States have been driven to Arms. The injuries and aggressions, the insults and indignities of Great Britain have *once more* left them no alternative but manly resistance or unconditional submission. The army under my Command has invaded your Country and the standard of the United States waves on the territory of Canada. To the peaceful, unoffending inhabitant, It brings neither danger nor difficulty I come to *find* enemies not to *make* them, I come to *protect* you not to *injure* you.

Separated by an immense ocean and an extensive Wilderness from Great Britain you have no participation in her counsels no interest in her conduct. You have felt her Tyranny, you have seen her injustice, but I do not ask *you* to avenge the one or to redress the other. The United States are sufficiently powerful to afford you every security consistent with their rights & your expectations. I tender you the invaluable blessings of Civil, Political, & Religious Liberty, and their necessary result, individual, and general, prosperity: That liberty which gave decision to our counsels and energy to our conduct in our struggle for INDEPENDENCE and which conducted us safely and triumphantly thro' the stormy period of the Revolution....

In the name of my *Country* and by the authority of my Government I promise you protection to your *persons, property, and rights*, Remain at your homes, Pursue your peaceful and customary avocations. Raise not your hands against your brethern, many of your fathers fought for the freedom & *Indepennce* we now enjoy Being children therefore of the same family with us, and heirs to the same Heritage, the arrival of an army of Friends must be hailed by you with a cordial welcome, You will be emancipated from Tyranny and oppression and restored to the dignified status of freemen.... If contrary to your own interest & the just expectation of my country, you should take part in the approaching contest, you will be considered and treated as enemies and the horrors, and calamities of war will Stalk before you.

If the barbarous and Savage policy of Great Britain be pursued, and the savages are let loose to murder our Citizens and butcher our women and children, this war, will be a war of extermination.

The first stroke with the Tomahawk the first attempt with the Scalping Knife will be the Signal for one indiscriminate scene of desolation, *No white man found fighting by the Side of an Indian will be taken prisoner* Instant destruction will be his Lot....

I doubt not your courage and firmness; I will not doubt your attachment to Liberty. If you tender your services voluntarily they will be accepted readily.

The United State offers you *Peace*, *Liberty*, and *Security* your choice lies between these, & *War, Slavery, and destruction*, Choose then, but choose wisely; and may he who knows the justice of our cause, and who holds in his hand the fate of Nations, guide you to a result the most compatible, with your rights and interests, your peace and prosperity.

WM. HULL

The General, who is afraid of the Indians, hopes that this document will force his opposite number at Fort Amherstburg to follow the lead of the United States and adopt a policy of native neutrality, at least temporarily. At the very minimum it ought to frighten the settlers and militia into refusing to bear arms. That is its immediate effect. In Brock's phrase, "the disaffected became more audacious, and the wavering more intimidated." The proclamation terrifies the militia. Within three days the force of newly recruited soldiers has been reduced by half as the farm boys desert to their homes.

Yet Hull has overstated his case. These are farmers he is addressing, not revolutionaries. The colonial authoritarianism touches very few. They do not feel like slaves; they already have enough peace, liberty, and security to satisfy them. This tax-free province is not America at the time of the Boston Tea Party. Why is Hull asking them to free themselves from tyranny? In the words of one, if they had been under real tyranny, "they could at any time have crossed the line to the United States."

130

Hull has made another error. He threatens that anyone found fighting beside the Indians can expect no quarter. That rankles. *Everybody* will be fighting with the Indians; it will not be a matter of choice. Some of the militiamen who secretly hoped to go over to Hull in the confusion of battle have a change of heart. What is the point of deserting if the Americans intend to kill them on capture?

Precipitate action does not fit the Upper Canadian mood. This is a pioneer society, not a frontier society. No Daniel Boones stalk the Canadian forests, ready to knock off an Injun with a Kentucky rifle or do battle over an imagined slight. The Methodist circuit riders keep the people law abiding and temperate; prosperity keeps them content. The Sabbath is looked on with reverence; card playing and horse racing are considered sinful diversions; the demon rum has yet to become a problem. There is little theft, less violence. Simple pastimes tied to the land – barn raisings, corn huskings, threshing bees – serve as an outlet for the spirited. The new settlers will not volunteer to fight. But most are prepared, if forced, to bear arms for their new country and to march when ordered. In the years that follow some will even come to believe that they were the real saviours of Upper Canada.

●

MONTREAL, LOWER CANADA, July 4, 1812. Sir George Prevost has moved up from his capital at Quebec to be closer to the scene of action. An American army is gathering at Albany, New York, poised to attack Montreal by the traditional invasion route of the Lake Champlain water corridor. If it succeeds, Sir George is perfectly prepared to abandon all of Upper Canada and withdraw to the fortress of Quebec.

At this moment, however, the Captain-General, Governor-in-Chief, Vice-Admiral, Lieutenant-General and Commanding Officer of His Majesty's Forces in Upper Canada, Lower Canada, Nova Scotia, New Brunswick, Cape Breton, Newfoundland and the Bermudas is faced with a crisis on his own doorstep. A riot has broken out at Lachine over the Militia Law, which provides for the drafting of two thousand bachelors for three months' training. Some of the men from the parish at Pointe Claire have refused to go, believing – or pretending to believe – that the act has not been properly passed and the government is simply seizing an excuse to turn young French Canadians into soldiers.

When the army tries force, a mob resists and marches off to Lachine to seize a flotilla of boats in which the draftees hope to escape. The Riot Act is read; shots whistle over the insurgents' heads and are returned; two civilians are killed. Four hundred and fifty soldiers invade the community and begin taking prisoners – so many, indeed, that they are finally released on the promise that they will "implore the pardon of His Excellency the Governor."

His Excellency is a suave diplomat whose forte is conciliation. He has learned that delicate art as governor of St. Lucia and later of Dominica, French-speaking islands in the Caribbean wrested from the mother country by the British but soothed into passivity by a man who has none of the hauteur of a British colonial bureaucrat. Born of a Swiss father and perfectly at home in the French language, Prevost has the exact qualifications needed to win over a race who also consider themselves a conquered people.

Now, before some three hundred insurgents, the Great Conciliator appears and turns on his considerable charm.

"His Excellency expostulated with them as a Father and pointed out to them the danger of their situation in a style truly honourable to his own feelings, assuring them of his forgiveness on delivering up those who had been promoters of the insurrection...which they cheerfully agreed to do...."

Thus with the crisis defused and the approving comment of the Montreal *Herald* putting the seal on his actions, the Governor General can turn to graver matters. He is resolved to fight a defensive war only; he does not have the resources to go on the attack, even if he wished to. But he does not wish to. His own natural caution has been sustained by specific instructions from Lord Liverpool, the Secretary of State for War and the Colonies, to do nothing rash.

Rashness is not Sir George's style. He finds it difficult to countenance it in others. Surely the United States will do nothing rash! He is half convinced that the Americans do not actually mean to fight; that some accommodation can be made with them; that the war is not a real war; and that, in any event, it cannot possibly last for more than a few weeks. "Prudent" is a word that slips comfortably into his correspondence. He considers it "prudent and politic to avoid any measure which can in its effect have a tendency to unite the people in the American States," for "whilst disunion prevails among them, their attempts on these provinces will be feeble." Therefore it is important not to anger the enemy. Brock, specifically, is enjoined from "committing any act which may even by construction tend to unite the Eastern and Southern states."

Brock, with his reputation for dash and daring, worries Prevost. The impetuous subordinate is more than a week away by express courier and a month away by post. His audacity is legendary. Prevost has certainly heard the stories. One goes all the way back to Brock's early days, when his regiment, the 49th, was stationed at Bridgetown in Barbados. There was in that company a confirmed braggart and duellist whose practice was to insult fellow officers and finish them off at twelve paces. Brock, when accosted, accepted the challenge but refused to fire at the regulation distance. Instead, he produced a handkerchief and demanded that both men fire across it at point-blank range, thus equalling the odds and making the death of at least one of them a virtual certainty. His adversary panicked, refused to fire, and thus shamed was forced to leave the regiment.

There are other tales: Brock in the saddle, insisting on riding to the very pinnacle of Mount Hillaby, twelve hundred feet above the Caribbean – a feat most horsemen consider impossible; or, in 1803, personally leading an eight-hour chase in an open boat across Lake Ontario to apprehend six deserters, a venture that brought him a reprimand.

To a prudent commander, Brock's presence can be disquieting, even alarming. He is known as a man who believes that "nothing should be impossible to a soldier; the word impossible should not be found in a soldier's dictionary!" Will Brock attempt the impossible in Upper Canada? Prevost is determined that he shall not.

The contrast between the two commanders can be seen in their official portraits. At forty-four, Prevost is a handsome man, his lean face framed by dark sideburns; yet even in his painted likeness there is a furtiveness. The eyes swivel back as if to watch the artist; little furrows crease the brow. There is a slackness of mouth, a hesitancy of stance, none of the knife-edge sharpness that distinguishes the features of his subordinate who, in his portraits, looks off resolutely and serenely into the middle distance.

If Prevost is more diplomat than soldier, Brock is more soldier than diplomat. He remains disdainful of civilians, though he has learned to curb in public the tactlessness that once marked his dealings with the administration in Quebec. Prevost on the other hand has, in less than a year, worked a miracle in Lower Canada by managing to conciliate the French Canadians whose loyalty to the Crown had been placed in jeopardy by the racial arrogance of his predecessor. Under Sir James Craig, the Québécois found themselves shut out of all important government posts.

In contrast to Craig, who believed the French Canadians disloyal, Prevost is convinced they will fight to retain their land. The bombast in Washington prophesying the easy conquest of the Canadas will, he believes, help swell the ranks of the militia. Nonetheless, diplomacy will be needed: "The Canadians in general are grossly ignorant, it will therefore require vigilance and circumspection to prevent the proposed changes from being attended by any circumstance prejudicial to the tranquillity of the colony."

Circumspection Prevost has in quantity; but circumspection does not win wars. In material supplies he is hopelessly deficient. He has no coin with which to pay his troops and will have to persuade the legislature to issue paper money. He is embarrassed that he cannot supply the militia with enough rifles, let alone other equipment. A ship has set out from Bermuda to Halifax with six thousand stands of arms; apparently it has foundered in a storm. The mother country's priorities are Wellington's; she can supply Prevost with little to repel invasion – neither money, nor arms, nor men. He is short of officers; there are only two generals in Lower Canada, himself and Baron Francis de Rottenburg, and in Upper Canada two more: Roger Sheaffe and Isaac Brock.

Brock! In many ways he is worth five generals; Prevost admires and likes him. But – one can see the pursed lips, the furrowed brow – how to keep him in check? Overall British strategy does not envisage the seizure of American territory. Prevost does not wish to provoke the enemy. There is only one way to contain Brock, dictated as much by circumstance as by design, and that is to keep his regular force to a minimum. Upper Canada will get five hundred reinforcements, no more. And Brock must be convinced that these numbers will not "justify offensive operations being undertaken, *unless they were solely calculated to strengthen a defensive attitude*."

The italics are not Prevost's. But the phrase is one that undoubtedly burns its way into the mind of the military commander of Upper Canada. When the moment comes, he will place the broadest possible interpretation on Sir George Prevost's cautious instructions.

SANDWICH, UPPER CANADA, July 23, 1812; with General
Hull's Army of the Northwest.

"Why does the army dally?" Robert Lucas asks rhetorically, as he
scratches away in his diary. "Why do they not make the Stroke on
Maldon [Amherstburg] at once, had proper energy been used, we
might have been in Maldon now, we are tampering with them untill
they will be able to drive us back across the river...."

Why indeed? Hull's troops are eager to maintain some momentum,
have been since the day of the landing when it was expected Hull would
sweep down the river to attack the British fort at Amherstburg – a place
name that has a sinister connotation for western Americans who have
suffered at the hands of the Indians. For this has been the headquarters of Elliott, McKee and Girty, whom the frontiersmen believe
were behind the raids on white settlements in the Northwest.

Like his fellow volunteers, Lucas wants to get on with it. Once Fort
Amherstburg's guns are silenced, the way to Upper Canada lies wide
open. The only other British forts on the western frontier are at the
other end of Lake Erie and along the Niagara River. A second
American army has been dispatched to attack these strong points. Its
task is to cause a diversion, pin down the defending British and prevent reinforcements from reaching Fort Amherstburg.

To Lucas, speed is essential. Amherstburg must be attacked and
taken before Brock can divert more men to its defence. Lucas is used
to swift, flexible movements, for he has been acting as a scout for
Hull. In the General's mixed bag of raw recruits, untrained civilians,
professional commanders, and elected leaders, he is a hybrid –
general, captain, and private soldier rolled into one. The anomaly
springs out of his country's awkward military philosophy, which disdains the idea of a standing army and relies on volunteers for the
nation's defence. Lucas had been for some time a brigadier-general in
the Ohio state militia. Eager to serve in the regular army, he applied
in April for a captain's commission. A few days later, before it came
through, McArthur ordered him to transmit from his brigade a proportion of the twelve hundred men required from the state in the coming war. What to do? Lucas, thirsty for action, set an example to his
men by enrolling as a private in a volunteer company. To add to the
confusion, the men elected his younger brother John as their captain.

Now, at Sandwich, Lucas vents his disgust in his diary: *Why does the army dally?* Hull is not short of supplies, for he has sent McArthur foraging up the Thames, raiding the farms, the barns, and the fields for food and equipment. McArthur and his men, moving without blankets or provisions, living off the land, penetrate sixty miles into the heart of Upper Canada: a land of stump and snake fences; of cabins and shanties of basswood and cedar; of Dutch lofts and clay ovens; of grist mills, fanning mills, and windmills; of chicken hutches, corn cribs, hog pens, and cattle sheds; of pickled pork and pigeon pie and fresh milk kept cool in underground sheds; of oxen hitched in tandem, furrowing the glistening fields, and raw-boned men in homespun linsey-woolsey scything the tawny harvest of midsummer. The raiding party leaves a trail of devastation in its wake, returning in five days with two hundred barrels of flour, four hundred blankets, and wagons loaded with whiskey, salt, cloth, guns, ammunition, household goods, tools – even boats. Grain fields are destroyed, homes ransacked, orchards levelled, corn trampled, fences burned or shattered – actions that enrage the settlers and help to turn them against their former compatriots.

John McGregor, a trader and merchant who has removed his goods to Matthew Dolsen's house and mill on the Thames for safety, loses everything – flour, merchandise, grain, livestock, and boats – and almost loses his life. He and Dolsen are forced to flee when it is learned that McArthur intends to shoot them on sight in the belief that they are rousing the Indians and militia to resistance.

Farmers and townspeople are beggared by the raiders. Jean-Baptiste Beniteau's orchard of sixty fruit trees is destroyed, his fences and pickets reduced to ashes. His neighbour, Jean-Baptiste Ginac, is looted of all his livestock, pork, flour, oats, and corn. Another Jean-Baptiste – Fourneaux – loses 480 bushels of grain, all his cider, as well as his winter's wood supply and furniture. A fourth, Jean-Baptiste Boismier, a fur trader, sees his entire fortune of 620 skins together with his livestock, tools, utensils, and harvested corn go to the enemy.

Hull's men make no allowance for old friends. Lieutenant-Colonel François Bâby, whose house has become Hull's headquarters, has tried to save some of his chattels by hauling them off to Jean-Baptiste Goyeau's home, three miles distant. But Hull dispatches a party of dragoons with six wagons who remove everything at gunpoint, then, emboldened by conquest, slice up one of Bâby's finest coats with their sabres. Bâby's loss is staggering; he reckons it at 2,678 pounds sterling.

Another raiding party ransacks the estate of the Earl of Selkirk at Baldoon on Lake St. Clair, seizing a thousand pounds' worth of booty, from pewter plates to pitchforks, including the greatest prize of all, more than nine hundred prize Merino sheep, which are ferried across the river to Fort Detroit along with the aged Scot who is their shepherd.

McArthur brushes all complaints aside with the promise that everything will eventually be paid for because, he says, Hull has such a footing in Canada that the British will never be able to drive him out.

And so it appears. At Fort Amherstburg the situation is deteriorating. Militia service works real hardship on those families who depend upon the able-bodied for their livelihood. Hundreds desert. Those who remain loyal – men like Robert Pike of Port Dover or John Williams on the Thames – have no one to harvest their wheat and so lose it all to rot. St. George, the commander at the fort, feels himself obliged to release the oldest and least efficient to return to their farms. Others slip away. On July 8, St. George counts 850 militiamen under his command. A week later the number has dropped to 471. "I expect that in two or three days we shall have very few of them at the post," Matthew Elliott informs his superior, adding that there is no ammunition left in the Indian stores "and, if more Indians come, I really do not know how to act." St. George expects an attack almost hourly, but it does not come. In Robert Lucas's rueful belief, Hull's dallying has given the British hope. "Our conduct has at least incouraged them much," he notes.

One of the keenest soldiers in Hull's army, Lucas has managed to see more action than most of his followers. As a ranger and scout he has always been in the vanguard of the main army, often in danger. He is one of those natural soldiers, found in every army, who thrive on action. When Hull's boats crossed over to Sandwich, Lucas arranged to switch companies temporarily in order to be one of the first to set foot on Canadian soil because he "could not endure to be behind."

On July 16, Lucas volunteers again: Colonels Cass and Miller are ordered to reconnoitre enemy country up to the River aux Canards, a deep but sluggish stream that winds through the marshes three miles above Amherstburg. Lucas immediately offers to go along. This war will help to make his reputation; one day he will be governor of Ohio and later of Iowa Territory.

Colonel Cass is as eager for glory and for action as Lucas. The bridge at the Canard is held by a detachment of British regulars and Indians – the same Menominee dispatched to Amherstburg from the Wisconsin country the previous month by Robert Dickson. Cass resolves to ford the river upstream and attack in a flanking movement while Miller pins down the sentries. Again Lucas and the rangers are in the vanguard.

Faced with an attack on their rear, the British retire. Cass cannot pursue, for a tributary stream blocks the way. But the British sentries – John Dean and James Hancock of the 41st – stubbornly hold their ground and become the first soldiers to shed their blood on Canadian soil in the War of 1812. Dean, one arm broken by a musket ball, fights on with his bayonet until he is knocked to the ground and disarmed. Hancock, bleeding from at least two wounds, unable to support himself, continues to fight on his knees until he is captured. He dies that night and is scalped by one of the Indians, who sells the trophy to the British – "a good trick for an Indian to make the British Gov. pay for their own Soldiers Scalps," comments Robert Lucas.

This is the first time the Americans have come up against British regulars, that tough, stubborn, hard-drinking, somewhat unimaginative breed whom Wellington has called, not without affection, "the scum of the earth." America, nurtured on the ideal of a free-wheeling grassroots democracy, scorns the British professional as a semi-robot and mercenary, wedded to no political ideal. It is true, certainly, that many a British working man joins for the money: the handsome bounties offered those who transfer from the militia, the prospect of a substantial prize after a successful engagement. But there are other reasons. Wellington believes, not without considerable evidence, that "they have all enlisted for drink." Yet drink is only a symptom; like enlistment, it is a form of escape from the appallingly drab conditions of the British lower classes. The army is composed of men fleeing from a variety of bedevilments – brutal taskmasters, nagging wives, pregnant girl friends, intolerable parents, constables and judges, or simple boredom. Black-sheep sons of well-born families ("gentlemen rankers") rub shoulders with footpads, pickpockets, roustabouts, poachers, smugglers, or plain, resolute English labouring men hungry for adventure in a far-off land, even if that be nothing more glamorous than garrison duty with the 41st in the backwater of Amherstburg.

Wellington's scum are actually in a minority. It is estimated that in a battalion of some three or four hundred men, perhaps fifty are rogues – drunkards, stragglers, potential deserters. A harsh system of discipline keeps them in line. In the summer of 1812, for instance, the 103rd Regiment in Quebec holds thirty-seven courts martial and sentences thirty-one men to a total of 5,725 lashes, of which at least 1,589 are actually laid on the bare back, the others being remitted. (One unfortunate is lashed three hundred times.) But it is the parade-ground drill, hammered into the rankers' subconscious, that trains the men to act automatically – to stand fast as the enemy advances, to hold their fire until ordered, to discharge their muskets in a single shattering volley without flinching, even as the cavalry sweeps down upon the square or hostile bayonets attempt to break the scarlet line. The wounded Dean, now a prisoner of war, and the dying Hancock are products of this system. It simply does not occur to them to desert their posts.

The Americans now hold the bridge that can lead the army to Amherstburg. It appears to Cass and Miller that the entire force should immediately move up to within striking distance of its objective. But Hull dithers. He is going by the book, planning a careful set-piece siege of the British fort. That he will not undertake until his heavy artillery is ready. The fort might be taken by an infantry assault, but the slaughter would be appalling; and that the former divinity student cannot abide. The bridge is abandoned.

He has other concerns. What is happening on the Niagara frontier? It is essential that an American army be in place along that river. Otherwise there is nothing to stop the British from deploying all their resources against him. Eustis and Dearborn have promised a diversion on the Niagara to support his invasion, but communications are such that the General has no way of knowing whether this has been done.

A closer problem torments him. He is certain that Colonel Cass is trying to pressure him for reasons of personal ambition. He feels his authority slipping away; his officers' complaints are beginning to destroy his influence. He calls council after council to try to quell their impatience; it only erodes his command. "They seem to have thought," he will later argue, "that when a council of war was called, it was to be governed by the laws of a town meeting."

He is determined not to advance until there is "an absolute certainty of success." How long will it take to prepare the cannon? Two days? Two weeks? After each meeting, the time stretches. Hull fears defeat. Defeat will mean starvation for the troops and, worse, devastation by the Indians. The militia fear the Indians. At the bridge over the Canard and also at Turkey Creek and Petite Coté, where desultory skirmishing continues almost daily, Dickson's Menominee and Tecumseh's followers terrify the raw recruits. One regular officer writes to the New York *Gazette*:

"Had it not been for the dastardly conduct of the drafted Ohio militia who composed one half of the party and who took to their heels when they evidently had the advantage, the whole of the Indians would have been killed or taken. The officers endeavoured to rally them and said they would be fired at by their own party if they did not stand. They replied that they would rather be killed by them than by the damned Indians."

There is savagery on both sides. The first Indian scalp is taken by Captain William McCullough of the Rangers, who describes in a letter to his wife how he tore it from the corpse's head with his teeth.

Word of these skirmishes reaches William K. Beall and his fellow prisoners aboard the *Thames*, docked at Amherstburg. It fuels their hope for speedy deliverance. On the night of the encounter at the Canard bridge, Beall learns that Hull's army is camped within reach. Glorious news! But instead of seeing American soldiers marching into town he is greeted by a more macabre spectacle: Thomas McKee of the Indian Department (the perennial drunkard whom Elliott has replaced) arrives at the head of about fifty Indians, all naked except for their breech cloths. McKee, who is also dressed as a native, halts opposite the gaping prisoners and hoists a fresh scalp, fastened to a long pole, which he shakes exultantly, all the time taunting the prisoners with savage cries.

For this spectacle, "which would have chilled the frigid blood of a Laplander or...crimsoned the tawny cheek of an unrelenting Turk," Beall abuses everything British, from the King on down. His fury is misplaced, for the scalp is undoubtedly that of the unfortunate British sentry Hancock.

Beall and his fellow prisoners have other concerns. Where is Hull? What can be keeping him? Gone now is the optimism, the good humour, the gallantry of those first days in captivity. Beall no longer sees the British as gentlemen but as monsters. And he is desperately homesick. His nights are troubled by visions of his young wife, far away on their estate of Beallmont in Kentucky. "In my sleep the air drawn figure of my Melinda often rises to my view: beautious as an Angel, gentle as the spring, smiling on me with enchanted tenderness and yealding to my fond embrace. In dreams, with rapturous fondness, I have pressed her to my bosom, felt her soft touch, heard the sweet accents of her voice, and gazed upon her lovely countenance till every sense was lost in extacy and love."

These visions are rendered more poignant by Beall's disillusionment with his general: "The British officers and soldiers begin to laugh at Hull.... He is now the object of their jest and ridicule instead of being as he was formerly their terror and greatest fear."

Even as Beall is committing these thoughts to paper, on July 26, Hull, at Sandwich, is shaken by an alarming piece of intelligence. A ship, the *Salina*, flying British colours, is brought about by a shot from the shore. Aboard is a group of American citizens and soldiers, led by Lieutenant Porter Hanks, the former commander at Michilimackinac, paroled by his adversary, Roberts. Now, for the first time, Hull learns of Mackinac's fall. It is a major disaster. "I can scarcely conceive of the impression made by the fall of Mackanac," Colonel Cass writes to a relative. For the western anchor on the American frontier has come unstuck, releasing, in Hull's phrase, "the northern hive of Indians," who will shortly come "swarming down in every direction."

Hull feels himself surrounded by Indians. He reasons that there must be two or three thousand Ottawa, Chippewa, and Sioux at his rear, advancing from Mackinac. On his left are the Iroquois of the Grand Valley. They are still neutral, as far as he knows, but he also has news that Brock has sent a detachment to try to bring them into the fight – a task rendered less difficult by the news of Mackinac's fall. In front of him, at Amherstburg, lies another potent force: hundreds more Indians led by the great Tecumseh. Hull fears these more than he does the handful of British regulars.

Within the fort, by the end of the month William Beall and the other American officers have lost all hope of rescue. "I can scarcely think that Genl. H. will be defeated," Beall writes, "but appearances justify such a belief. I am confident that he will not take Malden, though 300 men could do it.... Why does he not, by taking Malden, silence and drive the Indians away who infest the Country and secure a safe communication with the States, and safety to our Frontiers. Heaven only knows. I for a Harrison, a Daviess or a Wells."

•

YORK, UPPER CANADA, July 28, 1812. Isaac Brock, administrator of Upper Canada, resplendent in military crimson and gold, is opening the legislature and managing to mask the emotions of contempt, frustration, and even despair that boil up within him.

...when invaded by an Enemy whose avowed object is the entire Conquest of this Province, the voice of Loyalty as well as of interest calls aloud to every Person in the Sphere in which he is placed, to defend his Country.

Our Militia have heard that voice and have obeyed it, they have evinced by the promptitude and Loyalty of their Conduct, that they are worthy of the King whom they serve, and of the Constitution which they enjoy...

This is hokum, and Brock knows it. He has already written a private note to Prevost declaring his belief that it seems impossible "to animate the militia to a proper sense of duty" and that he almost despairs of doing anything with them. Worse, at Long Point on Lake Erie, where he has attempted to muster five hundred men to march to the relief of Fort Amherstburg, there has been open mutiny. The men have refused to march under Lieutenant-Colonel Thomas Talbot, the eccentric and domineering Irish aristocrat who controls some sixty thousand acres of land in the area. One reason for the mutiny has been the wives' fear of being left alone to the mercy of the neutral Iroquois at the Grand River. Another has been the inflammatory speeches made to them by pro-American civilian dissidents. A third, one suspects, has been Talbot himself, a curious specimen, tyrannical in his control over the settlers—a man who once lived in luxury but who now dresses in homespun, bakes his own bread, labours like a peasant, drinks like a toper, and affects a harsh mode of life which, in the words of a former lieutenant-governor, "might suit a Republic but is not fitted to a Monarchical Government."

In spite of this disaffection, Brock continues the charade:

...it affords me particular satisfaction, that while I address You as Legislators, I speak to men who in the day of danger, will be ready to assist, not only with their Counsel, but with their Arms...

He does not believe it, and his private correspondence reflects his dismay and cynicism. The people and their leaders appear convinced that the war is lost: "...a full belief possesses them that this Province must inevitably succumb.... Legislators, magistrates, militia officers, all have imbibed the idea, and are so sluggish and indifferent in their respective offices that the artful and active scoundrel is allowed to parade the country without interruption and commit all imaginable mischief."

The artful and active scoundrels include a big, ginger-haired blacksmith named Andrew Westbrook and a land surveyor from Montreal named Simon Z. Watson. Westbrook, a recent arrival from the United States, has enthusiastically espoused Hull's cause, helped distribute his proclamation, and volunteered to fight with the Detroit militia. Watson, "a desperate character" in Brock's view, is a bitter enemy of Thomas Talbot, and thus of the government, because of a long-standing rivalry over land fees and speculation. Created a temporary colonel by Hull, he has "vowed the most bitter vengeance against the first characters of the Province." There are other dissidents, such as John Beamer, a justice of the peace, who has chaired a meeting in Norfolk County urging the militia not to fight.

But Brock plays all this down:

A few Traitors have already joined the Enemy.... Yet the General Spirit of Loyalty which appears to pervade the Inhabitants of this Province, is such as to authorize a just expectation that their efforts to mislead and deceive, will be unavailing...

In private he reports:

"A petition has already been carried to Genl. Hull signed by many inhabitants about Westminster inviting him to advance with a promise to join him – What in the name of heaven can be done with such a vile population?"

Yet who can blame the mass of the people? The nature of the colonial aristocracy denies them a say in their own destiny, even though they are required to swear allegiance to the King, George III, who being certifiably insane is king in name only, the real monarch being his son, the Prince Regent, known to the irreverent masses as Prinny. The province is administered by the Prince Regent's appointee, Francis Gore, and in his absence by Isaac Brock, who also commands the army and the militia and is thus a near dictator. He sits at the head of a seven-man council, which, being appointed for life, can be said to be almost as conservative as the mad king himself, and a fourteen-man assembly, elected by freeholders, whose members serve for four years – or less, at the governor's pleasure. Anyone who dares speak disrespectfully of the King, the government, or its officers is treading perilously close to sedition.

The Church of England clergy, the military, and the leading

officeholders form a ruling elite, the legacy of the first lieutenant-governor, John Graves Simcoe, who was convinced that a landed aristocracy, conservative in its attitudes and British in its antecedents, was the only way to combat the twin viruses of democracy and republicanism creeping across the border. The tight little group that forms the apex of the social triangle in Upper Canada, entrenched by nepotism and by an educational system that ignores the masses, will shortly become known as the Family Compact. It does not tolerate opposition.

The "vile population" wants to be left alone. Militia service deprives the farms of their greatest asset, able-bodied men. Loyalists and the sons of the Loyalists – men like John Beverley Robinson, or the Ryersons of Norfolk County – will flock to the colours because their whole heritage represents a rejection of American values. And there are others who see in war a chance for adventure or escape. But these are in a minority. Brock is determined to rally the rest by Draconian methods, if need be. He wants to suspend habeas corpus and establish martial law but finds that in spite of his impressive authority he has little hope of either. The legislature will not vote for the first, and if he attempts the second "I am told the instant the law is promulgated the Militia will disperse...."

He is convinced that the legislators, expecting an American victory, are fearful of taking any overt action that might displease the conquerors. "I really believe it is with some cause that they dread the vengeance of the democratic party, they are such a set of unrelenting villains."

Pinned down at York by his civilian duties, he has taken what action he can to stiffen the defence at Fort Amherstburg, dispatching a younger and more energetic officer, Lieutenant-Colonel Henry Procter, to take over from the confused and harassed St. George.

Amherstburg is vital. If Hull seizes it – as he seems likely to do – he can sweep up the Thames or turn eastward to attack the British rear at Fort George on the Niagara and link up with the second American army already forming along that gorge. Brock *must* maintain a strong defence on the Niagara, yet his force at Amherstburg is distressingly thin. His only immediate solution is to move some men from Fort George to Fort Erie, a mid-point between the two bastions. From there they can be dispatched swiftly in either direction, depending upon the threat. Fortunately, he commands the Lakes.

He has also sent detachments down the valley of the Thames, recalling the militia from the harvest fields, attempting to waken the countryside to action, and distributing a proclamation of his own designed to counter Hull's. In this paper battle with the enemy, Brock, conjuring up the spectre of Napoleon, shows that he is no stranger to the art of magniloquence:

...it is but too obvious that once estranged from the powerful protection of the United Kingdom you must be reannexed to the dominion of France, from which the Provinces of Canada were wrested by the Arms of Great Britain, at a vast expense of blood and treasure, from no other motive than to *relieve* her ungrateful children from the oppression of a cruel neighbor: this restitution of Canada to the Empire of France was the stipulated reward for the aid offered to the revolted Colonies, now the United States; The debt is still due, and there can be no doubt but that the pledge has been renewed.... Are you prepared Inhabitants of Upper Canada to becoming willing subjects or rather slaves to the Despot who rules the nations of Europe with a rod of Iron? If not, arise in a Body, exert your energies, co-operate cordially with the King's regular Forces to repel the invader, and do not give cause to your children when groaning under the oppression of a foreign Master to reproach you with having too easily parted with the richest Inheritance on Earth – a participation in the name, character and freedom of Britons...

In his proclamation, Brock praises "the brave bands of Natives who inhabit this Colony," but the ink is scarcely dry on the paper when he learns that one brave band – the Iroquois of the Grand Valley – remains totally uninterested in fighting the Americans. Brock is infuriated. Their conduct is "ungrateful and infamous...mortifying." He would like to see them all expelled from their land. By refusing to take sides, the Iroquois "afford the Militia a plausible pretext for staying at home – They do not like leaving their families within the power of the Indians...."

Honourable Gentlemen of the Legislative Council and Gentlemen of the House of Assembly.

We are engaged in an awful and eventful Contest. By unanimity and despatch in our Councils, and by vigour in our Operations, we may teach the Enemy this lesson – that a Country defended by Free men, enthusiastically devoted to the cause of their King and Constitution, can never be Conquered.

Brock's closing words have a hollow ring. According to inviolable ritual, they will be parroted back to him twice: first by the Speaker of the Council and on the following day by the Speaker of the House, while Brock frets. He yearns to be at Amherstburg in the thick of things, away from the stuffy corridors of York and in sight of the enemy. Words are not his long suit, though in his loneliness he has become a voracious reader, devouring Plutarch's *Lives*, Hume's *Essays*, Pope's *Homer*, and dozens of military volumes. It is even said that much of his proclamation is the work of his friend Mr. Justice William Dummer Powell. Action is his forte, and it is action he craves. On the Iberian peninsula, Wellington has just won the battle of Salamanca and is basking in the approbation of Francisco Goya, the irascible Spanish court painter who has somehow got through the lines to commence an equestrian portrait of the victor. But it is thirteen years since Brock has seen real action (setting aside the naval attack on Copenhagen when he was sequestered aboard one of Nelson's ships, *Ganges*). He is not likely to forget that October afternoon at Egmont-op-Zee when death whispered to him as a musket ball, happily near spent, buried itself in his silk cravat, knocking him insensible from his horse. He was a lieutenant-colonel of the 49th then, a regiment that he had thoroughly shaken up, transforming it (in the Duke of York's opinion) from one of the worst to one of the best in the service. Now a whole country needs shaking up. Defeatism, timidity, irresolution, and treason stalk the land. It is Brock's task to achieve another miracle, and he cannot accomplish that in the dust and gumbo of provincial York. Duty calls. Immortality beckons. A new October awaits.

•

AUGUST 5, 1812. At the River aux Ecorces, on the American side of the Detroit, Robert Lucas the scout lies hidden in the bushes, waiting for the dawn, watched by unseen eyes. Two fellow rangers lie beside him along with the ranger captain McCullough, who has the dubious distinction of being the only American thus far to take an Indian scalp.

The four men lie on the left flank of an armed body sent across the river by Hull to make contact with the wagon train of supplies, which he desperately needs to feed his army. The supply train, under the command of a young Chillicothe lawyer, Captain Henry Brush, has reached the Rapids of the Maumee and is moving on to the River Raisin after a gruelling march through dense thickets and treacherous mires. But Brush does not dare continue to Detroit without an escort, for his cattle train and pack animals must pass within cannon shot of Fort Amherstburg. Hull has answered his plea by dispatching two hundred Ohio volunteers under Major Thomas Van Horne. Some of these are the same men who refused to cross the river in July; Van Horne has picked them up at Detroit along with their company commander, the recalcitrant Captain Rupes, who, astonishingly, is still in charge, having been re-elected by democratic vote after a court martial ordered him cashiered.

Dawn breaks. McCullough and his scouts rise and mount their horses, making a wide reconnaissance sweep around the detachment. They scent trouble, noting tracks on the road and trails in the grass—evidence that a party of Indians has been watching them during the night. Out on the river, a faint splish-splash penetrates the shroud of mist that hangs over the water. Oars! Hull's army cannot remain long on Canadian soil unless its supply lines are secured. The British, who control the river, intend that this shall not be.

The detachment moves, McCullough, Robert Lucas, and Van Horne's black servant riding out in front. Lucas continues to eye the river. Is a British force crossing over from Fort Amherstburg? The mist frustrates his view.

They ride through the Wyandot village of Maguaga. It is deserted, the houses empty. Tecumseh and Matthew Elliott have preceded them and persuaded the wavering Walk-in-the-Water to cross to British territory with his followers. Brock's assessment has been correct: news of the victory at Michilimackinac has tipped the scales, and the tribe wants to be on the winning side.

The road forks around a corn field. Lucas and a companion take the right fork; McCullough takes the left and rides into an ambush. Lucas hears a volley of shots, but before he can reach him, the scalper is himself scalped, tomahawked, riddled with musket balls. The rear guard is in a panic, but the Indians have already vanished into the tall corn.

Shaken, the detachment moves on, leaving three corpses under a cover of bark and ignoring a Frenchman's warning that a large force of Indians is waiting for them at Brownstown. The Americans do not trust the French settlers, some of whom are pro-British and seek to confuse them with false reports.

The war party moves in double file. Between the files, mounted men escort the mail—a packet of personal letters written by Hull's soldiers to their families and friends, many of them critical of their general, and, more significantly, Hull's official dispatches to Washington, revealing both his plans and his pessimism.

Brownstown village lies ahead, but Brownstown Creek must first be crossed. The only practical ford lies in a narrow defile with thick bushes on the right and fields of tall corn on the opposite bank and on the left. It is the perfect spot for an ambush; Lucas recognizes the danger and rides along the right column warning the men to see that their muskets are freshly primed. Tecumseh has recognized it, too. He and his followers are flat on their bellies directly ahead – twenty-four Shawnee and Ottawa and one white man, Matthew Elliott's son Alexander.

As Tecumseh silently waits, the American files close up to cross the creek. Then, at a range of no more than twenty-five yards, the Indians rise out of the corn, their high-pitched war cries mingling with the explosion of their weapons. Lucas's horse is shot, topples sideways against another wounded animal, pitches its rider onto the ground, his musket flying from his hand. Weaponless, Lucas tries with little success to rally the men. The odds are twenty to one in favour of the Americans, but the Indians are shouting so wildly that Van Horne believes himself outnumbered. It is scarcely necessary to order a retreat; his men fling down their weapons, scatter the mail, and plunge headlong back the way they came, actually outrunning their pursuers, who follow them for three miles before giving up the chase. Robert Lucas, covering the retreat as best he can, is the last man to escape.

The Battle of Brownstown, as it will be called, represents a serious setback for Hull. Van Horne has lost eighteen men killed and twenty wounded. Some seventy are missing, many hiding in the bushes; the following day, most straggle back. Worse than the loss of seven officers is the abandoning of the mail. This will raise Brock's spirits, for here, in letters home, is strong evidence of the discontent and illness in the ranks, of a lack of confidence in the leadership, and, even more important, Hull's letter of August 4 to the Secretary of War, outlining the critical situation of his army, pleading for another two thousand men, and expressing his deep-seated fear of the Indians who he believes will shortly be swarming down from Mackinac Island.

At Brownstown, meanwhile, a strong detachment of the British 41st accompanied by militia and civilian volunteers under Major Adam Muir has crossed the river, too late to take part in the skirmish but prepared to frustrate any further attempt by Hull to open the supply line. The men have waited all night, unable to light a fire, shivering in the damp, without blankets or provisions. Now they are exposed to a spectacle calculated to make them shudder further.

The Indians hold a young American captive and are intent on killing him. Muir does his best to intervene, offers a barrel of rum and articles of clothing if the prisoner's life is spared. But then a series of piercing cries issues from the forest – the funeral convoy of a young chief, Blue Jacket, the only casualty among Tecumseh's followers. Four tribesmen carry in the body. Thomas Verchères de Boucherville, a citizen volunteer and experienced fur trader from Amherstburg, realizes there is no hope for the American, for the Indians are intent on avenging their chief. They place his corpse at the captive's feet and he, too, seems to understand his fate.

The American turns pale, looks about him, asks in a low voice if it is possible that the English allow such acts of barbarity. The cries of the Indians drown out the response.

The oldest Potawatomi chief raises his hatchet over the prisoner; a group of Indian women draw near. At the chief's signal, one plunges a butcher knife into the victim's head; a second stabs him in the side while the chief dispatches him with a tomahawk. Tecumseh, who would surely have prevented the execution, is not present.

The white witnesses including Alexander Elliott (himself in Indian dress) are stunned. They feel impotent, knowing that these dark allies hold the keys to British success. Young Thomas de Boucherville, the fur trader, who will never shake the incident from his memory, puts their dilemma into words:

"We all stood around overcome by an acute sense of shame. We felt implicated in some way in this murder…and yet, under the circumstances what could we do? The life of that man undoubtedly belonged to the inhuman chief. The government had desperate need of these Indian allies. Our garrison was weak and these warriors were numerous enough to impose their will upon us. If we were to rebuke them in this crisis…they would withdraw from the conflict, and retire to their own country on the Missouri whence they had come to join us."

De Boucherville is coming to realize what others will soon grasp – that the British are, in a subtle way, as much prisoners of the Indians as the young American whose tomahawked corpse lies stretched out before them.

●

SANDWICH, UPPER CANADA, August 6, 1812. In his head-quarters in François Bâby's half-finished mansion, General Hull continues to vacillate. He has promised his impatient officers that he will attack the fort whether the artillery is ready or not. Now he has second thoughts. In Washington he allowed himself to be talked out of his original proposal: that America take steps to control the water routes. Now he himself is paying the price for that negligence. He cannot float his artillery downriver in the teeth of British gunboats. But his enemies can cross the river at will to harass his supply lines and herd Walk-in-the-Water's Wyandot followers into Canada to reinforce Fort Amherstburg.

He seriously considers retreat but backs off after a stormy meeting with Colonel McArthur. He broods, changes his mind, calls a council of his commanders, finally agrees to adopt their plan of attacking Fort Amherstburg. He will move against it at the head of his troops "and in whatever manner the affair may terminate, I will never reflect on you, gentlemen."

Dazzling news! Robert Lucas, back from the debacle at Browns-town, is exultant: the long faces of his comrades have been replaced by smiles. A wave of good cheer surges over the camp. The sick rise from their beds and seize their muskets; the wounded urge the sur-geons to pronounce them fit for duty. Orders are issued for five days' rations, three to be cooked – pork the staple fare. Ammunition and whiskey (twelve barrels) are loaded into wagons, axes, picks, and spades requisitioned, cannon placed on floating batteries. All unneces-sary tents, baggage, and boats are sent back to Detroit.

Then, on the afternoon of August 7, hard on the heels of the news from Brownstown, comes an express rider with dispatches for Hull from two American commanders on the Niagara frontier. Boats loaded with British troops have been seen crossing Lake Erie and heading for Amherstburg; more British regulars accompanied by Canadian militia and Indians are en route from Niagara by boat to the fort. Since the British control the lakes, there is nothing the Americans can do to stop them.

Hull is badly rattled. What is happening? Washington's over-all strategy was to pin down the British forces on the Niagara frontier by a series of attacks that would leave Fort Amherstburg lightly held. Now the British are taking troops from Fort George and Fort Erie, leaving that frontier exposed to attack. That may be of some comfort to his colleagues on the Niagara River, but it is disastrous for Hull; it is impossible for him "to express the disappointment which this information occasioned." What he does not know is that Prevost has sent an emissary to discuss an immediate armistice with General Henry Dearborn, the American commander-in-chief. Brock does not know this, either, but things are so quiet on the Niagara frontier that he feels justified in taking a gamble; he will reduce his forces there to a minimum in order to bolster his defence at Amherstburg and frustrate any attack by General Hull.

Both commanders—Hull at Sandwich, Brock at York—are suffering from bouts of gloom and frustration. Half blinded by the myopia of war, each believes his own position to be untenable, his adversary's superior. Brock, thwarted by timid civilians and a lukewarm militia, expects Hull to attack his weak garrison at Fort Amherstburg at any moment. He is desperate to reinforce it but despairs of holding it against greater numbers. Hull, isolated on Canadian soil, is convinced that Brock's combined force is not only stronger but also growing at an alarming rate.

Unlike Brock, Hull is no gambler. He feels doomed by bad fortune: the supposedly friendly Indians turning their coats and crowding into Amherstburg; the blocking of his supply train; now a fresh onslaught of fighting men. The General sees himself and his troops suddenly trapped in an unfriendly country, their backs to the river, their food running out, surrounded by Indians, facing Brock's regulars and Tecumseh's braves. Irresolution at last gives way to decision, but a decision tainted with panic. He must get his army back onto American soil, with the barrier of the river between him and his enemies—to Detroit at the very least, and perhaps all the way to the Maumee.

He sends again for his officers and breaks the news. It is his responsibility, and his alone, he declares, to decide the ultimate fate of the army. "Well, General," says the swarthy McArthur, "if it is your opinion, it must be so, but I must beg leave to decline giving any further opinion as to the movements of the army."

Hull suggests, hesitantly, that the army might be well advised to withdraw as far as the Maumee. Cass retorts that if he does that, every man in the Ohio militia will leave him. That puts an end to it: the army will withdraw across the river to Detroit, but no farther.

Lewis Cass is beside himself. In his eyes, Hull's decision is both fatal and unaccountable; he cannot fathom it. Coming after a series of timid, irresolute, and indecisive measures, this final about-face has dispirited the troops and destroyed the last vestige of confidence they may have had in their commander. Cass is undoubtedly right; far better if Hull had never crossed the river in the first place – at least until his supply lines were secure. A sense of astonishment, mingled with a feeling of disgrace, ripples through the camp. Robert Lucas feels it: the orders to cross the river under cover of darkness are, he thinks, especially dastardly. But cross the army must, and when night falls the men slink into their boats. By the following morning there is scarcely an American soldier left on Canadian soil.

●

WHILE BROCK is advancing toward the Detroit frontier, intent on attack, his superior, Sir George Prevost, is doing his best to wind down the war. He informs Lord Liverpool that although his policy of conciliation has not prevented hostilities, he is determined to do nothing to exacerbate the situation by aggressive action:

"...Your Lordship may rest assured that unless the safety of the Provinces entrusted to my charge should require them, no measures shall be adopted by me to impede a speedy return to those accustomed relations of amity and goodwill which it is the mutual interest of both countries to cherish and preserve."

Sir George, who has never believed in the reality of the war, is now convinced it will reach a swift conclusion. Augustus Foster has written from Halifax, en route home from Washington, with the news that Britain has revoked the hated Orders in Council. American ships may now trade with continental Europe without fear of seizure. Madison in June made it clear that the Orders were America's chief reason for going to war. Surely, then, with Britain backing off, he will come to his senses and halt the invasion.

Sir George sees no reason to wait for the President. Why not suspend hostilities at once – at least temporarily? Why spill blood senselessly if the war is, in effect, over?

On August 2, he dispatches his aide, Lieutenant-Colonel Edward Baynes, with a flag of truce to treat with Major-General Henry Dearborn, the U.S. commander, at his headquarters at Greenbush, across the river from Albany, New York.

The American in charge of the overall prosecution of the war in the north has not seen military service for two decades. A ponderous, flabby figure, weighing two hundred and fifty pounds, with a face to match, Dearborn does not look like a general, nor does he act like one. He is a tired sixty-one. His soldiers call him Granny.

His reputation, like Hull's, rests on the memory of another time. As a Revolutionary major he fought at Bunker Hill, then struggled, feverish and half-starved, with Arnold through the wintry forests of Maine to attack Quebec, was captured and exchanged to fight again – against Burgoyne at Saratoga, at Monmouth Court House in '78, with General John Sullivan against the Indians in '79, at Yorktown in '81. A successful and influential Massachusetts politician in the post-war era, Secretary of War for eight years in Jefferson's cabinet, he is now an old soldier who was slowly fading away in his political sinecure until the call to arms restored him to command.

The American strategy, to attack Canada simultaneously at Detroit, Niagara, Kingston, and Montreal, is faltering. Given the lack of men and supplies it is hardly likely that these thrusts can occur together. It is assumed, without anybody quite saying so, that Dearborn will co-ordinate them, but General Dearborn does not appear to understand.

Strategically, the major attack ought to be made upon Montreal. A lightning thrust would sever the water connection between the Canadas, deprive the upper province of supplies and reinforcements, and, in the end, cause it to wither away and surrender without a fight. The problem is that the New Englanders, whose co-operation is essential, do not want to fight, while the southerners and westerners in Kentucky, Tennessee, South Carolina, and Ohio are eager for battle. There is also the necessity of securing America's western flank from the menace of the Indians. Thus, the American command pins its initial hopes on Hull's army while the forces on Lake Champlain remain stagnant.

To describe Dearborn's prosecution of the war as leisurely is to understate that officer's proclivity for sluggish movement. He has spent three months in New England, attempting in his bumbling fashion to stir the people to belligerence with scarcely any success. The governors of Massachusetts and Connecticut are particularly obdurate. When Dearborn asks Caleb Strong to call out fourteen companies of artillery and twenty-seven of infantry for the defence of his Massachusetts ports and harbours, Governor Strong declares that the seacoast does not need defending since the government of Nova Scotia has "by proclamation, forbid[den] any incursions or depredations upon our territories." Governor John Cotton Smith of Connecticut points out that the Constitution "has ordained that Congress may provide for calling forth the militia *to execute the laws of the Union, suppress insurrections, and repel invasions.*" Since there has been neither insurrection nor invasion, he argues, no such emergency exists. Of course, Governor Smith adds, the militia stands ready to repel any invasion should one take place. Clearly, he believes that will never happen.

Dearborn dawdles. Eustis tries to prod him into returning to his base at Albany to get on with the invasion of Canada, but Eustis is not much of a prodder. "Being possessed of a full view of the intentions of government," he starts out – then adds a phrase scarcely calculated to propel a man of Dearborn's temperament into action; "take your time," he finishes, and Dearborn does just that.

It is an odd coincidence that the Secretary of War and his predecessor, Dearborn, are both medical men, former physicians trained to caution, sceptical of haste, wary of precipitate moves that might cause a patient's death. One of Dearborn's tasks is to create diversions at Kingston and at Niagara to take the pressure off Hull; but when Hull crosses the Detroit River, Dearborn is still in Boston. "I begin to feel that I may be censured for not moving," he remarks in what must be the understatement of the war, but he doubts the wisdom of leaving. To which Eustis responds: "Go to Albany or the Lake. The troops shall come to you as fast as the season will admit, and the blow must be struck. Congress must not meet without a victory to announce to them." Dearborn ponders this for a week before making up his mind, then finally sets off, reaching Greenbush on July 26, where some twelve hundred unorganized troops await him.

His letters to Washington betray his indecision ("I have been in a very unpleasant situation, being at a loss to determine whether or not I ought to leave the seacoast"). He is woefully out of touch with his command, has no idea who runs his commissary and ordnance departments, is not even sure how far his authority extends, although this has been spelled out for him. In a remarkable letter he asks Eustis: "Who is to have command of the operations in Upper Canada? I take it for granted that my command does not extend to that distant quarter." These are the words of a man trying to wriggle out of responsibility, a man for whom the only secure action is no action at all. He has been ordered to keep the British occupied while Hull advances. But he does nothing.

This, then, is the character of the commander who is to receive an offer of truce brought to his headquarters by the personable Lieutenant-Colonel Baynes.

It takes Baynes six days to reach Albany from Montreal. An experienced officer with thirty years' service behind him, he keeps his eyes open, recording, in the pigeon-holes of his mind, troop dispositions, the state of preparedness of soldiers, the morale of the countryside. At Plattsburg he is greeted cordially by the ranking major-general, a farmer named Moore, who gets him a room at the inn. Baynes notes that the militia have no uniforms, the only distinguishing badge being a cockade in their hats, and that they do not appear to have made any progress in the first rudiments of military drill. All the officers at Plattsburg express approval of Baynes's mission and one of them, a Major Clarke, is ordered to accompany him by boat to Burlington near the southern end of Lake Champlain. From this point on Baynes proceeds with more difficulty; the commander at Burlington is not enchanted by the spectacle of an enemy officer coolly looking over his force. But Baynes finally persuades him to let him proceed to Albany, 150 miles to the south.

For Lieutenant-Colonel Baynes the journey is salutary. He fails to see any military preparation but forms a strong opinion of the mood of the people, which he reports to Prevost:

"My appearance travelling thro' the country in uniform excited very great curiosity and anxiety. The Inns where the coach stopt were instantly crowded with the curious and inquisitive. I did not hear a single individual express a wish but for the speedy accommodation of existing differences and deprecating the war, in several instances these statements were expressed in strong and violent language and on Major Clarke endeavouring to check it, it produced a contrary effect. The universal sentiment of this part of the country appears decidedly adverse to war. I experienced everywhere respect and attention."

On the evening of August 8, Baynes reaches Albany and goes immediately to Dearborn's headquarters at nearby Greenbush. The American commander receives him with great affability, says he personally wants an armistice on honourable terms, and admits that "the burden of command at his time of life was not a desirable charge." Baynes finds him in good health but shrewdly concludes that he "does not appear to possess the energy of mind or activity of body requisite for the important station he fills."

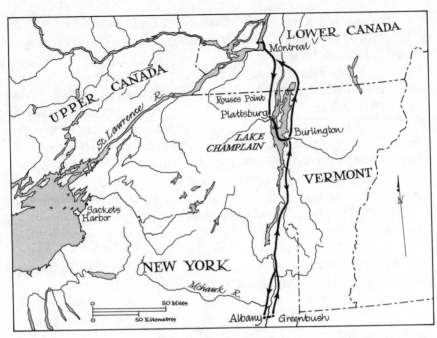

Baynes's Journey to Albany

An agreement of sorts is quickly concluded. Dearborn explains that his instructions do not allow him to sign an armistice, but he can issue orders for a temporary cessation of hostilities. The two men agree that should Washington countermand this order, four days' notice will be given before hostilities are resumed. Under this arrangement, the troops will act only on the defensive until a final decision is reached. To Dearborn, the procrastinator, this agreement has the great advantage of allowing him to recruit his forces and build up his supplies without fear of attack. "It is mutually understood that...no obstructions are to be attempted, on either side, to the passage of stores, to the frontier posts."

And Hull, who is desperate for both supplies and men? Hull is not included, specifically at Dearborn's request: "I could not include General Hull...he having received his orders directly from the department of war."

Thus is concluded a kind of truce, in which both sides are allowed to prepare for battle without actually engaging in one.

These arrangements completed, Lieutenant-Colonel Baynes prepares to take his leave. There is a brief altercation over the use of

156

Indians in the war. Dearborn, in strong language, attacks the British for using native warriors, implying that the Americans are free from reproach in this area. Baynes retorts that Hull's captured dispatches make it clear that he has been doing his best to persuade the Indians to fight for the Americans. That ends the argument. But Baynes has misread Hull's intentions. At Madison's insistence, the Americans use the Indians as scouts only. Hull's efforts have been designed only to keep the Indians neutral.

With great difficulty, Baynes convinces Dearborn to allow him to return to Montreal by a different route along the eastern shores of Lake Champlain; it allows him to size up American strength and assess the mood of the New Englanders.

The little coach clip-clops its way through Vermont's beguiling scenery, rattling down crooked clay roads and over rustic bridges, past stone mills perched above gurgling rivers, through neat, shaded villages hugging the sloping shoreline – a peaceful, pastoral land of farms, wayside inns, and the occasional classical courthouse, as yet untouched by battle. The war seems very far away and, Baynes notes, the people almost totally unprepared. The militia do not impress him.

"The men are independent in their habits and principles, their officers ignorant and totally uninformed in every thing relating to the possession of arms and possess no influence over the militia but in proportion as they court it by popular and familiar intercourse." A few, he notes, are prepared to march on Montreal; the rest just want to go home. More than half of them are absent with or without leave, and nobody seems able to control them.

Recruiting for the regular army, he reports to Prevost, is proceeding very slowly, even though the term of service is only five years and the bounty pay for signing up very liberal:

"There appears to exist in the United States the greatest contempt and repugnance to the restraint and discipline of a military life and few gentlemen of respectability are willing to become officers but prefer the militia where they obtain high rank without serving."

As the coach moves on along the maple-shaded roads, Baynes is subjected to a series of minor astonishments. He learns that one militia general is a farmer, another a sawmill keeper, a third a millwright. The coach pulls up at a tavern. Out comes the innkeeper to take the reins and water the horses. Baynes's sense of military decorum is severely shaken when he discovers that this servitor is a colonel and second-in-command of the entire Vermont militia. The gap between the British and the American attitudes toward their military is obviously wider than Baynes suspected, and he has more than a little trouble absorbing it. He concludes that of all the officers he has observed there is only one with any real military talent – the same commander at Burlington who vigorously opposed his presence in the United States.

As for the American people, they "have a very high and overrated opinion of their military prowess, conceiving it to be in their power to pillage Montreal and to march to Quebec whenever they think proper. The siege of the fortress alone they consider as a task of difficulty. From the actual state of the American forces assembled on Lake Champlain, I do not think there exists any intention of invading this part of the province."

As Baynes moves back to Canada, Dearborn dispatches a note to Hull, dated August 9, explaining what has happened and suggesting that the General of the Army of the Northwest make his own decision as to whether he should join in the truce. (Hull has just withdrawn from his beachhead at Sandwich, but Dearborn has no knowledge of that.) Reinforcements are, of course, out of the question. "The removal of any troops from Niagara to Detroit, while the present agreement continues, would be improper and incompatible with the true interest of the agreement."

Thus does Dearborn relieve himself of the responsibility of reinforcing Hull or of creating the promised diversion along the Niagara frontier that might prevent Brock from reinforcing Amherstburg. Communications being what they are, Hull cannot know this. And by the time Dearborn's letter reaches him, it will not matter.

●

BROWNSTOWN, MICHIGAN TERRITORY, August 9, 1812. Thomas Verchères de Boucherville, the fur trader and Amherstburg storekeeper, is weary of waiting. On and off for four days he and his comrades have been on the alert on the American side of the river, expecting to surprise another of Hull's armed escorts seeking to bring in the wagon train of supplies held up at the River Raisin. But the Americans do not come and finally Major Muir gives the order to embark for the Canadian shore.

The men are clambering into the boats when from the woods there issues a series of piercing cries. In a few minutes Tecumseh's scouts come bounding out of the thickets to report that a detachment of Long Knives has been spotted upriver "like the mosquitoes of the swamp in number." This is no minor force of the kind that was routed a few days before; Hull has sent six hundred men including two hundred regulars, supported by cavalry and cannon. He is determined that this time the supply train will get through.

Muir puts into action a plan proposed by Tecumseh: his troops will march to a ravine near the Indian village of Maguaga, three miles upriver from Brownstown, and there lie in wait. Their orders are to charge with the bayonet as soon as the first volley of musket balls is fired. The Indians will conceal themselves in the corn fields on the right and the left, securing the flanks.

De Boucherville and his companions, having no uniforms, stick sprigs of basswood into their caps for identification and set out along the muddy track for Maguaga. Soon an odour, sickly sweet, assails their nostrils, and a horrifying spectacle comes into view at the turn of the trail – the battlefield of the previous week. De Boucherville shudders and is seized with revulsion as he sees displayed before him the corpses of the cavalrymen, already decomposed and impaled on stakes by Tecumseh's men, who have left the cadavers in full view to terrify the Americans. Gnawed and mangled by crows and animals, the rotting bodies give off an indescribable stench.

At almost the same moment, James Dalliba, a young American artillery officer in Lieutenant-Colonel Miller's advancing force, sees the bloated and scalped carcass of the luckless ranger captain, McCullough, lying beside the road under its covering of bark.

Marching with the British is an Amherstburg acquaintance of de Boucherville, young John Richardson, a member of the widespread Askin family (John, Senior, is his grandfather). Richardson, not yet turned sixteen, is a gentleman volunteer in the 41st and a future novelist – one of Canada's first. He will never forget this silent march to Maguaga; thirty years later it remains vividly in his mind:

"No other sound than the measured step of the troops interrupted the solitude of the scene, rendered more imposing by the wild appearance of the warriors, whose bodies, stained and painted in the most frightful manner for the occasion, glided by us with almost noiseless velocity...some painted white, some black, others half black, half red; half black, half white; all with their hair plastered in such a way as to resemble the bristling quills of the porcupine, with no other covering than a cloth around their loins, yet armed to the teeth with rifles, tomahawks, war-clubs, spears, bows, arrows and scalping knives. Uttering no sound, intent only on reaching the enemy unperceived, they might have passed for the spectres of those wilds, the ruthless demons which War had unchained for the punishment and oppression of man."

Screened by the forest, the two forces move blindly towards one another, neither side knowing when or where the clash will take place but all sensing that within minutes men will fall and some will die. Most have had no experience of battle; many have had no military training; save for Miller's Tippecanoe veterans, few have fired a musket at a living human.

At Maguaga, the British and Canadians take up their position behind a low rise, each man hugging the ground as he would a friend. De Boucherville finds himself next to another acquaintance, Jean-Baptiste Bâby, whose family home at Sandwich has been seized by Hull. Nervous, he asks Bâby for a pinch of snuff "to keep me in countenance a little." A moment later comes the sound of an enemy drum, the stroke wavering slightly as if the drummer, too, fears whatever lies ahead.

The British remain concealed, waiting for the signal. Suddenly an American officer, brilliant in blue and gold, riding a superb horse, his hat covered by a three-foot plume, appears on an eminence. A shot rings out; the American falls dead at his horse's feet, and the battle is joined.

Confusion! A melee of painted bodies, scarlet tunics, snorting horses, flying tomahawks, splintered foliage, black musket smoke. On the left, Tecumseh leads his men forward in an attempt to turn the American flank. Five hundred yards to the right, another group of Indians, trying a similar manoeuvre, is forced back. To the British volunteers all Indians look alike; they believe the retreating natives to be part of the advancing enemy and fire on them. Ally battles ally as the skirmish grows hotter.

"Take care, de Boucherville!" cries an officer on the left. "The Kentuckians are aiming at you." Even as he speaks a ball strikes him in the head, and he falls into de Boucherville's arms. "Well, old fellow," thinks the volunteer to himself, "you came out of that all right." But a moment later he is hit in the thigh by a musket ball.

Muir, the British commander, seeing an American taking deliberate aim at him, hastily raises his short rifle and lays it across the shoulders of a fellow officer, Lieutenant Charles Sutherland. Both adversaries fire at the same time. The American drops dead; his rifle ball enters Sutherland's cheek, comes out the back of his neck and passes through Muir's shoulder. (Sutherland's wound is not mortal, but he will shortly die of loss of blood as a result of brushing his teeth before it is properly healed.)

Now occurs one of those maddening misunderstandings that frustrate the best-laid plans. Brock's reinforcements from the Niagara frontier, hustled across the river by Procter, arrive on the scene, sixty strong, just as Muir's bugler, by pre-arrangement, sounds the bayonet charge.

The new troops, confused, take this as a signal to retreat, and the British centre begins to break. Muir receives a second wound in the leg but carries on.

By now the American six-pounder is in action spraying grape-shot, its initial discharge so terrifying Lieutenant-Colonel Miller's horse that it throws the American commander to the ground. Tecumseh's warriors rush forward to take his scalp but are forced back. Miller remounts, cries for a cavalry charge. But the cavalry fails to respond, and the main advance is made by foot soldiers. The smoke is now so dense that no one can see for more than twenty paces.

Tecumseh is making a strategic withdrawal toward the west, drawing the American fire away from the retiring British and forcing Miller to divide his forces. The manoeuvre slows down the American advance, allows the British to reach the boats they have concealed on the beach and make their escape out of range of the American muskets.

Miller draws his men up in line and utters the obligatory words of commendation:

"My brave fellows! You have done well! Every man has done his duty. I give you my hearty thanks for your conduct this day; you have gained my highest esteem; you have gained fresh honor to yourselves and to the American Arms; your fellow soldiers will love you and your country will reward you...."

With this accolade ringing in their ears, the Americans move through the woods, seeking the dead and the wounded. Hidden in a cedar swamp under a gigantic deadfall lie three men – Thomas Verchères de Boucherville, his friend Jean-Baptiste Berthe (another member of the Askin family and a civilian volunteer), and a regular soldier. Caught in the crossfire between the British rear and the advancing Americans, they have run into the woods to escape the shower of musket balls. It is now four in the afternoon, but they cannot leave their soggy retreat for the enemy is only a few feet away. Finally, at ten, under cover of a violent thunderstorm, they crawl out of the water onto a drier knoll, guided by lightning flashes, and here they crouch, soaked through, for the rest of the night, while the rain beats down on them and a violent gale, wrenching the branches from the trees, puts them in as much danger as the battle itself.

De Boucherville's wound is bleeding but painless. He cakes earth over it as he has seen the Indians do, binding it with a towel brought along for just such a misfortune, and considers his plight. Only a few days before he was at dinner with some guests when he heard a drummer parading the streets of Amherstburg, beating the call to arms. With his friend Berthe and several others he answered the summons for volunteers, not pausing to finish his meal but taking care to bury all his money, secretly, in his backyard. Now here he is, wounded, wet, and miserable, waiting for the dawn.

At first light, he and his two companions set out for the river, watching all the time for the enemy. They reach it at four o'clock, gather some planks and strands of basswood from a deserted Indian village, construct a crude raft, and cross to an island in midstream. Here they do their utmost to attract attention, wiping their muskets dry and firing them off, making flags of their shirts and waving them on long poles. Eventually a boat rescues them. On the dockside are friends, officers, natives, civilians, all cheering. They had given de Boucherville and Berthe up for dead.

De Boucherville stumbles home, flops onto a sofa, falls into a dead sleep. When he wakes he is astonished to find an Indian by his bedside. It is Tecumseh himself, who has been sitting silently for hours waiting for him to wake.

A surgeon removes the ball from de Boucherville's thigh but cannot extract a quantity of shot. Tecumseh fetches a Shawnee healer, who prescribes a herbal remedy. In ten days the wound is healed, de Boucherville is back behind the counter of his store, and the Battle of Maguaga is a memory to be savoured in the retelling for the remainder of his days.

Hull, in his message to Washington, treats the battle as a stunning victory. It is scarcely that, for it has failed in its purpose of opening his line of supply. Captain Brush's wagon train still cannot get through, and Lieutenant-Colonel Miller, even in victory, cannot help. In the heat of the battle his troops have thrown away their knapsacks and are without rations, forced to lie all night in the open in the same driving thunderstorm that poured down on de Boucherville. Miller himself is tottering with fatigue, ague, and two wounds; he has been on and off the sick list for weeks. He sends to Hull for reinforcements and provisions in order to move on. Colonel McArthur arrives with a fleet of bateaux bringing two barrels of flour, one of pork, and considerable whiskey, all of which the troops devour in a single breakfast. The wounded are loaded into bateaux for the return voyage. But the British, who have control of the river, seize twelve boats, capture some fifty Americans, and recapture two of their own men held as prisoners.

At sunset an express arrives from Hull: because he cannot spare further reinforcements, Miller and his men are ordered to return to Detroit without completing their mission. They make their way to the river in the driving rain, soaking wet, shoeless, sleeping that night as best they can in dripping blankets. They reach Detroit at noon on August 11. Brush and the supply train remain pinned down at the River Raisin.

Miller has lost eighteen men killed and some sixty wounded. The British casualties are fewer: six killed, twenty-one wounded. But Hull writes to Eustis that "the victory was complete in every part of the line," and that is the way the history books will record it.

●

ISAAC BROCK has no time for democratic chatter. He prorogues the legislature on August 5 and, with the consent of his appointed council, declares martial law. He has decided on a mighty gamble: he will gather what troops he can, speed post-haste to Amherstburg at their head, and, if that fort has not fallen, provoke Hull into a fight, then try to get back to the Niagara frontier before the Americans attack. He is taking a long chance, but he has little choice. Off he goes, moving swiftly southwest through the province, calling for volunteers to accompany him to Amherstburg. Five hundred rush to apply, "principally the sons of Veterans, whom His Majesty's munificence settled in this country." He can take only half that number. The York Volunteers will become Brock's favourite militia unit, including among its officers such names as Ridout, Jarvis, and Robinson, all of them scions of the tight Upper Canada aristocracy, trained at the Reverend John Strachan's famous school at Cornwall. The war will entrench them in the Family Compact.

Brock reaches Port Dover on the north shore of Lake Erie on August 8, where he hopes enough boats have been commandeered to move his entire force to Amherstburg. The British have the immense advantage of being able to move troops swiftly by water in contrast to the Americans' slow drive through the wilderness. But at Dover, Brock finds that not nearly enough boats have been provided, while those available are leaky, uncaulked, dilapidated. A day is required to make ten of them ready, and these are in such bad shape that the men grow exhausted from constant bailing.

The flotilla can move no faster than the slowest vessel, the hundred-ton schooner *Nancy*, which must be manhandled over the narrow neck of the Long Point peninsula—a backbreaking task that requires the energy of all the boat crews—and later dragged by ropes onto the beach at Port Talbot. Here the troops take refuge from the same thunderstorm that is drenching the Americans after the battle of Maguaga.

All that day the men, joined by sixty volunteers from the village of Queenston on the Niagara, lie in the boats or on the sand as the rain pelts down.

Yet they remain in good spirits. Brock notes it: "In no instance have I witnessed greater cheerfulness and constancy than were displayed by these Troops under the fatigue of a long journey in Boats and during extremely bad Weather...their conduct throughout excited my admiration."

The admiration is mutual. At one point Brock's own boat strikes a sunken rock. His boat crew goes to work with oars and poles. When they fail to push her free, the General, in full uniform, leaps over the side, waist deep in water. In an instant the others follow and soon have the boat afloat. Brock climbs aboard, opens his liquor case, gives every man a glass of spirits. The news of this act, spreading from boat to boat, animates the force.

On August 11, the weather again turns capricious. The wind drops. The men, wet and exhausted from lack of sleep, are forced to row in relays for hours. Then a sudden squall forces the flotilla once more in to shore. That night the weather clears, and the impatient general makes another attempt to get underway, this time in the dark, his boat leading with a lantern in the stern. They sail all night, the boats too crowded for the men to lie down. The following day they hear that Hull has re-crossed the river to Detroit and that there has been a skirmish (Maguaga) on the American side. At Point Pelee that after-

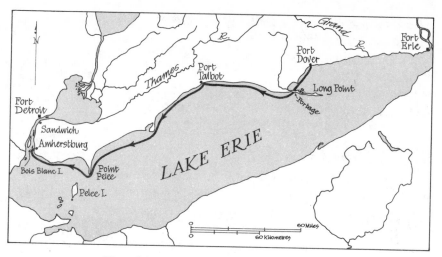

Brock's Passage to Amherstburg

noon, some of the men boil their pork; others drop exhausted onto the beach. Early next morning they set off again and at eight in the forenoon straggle into Amherstburg, exhausted from rowing, their faces peeling from sunburn.

Brock has preceded them. Unable to rest, the General and a vanguard of troops have departed the previous afternoon and reached their objective shortly before midnight on August 13. Lieutenant-Colonel Procter and Matthew Elliott are waiting on the quayside. Across the water from Bois Blanc Island comes the rattle of musketry. It startles Brock. When Elliott explains that the Indians, bivouacked on the island, are expressing their joy at the arrival of reinforcements, the General expresses concern over the waste of ammunition: "Do, pray, Elliott, fully explain my wishes and motives, and tell the Indians that I will speak to them to-morrow on this subject."

Midnight has passed. But before Brock can sleep he must read the dispatches and mail captured at Brownstown. He sits in Elliott's study with his aide, Major J.B. Glegg, the yellow light from tallow candles flickering across a desk strewn with maps and papers. Suddenly the door opens and Elliott stands before him accompanied by a tall Indian dressed in a plain suit of tanned deerskin, fringed at the seams, and wearing leather moccasins heavily ornamented with porcupine quills. This is clearly a leader of stature. In his nose he wears three silver ornaments in the shape of coronets, and from his neck is hung, on a string of coloured wampum, a large silver medallion of George III.

The Indian is beaming. Glegg gets an instant impression of energy and decision. This must be Tecumseh.

Brock rises, hand outstretched to his ally. The contrast is striking: the British general — fair, large-limbed, blue-eyed, impeccable in his scarlet jacket, blue-and-white riding trousers, and Hessian boots — towers over the lithe figure of the Shawnee. Brief salutations follow. Brock explains about the waste of ammunition. Tecumseh agrees. Each man has taken the other's measure and both are impressed. Brock will write to Lord Liverpool that "a more sagacious and gallant Warrior does not I believe exist. He was the admiration of every one who conversed with him...." Tecumseh's comment, delivered to his followers, is blunter. "This," says Tecumseh, "is a *man*!"

Brock calls a council of his officers, asks for a military appreciation. Tecumseh urges an immediate attack on Detroit, unrolls a strip of elm bark, pulls his scalping knife from his belt, and proceeds to scratch out an accurate map of the fort and its surroundings.

Brock points out that the British and Indians will be outnumbered by the Americans: "We are committed to a war in which the enemy will always surpass us in numbers, equipment and resources." One by one his officers are polled. One by one they opt for caution: a crossing is too dangerous to attempt. Lieutenant-Colonel Henry Procter, who will one day clash with Tecumseh over tactics, is particularly cautious. Only one man, Colonel Robert Nichol, the diminutive ex-storekeeper who has just been named quartermaster general of the militia, supports Brock. Nichol has lived in Detroit, knows every cranny of town and fort, boasts that he can lead the troops to any point that Brock wants to attack. He and the commander are old friends, their acquaintance going back to 1804 when Brock commanded at Fort Erie and Nichol ran a general store. Nichol's sudden appointment to field rank has offended some of the political higher-ups, but Brock knows his man. It is said that Nichol would follow his general into Vesuvius if need be.

At this midnight council the contrast between Brock and Hull is starkly clear. Brock listens carefully to his subordinates' reservations, then speaks: nothing, he says, can be gained by delay. "I have decided on crossing, and now, gentlemen, instead of any further advice, I entreat of you to give me your cordial and hearty support."

The following morning, standing beneath a great oak on the outskirts of the fort, he addresses several hundred Indians representing more than a dozen tribes on both sides of the border. (Even the recalcitrant Iroquois are here, though only thirty in number.) He has

166

come, says Brock, to battle the Long Knives who have invaded the country of the King, their father. The Long Knives are trying to force both the British and the Indians from their lands. If the Indians will make common cause with the British, the combined forces will soon drive the enemy back to the boundaries of Indian territory.

Tecumseh rises to reply. This polyglot assembly is of his making – the closest he will ever get to achieving the confederacy of which he dreams. The hazel eyes flash, the oval face darkens as he conjures up the memory of Tippecanoe:

"They suddenly came against us with a great force while I was absent, and destroyed our village and slew our warriors."

All the bitterness against the land-hunger of the frontier settlers is revived:

"They came to us hungry and cut off the hands of our brothers who gave them corn. We gave them rivers of fish and they poisoned our fountains. We gave them forest-clad mountains and valleys full of game and in return what did they give our warriors and our women? Rum and trinkets and a grave!"

Brock does not intend to reveal the details of his attack plan to such a large assembly. The oratory finished, he invites Tecumseh and a few older chiefs to meet at Elliott's house. Here, through interpreters, he explains his strategy as the chiefs nod approval. The General is concerned, however, about alcohol: can Tecumseh prevent his followers from drinking to excess? The Shawnee replies that before his people left the Wabash they promised to abstain from all spirits until they had humbled the Long Knives. Brock responds with satisfaction: "If this resolution be persevered in, you must conquer."

He has one further act of diplomacy before he leaves for Sandwich. He issues a general order intended to heal the wounds caused by Hull's divisive proclamation:

"The major-general cannot avoid expressing his surprise at the numerous desertions which have occurred from the ranks of the militia, to which circumstance the long stay of the enemy on this side of the river must in great measure be ascribed. He is willing to believe that their conduct proceeded from an anxiety to get in their harvest, and not from any predilection for the principles or government of the United States."

This pretty fiction serves its purpose of uniting the people behind him. Hull has deserted them: Brock, by implication, has promised an amnesty. As he rides that same afternoon past the ripening apple trees to Sandwich he knows he is passing through friendly country.

•

DETROIT, MICHIGAN TERRITORY, August 12, 1812. Colonel Lewis Cass is seething with frustration over what he conceives to be the inadequacies and follies of his commander. He can contain himself no longer and finds a temporary outlet for his anger in a letter to his brother-in-law:

"Our situation is become critical. If things get worse, you will have a letter from me giving you a particular statement of this business. As bad as you may think of our situation it is still worse than you believe. I cannot descend into particulars for fear this should fall into the hands of the enemy."

From the outset he has thought of Hull as a weak old man. Now other, more sinister epithets begin to form in his mind. Cass is contemplating something very close to treason, a word he will shortly apply to his commanding officer.

His style is as blunt as his body. He has powerful arms and legs and a trunk like an ox. Nobody would call him handsome. Long, unruly hair dominates a coarse face. A later official portrait shows him scowling blackly at the artist, one hand thrust into his tunic, Napoleon-fashion. At thirty, he has the resonant voice of a frontier lawyer, toughened on the court circuit, his endurance tested by years spent on horseback on old Indian trails or on pitching flatboats in wilderness rivers, arguing and pleading in primitive courthouses where the judge, on occasion, has been known to descend from the bench to wrestle a pugnacious spectator into submission.

He is an ambitious man, Cass. He has been a member of the Ohio House, a state marshal, a brigadier-general in the militia. He loves the military life, likes to wear splendid uniforms (his officer's plume is the highest of any), insists on parading his men whenever the opportunity allows, believes in regular, arduous drilling. For all that he is popular, for his is the easy camaraderie of the circuit court. He mixes freely with his men, who respect him in spite of a certain humourlessness. Unlike Hull, Cass conveys an air of absolute conviction; he *knows* he is right; and the fact that Hull, in Cass's view, is wrong drives him to distraction. In spite of his ponderous appearance he has all the nervous energy of a tomcat – not the kind of man to sit quietly by and watch the enemy preparing for an assault.

Cass's disillusionment with Hull is shared by his fellow officers and has filtered down through the ranks. On this same day (the very day on which Wellington's forces enter Madrid), the scout Robert Lucas is writing to a friend in Portsmouth, Ohio, in much the same vein:

"Never was there a more Patriotic army...neither was there ever an army that had it more completely in their power to have accomplished every object of their Desire than the Present, And must now be sunk into Disgrace for want of a General at their head —

"Never was there officers...more united than our Patriotic Colonels...to promote the Public good neither was there ever men of talents as they are so shamefully opposed by an imbesile or Treacherous Commander as they have been.... Would to God Either of our Colonels had the command, if they had, we might yet wipe off the foul stain that has been brought upon us...."

The army is close to mutiny. A round robin is circulating among the troops urging that Hull be replaced by McArthur. Cass, Findlay, and McArthur meet with Miller and offer to depose Hull if he will take command. Miller refuses but agrees to unite with the others to oppose Hull and give the command to McArthur. McArthur, who has already said privately that Hull will not do, also refuses — nobody wants to bell the cat. All three turn to Cass, who agrees to write secretly to Governor Meigs of Ohio, urging him to march at once with two thousand men. The assumption is that Meigs will depose Hull.

"From causes not fit to be put on paper but which I trust I shall live to communicate to you, this army has been reduced to a critical and alarming situation," Cass writes. When he finishes the letter, he, McArthur, Gaylor (the Quartermaster General), and Elijah Brush of the Michigan state militia all affix their signatures to a cryptic postscript:

"Since the other side of this letter was written, new circumstances have arisen. The British force is opposite, and our situation has nearly reached its crisis. Believe all the bearer will tell you. Believe it, however it may astonish you; as much as if told by one of us. Even a c—— is talked of by the ———! The bearer will supply the vacancy. On you we depend."

The missing words are "capitulation" and "commanding officer." The signature of Lieutenant-Colonel Miller, the career officer, is conspicuously absent.

Hull by this time knows of the incipient plot against him but hesitates to arrest the ringleaders, fearing perhaps a general uprising. He has, however, the perfect excuse for ridding himself temporarily of the leading malcontents. Captain Henry Brush, still pinned down at the

River Raisin, has discovered a back-door route to Detroit; it is twice as long as the river road but hidden from Fort Amherstburg. When he asks again for an escort for his supply train, Hull is only too pleased to dispatch both Cass and McArthur with 350 men for this task. They leave Detroit at noon on August 14.

The General has, of course, weakened his own garrison in spite of strong evidence that the British, now directly across the river at Sandwich, are planning an attack. What is in Hull's mind? Has he already given up? He has in his possession a letter, intercepted from a British courier, written by Lieutenant-Colonel Procter to Captain Roberts at Michilimackinac, informing him that the British force facing Detroit is so strong that he need send no more than five thousand Indians to support it!

It is a sobering revelation. Brock and Tecumseh face Hull across the river; now at his rear he sees another horde of painted savages.

He cannot know that the letter is a fake, purposely planted by Brock and Procter, who already have an insight into his troubled state of mind through captured documents. There are only a few hundred Indians at Mackinac, and on August 12 they are in no condition to go anywhere, being "as drunk as Ten Thousand Devils" in the words of John Askin, Jr. But Brock well knows that the threat of the Indians is as valuable as their presence and a good deal less expensive.

Many months later, when his peers sit in judgement upon him, Hull will swear to his firm belief that the British had no intention of attacking Detroit. He believes their conduct of the war will be entirely defensive. He has put himself in Prevost's shoes but certainly not in those of Isaac Brock who, contrary to all instructions, is preparing to invade the United States.

Brock is completing the secret construction of a battery directly across from Detroit – one long eighteen-pound gun, two long twelve-pounders, and a couple of mortars – hidden for the moment behind a building and a screen of oak. Lieutenant James Dalliba of Hull's ordnance department suspects what is going on. Dalliba, who has twenty-eight heavy guns and has constructed his own battery in the centre of town, asks Hull if he may open fire.

"Sir, if you will give permission, I will clear the enemy on the opposite shore from the lower batteries."

Dalliba will not soon forget Hull's reply:

"Mr. Dalliba, I will make an agreement with the enemy that if they will never fire on me I will never fire on them," and rides off, remarking that "those who live in glass houses must take care how they throw stones."

The following morning, to the army's astonishment, Hull has a large marquee, striped red and blue, pitched in the centre of camp, just south of the walls of the fort. It is a measure of the army's low morale and lack of confidence in their general that many believe Hull is in league with the British and that the coloured tent is intended as a signal.

In a barrack room, a court of inquiry under the ailing Lieutenant-Colonel Miller is investigating Porter Hanks's surrender of Mackinac. Hanks has asked for a hearing to clear his name. But part way through the testimony an officer looking out onto the river spies a boat crossing from the opposite shore under a white flag. Miller adjourns the hearing. It will never be reopened.

Up the bank come Brock's two aides, Major J.B. Glegg and Lieutenant-Colonel John Macdonell, with a message for Hull. They are blindfolded and confined to a house in the town near the fort while Hull ponders Brock's ultimatum:

"The force at my disposal authorizes me to require of you the immediate surrender of Fort Detroit...."

The force at his disposal! Brock has at most thirteen hundred men; Hull has more than two thousand. Brock is proposing to attack a fortified position with an inferior force, an adventure that Hull, in declining Amherstburg, has said would require odds of two to one.

But Brock has studied his man, knows his vulnerable spot:

"It is far from my intention to join in a war of extermination; but you must be aware that the numerous body of Indians who have attached themselves to my troops will be beyond my control the moment the contest commences.... Lieutenant-Colonel M'Donnell and major Glegg are fully authorised to conclude any arrangement that may lead to prevent the unnecessary effusion of blood."

What Brock is threatening *is* a war of extermination – a bloody battle in which, if necessary, he is quite prepared to accept the slaughter of prisoners and of innocent civilians, including women and children. He is, in short, contemplating total war more than a century before the phrase comes into common use. The war is starting to escalate as all wars must; a zeal for victory clouds compassion; the end begins to justify the means.

Like other commanders, Brock salves his conscience with the excuse that he cannot control his native allies; nonetheless he is quite happy, in fact eager, to use them. It is sophistry to say they have "attached themselves" to his troops; he and his colleagues have actively and consistently enlisted their support. The Americans are equally hypocritical; they pompously upbraid the British for waging uncivilized warfare, but their own men take scalps indiscriminately. The conflict, which began so softly and civilly, is beginning to brutalize both sides. The same men who censure the Indians for dismembering non-combatants with tomahawks are quite prepared to blow the limbs off soldiers and civilians alike with twenty-four-pound cannonballs. Though it may offer some comfort to the attacker, the range of the weapon makes little difference to its victim.

Hull mulls over Brock's extraordinary document for more than three hours while the General's two aides fidget behind their blindfolds. At last he summons up an answer:

"...I have no other reply than to inform you, that I am prepared to meet any force which may be at your disposal, and any consequences which may result from any exertion of it you may think proper to make."

At about three that afternoon, Major Josiah Snelling of Miller's 4th Infantry steps out onto the street to see the General's son and aide, Captain Abraham Hull, heading off with his father's reply in his pocket. The little village is alive with people running toward the fort carrying their family possessions or burying their valuables. Snelling picks up his glass and sees that the British across the river are chopping down the oaks and removing the building that masks their battery. He forms up his men, marches them through the gates of the fort, and, on Hull's orders, mans the ramparts.

Hull's back seems to have stiffened.

"The British have demanded the place," he says. "If they want it they must fight for it."

He sends a messenger to recall the party under Cass and McArthur, who have become entangled in a swamp some twenty-five miles away. The troops in Detroit, knowing their force to be superior, are astonished at what they consider the insolence of the British.

The boat carrying Brock's aides has no sooner reached the Canadian shore than the cannonade commences. Hundreds of pounds of cast iron hurtle across the mile-wide river, tearing into walls and trees and plunging through rooftops but doing little damage. James Dalliba with his battery of seven twenty-four-pounders replies immediately to the first British volley. He stands on the ramparts until he sees the smoke and flash of the British cannon, then shouts "Down!" allowing his men to drop behind the parapet before the shot strikes. The British are aiming directly at his battery, attempting to put it out of action.

A large pear tree near Dalliba's battery is blocking the guns and giving the British a point to aim at. Dalliba orders a young Michigan volunteer, John Miller, to cut it down. As he is hacking away, a cannonball finishes the job for him. Miller turns and shouts across the water: "Send us another, John Bull; you can cut faster than I can!"

The artillery duel continues until well after dark. The people scramble after every burst, ducking behind doors, clinging to walls, until they become used to the flash and roar. In the doorway of a house by the river a *Canadien* stands unconcerned, puffing on his pipe, as the hot metal screams by him until a shell fragment tears the stem from his mouth. Infuriated, he seizes his musket, wades out into the river, and fires back at the British battery until his ammunition is exhausted.

A mortar shell, its fuse burning brightly, falls upon the house of Augustus Langdon on Woodward Avenue. It tears its way through the roof, continues through the upper storey and into the dining room, dropping directly upon the table around which Langdon and his family are sitting. It rips through the table, continues through the floor and into the cellar as the family dashes for safety. They are no sooner clear than the shell explodes with such power that it tears the roof away.

Hull's brigade major, Thomas Jesup, reports that two British warships are anchored in midstream just opposite Spring Wells, two miles from the fort, and that the British appear to be collecting boats for an invasion. At sundown, Hull sends Major Snelling to Spring Wells to report on the British movements. Snelling reports that the *Queen Charlotte* is anchored in the river but can be dislodged by one of the fort's twenty-four-pounders. Hull shakes his head, finds reasons why the gun can't be moved. Something odd is happening to the commander. To Jesup he seems pale and very much confused.

At ten that evening the cannonade ceases. Quiet descends upon the American camp. The night is clear, the sky tinselled with stars, the river glittering in the moonlight. At eleven, General Hull, fully clothed, his boots still laced, slumps down in the piazza of the barracks and tries to sleep. Even as he slumbers, Tecumseh and his Indians are slipping into their canoes and silently crossing to the American side.

SANDWICH, UPPER CANADA, August 16, 1812. Dawn.

The moment is at hand. Brock's couriers have scoured the country-side, roused the militia from the farms, emptied the mills and harvest fields. Now these raw troops gather on the shore at McKee's Point, four hundred strong, waiting their turn to enter the boats and cross to the enemy side. Three hundred have been issued the cast-off crimson tunics of the 41st to deceive Hull into believing that Brock's force of regular soldiers is double its actual strength.

The Indians are already across, lurking in the forest, ready to attack Hull's flank and rear should he resist the crossing. Thomas Verchères de Boucherville has watched their war dance the night before; he finds it an extraordinary spectacle – six hundred figures, leaping in the firelight, naked except for their breech cloths, some daubed in vermilion, others in blue clay, and still others tattooed with black and white from head to foot. Even to de Boucherville, with his years of experience in the fur trade, the scene is macabre – frightful and horrifying beyond expression. It occurs to him that a stranger from Europe witnessing it for the first time would believe he was standing at the very entrance to Hell "with the gates thrown open to let the damned out for an hour's recreation on earth!"

But on this calm and beautiful Sunday morning, a different spectacle presents itself. A soft August sun is just rising as the troops climb into the boats and push out into the river, their crimson jackets almost perfectly reflected in the glassy waters. Behind them, the green meadows and ripening orchards are tinted with the dawn light; ahead, in the lead boat, stands the glittering figure of their general. Charles Askin thinks it the handsomest sight he has ever seen, even though in a few hours he may well be fighting his own brother-in-law. Already cannonballs and mortar bombs are screaming overhead.

On the far bank, pocked and riven by springs (hence the name Spring Wells), the figure of Tecumseh can be discerned, astride a white mustang, surrounded by his chiefs. The enemy is not in sight and the troops land without incident or opposition.

Brock's plan is to outwait Hull, draw him out of his fort, and do battle in the open where, he believes, his regulars can devastate the wavering American militia. But now an Indian scout rides in with word that enemy horsemen have been spotted three miles to the rear. This is the detachment, 350 strong, that Hull has sent to the River

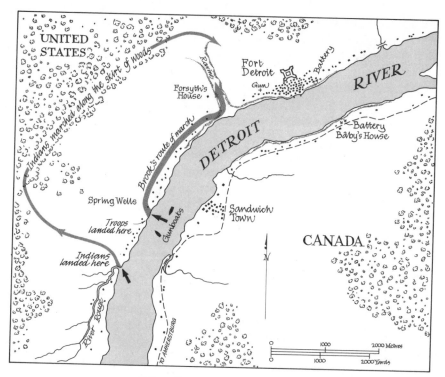

The Capture of Detroit

Raisin and recalled to reinforce Detroit. Brock's position suddenly becomes precarious. His men are caught between a strong fortification and an advancing column in their rear. Without hesitation Brock changes his plans and decides to attack immediately.

He draws up his troops in column, doubling the distance between the sections to make his diminutive force seem larger. His route to Detroit hugs the river bank at his right, protected by the guns of the *Queen Charlotte* and the *Hunter* (Frederic Rolette's command) and by the battery at Sandwich. On his left, slipping through the corn fields and the woods, are Tecumseh's Indians. To many of the militia this is familiar territory. Charles Askin, marching with the 2nd Brigade, greets and waves to old friends along the road, many of whom seem happy to see him.

At the town gate, the forward troops can spot two long guns — twenty-four-pounders — positioned so that they can enfilade the road. A single round shot, properly placed, is capable of knocking down a file of twenty-five men like dominoes. American gunners stand beside their weapons with matches burning. William McCay, who has come up from Queenston as a volunteer and is marching with Captain Hatt's company just behind the British 41st, screws up his courage, expecting to be fired upon at any moment. Young John Richardson, the future novelist, cannot help a sinking feeling in the pit of his stomach that he and his comrades are marching directly into the jaws of death, for the road "is as bad as any cul-de-sac."

Brock, at the head of the line, rides impassively forward, a brilliant target in his cocked hat and gold epaulettes. His old friend, little Colonel Nichol, trots up to remonstrate with his commander:

"Pardon me, General, but I cannot forbear entreating you not to expose yourself thus. If we lose you, we lose all; let me pray you to allow the troops to pass on, led by their own officers."

To which Brock replies: "Master Nichol, I duly appreciate the advice you give me, but I feel that in addition to their sense of loyalty and duty, many here follow me from a feeling of personal regard, and I will never ask them to go where I do not lead them."

Why have the guns not fired? There is a host of explanations after the fact. One is that Hull refuses to give the order for reasons of cowardice or treason. Another, more plausible, is that the British are still out of effective range and the American artillery commander is waiting until they draw closer so that his grape-shot—a large number of musket balls packed in canvas bags—can mow down the column.

If so, Brock outwits him, for suddenly, the British wheel to the left through an orchard and into a ravine protected from the enemy guns. John Richardson, for one, breathes more freely. Brock, meanwhile, commandeers William Forsyth's farmhouse as a headquarters, then climbs up the bank to reconnoitre his position.

The town of Detroit, a huddle of some three hundred houses, lies before him. Its population, three-quarters French-speaking, is inured to siege and plunder. It has been transferred three times by treaty, twice besieged by Indians, burned to the ground only a few years previously. It is enclosed on three sides by a wooden stockade of fourteen-foot pickets. Entrance can be gained only by three massive gates. On the high ground to the northeast, covering three acres, sprawls the fort, built originally by the British, repaired by the Americans. The parapet is eleven feet high, twelve feet thick. A ditch, six feet deep and twelve feet across, together with a double row of pickets, each twice the height of a man, surrounds the whole. It is heavily armed with long guns, howitzers, and mortars. Most of the troops are quartered outside the walls.

The American position seems impregnable, but Brock has a secret weapon – psychology. Hull has already been led to believe that three hundred militiamen are regulars. Now Tecumseh and his Indians are ordered to march in single file across an open space, out of range but in full view of the garrison. The spectacle has some of the quality of a vaudeville turn. The Indians lope across the meadow, vanish into the forest, circle back and repeat the manoeuvre three times. Hull's officers, who cannot tell one Indian from another, count fifteen hundred painted savages, screeching and waving tomahawks. Hull is convinced he is outnumbered.

Brock is still scrutinizing his objective, all alone, some fifty yards in front of his own troops, when an American officer suddenly appears, waving a white flag and bearing a note from his general. The American commander, it seems, is on the verge of giving up without a fight.

●

INSIDE THE PALISADE, William Hull appears on the edge of nervous collapse. Except for Colonel Findlay, he has no battalion commanders to fall back on. Cass and McArthur have not yet returned. Miller is too ill to stand up. Hull's son and aide, Abraham, is not only drunk but has picked a fight with a senior officer, in his father's presence, and challenged him to a duel. A dozen Michigan volunteers on picket duty at the rear of the fort have allowed themselves to be captured by Tecumseh's Indians. Elijah Brush, in charge of the Michigan militia, believes that if attack comes his men will flee. The fort itself is so jammed with soldiers, civilians, and cattle, all seeking refuge from the bombardment, that it is difficult to manoeuvre.

The cannonade has unnerved Hull. He saw blood enough in his Revolutionary days, but now he is transfixed by a spectacle so horrifying that it reduces him to jelly. Lieutenant Porter Hanks, relieved for the moment of appearing at his court of inquiry, has come into the fort to visit an old friend and is standing in the doorway of the officers' mess with several others when a sixteen-pound cannonball comes bouncing over the parapet and skipping across the open space. It strikes Hanks in the midriff, cutting him in two, then tears both legs off Cass's surgeon's mate, Dr. James Reynolds, instantly killing him and mangling a second man with the appropriately grisly name of Blood.

A second cannonball dispatches two more soldiers. Blood and

brains spatter the walls and the gowns of some women who have sought refuge nearby. One drops senseless to the ground; others begin to scream. Hull cannot be sure from a distance who is dead, but a frightful thought crosses his mind: can it be his own buxom daughter, Betsey? It is more than possible. She and her child have taken refuge in the fort with most of the civilians, all of whom Hull knows as well as his own family.

Something very odd is happening to Hull: he is becoming catatonic; his brain, overloaded by too much information, refuses to function. It has happened before to better commanders when events crowded in too quickly, to Washington at the Battle of Brandywine, for one, and it will happen again – to Napoleon at Waterloo, to Stonewall Jackson at White Oak Swamp, to Douglas MacArthur at Manila.

Hull's brigade major, Jesup, finds his commander half-seated, half-crouched on an old tent that is lying on the ground, his back to the ramparts under the curtain of the fort that faces the enemy. Save for the movement of his jaws he seems comatose. He is chewing tobacco at a furious rate, filling his mouth with it, absently adding quid after quid, sometimes removing a piece, rolling it between his fingers and then replacing it, so that his hands run with spittle while the brown juice dribbles from the corners of his mouth, staining his neckcloth, his beard, his cravat, his vest. He chews as if the fate of the army depended upon the movement of his jaws, rubbing the lower half of his face from time to time until it, too, is stained dark brown. Jesup, who has reconnoitred the British position, asks for permission to move up some artillery and attack their flank with dragoons. Hull nods, but he is clearly not in control. All he can say, as much to himself as to Jesup, is that a cannonball has killed four men.

It is the future as much as the present that renders him numb. A procession of ghastly possibilities crowds his mind; his troops deserting pell-mell to the enemy; the women and children starving through a long siege; cannon fire dismembering more innocent bystanders; and finally – the ultimate horror – the Indians released by Brock and Tecumseh, bent on revenge for Tippecanoe and all that came before it, ravaging, raping, burning, killing. He sees his daughter scalped, his grandchild mutilated, his friends and neighbours butchered. He believes himself outnumbered and outmanoeuvred, his plea for reinforcements unheeded. Sooner or later, he is convinced, defeat is inevitable. If he postpones it, the blood of innocent people will be on his hands. If he accepts it now, before the battle is joined, he can save hundreds of lives. He can, of course, fight on to the last man and go into the history books as a hero. But can he live with himself, however briefly, if he takes the hero's course?

There is another thought, too, a guilty thought, lurking like a vagrant in the darker recesses of that agitated mind. The memory of the notorious proclamation has returned to haunt him. He himself has threatened no quarter to any of the enemy who fight beside the Indians. Can he or his charges, then, expect mercy in a prolonged struggle? Might the enemy not use his own words to justify their allies' revenge?

The shells continue to scream above his head and explode. Six men are now dead, several more wounded, the fort in a turmoil. Hull determines to ask for a cease-fire and a parley with Brock, scrawls a note, hands it to his son, asks him to have Major Snelling take it across the river. (Incredibly, it does not occur to him that Brock may be with his troops outside the palisade.) At the same time he orders a white tablecloth hung out of a window where Dixon, the British artillery commander on the Canadian shore, can see it. He will not fight to the last man; in the future metropolis of Detroit there will be no Hull Boulevard, no Avenue of the Martyrs.

Abraham Hull ties a handkerchief to a pike and gives it to Snelling, who declares he'll be damned if he'll disgrace his country by taking it out of the fort. Young Hull takes it himself and crosses the river, only to discover that Brock is on the American side. When he returns, Snelling is persuaded to seek out the British general.

Outside the fort, Jesup, seeking to take command of the dragoons to meet Brock's expected attack, finds the whole line breaking up, the men marching back toward the fort by platoons. Baffled, he asks what on earth is going on. An officer riding by tells him: "Look to the fort!" Jesup for the first time sees the white flag.

He rides back, accosts Hull, demands to know if surrender is being considered. Hull's reply is unintelligible. Jesup urges Hull to hold out at least until McArthur and Cass return. But all Hull can exclaim is, "My God, what shall I do with these women and children?"

Hull has ordered the Ohio volunteers to retreat into the fort. Their commander, Colonel Findlay, now rides up in a rage and asks, "What the hell am I ordered here for?" Hull replies, in a trembling voice, that several men have been killed and that he believes he can obtain better terms from Brock if he capitulates now than if he waits for a storm or a siege.

"Terms!" shouts Findlay. "Damnation! We can beat them on the plain. I did not come here to capitulate; I came here to fight!"

He seeks out the ailing Miller.

"The General talks of surrender," says Findlay. "Let us put him under arrest."

But Lieutenant-Colonel Miller, a regular officer, is no mutineer:

"Colonel Findlay, I am a soldier; I shall obey my superior officer."

By now the shelling has ceased. Hidden in the ravine, Brock's men are enjoying breakfast provided by William Forsyth, one of 120 British males who refused to change their allegiance when Detroit became an American community in 1796. Forsyth's house lies in the ravine, and its owner, who has been plundered by Hull, is glad to open his doors to Brock's officers and the contents of pantry and cellar to his troops, who manage in this brief period to consume twenty-four gallons of brandy, fifteen gallons of madeira and nine of port.

In the midst of this unexpected revel, some of the men spot Brock's two aides, Glegg and Macdonell, moving toward the fort with a flag of truce. A buzz of excitement: is it all to be over so quickly? Some – especially the younger officers – hope against hope that Hull will not give in. They thirst for glory and for promotion, which can only be gained in the smoke of battle and (a thought swiftly banished) the death or incapacity of their superiors. In this they resemble Tecumseh's young men, who have flocked to his side also seeking glory and hoping, some of them, to gain precedence over the older chiefs who try to dissuade them from rashness. But most of Brock's followers breathe a little more freely. Charles Askin, a seasoned son of the frontier, wishes for a cease-fire for the sake of the women and children who, he believes, will be massacred by the Indians once the action commences.

Hull wants a truce, has asked for three days. Brock gives him three hours: after that he will attack.

After this no-nonsense ultimatum it becomes clear that Hull is prepared for a full surrender. He will give up everything – the fort, its contents, all the ordnance, all supplies, all the troops, even those commanded by the absent Cass and McArthur and by Captain Henry Brush at the River Raisin. *Everything.* When Hull tries tentatively to make some provision for those Canadian deserters who have come over to his side, Macdonell replies with a curt "Totally inadmissible." Hull makes no further remonstrance. The surrender details he leaves to Elijah Brush and Miller, actually to Brush alone, since Miller, trembling with ague, is now prostrate on the ground. But sick or not, he is in no mood to sign any surrender document and does so only reluctantly.

Two more signatures are required – those of Hull and Brock. The British general now rides into the fort accompanied by a fife and drum corps playing "The British Grenadiers" and by his advance guard, which includes John Beverley Robinson, the future chief justice of Upper Canada, Samuel Peters Jarvis, whose family will give its name to one of Toronto's best-known streets, and two members of the Askin family, Charles and his fifteen-year-old nephew, John Richardson. Askin, for one, has never felt so proud as at this moment.

The advance guard, however, has advanced a little too quickly. The articles of surrender stipulate that the Americans must leave the fort before the British enter. A confused melee follows. The American soldiers are in a turmoil, some crying openly, a few of the officers breaking their swords and some of the soldiers their muskets rather than surrender them. Others cry "Treason!" and "Treachery!" and heap curses and imprecations on their general's head. One of the Ohio volunteers tries to stab Macdonell before the advance guard moves back across the drawbridge.

Within the fort, Abraham Hull wakens in his quarters from a sound sleep, doubtless brought on by his earlier inebriation, to discover enemy soldiers entering the fort. He breaks through a window and, hatless, rushes up to a British officer to demand his business there with his "redcoat rascals." The officer raises his sword and is about to run him through when an American runs up to explain that the General's son is temporarily deranged.

Finally the tangle is straightened out. The Americans stack their arms and move out of the fort. The 4th Regiment of regulars, its members in despair and in tears, gives up its colours, sewn by a group of Boston ladies and carried through the Battle of Tippecanoe. Charles Askin, watching them shamble past, wonders at the legend of their invincibility. To him they look like the poorest set of soldiers he has seen in a long time, their situation and their ragged clothing making them appear as sick men.

Now the British and Canadians officially enter the fort, the regulars in the lead, followed first by the uniformed militia, then by those not in uniform and, bringing up the rear, Tecumseh's followers led by the chiefs and the officers of the British Indian Department, themselves dressed and painted as Indians.

Down comes the Stars and Stripes. A bluejacket from one of the gunboats has tied a Union Jack around his body in preparation for this moment. It is hoisted high to the cheers of the troops. John Richardson, whose musket is taller than himself, is one of those chosen to mount the first guard at the flagstaff. He struts up and down his post, peacock proud, casting his eyes down at the vanquished Americans on the esplanade below the fort. Almost at this moment, in Kentucky, Henry Clay is predicting the fall of Fort Amherstburg and the speedy conquest of Upper Canada.

As the flag goes up, the Indians pour through the town, cheering, yelling, firing off their guns and seizing American horses. There is looting but no savagery; Tecumseh keeps his promise to Brock that his people will not molest the prisoners. As the two ride together through the fort, the general seems larger than life in his black cocked hat – his crimson uniform and gilt epaulettes contrasting sharply with the fringed buckskin of his lither Shawnee ally. It is a moment for legend: a story will soon spring up that Brock has torn off his military sash and presented it to Tecumseh. If so, Tecumseh is not seen to wear it. Perhaps, as some say, he has turned it over to Roundhead, who as senior member of the senior tribe of Wyandot is held by the Shawnee to be more deserving. Perhaps Tecumseh feels the gaudy silk is too much out of character for the plain deerskin garb that, in a kind of reverse vanity, he has made his trademark. Perhaps. The incident becomes part of the myth of Tecumseh, the myth of Brock.

Brock has one more symbolic act to perform. He goes directly to the guardroom to release John Dean, the British regular who struggled to hold the bridge during the first engagement at the River aux Canards. He releases him personally, shakes his hand, and in the presence of his men, his voice breaking a little with emotion, tells Dean he is an honour to his military calling.

These and other formalities observed, he turns the command of the captured territory over to Lieutenant-Colonel Procter and prepares to leave for York, where he will be hailed as the saviour of the province. In just nineteen days he has met the legislature, arranged the public affairs of Upper Canada, travelled three hundred miles to invade the invader, captured an entire army and a territory as large as the one he governs. Now he must hurry back to the capital and return the bulk of his troops as swiftly as possible to the sensitive Niagara frontier, under threat of imminent attack.

On this triumphant journey across the lake he makes a remark to a captain of the York Volunteers, Peter Robinson, that is both self-revealing and prophetic.

"If this war lasts, I am afraid I shall do some foolish thing," says General Brock, "for I know myself, there is no want of courage in my nature – I hope I shall not get into a scrape."

●

ONCE THE SURRENDER is accomplished, Hull emerges from his catatonic state like a man coming out of an anaesthetic. Scarcely able to speak or act that morning, he is now both lucid and serene. "I have done what my conscience directed," he declares. "I have saved Detroit and the Territory from the horrors of an Indian massacre." He knows that his country will censure him (though he cannot yet comprehend the magnitude of that censure), knows that he has "sacrificed a reputation dearer to me than life," but he is by no means downcast. A prisoner of the British, he no longer carries on his shoulders the crushing burden of command. As his former friend Lieutenant-Colonel Bâby remarks to him in his captivity – echoing Hull's own brittle comment of the previous month – *"Well, General, circumstances are changed now indeed."*

Of his surrender, Hull says, "My heart approves the act." His colleagues are of a different mind. McArthur and Cass, trotting to the relief of Detroit, their exhausted and famished troops riding two to a horse after a forced march of twenty-four miles, have heard the cannonade cease at 10 A.M. and are convinced that Hull has repulsed the British. The astonishing sight of the Union Jack flying over the fort changes their minds, and they move back several miles. Their men have had nothing to eat for forty-eight hours except green pumpkins and unripe corn garnered in the fields. Now they spy an ox by the roadside, slaughter and roast it. In the midst of this feast they are accosted by two British officers bearing a flag of truce who inform them that by the terms of their commander's surrender they are all prisoners.

"Traitor!" cries Cass. "He has disgraced his country," and seizing his sword from its sheath proceeds to break it in two.

It does not, apparently, occur to either of these commanders, so eager now to have at the enemy, that they might make their way back to Urbana without much fear of pursuit. Tired and dispirited, they meekly lay down their weapons and are marched into captivity.

Captain Henry Brush, at the River Raisin, is an officer of different mettle. When Matthew Elliott's son William, a militia captain, arrives to inform him of the surrender, Brush denounces the document of capitulation as a forgery, calls Elliott an imposter and spy, places him under arrest, and with all of his men except the sick decamps to the Rapids of the Maumee and thence through the Black Swamp to Urbana, where his followers disperse in small groups to their homes in Chillicothe. Tecumseh gives chase with three hundred mounted Indians, but Brush's men are too far in the lead to be captured. It makes little difference: the war still has rules of a sort, and under the terms of the surrender document, the United States officially recognizes Brush's men as prisoners. They cannot fight again until they are exchanged for an equal number of captured British.

Hull, who is worth thirty privates in a prisoner exchange, is shipped off to Quebec with his officers and the regular troops of Miller's 4th Infantry. Some of these men, hungry and emaciated, do not survive the journey. One regular, the enterprising Robert Lucas, has no intention of making it. The instant the British flag replaces the Stars and Stripes over the fort, he slips out of his uniform, hides his sword in his brother's trunk, and disguised as a civilian volunteer boards the vessel that is taking the Ohio militia on parole to Cleveland. Twenty years from now the Democratic party of Ohio will nominate him for governor over his only rival – Colonel James Findlay, his fellow prisoner.

Tecumseh knows many of the American prisoners by sight and greets them in Detroit without apparent rancour. This is his supreme moment. One of the militia engineers, Lieutenant George Ryerson (older brother of the great educator, Egerton) sees the buckskin-clad Shawnee chief shortly after the surrender, sitting with his brother, the Prophet, smoking his pipe "with his face perfectly calm, but with the greatest satisfaction beaming in his eye."

Now, in the aftermath of the bloodless victory, a number of tales are added to the legend of Tecumseh.

There is, for instance, the story of Father Gabriel Richard, the priest of Ste Anne's parish, who refuses to take the oath of allegiance to the British Crown because, he says, he has already sworn an oath to support the American Constitution. Procter, whom Brock has left in charge, imprisons the priest at Sandwich. When Tecumseh insists upon his release, Procter snubs him. Tecumseh swiftly assembles his followers, warns Procter that he will return to the Wabash if the priest is not freed. The Colonel gives in. It is the first but not the last time that he will clash with the Shawnee.

There are other tales: Tecumseh is speaking to his followers at the River Raisin when he feels a tug at his jacket, looks down, sees a small white girl. When he continues to speak, she tugs again: "Come to our house, there are bad Indians there."

He stops at once, follows her, seizes his tomahawk, drops the leader with one blow and, as the others move to attack, shouts out: "Dogs! I am Tecumseh!" The Indians retreat. Tecumseh, entering the house, finds British officers present. "You are worse than dogs to break faith with your prisoners!" he cries, and the British apologize for not having restrained the Indians. They offer to place a guard on the house, but that is not necessary, the child's mother tells them. So long as Tecumseh is near she feels safe.

Another incident occurs about the same time. Tecumseh's followers are ravenous. The game has fled; the settlers are short of supplies. Near the River Raisin, Tecumseh approaches a boy working with two oxen.

"My friend," says Tecumseh, "I must have these oxen. My young men are very hungry. They have nothing to eat."

The youth remonstrates. His father is ill. The oxen are their only farm animals. Without them they will die.

"We are the conquerors," Tecumseh says, "and everything we want is ours. I *must* have the oxen, but I will not be so mean as to rob you of them. I will pay you one hundred dollars for them, and that is more than they are worth."

He has his interpreter write out an order on Matthew Elliott for that sum, then takes the beasts, which his men roast and eat. But Elliott will not pay: Hull, after all, has stolen quantities of Canadian cattle, not to mention a herd of fine Merino sheep. When Tecumseh hears this he drops everything, takes the boy to Elliott, insists on payment. The Shawnee's anger rises when Elliott remains stubborn:

"You can do what you please, but before Tecumseh and his warriors came to fight the battles of the great King they had enough to eat, for which they only had to thank the Master of Life and their good rifles. Their hunting grounds supply them with enough food, and to them they can return."

"Well," Elliott responds, "if I *must* pay, I will."

"Give me hard money," says Tecumseh, "not rag money."

Elliott counts out one hundred dollars in coin. Tecumseh gives it to the boy, then turns to Elliott.

"Give me one dollar more," he says.

Elliott grudgingly hands him an extra coin.

"Here," says Tecumseh to the boy, "take that. It will pay you for the time you have lost getting your money."

There are many such tales growing out of the victory at Detroit. The Americans believe Tecumseh to be a brigadier-general in the British Army. He is not, but he dines with the officers at the victory dinner in Amherstburg, ignoring the wine in which the toasts are drunk yet displaying excellent table manners while his less temperate followers whoop it up in the streets of Detroit.

When news of Prevost's armistice reaches him, he is enraged. The action confirms his suspicions that the British are not interested in prosecuting the war to its fullest. If they will not fight, then the Indians will. Already the tribes are investing the American wilderness block-houses – Fort Harrison, Fort Wayne, Fort Madison. Tecumseh leaves them to it and heads south on a new journey, attempting once again to rally new tribes to his banner.

For the British, if not for the Indians, the results of Detroit's surrender are staggering. Upper Canada, badly supplied and even worse armed, now has an additional cache of 2,500 captured muskets, thirty-nine pieces of heavy ordnance, forty barrels of gunpowder, a sixteen-gun brig, *Adams* (immediately renamed *Detroit*), a great many smaller craft, and Henry Brush's baggage train of one hundred pack animals and three hundred cattle, provisions and stores. The prize money to be distributed among the troops is reckoned at $200,000, an enormous sum considering that a private's net pay amounts to about four shillings, or one dollar, a week.

As a result of the victory at Detroit, every private soldier receives prize money of more than four pounds – at least twenty weeks' net pay. The amount increases according to rank and unit. Sergeants of the 41st Foot receive about eight pounds, captains, such as Adam Muir, forty pounds. General Brock is due two hundred and sixteen pounds. One luckless private bearing the Biblical name of Shadrach Byfield is left off the list by mistake and does not receive his share until May of 1843.

More significant is the fact that Brock has rolled back the American frontier to the Ohio River, the line that the Indians themselves hold to be the border between white territories and their own lands. Most of Michigan Territory is, for practical purposes, in British hands. A council of tribal leaders called by the U.S. government at Piqua, Ohio, for the express purpose of maintaining native neutrality collapses with the news of Hull's surrender. Many Indians, such as the Mohawk of the Grand Valley, who have been reluctant to fight on either side, are now firmly and enthusiastically committed to the British. The same can be said for all the population of Upper Canada, once so lukewarm and defeatist, now fired to enthusiasm by Brock's stunning victory. In Montreal and Quebec, the spectacle of Hull's tattered and ravaged followers provokes a wave of patriotic ardour.

The General, who has to this point treated the militia with great delicacy, reveals an iron fist. Now he has the power and the prestige to enforce the oath of allegiance among the citizen soldiers and to prosecute anybody, militiaman or civilian, for sedition, treason, or desertion.

In Canada Brock is the man of the hour, but in America the very word "Hull" is used as a derogatory epithet. In their shame and despair, Americans of all political stripes – civilians, soldiers, politicians – lash out blindly at the General, who is almost universally considered to be a traitor and a coward. On his drooping shoulders will be laid all the guilt for his country's singular lack of foresight and for its military naïveté. Forgotten now are Hull's own words of advice about the need for controlling the Lakes before attempting to invade Canada. Ignored is Major-General Dearborn's dereliction in refusing to supply Hull with the reinforcements for which he pleaded or launching the diversionary attacks at Niagara and Kingston, which were key elements in American strategy.

Hull is to be made the scapegoat for Dearborn's paralysis and Washington's bumbling. When he is at last exchanged (and Prevost is anxious to release him because he believes Hull's return will cause dissension in America), he faces a court martial that is a travesty of a trial. Here he comes up against his old adversaries, McArthur, Cass, Findlay, Miller. But his lawyer is not permitted to cross-examine these officers or to examine other witnesses; the old general, unschooled in law, must perform that task himself.

Though his papers were burned on their way from Detroit to Buffalo after the surrender, he is not allowed to examine copies at Washington. The court is packed against him: Henry Dearborn is the presiding judge. He is unlikely to be sympathetic, for if the court acquits Hull of the twin charges of cowardice and treason, Dearborn himself and his superiors in Washington must be held culpable for the scandal at Detroit.

The charge of treason is withdrawn on the grounds that it is beyond the court's jurisdiction. Three months later, when the weary process is at last completed and Hull is found guilty of cowardice, the court adds a rider saying that it does not believe him to be guilty of treason. There is more to this than simple justice, for the charge is based entirely on the loss of the *Cuyahoga* and all Hull's baggage before he knew war was declared. That misfortune cannot be laid at the ill-starred general's door but at that of Dr. Eustis, the Secretary of War, who was scandalously remiss in informing his outposts of the outbreak of hostilities.

Hull, officially branded as a coward, is sentenced to be shot. The President, taking into account the General's Revolutionary gallantry and perhaps also pricked by a guilty conscience, pardons him. Hull spends the rest of his life attempting to vindicate his actions. It is an irony of war that had he refused to surrender, had he gone down to defeat, his fort and town shattered by cannon fire, his friends and neighbours ravaged by the misfortunes of battle, his soldiers dead to the last man, the civilians burned out, bombed out, and inevitably scalped, the tired old general would have swept into the history books as a gallant martyr, his name enshrined on bridges, schools, main streets, and public buildings. (There is also the possibility that he might have beaten Brock, though somehow one doubts it.) But for the rest of their lives the very soldiers who, because of him, can go back whole to the comfort of their homesteads, and the civilians who are now able to pick up the strings of their existence, only briefly tangled, will loathe and curse the name of William Hull who, on his deathbed at the age of seventy-two, will continue to insist that he took the only proper, decent, and courageous course on that bright August Sunday in 1812.

5

CHICAGO
Horror on Lake Michigan

The wretchedness of that night who can tell! the
despondency that filled the hearts of all, not so
much in regard to the present as from apprehension for the future, who...can comprehend?...
Alas, where were their comrades – friends, nay,
brothers of yesterday? Where was the brave,
the noble-hearted Wells...the manly Sergeant
Nixon...the faithful Corporal Green – and nearly
two-thirds of the privates of the detachment?

– From Wau-nan-gee, *by John Richardson.*

FORT DEARBORN, ILLINOIS TERRITORY, August 15, 1812. Billy Wells has blackened his face in the fashion of a Miami warrior. It is a sign that he expects to be killed before sundown.

He has come to escort the garrison and the people of Chicago from the protection of the fort to the dubious security of Fort Wayne on the Maumee. It is not his doing; the move has been explicitly ordered by General Hull, who is himself only a day away from defeat and disgrace. Billy Wells has greater reason than Hull for pessimism; his blackened face betrays it.

Billy Wells is that curious frontier creature, a white man who thinks like an Indian – citizen of a shadow world, half civilized, half savage, claimed by two races, not wholly accepted by either. His story is not unusual. Captured by the Miami as a child, raised as a young warrior, he grew to manhood as an Indian, took the name of Black Snake, married the sister of the great war chief Little Turtle, became a leader of his adoptive people. As the years drifted by, the memories of his childhood – he is a descendant of a prominent Kentucky family – began to blur. Did he dream them? Was he really white? In the successful attacks on the Maumee against Harmar in 1790 and St. Clair in 1791 he fought with tomahawk and war club by the side of his brother-in-law. In that last battle – the greatest defeat inflicted on any American force by Indians in pre-Custer days – he butchered several white soldiers. But when the grisly work was done, old memories returned, and Billy Wells was haunted by a nagging guilt. Was it possible that he had actually killed some of his own kinsmen? Guilt became obsession. The call of blood defeated the bonds of friendship. Wells could no longer remain an Indian: he must leave his wife, his children, his old crony Little Turtle and return to his own people. There was a legendary leave-taking: "We have long been friends [to Little Turtle]; we are friends yet, until the sun stands so high [pointing to the sky] in the heavens; from that time we are enemies and may kill one another."

Billy Wells joined General Anthony Wayne, advancing down the Maumee, became chief of Wayne's scouts, fought on the white side in the Battle of Fallen Timbers. The battle over, his wife and family rejoined him. Billy Wells was appointed government agent and interpreter at Fort Wayne; Little Turtle, rendered docile by defeat, continued as his friend and confidant.

Yet no one can be quite sure of Billy Wells, who, like Matthew Elliott, prospers from his government and Indian connections. William Henry Harrison does not trust him, believes him to be secretly conniving with his former people. Tecumseh despises him and Little Turtle as turncoats. Billy Wells is history's captive, and today he will become history's victim.

As the heavy stockade gate swings open, he leads a forlorn group down the road that will become Michigan Avenue in the Chicago of the future. He has brought along an escort of thirty Miami warriors to lead to safety the entire population of the fort and the adjacent village of Chicago – some hundred soldiers and civilians. Half of his Miami escort rides beside him. Directly behind is Captain Nathan Heald, commander of the fort (the same man who, the previous spring, intercepted Brock's couriers to Robert Dickson), with his wife Rebekah, who is Billy Wells's niece, and his garrison of regular soldiers. A wagon train follows with the women and children of the settlement, the younger children riding in one of the covered carts. The Chicago militia and the remainder of Wells's Miami bring up the rear.

Why are these people leaving the sturdy protection of an armed stockade and venturing into hostile Indian territory? Simply because General Hull, dismayed by the loss of Michilimackinac, has decided to evacuate the area. He has instructed Heald to destroy all arms and distribute the supplies, provisions, food, and blankets among the neighbouring Indians. The gesture, designed to placate the natives, has the opposite effect, especially as Heald decides to destroy all the garrison's liquor as well as its arms. Since whiskey and guns are what the Indians desire most, the deliberate destruction of these prizes has put them in an ugly mood. Moreover, one of Tecumseh's runners has arrived with news of Hull's crumbling position at Detroit. The momentum of British success and American failure has got their blood up. Just ahead, concealed behind a ridge of sand dunes, lurks a war party of six hundred Potawatomi, the tribe so prominent at the Battle of Tippecanoe.

Billy Wells's trained eye spots the ambush. He gallops back to warn Heald, swings his hat in a circle to indicate that the force is surrounded, then leads a bayonet charge up the bank.

It is a tragic error of judgement, bold but foolhardy, for it leaves the wagon train unprotected. Heald's two junior officers, together with twelve newly recruited militiamen and a handful of regulars, fight furiously with bayonet and musket butt but are quickly subdued by the superior force of Indians. Only one white civilian, John Kinzie, the Chicago trader, survives, spared, perhaps, by the same Indians with whom he is accustomed to do business. At the wagon train, the soldiers' wives, armed with their husbands' swords, fight as fiercely as the men. Two are hacked to pieces: a Mrs. Corbin, wife of a private, who has vowed never to be taken prisoner, and Mrs. Heald's black slave, Cicely, who is cut down with her infant son.

Within the wagons, where the younger children are huddled, there is greater horror. One young Indian slips in and slaughters twelve single-handed, slicing their heads from their bodies in a fury of blood lust.

Billy Wells, a musket ball in his breast, his horse wounded and faltering, hears the clamour at the wagons and attempts to turn back in a last effort to save the women and children. As he does so, the horse stumbles, and he is hurled to the ground, one leg caught under the animal's body. The Indians are bearing down, and Billy Wells knows that his hour has come. He continues to fire, killing at least one man. As he does so, he calls out to his niece Rebekah, bidding her goodbye. An Indian takes deliberate aim. Billy Wells looks him square in the eye, signals him to shoot.

A short distance away, Heald's sergeant, Hayes, is engaged in a death struggle with a Potawatomi warrior. Their muskets have been discharged; there is no time to reload. The Indian rushes at Hayes, brandishing his tomahawk. As the blow falls, the sergeant drives his bayonet up to the socket into his enemy's breast. They die together.

Walter Jordan, one of Wells's men, has a miraculous escape. One ball takes the feather off his cap, another the epaulette from his shoulder, a third the handle from his sword. He surrenders to the Indians and is recognized by a chief:

"Jordan, I know you. You gave me tobacco at Fort Wayne. We won't kill you, but come and see what we will do to your captain." He leads him to where Wells's body lies, cuts off the head, and places it on a long pole. Another cuts out the heart and divides it among the chiefs, who eat it raw, hoping thereby to absorb some of Wells's courage.

Heald, wounded in arm and thigh, abandoned by Wells's escort of Miami, half his force of regulars dead, all his officers casualties, decides to surrender. He approaches the Potawatomi chief, Black Bird, promises a ransom of one hundred dollars for everyone left alive if the Indians will agree not to kill the prisoners. Black Bird accepts; the soldiers lay down their arms and are marched back past the naked and headless bodies of the women and children. Heald, thinking he recognizes the torso of his wife, briefly repents the surrender, then is overjoyed to find that she is alive at the fort, weeping among a group of Indian women, saved apparently by the intervention of a friendly chief, Black Partridge.

Black Bird does not keep his promise. One of the wounded soldiers, Sergeant Thomas Burns of the militia, is killed almost immediately by the squaws. His is a more fortunate fate than that of five of his comrades who are tortured to death that night, their cries breaking the silence over the great lake and sending shivers through the survivors.

More than half the band that left the fort in the morning are dead by the following day. The remainder, twenty-nine soldiers, seven women, and six children, are captives of the Indians, destined to be distributed among the various villages in the area. Thus begins their long travail.

The Healds' captivity is short-lived. After a few days, with Michigan now in British hands, most of the Indians take off to attack Fort Wayne, and Heald is able to buy his way to St. Joseph's Island in British territory, where Captain Roberts sends them home under parole. At Detroit, Mrs. Heald's "inimitable grace and fulness of contour" together with her "magnificence of person and brilliancy of character" make a lasting impression on the fifteen-year-old John Richardson, who, at the end of his life, gives her a certain immortality by making her the heroine of his novel *Wau-nan-gee*.

Others are less fortunate. That winter one captive freezes to death on the trail; two more, who cannot keep up, are tomahawked; nine exist as slaves for almost a year before they are ransomed through the efforts of the red-headed trader, Robert Dickson.

The family of John Needs, one of Heald's regular soldiers, manages to survive the massacre only to die in captivity. The Needs's only child, crying with hunger, so annoys the Indians that they tie it to a tree to perish from starvation. Needs also dies of cold and hunger. His wife expires the following January.

The family of the murdered Sergeant Burns is shattered. One grown son is killed in the fighting; two small children are victims of the wagon massacre. A nine-year-old daughter, though scalped, succeeds in freeing herself. She, her mother, and an infant in arms survive for two years among the Indians before being ransomed by a white trader. For the rest of her life the scalped girl is marked by a small bald spot on the top of her head.

In the fate of the Lee family are all the ingredients of a nineteenth-century frontier novel. All its members except the mother and an infant daughter are killed in the fighting. The two survivors are taken by Black Partridge to his camp. Here the baby falls ill and Black Partridge falls in love – with Mrs. Lee. In order to win her hand he determines to save the infant's life. He takes her back to Chicago where a newly arrived French trader named Du Pin prescribes for her and cures her. Learning of Black Partridge's romantic intentions, Du Pin ransoms Mrs. Lee, then marries her himself.

These stories pale before the long odyssey of Mrs. John Simmons, whose husband also perishes during the defence of the wagons. Believing that the Indians delight in tormenting prisoners who show any emotion, this remarkable woman resolves to preserve the life of her six-month-old child by suppressing all outward manifestations of grief, even when she is led past a row of small, mutilated corpses which includes that of her two-year-old boy, David. Faced with this grisly spectacle, she neither blinks an eye nor sheds a tear, nor will she during the long months of her captivity.

Her Indian owners set out for Green Bay on the western shore of Lake Michigan. Mrs. Simmons, carrying her baby, trudges the entire distance, working as a servant in the evenings, gathering wood and building fires. When the village is at last reached, she is insulted, kicked, and abused. The following day she is forced to run the gauntlet between a double line of men and women wielding sticks and clubs. Wrapping the infant in a blanket and shielding it in her arms, she races down the long line, emerging bruised and bleeding but with her child unharmed.

She is given over to an Indian "mother," who feeds her, bathes her

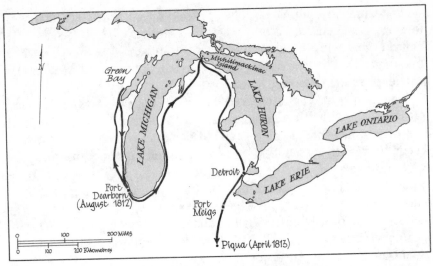

Mrs. Simmons's Trek

wounds, allows her to rest. She needs such sustenance, for a worse ordeal faces her—a long tribal peregrination back around the lake. Somehow Mrs. Simmons, lightly clad, suffering from cold, fatigue, and malnutrition, manages to carry her child for the entire six hundred miles and survive. She has walked with the Indians from Green Bay back to Chicago, then around the entire eastern shore of the lake to Michilimackinac. But a second, even more terrible trek faces her—a three-hundred-mile journey through the snow to Detroit, where the Indians intend to ransom her. Ragged and starving, she exists on roots and acorns found beneath the snows. Her child, now a year old, has grown much heavier. Her own strength is waning. Only the prospect of release sustains her.

Yet even after her successful ransom her ordeal is not over. The route to her home near Piqua, Ohio, is long and hard. By March of 1813 she reaches Fort Meigs on the Maumee. Here she manages to secure passage in a government wagon, part of a supply train that winds its way through swampy roads, depositing her, in mid-April, four miles from her father's farm.

Mother and child walk the remaining distance to find that the family, which has long since given her up for dead, has taken refuge in a blockhouse against Indian marauders. Here, safe at last, she breaks down and for several months cannot contain her tears. In August, she has further reason to weep. Her sister and brother-in-law, working in a nearby flax field, are surprised by Indians, shot, toma-hawked, and scalped in front of their four horrified children. Such, in part, is the legacy of Tippecanoe and all that preceded it.

To these tales of horror and heroism must be added a bizarre coda:

It is October, 1816; the war has been over for two years. Two workmen helping to rebuild Fort Dearborn are travelling by skiff up the north branch of the Illinois, searching out suitable timber, probing deep into the wilderness, far from human habitation. Suddenly they hear the cries of Indian women and, above that gabble, the sound of English words. They spy, half-hidden in the underbrush, an Indian hut and then a white man, standing on the bank, who pleads with them to stop and talk, for he has heard no English for four years. This is the tale he tells:

He is one of Heald's force of soldiers, badly wounded in the battle with the Potawatomi and saved by an aging Indian woman, to whom he has previously been kind. She prevents her people from scalping him and, with the help of her three daughters, moves him across the river, hides him in the undergrowth, and tends his wounds until he is well enough to be moved.

The four women secure a piece of timber from the ruined fort, tie him to it, and tow the makeshift raft forty miles northward to the shores of a small lake. And here all five live together. He marries his benefactor, Indian fashion. When she dies he takes the two older daughters as his wives. Since that day they have been living here together in the wilderness.

The workmen return to Chicago to report their strange discovery. Next day, the army surgeon accompanies them upriver with a boat-load of presents for the quartet, only to discover that the women are on the point of spiriting their joint husband away, deeper into the wild. He, for his part, has made no objection; indeed, he has decided to take their younger sister as his third common-law wife.

The doctor examines his wounds. They have healed; but one leg is shorter than the other, and one arm is useless. Does he wish to return to his own kind? The old soldier shakes his head: not as long as his harem will live with him and care for him, he says. He is already preparing to move further from civilization, further into the unpopu-lated forest. Perhaps he will visit the fort some day, he remarks, but only if the soldiers solemnly promise not to make fun of his little teen-aged bride.

But he does not come. No white man ever sees or hears of him again. He and his little family melt away into the recesses of the coniferous jungle that clothes the territory. No pen records his odyssey; no stone marks his grave; nor can anyone recall his name. Like so many others he is the faceless victim of a war not of his making; and, again like so many others, he has managed to come to terms with his fate and in that process to survive and even prosper in his fashion, a creature of the wild, at once its prisoner and its conqueror, master and servant of all he surveys, monarch of an empty empire.

6

QUEENSTON HEIGHTS
The End of Isaac Brock

No tongue shall blazon forth their fame —
The cheers that stir that sacred hill
Are but the promptings of the will
That conquered then, that conquers still
And generations shall thrill
At Brock's remembered name.

— Anon.

LEWISTON, NEW YORK, August 15, 1812; with the United States Army of the Centre.

Major John Lovett, who is more poet than soldier, leaps out of his quarters to the roar of musket fire on the heights above the Niagara River, flings himself onto his horse, and dashes off. The cries of his commanding officer, Major-General Stephen Van Rensselaer, echo behind him: *Come back! Come back!* But Lovett gallops on. Later, the General will tell him that he fully expected he was about to run away, never to be seen again; but this is mere badinage, for the two are old friends. Lovett serves the American commander officially as military aide and secretary; he is also confidant, political ally, and something of a court jester – an antidote against the loneliness and burden of command. To Lovett, soldiering is a new experience, war is something of a lark, the sound of musketry exciting.

As the Major gallops for the cliffs, he realizes that two other riders are close behind him. Both are high-ranking officers. Lieutenant-Colonel Solomon Van Rensselaer is the General's aide-de-camp, kinsman, and friend. Brigadier-General William Wadsworth of the Upper New York State militia has been in charge of recruiting for the coming thrust against Queenston – a difficult and thankless task, given the mood of the region.

As they run their horses up the broken rock of the precipice (the worst terrain Lovett has ever known), the musket fire increases. They burst out of a copse into open land; a soldier runs up crying, "General, do ride into that hollow, for the balls fly dreadfully here!" but they gallop in, seeking to discover the cause of the gunfire. One of the guards posted on the cliff starts to explain just as a ball fans his face. He leaps behind a great oak, pulling his arms close in to his body to make himself invisible, and then, seeing the ludicrousness of his position, grins ruefully, causing Lovett to burst out laughing. General Wadsworth maintains a straight face and is careful to present his breast to the enemy at all times, for he does not intend, he says, "that a Wadsworth should be shot through the back." A few minutes later the skirmish ends inconclusively. It has been caused, significantly, by the attempts of two Americans to desert to the Canadian side of the Niagara River by boat.

That evening, Lovett takes pains to write his friend and confidant, John Alexander of Albany, a breathless account of the incident "principally for the purpose of enabling you to meet the *lye* should any fool or scoundrel manufacture one, out of what little did actually take place." He does not want it "conjured up as to another *Sackett's Harbor Battle*." Lies there have been and rumours aplenty, including one monstrous falsehood, heard during the army's march north through Utica, that the American post at Sackets Harbor had been attacked and blockaded by the British – a piece of fiction that caused the General to abandon his route to the Niagara River and march to the relief of the town, only to find that nothing untoward had taken place.

Now, Stephen Van Rensselaer has set up his headquarters at Lewiston, concentrating his forces here, directly across from the Canadian village of Queenston. This very day, Dr. Eustis, the Secretary of War, has sent an order to Van Rensselaer's superior, General Dearborn, at Albany: "Considering the urgency of a diversion in favour of General Hull under the circumstances attending his situation, the President thinks it proper that not a moment should be lost in gaining possession of the British posts at Niagara and Kingston, or at least the former, and proceeding in co-operation with General Hull in securing Upper Canada." Both Eustis and Dearborn cling to the fancy that Hull has been victorious in Upper Canada and that Fort Amherstburg has already fallen.

In Lewiston, General Van Rensselaer is under no such illusion, though he will not learn of Hull's situation for several days. There is not much he can do to aid Hull. It is all very well for Eustis to talk of an attack on the Niagara frontier; it is quite a different matter to put his strategy into practice. The British control not only the far shore but also the Niagara River and the two lakes. Van Rensselaer has less than a thousand men to guard a front of thirty-six miles. One-third of his force is too ill to fight. None has been paid. His men lie in the open without tents or covering. Ammunition is low; there are scarcely ten rounds per soldier. There are no heavy ordnance, no gunners, no engineers, scarcely any medical supplies.

And even if, through some miracle of logistics, these deficiencies were rectified, it is questionable whether the state militia will agree to fight on foreign soil. On July 22, a humiliating incident at Ogdensburg made the General wary of his civilian soldiers. Across the St. Lawrence at Prescott lay a British gunboat. The General's aide and cousin, Solomon, had planned a daring raid to capture her; he and 120 men would row silently upriver at three in the morning, cross to the Canadian shore, seize the wharf buildings, and attack the ship simultaneously from land and water. At two, everything was in readiness; four hundred men were paraded and volunteers called for, but when only sixty-six agreed to go, the expedition had to be aborted.

If the troops are reluctant, their militia leaders, with the exception of Solomon Van Rensselaer, are inexperienced. Wadsworth, the militia general, knows so little of war that he has pleaded to be released from his assignment of assembling volunteers: "I confess myself ignorant of even the minor details of the duty you have assigned to me, and I am apprehensive that I may not only expose myself but my Government," he tells the Governor of New York.

Stephen Van Rensselaer is himself a militiaman without campaign experience. When the crunch comes, colleagues in the regular forces will refuse to co-operate with him. The irony is that the General is totally and unequivocally opposed to a war that he now intends, as a matter of honour, to prosecute to the fullest—even at the risk of his own reputation. He is a leading Federalist politician, a candidate for governor with a strong following in New York State, and that is precisely why he is here at the head of a thousand men, very much against his will.

For his appointment he has his political rival to thank—the iron-jawed incumbent, Governor Daniel D. Tompkins, an able administrator and machine politician who is up for re-election the coming spring. As the Republican standard-bearer, Tompkins is as interested in getting his Federalist opponent out of the way as he is in prosecuting the war, and there is little doubt that Stephen Van Rensselaer will be a formidable rival.

He is the head of one of the first families in New York, and in his name one hears the ring of history. He is the eighth and last patroon of the feudal estate of Rensselaerwyck on the outskirts of Albany, a vast domain close to twelve hundred square miles in size and after almost two centuries still in the hands of the original family. A relic of the early Dutch immigration to America, the General is a Harvard graduate, a farmer, a millionaire, a philanthropist, and, more from a sense of duty than from ambition, a politician. He has served in the state assembly, in the state senate, and as lieutenant-governor of New York. Though he is entitled to feudal tithes, he does not collect them. He is liberal enough to vote against his own class in favour of extending the suffrage. His military training and experience as a militia general are all but non-existent, but that does not bother Governor Tompkins. By appointing his rival to the command of the army on the state's northern frontier he has everything to gain and nothing to lose – except, possibly, the war.

Politically, it is a masterstroke. Stephen Van Rensselaer can scarcely refuse the post; if he does he will be discredited in the eyes of the voters. If he accepts, he ends Federalist opposition to the war in New York State. If he blunders, he will undoubtedly be relieved of his command, and that will work against him in the political contest to come. If he performs brilliantly he will not be able to relinquish command and so will pose no political threat.

He accepts – but under one condition: he insists that his cousin Solomon be his aide-de-camp. For Solomon, in the words of his friend Lovett, "is all formed for war." Unlike the General, with his pert and amiable Dutch features, the Lieutenant-Colonel looks like a soldier – "the handsomest officer I ever beheld," in the words of a contemporary. The son of a Revolutionary general, ensign at seventeen, he fought with distinction under Wayne at Fallen Timbers. (Though seriously wounded, he took command of his shattered force and for his gallantry was promoted to major.) For most of the intervening years since leaving the regular army at the century's turn he has been adjutant-general for the state of New York. Now thirty-eight, he is ten years younger than his commanding officer.

The two cousins with Lovett form a close triumvirate – "our little family," Lovett calls it. They can rely on no other counsel than their own, for their politics render them suspect, especially to such fire-breathing War Hawks as Peter B. Porter, chairman of the House committee on foreign relations, who has been appointed quartermaster general for the state of New York. (Porter and his brother are themselves in the contracting and provisioning business and thus in a position to profit from supplying the army, but no one worries about that; the phrase "conflict of interest" has yet to enter the language.) In Albany, Governor Tompkins and General Dearborn show no great eagerness to assist the beleaguered force along the Niagara. Solomon, for one, is convinced that his political enemies are deliberately trying to sabotage him.

Lovett is determined to keep a careful record of everything that happens (or does not happen) – "the history of every occurrence that can possibly be tortured into a lie" – in the event of later distortions or misunderstandings. He does so in a series of breathless letters to his friend John Alexander, scribbling away at night, even though exhausted from his unaccustomed soldiering. He has neither stamina nor time to scrawl out a sentence to his wife, Nancy; that duty he leaves to his friend: "Tell my good wife, I have not another moment to write, that I am neither homesick, crop-sick, war sick, nor sick of my Wife," he writes. And again: "Don't let my wife get alarmed" and "Don't forget my Wife and Children, nor suffer them to be lonely. Keep their spirits up" and so on. It does not seem to occur to Lovett that the best way to keep up the family spirits might be to send off a letter in his own hand. But then Mrs. Lovett, herself a general's daughter, prefers to relay her own messages to her husband through their chosen intermediary, Alexander.

To Alexander, Lovett pours out his own pessimism and despair, which he shares with his two friends, the Van Rensselaer cousins. The war, to him, is foolish:

"If any man wants to see folly triumphant, let him come here, let him view friends by friends stretched for hundreds of miles on these two shores, all loving and beloved; all desirous of harmony; all wounded by being coerced, by a hand unseen, to cut throats. The People must awaken, they will wake from such destructive lethargy and stupor....

"What might not the good spirit of this great People effect, if properly directed. History while recording our folly, will dress her pages in mourning, the showers of Posterity's tears will fall in vain; for the sponge of time can never wipe this blot from the American Name...."

And yet, when the men under his friends' command refuse to leave the boundaries of the state to attack the British gunboat on the opposite shore, he is "mortified almost to death." For John Lovett is torn by conflicting emotions. He hates the idea of the war but badly wants to win it. He adjures his friend Alexander not to breathe a word about the defections of the militia lest the news cause further defections. He worries about Hull, hoping against hope that he can hold out, but expecting the worst. His despair over the outbreak of war is accompanied by a despair over his general's inability to strike a decisive blow against the enemy. To him, this war is "the Ominous Gathering of folly and madness," yet he deplores the lack of two thousand disciplined troops who, he has been told, are necessary for a successful attack on Fort George, the British post at the Niagara's mouth.

He is a lawyer by profession, a *bon vivant* by inclination, a satirical poet, a dinner wit, an amateur politician. He is good with juries, bad with law, for he cannot abide long hours spent with dusty tomes in murky libraries. He is restless, always seeking something new, changing employment frequently. It is doubtful, however, that he ever expected to become a soldier.

"I am not a soldier," he tells his friend the General when he seeks to employ him. To which Stephen Van Rensselaer replies, "It is not your *sword*, but your *pen* I want."

Now, in spite of himself, in spite of his hatred of war and bloodshed, in spite of his aching back and his head cold, in spite of long hours spent in the saddle and damp days on the hard ground, he discovers that he is actually enjoying the experience. It is for him a kind of testing, and his letters bubble with the novelty of it all.

"If flying through air, water, mud, brush, over hills, dales, meadows, swamps, on wheels or horseback, and getting a man's ears gnawed off with mosquitoes and gallinippers make a *Soldier*, then I have seen service for — one week," he boasts. And he revels in the tale of how he and his two friends, shipwrecked in a thunderstorm near Sackets Harbor, sought refuge in an abandoned house where he went to sleep in a large Dutch oven, aided by a sergeant of the guard who laid him on a large board and pushed him into its mouth "like a pig on a wooden shovel."

He worships the Van Rensselaer cousins (after all he is employed as a propagandist):

"One thing I can with great truth say; nothing but General Stephen Van Rensselaer's having the command of this campaign could have saved the service from confusion; the State from disgrace, and the cause from perdition; and nothing could have been more fortunate for the General than the man he has at his elbow, for Solomon in *fact* and *truth* does know everything which appertains to the economy of a camp – Stop: – Away we must all march, at beat of drum, and hear an old Irish clergyman preach to us, Amen. I have become a perfect machine; go just where I'm ordered."

●

LEWISTON, NEW YORK, August 16, 1812. Consternation in the American camp! Excitement – then relief. A red-coated British officer gallops through, carrying a flag of truce. Hull may be in trouble on the Detroit frontier. (He is, at this very moment, signing the articles of surrender.) But here on the Niagara the danger of a British attack, which all have feared, is over.

Major John Lovett cannot contain his delight at this unexpected reprieve. "Huzza! Huzza!" he writes in his journal, "...an Express from the Governor General of Canada to Gen. Dearborn proposing an Armistice!!!!" The news is so astonishing, so cheering, that he slashes four exclamation marks against it.

The following night, at midnight, there is a further hullabaloo as more riders gallop in from Albany bearing letters from Dearborn "enclosing a sort of three legged armistice between some sort of an Adjutant General on behalf of the governor general of Canada and the said Gen. Dearborn." Now the camp is in a ferment as messages criss-cross the river: "There is nothing but flag after flag, letter after letter."

A truce, however brief, will allow the Americans to buy time, desperately needed, and to reinforce the Niagara frontier, desperately undermanned, that stretches thirty-six miles along the river that cuts through the neck of land separating Lake Erie from Lake Ontario. At the southern end, the British Fort Erie faces the two American towns of Buffalo, a lively village of five hundred, and its trading rival, Black Rock. At the northern end, Fort George on the British side and Fort Niagara on the American bristle at each other across the entrance into Lake Ontario. The great falls, whose thunder can be heard for miles, lie at midpoint. Below the gorge that cuts through the Niagara escarpment are the hamlet of Lewiston, on the American side, where Van Rensselaer's army is quartered, and the Canadian village

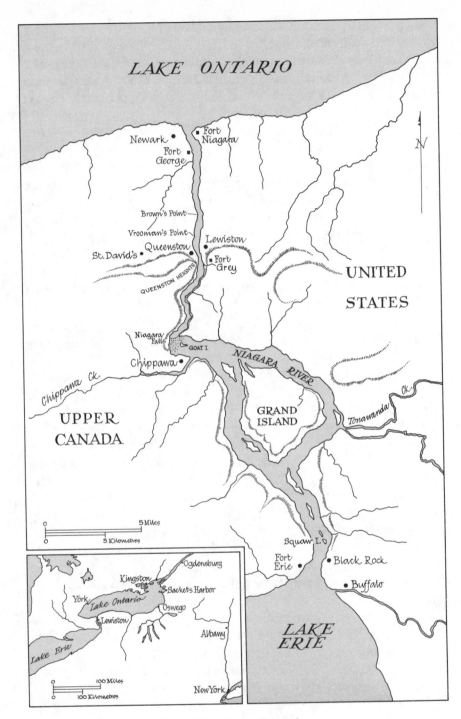

The Niagara Frontier

of Queenston, a partially fortified community, overshadowed physically by the heights to the south and economically by the village of Newark (later Niagara-on-the-Lake) on the outskirts of Fort George.

At Lewiston, the river can be crossed in ten minutes, and a musket ball fired from one village to the other still has the power to kill. For some time the Americans have been convinced that the British mean to attack across the river. It is widely believed that they have three thousand men in the field and another thousand on call. As is so often the case in war, both sides overestimate the forces opposite them; Brock has only four hundred regulars and eight hundred militia, most of the latter having returned to their harvest.

New York State is totally unprepared for war. The arms are of varying calibres; no single cartridge will suit them. Few bayonets are available. When Governor Tompkins tries to get supplies for the militia from the regular army, he is frustrated by red tape. From Bloomfield comes word from one general that "if Gen. Brock should attack...a single hour would expend all our ammunition." From Brownville, another general reports that the inhabitants of the St. Lawrence colony are fleeing south. From Buffalo, Peter B. Porter describes a state bordering on anarchy – alarm, panic, distrust of officers, military unpreparedness. If Hull is beaten at Detroit only a miracle can save Van Rensselaer's forces from ignoble defeat.

Now, when least expected, the miracle has happened and the army has been given breathing-space.

Lieutenant-Colonel Solomon Van Rensselaer, the old campaigner, immediately grasps the significance of the projected armistice, but he faces serious problems. All the heavy cannon and supplies he needs are far away at Oswego at the eastern end of Lake Ontario. The roads are mired; supplies can only be moved by water. At present the British control the lake, but perhaps the terms of the truce can be broadened to give the Americans an advantage.

The agreement with Dearborn is specific: the British will not allow any facility for moving men and supplies that did not exist before it was signed. In short, the Americans cannot use the lake as a common highway. Solomon is determined to force his enemies to give way; the security of the Army of the Centre depends upon it.

He goes straight to his cousin, the General.

"Our situation," he reminds him, "is critical and embarrassing, *something* must be done, we must have cannon and military stores from Oswego. I shall make a powerful effort to procure the use of the waters, and I shall take such ground as will make it impossible for me to recede. If I do not succeed, then Lovett must cross over and carry Gen. Dearborn's orders into effect."

"Van," says Lovett, "you may as well give that up, you will not succeed."

"If I do not," retorts his friend, "it will not be my fault."

He dons full military dress and crosses to the British fort. Three officers are there to meet him: Brock's deputy, Major-General Roger Sheaffe, Lieutenant-Colonel Christopher Myers, commanding the garrison, and the brigade major, Thomas Evans. Sheaffe agrees readily to the American's proposal that no further troops should move from the district to reinforce Brock at Amherstburg; the Americans do not know that most of the needed troops have already been dispatched. But when Van Rensselaer proposes the use of all navigable waters as a common highway, Sheaffe raps out a curt "Inadmissible!" The Colonel insists. Again the General refuses. Whereupon Solomon Van Rensselaer engages in Yankee bluff.

"There can be no armistice," he declares; "our negotiation is at an end. General Van Rensselaer will take the responsibility on himself to prevent your detaching troops from this district."

The British officers leap to their feet. Sheaffe grips the hilt of his sword.

"Sir," says he, "you take high ground!"

Solomon Van Rensselaer also rises to his feet, gripping his sword. "I do, sir, and will maintain it." Turns to Sheaffe and speaks directly: "You do not dare detach the troops."

Silence. The General paces the room. Finally: "Be seated and excuse me." Withdraws with his aides. Returns after a few minutes: "Sir, from amicable considerations, I grant you the use of the waters."

It is a prodigious miscalculation, but it is Prevost's as much as Sheaffe's. The British general has his orders from his cautious and over-optimistic superior. Brock, contemplating an all-out offensive across the Niagara River, is still in the dark at Detroit.

The truce, which officially begins on August 20, can be cancelled by either side on four days' notice. It ends on September 8 after President Madison informs Dearborn that the United States has no intention of ending the war unless the British also revoke their practice of impressing American sailors. By that time Van Rensselaer's army has been reinforced from Oswego with six regiments of regulars, five of militia, a battalion of riflemen, several batteries of heavy cannon and, in Brock's rueful words, "a prodigious quantity of Pork and Flower." As Lovett puts it, "we worked John Bull in the little Armistice treaty and got more than we expected." Not only has Lewiston been reinforced, but the balance of power on Lake Ontario has also been tilted. General Van Rensselaer, taking advantage of the truce, has shot off an express to Ogdensburg on the St. Lawrence to dispatch nine vessels to Sackets Harbor, a move that will aid the American naval commander, Captain Isaac Chauncey, in his attack on the Upper Canadian capital of York the following year.

In spite of his diplomatic coup, Solomon Van Rensselaer is not a happy man. Somehow, at the height of the negotiations with the British, he has managed to hold a secret and astonishing conversation with Sheaffe's brigade major, Evans, in which he has confided to his enemy his own disillusionment with the government at Washington, his hope that the war will speedily end, and his belief that the majority of Americans are opposed to any conflict. Solomon feels himself the plaything of remorseless fate – surrounded by political enemies, forced into a war he cannot condone, nudged towards a battle he feels he cannot win, separated from a loving wife whose protracted silence dismays him, and, worst of all, crushed by the memory of a family tragedy that he cannot wipe from his mind.

The vision of a sunlit clover lot near the family farm at Bethlehem, New York, is never far from his thoughts: his six-year-old son, Van Vechten, romps in the field with an older brother. Suddenly a musket shot rings out; the boy drops, shot through the ear, his brain a pulp. The senseless tragedy is the work of an escaped lunatic, and there is nothing anybody can do. Even revenge is futile, and Solomon Van Rensselaer is not a vengeful man. Again and again in his dreams and nightmares, he sees himself picking up the small bleeding corpse and struggling back across the field to his white-faced wife, Harriet.

It is she who worries him. The incident occurred on May 29, not long before he was forced to leave his family to take up arms. Why has she not written? Has the tragedy deranged her? Since leaving home he has sent her at least a dozen letters but has received no answer. "Why under the Heavens is the reason you do not write me?" he asks on August 21. Silence. A fortnight later he asks a political friend in Albany to tell him the truth: "The recollection of that late overwhelming event at home, I fear has been too much for her...." No doubt it has. But what he apparently does not know, and will not know until the affair at Queenston is over, is that Harriet is in the final stages of pregnancy and about to present him with a new son.

His unhappy state of mind is further agitated by his political opponents, "who even pursue me to this quarter of the Globe." The chief of these is Henry Clay's supporter Peter B. Porter, who, in Solomon's opinion, has with some Republican friends been causing "confusion and distrust among the Troops on this Frontier to answer party purposes against the Commander." The Lieutenant-Colonel blames Porter, as quartermaster general of the army, for "speculating and attending to mischief and his private affairs" when the army is in such want of supplies. The camp is short of surgical instruments, lint, bandages, hospital stores.

In Solomon's view, Porter is "an abominable scoundrel." He makes so little attempt to hide that opinion that Porter eventually challenges him to a duel. Solomon chooses Lovett as his second, but when his cousin, the General, hears of the affair he threatens to court-martial both antagonists. Their job, he points out, is to fight the British, not each other. Yet this quarrel reveals only the tip of an iceberg of dissension, which in the end will force the Van Rensselaers into rash action. For after the truce ends on September 8, Porter and his hawkish friends begin to whisper that the General is a coward and a traitor who does not really want to attack the heights of Queenston.

•

WITH ISAAC BROCK, aboard the schooner *Chippewa*, Lake Ontario, August 23, 1812.

Euphoric after his capture of Detroit, the General is hastening back to his capital at York when a provincial schooner, *Lady Prevost*, approaches and fires a seventeen-gun salute. The ceremony over, her commander comes aboard and presents Brock with a dispatch – his first intimation of the armistice that Prevost and Dearborn have concluded on the Niagara frontier.

The General's elation dissolves. He is stunned, mortified, disillusioned. He had planned to continue the relentless momentum of his victory, to roll up the entire New York frontier from Buffalo to Sackets Harbor, to hammer at the Americans while they were still off balance and poorly supplied. Now his hands are tied by Prevost, and he cannot conceal his bitterness. He does not share his superior's optimism that the armistice is the first step towards a permanent cessation of hostilities. He is convinced that the sharp Yankees are buying time to reinforce their own position, that John Bull has been gulled by Brother Jonathan.

What he desires most of all is a quick victory, one that will allow him to leave the stifling colonial atmosphere of the Canadas and return to Europe to serve under Wellington and to visit with his several brothers, to whom he writes regularly. Indeed, on the very day of Detroit's fall, while plagued by a score of problems, he has managed to send them a brief dispatch: "Rejoice at my good fortune, and join me in prayers to Heaven," adding, somewhat cryptically, "Let me hear that you are all *united* and happy."

For there has been a family falling out, which disturbs him mightily. It springs from the collapse of the banking firm of which his brother William was senior partner, a financial blow that has all but beggared the family, including the General himself. Years before, his brother advanced him three thousand pounds with which to purchase his commission in the 49th. William Brock, who has no close relatives except his brothers, had no intention that the money should be paid back; nonetheless, it remains on the books of the bankrupt firm as a debt, and the assignees are clamouring for it, even threatening legal action. Brock has pledged his entire civil salary as governor of Upper Canada – one thousand pounds a year – to pay off the debt ("Depend on my exercising the utmost economy.... Did it depend on myself, how willingly would I live on bread and water"). Typically, he is less concerned about this loss than about the estrangement between William Brock and his brother Irving, also connected with the firm.

On September 3, after stopping at York en route to Kingston (he is never still in these last days), he finds time aboard ship to write a longer letter, making use of the example of his recent victory to heal the family rift: "Let me know, my dearest brothers, that you are all again united. The want of union was nearly losing this province, without even a struggle, and be assured that it operates in the same degree in regard to families."

In spite of the depressing news of Prevost's armistice, he cannot conceal his ecstasy over the bloodless victory at Detroit. He knows he has taken a desperate gamble, but "the state of the province admitted of nothing but desperate remedies." He is irked that his enemies should attribute his success to blind luck. He believes in careful preparation, not luck. His victory has proceeded from "a cool calculation of *pours* and *contres*" and it is his alone, for he crossed the river against the advice of the more conservative Procter, who now commands at Detroit, and other advisers. "I have," he exults, "exceeded beyond expectation."

The best news is that as general he will receive the largest share of the Detroit prize money. The value of captured articles is now reckoned at between thirty and forty thousand pounds and may go higher. He does not want it for himself, but if it will enable him to contribute to the comfort and happiness of his nearly destitute family, he will "esteem it my highest reward." At the moment of victory, "when I returned Heaven thanks for my amazing success, I thought of you all; you appeared to me happy – your late sorrows forgotten; and I felt as if you acknowledged that the many benefits, which for a series of years I received from you, were not unworthily bestowed."

His brothers will, he believes, be able to see the colours of the U.S. 4th Regiment, which he expects his aide, Major Glegg, will bring to England. He doubts, however, that his fellow countrymen will hold the trophy in much esteem. "Nothing is prized," he writes acidly, "that is not acquired with blood."

In Canada he is a national hero, and he knows it. The plaudits pour in. The Chief Justice of Lower Canada hastens to send his congratulations "in common with every other subject of his majesty in British North America." General Alexander Maitland, the honorary colonel of the 49th, dispatches a gushing note from across the Atlantic, which Brock never receives. His old friend Justice William Dummer Powell cannot contain himself: "There is something so fabulous in the report of a handful of troops supported by a few raw militia leaving their strong post to invade an enemy of double numbers in his own fortress, and making them all prisoners without the loss of a man, that...it seems to me the people of England will be incredulous...." He can hardly wait to get the news in person from Brock when he reaches Kingston.

Brock himself is a little stunned by the adulation. He has received so many letters hailing his victory that he begins "to attach to it more importance than I was at first inclined." If the English take the same view as the Canadians, then "I cannot fail of meeting reward, and escaping the horror of being placed high on a shelf, never to be taken down."

He reaches Kingston on September 4, to be greeted by an artillery salute and a formal address of congratulation from the populace. As he has done at York a few days before, he replies with tact, praising the

York and Lincoln regiments of militia, now at Queenston, whose presence, he declares (stretching the truth more than a little), induced him to undertake the expedition that brought about the fall of Detroit.

He praises everybody – citizens, soldiers, magistrates, officers, militia – for he intends to squeeze every possible advantage out of his victory, uniting Canadians against the invader. The change in attitude is startling; he notes privately that "the militia have been inspired... the disaffected are silenced." People are calling him the Saviour of Upper Canada. It is an accurate title, and in more ways than one, for he has saved the province not only from the Americans but also from itself.

He cannot rest. Back he goes across the lake to Fort George on the Niagara to study the situation along the frontier. Lieutenant-Colonel Baynes has already written to him of his meeting with Dearborn, describing the mood at Albany where the Americans are convinced that the British are weak and their own resources superior, exaggerations that are both "absurd and extravagant." But Baynes has urged Prevost to send more reinforcements to Niagara, so that if matters come to a head the British force will be superior.

Brock reaches Fort George on September 6, chagrined to discover how heavily the Americans have been reinforced during the armistice, due to end in two days. He expects an immediate attack. "The enemy will either turn my left flank which he may easily accomplish during a calm night or attempt to force his way across under cover of his Artillery." He sends at once to Procter at Amherstburg and Lieutenant-Colonel John Vincent at Kingston asking for more troops.

There is one bright spot, the result again of the victory at Detroit: three hundred Mohawk Indians are on the ground and another two hundred on their way under the controversial John Norton of the Indian Department. Born a Scotsman, now an adopted Mohawk chief, Norton sees himself the successor of the great Joseph Brant and the arch-rival of William Claus, his superior in the service.

Brock has mixed feelings about Norton's followers, who have cast aside their neutrality only as a result of British victories. Any form of neutrality is, to Brock, little short of treason. He cannot forgive the Mohawk, cannot understand why they would not wish to fight for the British, cannot grasp the truth – that the quarrel is not really theirs, that its outcome cannot help them. Now, he notes, "they appear ashamed of themselves, and promise to whipe [sic] away the disgrace into which they have fallen by their late conduct." It is doubtful whether the Indians feel any sense of disgrace; they have simply been following a foreign policy of their own, which is to reap the benefits of fighting on the winning side.

Brock is a little dubious of their value: "They may serve to intimidate; otherwise expect no essential service from this degenerate race." Has he forgotten so quickly that the great value of the Indians at Michilimackinac and Detroit was not to fight but to terrify? In his account to Prevost of the capture of Detroit, he has mentioned both Elliott and McKee by name but not Tecumseh, without whose presence the state of affairs on the Canadian frontier might easily have been reversed. For Tecumseh and the Indians are also the Saviours of Upper Canada.

But Brock urgently needs to bolster the loyalty of the Indians on the western frontier in Michigan Territory, which the British hold. That loyalty has been badly shaken by Sir George Prevost's armistice; the natives, who have been suspicious of British intentions since the gates of the fort were closed to them after the Battle of Fallen Timbers, are growing uneasy again. Brock has ordered Procter to dispatch a force to invest Fort Wayne on the Maumee – the kind of aggressive move that is totally opposed to Prevost's wishes and intentions. He explains to Prevost that he has done this with the hope of preserving the lives of the garrison from an Indian massacre. This humanitarian motive is overshadowed by a more realistic if cynical objective. Brock wants to preserve the Indians' allegiance, to keep the native warriors active and at the same time demonstrate an aggressive policy on the part of the British against the Long Knives. If Tecumseh's followers desert him "the consequences must be fatal," and to preserve their loyalty he has pledged his word that England will enter into no negotiation with the United States in which the interest of the Indians is not consulted. He reminds Prevost of this and Prevost reminds Whitehall. The Governor General, who seems to believe that peace is just around the corner, revives the old British dream of an Indian buffer state – a kind of native no man's-land – separating British North America from the Union to the south.

But Prevost still believes that the path to peace lies in being as inoffensive as possible with the enemy. He wants to evacuate Detroit and indeed all of Michigan Territory – a possibility that appalls Brock, for he knows that it would cause the Indians to desert the British cause and make terms with the Americans. "I cannot conceive of a connexion so likely to lead to more awful consequences," he tells Prevost.

The Governor General backs down, but relations between the two men are becoming increasingly strained. Brock is prepared to attack across the Niagara River, is, in fact, eager to attack, convinced that he can sweep the Americans from the frontier and make himself master of Upper New York State, even though "my success would be transient." But Prevost has him shackled. Even after the armistice ends on September 8 Sir George clings to the wistful fancy that the Americans will come to terms if only the British do nothing to annoy them. This is fatuous. American honour has been sullied, and nothing will satisfy it but blood. It is psychologically impossible for the Americans to break off the war after the ignominy of Detroit. Thus far the only bright spot in America's abysmal war effort has been the defeat and destruction of the British frigate *Guerrière* by the *Constitution* off the Grand Banks on August 19. This naval encounter by two isolated ships will have little effect on the outcome of the war, but it does buoy up America's flagging spirits and makes a national hero of the *Constitution*'s commander, Isaac Hull, at the very moment when his uncle William has become a national scapegoat.

Sir George makes one telling point in his instructions to his frustrated general: since the British are not interested in waging a campaign of conquest against the United States but only in containing the war with as little fuss as possible while battling their real enemy, Napoleon, it surely makes sense to let the enemy take the offensive "having ascertained by experience, our ability in the Canadas to resist the attack of a tumultuary force."

There is a growing testiness in Prevost's correspondence with Brock – more than a hint that he is prepared, if necessary, to write off the Niagara frontier. Sir George berates Brock obliquely for weakening the line of communication along the St. Lawrence between Cornwall and Kingston: by moving troops from those points to Niagara he has encouraged predatory raids by the enemy. Between the lines can be seen Prevost's fear of giving his impetuous subordinate too many troops lest he make an overt move that will upset the fine balance with which Prevost still hopes to conciliate the Americans.

But Brock has not been a soldier for the best part of three decades without learning to obey orders: "I have implicitly followed Your Excellency's instructions, and abstained, under great temptation and provocation, from every act of hostility." To his brother Savery he pours out his frustrations: "I am really placed in a most awkward predicament.... My instructions oblige me to adopt defensive measures, and I have evinced greater forbearance than was ever practised on any former occasion. It is thought that, without the aid of the sword, the American people may be brought to a full sense of their own interests. I firmly believe that I could at this moment sweep everything before me from Fort Niagara to Buffalo...."

At last he has some officers he can trust. These come not from the 41st, which he finds wretchedly officered, but from his old regiment, the 49th, six companies of which he has brought to Fort George from Kingston: "Although the regiment has been ten years in this country drinking rum without bounds, it is still respectable...."

Many U.S. regulars, tired of service, are deserting to him; more, he believes, would do so if the opportunity offered. Those deserters who do not drown in the swirling river report a state of poor morale on the opposite side. They complain of bad food, scanty pay, continual sickness, and they are jealous of the militia, which they believe to be better fed and better treated. Brock disdains the American militia. He sees them as an undisciplined rabble of "enraged democrats...who... die very fast."

His enemies cannot help but admire him. Years later, Winfield Scott will recall how the Canadian commander of a small provincial vessel made a landing on the Erie shore and plundered several farm families of their table silver, beds, and other possessions. The indignant Brock seized the vessel, sent her back under a flag of truce with all the property that had not been destroyed and the money for the remainder. "Such conduct could not fail to win all noble hearts on both sides of the line."

But Brock has not the temperament for the kind of bloodless warfare that has been his lot since hostilities began. He is impatient for action and, since he cannot initiate it, hopes and expects the Americans will. He is convinced (correctly) that the Americans will have to make a move soon to keep their restless and undisciplined militia in line. To warn of attack he has ordered a line of beacon signals along the frontier. Now he can only sit and wait. His sword has yet to be raised in combat, and this clearly irks as much as it puzzles him:

"It is certainly something singular that we should be upwards of two months in a state of warfare, and that along this widely extended frontier not a single death, either natural or by the sword, should have occurred among the troops under my command, and we have not been altogether idle, nor has a single desertion taken place."

Who, in Europe, can take this bloodless colonial fracas seriously? On September 9, the day after Prevost's armistice ends, Napoleon launches and, at great cost, wins the Battle of Borodino, thus opening the way to Moscow. The casualties on that day exceed eighty thousand – a figure greater than the entire population of Upper Canada. On the Niagara frontier, two tiny, untrained armies face each other across the boiling river, each afraid to make the first move, each expecting the other to launch an attack.

Brock is certain that something decisive will happen before the month's end. "I say decisive, because if I should be beaten, the province is inevitably gone; and should I be victorious, I do not imagine the gentry from the other side will be anxious to return to the charge."

In short, he will either be confirmed as the Saviour of Upper Canada or there will be no Upper Canada. And whatever happens, Brock is convinced, this brief and not very bloody war will come to a swift conclusion. There are, of course, other possibilities, both glorious and at the same time tragic, but these he does not consider.

●

IN LEWISTON, during these same weeks, General Stephen Van Rensselaer finds himself pushed to the brink of a battle for which he is inadequately prepared by a series of circumstances over which he has little control. Events pile up, one upon another, like ocean breakers, driving him unwillingly towards a foreign shore.

On August 27 the camp is subjected to a dreadful spectacle: across the river for more than half a mile straggle the remnants of Hull's defeated army, ragged, shoeless, dispirited, the wounded groaning in open carts, the whole prodded onward by their British captors.

"The sensations this scene produced in our camp were inexpressible," Lovett writes his friend. "Mortification, indignation, fearful apprehension, suspicion, jealousy, dismay, rage, madness." The effect on Van Rensselaer's force is twofold: the militia is cowed by this demonstration of British invincibility while the Hawks among the officers salivate for action.

"Alarm pervades the country and distrust among the troops," the General writes to Governor Tompkins. Like Hull's beaten soldiers, many of his own are without shoes; all are clamouring for pay. "While we are thus growing daily weaker, our enemy is growing stronger." The British are reinforcing the high ground above Queenston, pouring in men and ordnance and fortifying every prominent point from Fort Erie to Fort George.

Governor Tompkins, who is thunderstruck by the disaster, receives another letter from his political ally, the belligerent quartermaster general, Peter B. Porter:

"Three days ago we witnessed a sight which made my heart sick within me, and the emotions it excited throughout the whole of our troops along the line...are not to be described. The heroes of Tippecanoe, with the garrisons of Detroit and Michilimackinac...were marched like cattle from Fort Erie to Fort George, guarded by General Brock's regular troops with all the parade and pomp of British insolence, and we were incapacitated by the armistice and our own weakness from giving them the relief which they seemed anxiously to expect, and could only look on and sicken at the sight....

"...This miserable and timid system of defense must be abandoned or the nation is ruined and disgraced. Make a bold push at any one point and you will find your enemy....

"The public mind in this quarter is wrought up almost to a state of madness. Jealousy and distrust begin to prevail toward the general officers, occasioned perhaps by the rash and imprudent expressions on politics of some of the persons attached to them, but principally to the surrender of Detroit, which among the common people is almost universally ascribed to treachery...."

On September 7, a day before the armistice ends, Major Lovett, the General's eloquent aide, comes to the conclusion that "we must either fight or run.... There are some pretty strong reasons to believe that Brock is attempting to *Hull* us...." Yet nobody on the American side can guess Brock's intentions or even estimate the true strength of his force because it is impossible to persuade a single man to risk his neck by acting as a spy on the Canadian shore. Van Rensselaer must resort to the timeworn artifice of sending officers across under flags of truce to treat with the enemy on various pretexts while peering about at the fortifications.

At Albany, General Dearborn's resolve is wavering. As late as mid-August he stated his belief that Montreal and all of Upper Canada would fall to the Americans before winter. Now Hull's defeat has shaken him. He still insists that he will attack Niagara, Kingston, and Montreal, but his purpose is circumscribed by a hedgerow of "ifs." *If* the governors of the neighbouring states will supply enough reinforcements quickly; *if* the Quartermaster General can get him sufficient supplies, ammunition, and guns, then "I am persuaded we may act with effect." *If* he can muster some five thousand regulars and additional militia, he will push on to Montreal to support Van Rensselaer's offensive on the Niagara, hoping to cut communications between the two Canadas, "but whether I shall be able to effect anything or not depends on so many contingencies as to leave all in doubt."

He has dispatched some five thousand troops to Plattsburg on Lake Champlain and another two thousand (all militia) to Sackets Harbor and expects to have an army of seven thousand on the Niagara, including three thousand regulars. Unfortunately Brigadier-General Wadsworth, the New York militia commander, who has grossly overestimated Brock's forces, has warned him that anything fewer than ten thousand will not do.

In his reports to Washington, Dearborn manages to be gloomy and optimistic in the space of a single sentence: "I fear...that we shall meet with additional misfortunes on the borders of Upper Canada... but if we redouble our exertions and inspire a due degree of firmness and spirit in the country, all will ultimately go well."

He is an old man, indecisive, inexperienced, out of his depth, querulous and uninformed ("Will the militia consent to go into Canada?"), the victim of his country's military myopia, the prisoner of its bureaucratic confusion. Hampered by lack of supplies, lack of men, lack of money, he tells Eustis: "I have never found official duties so unceasing, perplexing and fatiguing as at this place" and then adds a sympathetic postscript: "I presume you are not on a bed of roses."

At Lewiston, while Dearborn vacillates, Peter B. Porter chafes for action. He and his cronies mount a whispering campaign against Van Rensselaer's command. The General's aide, Solomon, is convinced that "they have so far succeeded in the Camp and the Country that in the former it is only whispered, but in the Latter it is openly said, that Gen. Van Rensselaer is a traitor to his Country and the Surrender of the Army when it crosses the River is the price of his Infamy." As a result, "he cannot enforce the Subordination which is so necessary to the safety and glory of the Troops he Commands."

Reluctantly, Solomon writes to Morgan Lewis, a former Republican governor of New York and now the state's quartermaster general, suggesting that another commander – somebody of the same politics as the government – replace his cousin on the frontier. Nothing comes of it.

The General expects a British attack imminently and prepares to defend against it. He decides to maintain Fort Niagara, opposite Fort George, decrepit though it is, removes the roof from a stone building, sets up a battery of two twelve-pound cannon in its upper storey, establishes a second battery of three eighteen-pounders a mile upriver across from a similar British emplacement, builds a new communications road back of the river and beyond enemy fire, and co-opts an additional five hundred men stationed at Buffalo to strengthen his own force.

The British are also active. Gazing across the narrow river, General Van Rensselaer can see the *Royal George* arrive with two hundred gunners. He has learned that one hundred smaller boats loaded with stores for the enemy fort have passed up the St. Lawrence together with two regiments of troops. The situation, he admits, is critical, but "a retrograde movement of this army upon the back of that disaster which has befallen the one at Detroit would stamp a stigma upon the national character which time could never wipe away." He will hold out against superior strength until he is reinforced. There is no evidence that he contemplates an attack. It is the British who will attack, or so the General believes.

But the British do not attack, and the promised reinforcements do not arrive. In Van Rensselaer's army of two thousand, on September 22, one hundred and forty-nine are too sick to fight, including his cousin Solomon. The weather is dreadful; raw winds and cold rains harass the troops, soaking such blankets and tents as are available.

After suffering for six days with fever, Solomon attempts to return to duty, suffers a relapse, is bled thrice and doctored with enough salts, jalap, castor oil, and calomel to render an ordinary man insensible. It takes him another week to recover from the doctors' ministrations. By contrast Lovett, the amateur soldier, is in splendid condition, "hardened almost to the hide, muscles and houghs of an ox" and clearly having the time of his life:

"We are every few days, deluged in water, such storms of rain and wind I think I never experienced, the cloth of my Tent is mere sieve stuff; every third night I get wet as a Muskrat. But in the worst of it I sing, in proper tune: 'No burning heats by day, Nor blasts of evening air, Shall take my health away, If God be with me there.' ...I feel safe; for I feel myself in duty. I am glad I came...."

In Albany, General Dearborn continues to promise that money, men, and provisions are on the way, albeit tardily ("a strange fatality seems to have pervaded the whole arrangement" is the way he puts it), and urges aggressive action. His letter to Stephen Van Rensselaer bubbles with enthusiasm: on the western frontier, General Harrison is marching to the relief of Detroit with a new Army of the Northwest, six or seven thousand strong; two thousand more troops are stationed at Sackets Harbor; the American navy is operating in Lake Ontario. "In fact we have nothing to fear and much to hope."

Everything, however, depends on what happens on the Niagara River: *"By putting on the best face that your situation admits, the enemy may be induced to delay an attack until you will be able to meet him and carry the war into Canada. At all events, we must calculate on possessing Upper Canada before winter sets in."* Dearborn underlines this passage as if, by a pen stroke, he can will his ragtag army into victory.

At the end of September, the longed-for reinforcements arrive, including seventeen hundred soldiers under the command of one of the more curious specimens of American generalship, Brigadier-General Alexander Smyth. Smyth is bombastic, egotistical, jealous of his prerogatives. A regular officer, he disdains the militia and has no intention of co-operating with his nominal commander, Stephen Van Rensselaer. Though he knows nothing of the country and has only just arrived, he takes it upon himself to advise the General that the best place for a crossing of the Niagara would be above the falls and not below them. He has therefore decided not to take his troops to Lewiston but to encamp them near Buffalo, thus splitting the American force. Nor does he report personally to Van Rensselaer. He says he is too busy.

By now, General Stephen Van Rensselaer has, in the words of his cousin Solomon, "resolved to gratify his own inclinations and those of his army" and commence operations. The British show no inclination to attack. Dearborn has demanded action. For better or for worse, Stephen is determined that he shall have it.

If numbers mean anything, his chances for success are excellent. He now has some eight thousand troops under his command, half of them regulars, of whom forty-two hundred are encamped at Lewiston. (The remainder are at Fort Niagara and either at Buffalo or, in the case of some two thousand Pennsylvania volunteers, en route to Buffalo.) To counter this force Brock has about one thousand regular troops, some six hundred militia, and a reserve of perhaps six hundred militia and Indians, strung out thinly from Fort Erie to Fort George. The bulk of his strength he must keep on his wings to prevent the Americans from turning one of his flanks and attacking his rear. Thus his centre at Queenston is comparatively weak.

Yet numbers do not tell the whole story. Morale, sickness, discipline, determination – all these Van Rensselaer must take into account. By his own count he has only seventeen hundred *effective* militia men at Lewiston. The state of his army is such that he knows he must act swiftly, if at all:

"Our best troops are raw, many of them dejected by the distress their families suffer by their absence, and many have not necessary clothing. We are in a cold country, the season is far advanced and unusually inclement; we are half deluged by rain. The blow must be struck soon or all the toil and expense of the campaign will go for nothing, and worse than nothing, for the whole will be tinged with dishonor."

The key word is "dishonor." It creeps like a fog through the sodden tents of the military, blinding all to reality. It hangs like a weight over the council chambers in Albany and Washington. Stephen Van Rensselaer feels its pressure spurring him to action, *any* action. No purpose now in disputing the war and its causes, no sense in further recriminations or I-told-you-so's. Detroit must be avenged! "The national character is degraded, and the disgrace will remain, corroding the public feeling and spirit until another campaign, unless it be instantly wiped away by a brilliant close of this." The words might have sprung from the lips of Porter, the War Hawk; they are actually those of Van Rensselaer, the Federalist and pacifist.

He knows that with his present force at Lewiston it would be rash to attempt an attack. But Smyth has arrived with an almost equal number and that is enough. He plans a two-pronged assault: Smyth's regulars will cross the river near Newark and storm Fort George from the rear while he leads the militia from Lewiston to carry the heights above Queenston. This will divide the thinly spread British forces, cut their line of communications, drive their shipping from the mouth of the Niagara River (which will become an American waterway), provide the troops with warm and extensive winter quarters, act as a springboard for the following season's campaign, and – certainly not least – "wipe away part of the score of our past disgrace."

The scheme is plausible, but it depends on the co-operation of Brigadier-General Smyth; and Smyth has no intention of co-operating. He acts almost as if Van Rensselaer did not exist. The Commander invites him to a council of officers to plan the attack. Smyth does not reply. The General writes again, more explicitly. Still no reply. Several days pass. Nothing. A fellow officer now informs Van Rensselaer that he has seen Smyth, who is unable to name the day when he can come to Lewiston for a council. The General thereupon sends a direct order to Smyth to bring his command "with all possible dispatch." Silence.

In no other army would such insubordination be tolerated, but America is not yet a military nation. The amiable Van Rensselaer does not court-martial his recalcitrant underling; he simply proceeds without him. He has already told Dearborn that it would be rash to attack Queenston with the militiamen under his command at Lewiston. Now, with Smyth's regulars apparently out of the picture, he determines to do just that.

He has very little choice for, at this juncture, an incident occurs near Black Rock that reduces his options.

●

BLACK ROCK, NEW YORK, October 8, 1812. Lieutenant Jesse Elliott of the U.S. Navy, a veteran of the 1807 attack on *Chesapeake* (and said to be a nephew of Matthew Elliott), supervising the construction of three ships of war for service in Lake Erie, finds himself tempted by the sight of two British ships, newly anchored under the guns of Fort Erie. One is the North West Company's two-gun schooner *Caledonia*, which Captain Roberts impressed into service during the successful attack on Michilimackinac. The other is a former American brig, *Adams*, mounting six guns, captured at Detroit and renamed for that city by the British. Elliott conceives a daring plan: if he can capture both vessels and add them to the fleet under construction, the balance of power will shift to the American side on Lake Erie.

He needs seamen. Fortunately some ninety American sailors are on the march from Albany. Elliott sends a hurry-up call, selects fifty for the job. Isaac Roach, a young artillery adjutant (and a future mayor of Philadelphia), offers fifty more men from his own regiment. There is a scramble to volunteer. The battalion commander, Winfield Scott, then on the threshold of what will be a long and glorious career, warns his men that they can expect a hard fight, but this only excites them further. When Roach, a mere second-lieutenant, orders "Volunteers to the front: March!" the entire battalion steps forward. Officers senior to Roach attempt to resign their commissions in order to serve under him. Men are so eager for battle that Roach finds he must select ten more than his quota.

The attack is made in two longboats, each carrying about fifty armed men, who must track their craft against the rapid current of the Niagara to the mouth of Buffalo Creek – difficult work. Here the men are forced to wade into the freezing water to their shoulders to haul the empty longboats over the bar at the creek's mouth in order to enter Lake Erie. It is past midnight; the troops, soaking wet, with a chill sleet falling about them, must now row for three hours up the lake "and not allowed to even laugh to keep ourselves warm."

At three they come silently upon their unsuspecting quarry. A fire in the caboose of *Detroit* gives them a light to steer by. Roach and Elliott, in the lead boat, head straight for the vessel. Sailing Master George Watts and Captain Nathan Towson of Winfield Scott's regiment take their boat under the stern of *Caledonia*. It is not possible to achieve complete surprise for the sleet has ended, the night is calm, the lake glassy. Two volleys of musket fire pour into the lead boat from the deck of *Detroit*, whose captain is the same Lieutenant Frederic Rolette who captured *Cuyahoga* at the start of the war. Rolette and his crew are quickly overpowered as Elliott manages to loose the topsails in an attempt to get the ship underway. Suddenly a British cannon opens up; a heavy ball whizzes twenty feet above the heads of the boarding party ("John Bull always aims too high," says Roach), ricochets onto the opposite shore where half of Winfield Scott's men are lined up to watch the action and tears an arm off a Major Cuyler of the New York militia, knocking him from his horse, mortally wounded. Roach, with a bundle of lighted candles in his hand, touches off *Detroit*'s six-pound deck guns in reply.

Aboard *Caledonia*, the commander, a young Scot, Second-Lieutenant Robert Irvine, roused from his bed, has thrown himself down the gangway, calling on his inexperienced crew of a dozen men to follow him and discharging his blunderbuss into the attackers. He has time only for a second charge before he is felled by a cutlass stroke, but he has managed to kill or wound several of the boarding party. Watts and Towson get *Caledonia* underway – thus distracting the enemy fire from *Detroit*, whose attackers are axing through her cables – and sail her across the river, where she anchors under the protection of the American batteries at Black Rock. She is a considerable prize, being loaded with pork destined for Amherstburg, a rich cargo of furs, and a good many American prisoners captured at Michilimackinac and Detroit who now find themselves free men again.

Elliott and Roach, still facing a concentrated fire from Fort Erie, drift down the river, unable to manoeuvre *Detroit*. A half mile below Black Rock she grounds on the British side of Squaw Island. Exposed to enemy fire, the Americans abandon ship, taking the captured Lieutenant Rolette and his men and all but three American prisoners of war who had been held in the hold.

A seesaw battle ensues for the shattered *Detroit*. A British detachment crosses the river, seizes her, attempts to pull her off the shoal. This is too much for Winfield Scott, who dispatches another party to land on the northeast shore of Squaw Island and drive the British away. The Americans do their best to warp *Detroit* into open water, but she has lost her anchor and the British fire is so hot they are forced to abandon the attempt. They strip her of armament and supplies and burn her to the water line, thus denying her to the enemy.

It is a considerable blow to the British. The Americans have captured four cannon, two hundred muskets, and so much pork that Procter's men at Amherstburg will be forced on to half rations. But the real effect of the loss of one ship and the seizure of another will not be felt until the following year at the Battle of Lake Erie.

Brock, who gallops directly to the scene as soon as he receives the news, instantly sees the danger. The event, he tells Prevost, "may reduce us to incalculable distress. The enemy is making every effort to gain a naval superiority on both lakes, which, if they accomplish, I do not see how we can retain the country." Brock cannot resist a small gibe at Prevost's continuing policy of caution: "Three vessels are fitting out for war on the other side of Squaw Island, which I would have attempted to destroy but for Your Excellency's instructions to forbear. Now such a force is collected for their protection as would render any operation against them very hazardous."

Jesse Elliott's bold adventure has another equally far-reaching result. The only American victory on the frontier, its success will goad the Americans into premature attack. The newspapers seize upon it thirstily. The Buffalo *Gazette* headlines it as a GALLANT AND DARING EXPLOIT. Congress publicly thanks Elliott and presents him with a sword. A thrill runs through the nation. At Lewiston, General Van Rensselaer is presented with an ultimatum from his troops, who are now hot for action – or claim to be. The General is warned that if he does not take the offensive immediately, they will all go home. With Smyth sulking in his tent at Buffalo, Van Rensselaer decides to abandon his two-pronged attack and launch a single assault upon Queenston on October 11. What follows is high farce.

He has planned to cross the river at night in thirteen boats, each capable of carrying twenty-five men. Lieutenant-Colonel John Fenwick's artillery will come up from Niagara to support the attack, and it is hoped that Smyth will send further reinforcements. The crossing will be made from the old ferry landing directly opposite the heights of Queenston where the river is a tumult of eddies and whirlpools; thus experienced boatmen are mandatory. The best man for the job is one Lieutenant Sims, who is sent ahead in the darkness while the troops follow in wagons.

Now an extraordinary incident takes place which defies explanation. Sims, by accident or design, passes the embarkation point, lands his boat far upriver where it cannot be found, then, perhaps through panic at his error or perhaps from cowardice, abandons his boat and is not seen again. In the growing drizzle, the troops wait in vain for him to return. Solomon Van Rensselaer, roused from his sickbed to command the assault and shaking with fever, waits with them. Nothing can be done because, for reasons unexplained, the oars for all the boats are with the wretched Sims.

The troops wait all night as the storm rises in fury. (It will continue for twenty-eight hours, deluging the camp.) Finally, as daylight breaks, they are marched back to camp, the boats half-concealed in the rushes. Van Rensselaer calls a council, hoping that the incident will dampen the spirits of his eager officers. On the contrary, they are even keener to attack. Lieutenant-Colonel John Chrystie, newly arrived on the scene, has already reported that his officers and men are "full of ardor and anxious to give their country proof of their patriotism." Everybody, the General discovers, seems to "have gained new heat from the recent miscarriage." Events not of his making have him in their grasp. A friend in Albany, the Federalist congressman Abraham Van Vechten, realizes this and in a letter (delivered too late) warns Solomon that "the General's reputation forbids rashness. To shun the Enemy improperly would be censurable – but to seek him under manifest disadvantages would be madness." The time has long passed, however, when the General can accept such cool advice. The pressure on him is so great that he realizes that "my refusal to act might involve me in suspicion and the service in disgrace."

As his aide and friend John Lovett describes it, "the impetuosity of not only men but his first officers became such that he was absolutely compelled to go to battle or risk such consequences as no man could endure." It is not possible to wait, even though there is no proper plan of attack. He must strike the blow at once, this very night.

•

FORT GEORGE, UPPER CANADA, October 11, 1812. As Brock's brigade major, Thomas Evans, rises from his dinner at the officers' mess, his commander hands him an alarming note. It comes from Captain James Dennis, commanding one of the flank companies of the 49th at Queenston. Dennis's detachment is in a state of mutiny. The men have threatened to shoot their officers.

"Evans," says Brock, "you will proceed early in the morning and investigate this business, and march as prisoners in here half a dozen of the most culpable and I will make an example of them."

There can be little doubt what that example will be. Years before, Brock literally pounced on Fort George and in a few minutes seized and shackled a group of mutineers plotting to shoot their commander, Roger Sheaffe. The ringleaders were taken to Quebec, court-martialled, and shot by a firing squad in the presence of the entire company, a demonstration that shook everyone including Brock himself, who was seen to wipe the tears from his eyes as the order was executed.

Brock has a second instruction for Major Evans:

"You can also cross the river and tell Van Rensselaer I expect he will immediately exchange the prisoners taken in the *Detroit* and *Caledonia* for an equal number of Americans I released after the capture of Detroit."

Thus, on the very eve of the most famous battle on Canadian soil, a British officer will enter and reconnoitre the enemy camp.

Evans reaches Queenston the following morning to find the guardhouse gutted and Dennis in a state of alarm. The two repair to Dennis's quarters in the largest home in the village, a handsome stone edifice on the high bank above the river, built by the best-known trader on the frontier, the late Robert Hamilton. It is owned now by his son Alexander, sheriff of Queenston, member of the Legislative Council, and a lieutenant-colonel in the militia. Alexander is another of the many grandsons of John Askin of Amherstburg.

Just as Evans is about to leave the Hamilton house to arrest the ringleaders of the mutiny, he hears a scatter of musket fire from the opposite shore. A ball whizzes through the room, passing directly between the two officers. Evans is outraged and demands to know the meaning of "such unusual insolence." Dennis replies that sporadic firing has been going on for some days, making it hazardous to use the door on the river side of the building.

Evans decides to cross the river at once, musket balls or no, and orders Dennis to corral the prisoners for his return. Then, with the balls still hurtling past his ears, he walks over to the home of a militia captain, Thomas Dickson, the brother of Robert, the Red-Haired Man, and — such are the close-knit relationships of the frontier trade — a cousin of the late Robert Hamilton.

Evans asks Mrs. Dickson for a white kerchief to serve as a flag of truce and invites Dickson to join him in the river crossing. Mrs. Dickson expostulates. Others in the house join her: the venture is far too dangerous; the enemy is in a temper; they will no longer respect a white flag.

At this, Evans seizes Dickson by one hand, takes the flag in the other, descends the steep steps to a canoe at the water's edge, and starts off across the two-hundred-yard stream in an unceasing shower of musket balls. The canoe, battered by the eddies and filling with water, becomes unmanageable and seems about to founder when the American fire suddenly ceases and the two men are able to reach the far shore.

As Evans is about to leap to the ground, an American with a bayonet stops him. The Major asks to see the Adjutant-General, Solomon Van Rensselaer, but is told that Solomon is too ill to receive him. He replies that he carries an important message from Brock and is prepared to see either the General himself or somebody deputized by him. Eventually, Major Lovett appears, and Evans presents his request about the prisoner exchange. Lovett's reply is abrupt and curiously evasive. Nothing can be done, he says, "till the day after tomorrow."

Evans is instantly on the alert. What have the Americans planned for the morrow? When he presses his case, Lovett remains evasive. Evans urges him to consult the General. Lovett agrees and goes off.

It appears to Evans that Lovett is trying to delay his return to the Canadian side — it is already past midday. Lovett does not come back for two hours. He explains that the prisoners have been sent on to Albany and cannot quickly be brought back, but all will be settled "the day after tomorrow."

This constant harping on the morrow confirms Evans in his suspicions that the enemy is planning an immediate attack. Now he is anxious to get away and report to Brock. He has kept his eyes open and notices that the Americans' numbers have been "prodigiously swelled by a horde of half-savage troops from Kentucky, Ohio, and Tennessee." (The prevailing British opinion is that the American militia and volunteers consist of uncivilized wild men.) Even more significant, Evans spots more than a dozen boats half-hidden in fissures in the bank and partially covered with brush. This convinces him that "an attack on our shores could not be prudently delayed for a single day."

He and Dickson paddle swiftly to their own shore. Dickson's first task is to remove his family from their house on the river bank, clearly the site of any future battle. Evans, meanwhile, rushes to warn the 49th flank companies and the militia stationed at Queenston. It is now past three. Fort George is six miles away. Every man will be needed to defend the town, including the mutinous prisoners. On his own responsibility, Evans liberates them "on the specious plea of their offence proceeding from a too free indulgence in drink," appealing to their loyalty and courage, which he has no doubt will be tested by the following day.

Then, after making sure a fresh supply of ammunition has been distributed and "infusing all the spirit and animation in my power to impart," the harried brigade major sets off at a gallop for Fort George, alerting the various posts along the route to the coming danger. He reaches the fort at six, having been exposed for thirteen hours "to wet feet and extreme heat without refreshment of any kind." He is so exhausted he cannot speak. He takes some food, recovers his breath, and is ushered into the dining room before Brock and his senior officers.

At first they do not believe him, charge him with overreaction, offer to place bets against his predictions of an attack on the following day. Brock himself appears doubtful, then changes his mind as Evans talks on. With a grave face he asks Evans to follow him into his office where he questions him carefully on the day's occurrences. At last he is convinced. The two men return to the dining room where the General issues orders calling in all the militia in the neighbourhood that very evening; others in outlying districts are told to report as swiftly as possible. He thanks Evans, who is ordered to make all necessary preparations at headquarters to meet the coming assault. Brock then returns to his office to work late into the night. Evans toils until eleven, then slumps onto a mattress. A few hours later, his slumber is disturbed by the rumble of distant guns.

●

LEWISTON, NEW YORK, October 13, 1812. At 3 A.M. General Stephen Van Rensselaer opens the attack on Queenston, after some unfortunate skirmishing between his regular and militia officers on the touchy subject of seniority. Lieutenant-Colonel Winfield Scott refuses to serve under Solomon Van Rensselaer, who has been deputed to lead the first wave. Lieutenant-Colonel John Chrystie, another regular, also demurs. A solution is worked out that gives Chrystie a command equal to but separate from Solomon's. Chrystie will command the three hundred regular troops during the crossing; Solomon will be in charge of an equal number of militia – men picked carefully from the best-drilled battalions. Not all of the regulars are as touchy as Scott and Chrystie. Lieutenant-Colonel John Fenwick is so anxious to get into the battle that he drops his rank and puts himself under the command of the militia.

Stephen Van Rensselaer's attack plan and his preparations for the assault are both faulty. He has already lost the advantage of surprise; now he proposes to make the first crossing with only a handful of bateaux: two large boats, each holding eighty men, and a dozen smaller ones, each holding twenty-five. His initial attack force, which will cross in two waves, consists of some six hundred men, half of them militia. A few miles upriver are more boats, which could easily be floated down, but the General does not take advantage of these, believing that once the boats are emptied on the opposite shore they can quickly return for reinforcements. Half a dozen trips may serve to ferry the entire force across the river. It is a serious miscalculation.

Nor does Stephen Van Rensselaer think to make use of Jesse Elliott's bluejackets at Black Rock, men who might be considered experienced boatmen. His own militia, of course, know this part of the river well; they have been staring across it, sometimes navigating it under flags of truce, for some six weeks. But those who have just joined his force from Buffalo, Black Rock, and Fort Niagara are strangers to the area.

There are other problems. Van Rensselaer has failed to distribute enough ammunition. He has not insisted strongly enough on making use of Smyth's regular forces at Buffalo. Nobody has thought to find boats large enough to transport heavy field pieces across the river; the bateaux cannot handle cannon or caissons. Nor have the various commands been assigned to specific objectives. The orders are general: get across, seize the village, gain the heights.

It is still dark when the first boats push off in the teeth of a chill, sleety drizzle. To oppose the landing, the British have fewer than three hundred men in and about Queenston. But the defenders are on the alert. John Lovett, who has been placed in charge of the American battery at Fort Grey on the heights above Lewiston, notes that the Canadian shore is an incessant blaze of musketry and that his friend Solomon lands in what seems to be a sheet of fire. His own guns — eighteen-pounders — open up to cover the attack, aided by two six-pounders and a mortar on the Lewiston shore, the cannonballs and shells whistling over the heads of the troops in the bateaux.

At the same moment, the British open fire. Half-way up the heights, in an arrow-shaped emplacement known as a redan, a single cannon begins to lob eighteen-pound balls down on the boats. Darkness is banished as bombs burst and muskets flash. At Brown's Point, half-way between Queenston and Fort George, young Lieutenant John Beverley Robinson of the York Volunteers (the future chief justice) sees all of the village lit by gun fire.

In one of the boats approaching the shore sits the oldest volunteer in the American army, an extraordinary Kentucky frontiersman named Samuel Stubbs, sixty-two years old and scarcely five feet in height, gripping the rifle with which, in just three months, he has killed forty-five deer. Peering into the gloom illuminated now by the flash of cannon, Stubbs sees the opposite shore lined with redcoats "as thick as bees upon a sugar maple." In a few minutes he is ashore under heavy fire, "the damned redcoats cutting us up like slain venison," his companions dropping "like wild pigeons" while the musket balls whistle around him "like a northwest wind through a dry cane break."

Colonel Van Rensselaer's attack force has dwindled. Three of the boats, including the two largest containing almost two hundred men, have drifted downriver and turned back. On the bank above, Captain Dennis with forty-six British regulars and a handful of militia is keeping up a withering fire. Solomon Van Rensselaer is no sooner out of his boat than a ball strikes him in the right thigh. As he thrusts forward, waving his men on, a second ball enters his thigh — the British are purposely firing low to inflict maximum damage. As the Colonel continues to stumble forward, a third shot penetrates his calf and a fourth mangles his heel, but he does not stop. Two more strike him in the leg and thigh. Weak from loss of blood, his men pinned down by the killing fire, he totters back with the remnant of his force to the shelter of the steep bank above the river and looks around weakly for his fellow commander. Where is Chrystie? He is supposed to be in charge of the regulars. But Chrystie is nowhere to be seen.

Chrystie's boat has lost an oarlock and is drifting helplessly downstream while one of his officers attempts to hold an oar in place. None of these regulars is familiar with the river; all are dependent upon a pilot to guide them. But as they come under musket fire from the Canadian bank the pilot, groaning in terror, turns about and makes for the American side. Chrystie, wounded in the hand by grape-shot, struggles with him to no avail. The boat lands several hundred yards below the embarkation point, to which Chrystie and the others must return on foot.

In Solomon Van Rensselaer's later opinion, this is the turning point of the battle. Chrystie's return and the heavy fire from the opposite shore "damped the hitherto irrepressible ardor of the militia." The very men who the previous day were so eager to do battle – hoping, perhaps, that a quick victory would allow them to return to their homes – now remember that they are not required to fight on foreign soil. One militia major suddenly loses his zest for combat and discovers that he is too ill to lead his detachment across the river.

At the embarkation point, Chrystie finds chaos. No one, apparently, has been put in charge of directing the boats or the boatmen, most of whom have forsaken their duty. Some are already returning without orders or permission, landing wherever convenient, leaving the boats where they touch the shore. Others are leaping into bateaux on their own, crossing over, then abandoning the craft to drift downriver. Many are swiftly taken prisoner by the British. Charles Askin, lying abed in the Hamilton house suffering from boils, hears that some of the militia have cheerfully given themselves up in the belief that they will be allowed to go home as the militia captured at Detroit were. When told they will be taken to Quebec, they are distressed. Askin believes that had they known of this very few would have put a foot on the Canadian shore.

As Chrystie struggles to collect the missing bateaux, his fellow commander, Lieutenant-Colonel Fenwick, in charge of the second assault wave, arrives only to learn that he cannot cross for lack of boats. Exposed to a spray of grape- and canister-shot, Fenwick herds his men back into the shelter of the ravine until he manages to secure enough craft to move the second wave out onto the river. The crossing is a disaster. Lieutenant John Ball of the 49th directs the fire of one of his little three-pounders, known as "grasshoppers," against the bateaux. One is knocked out of the water with a loss of fifteen men. Three others, holding some eighty men, drift into a hollow just below the Hamilton house. All are slaughtered or taken prisoner, Fenwick among them. Terribly wounded in the eye, the right side, and the thigh, he counts nine additional bullet holes in his cloak.

None of the regular commanders has yet been able to cross the narrow Niagara. On the opposite shore under the sheltering bank, Solomon Van Rensselaer, growing weaker from his wounds, is attempting to rally his followers, still pinned down by the cannon fire from the gun in the redan and the muskets of Captain Dennis's small force on the bank above. Captain John E. Wool, a young officer of the 13th Infantry, approaches with a plan. Unless something is done, and done quickly, he says, all will be prisoners. The key to victory or defeat is the gun in the redan. It must be seized. Its capture could signal a turning point in the battle that would relieve the attackers while the fire could be redirected, with dreadful effect, among the defenders. But how can it be silenced? A frontal attack is out of the question, a flanking attack impossible, for the heights are known to be unscalable from the river side. Or are they? Young Captain Wool has heard of a fisherman's path upriver leading to the heights above the gun emplacement. He believes he can bring an attacking force up the slopes and now asks Solomon Van Rensselaer's permission to attempt the feat.

Wool is twenty-three, a lithe, light youth of little experience but considerable ambition. One day he will be a general. The fact that he has been shot through the buttocks does not dampen his enthusiasm. With his bleeding commander's permission, he sets off with sixty men and officers, moving undetected through a screen of bushes below the river bank. Solomon Van Rensselaer's last order to him is to shoot the first man in the company who tries to turn tail. Then, as Wool departs, the Colonel slumps to the ground among a pile of dead and wounded, a borrowed greatcoat concealing the seriousness of his injuries from his wet and shivering force. Shortly afterwards he is evacuated.

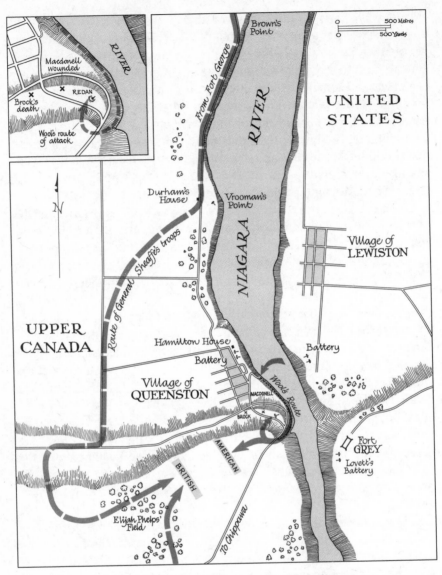

The Battle of Queenston Heights

Captain Wool, meanwhile, finds the path and gazes up at the heights rising almost vertically more than three hundred feet above him. Creased by gullies, blocked by projecting ledges of shale and sandstone, tangled with shrubs, vines, trees and roots clinging to the clefts, they look forbidding, but the Americans manage to claw their way to the crest.

Wool, buttocks smarting from his embarrassing wound, looks about. An empty plateau, bordered by maples and basswood, stretches before him. But where are the British? Their shelters are deserted. Below, to his right, half-hidden by a screen of yellowing foliage, he sees a flash of scarlet, realizes that the gun in the redan is guarded by the merest handful of regulars. Brock, who is a great reader of military history, must surely have studied Wolfe's famous secret ascent to the Plains of Abraham, yet, like the vanquished Montcalm, he has been assured that the heights are safe. He has brought his men down to reinforce the village, an error that will cost him dear. Wool's men, gazing down at the red-coated figures manning the big gun, cannot fail to see the tall officer with the cocked hat in their midst. It is the General himself. A few minutes later, when all are assembled, their young commander gives the order to charge.

●

AT FORT GEORGE, Brock has awakened in the dark to the distant booming of cannon. What is happening? Is it a feint near Queenston or a major attack? He is inclined to the former possibility, for he has anticipated Van Rensselaer's original strategy and does not know of Smyth's obstinacy. Brock is up in an instant, dressed, and on his grey horse Alfred, dashing out the main gate, waiting for no one, not even his two aides, who are themselves hurriedly pulling on their boots. Later someone will spread a story about Brock stopping for a stirrup cup of coffee from the hands of Sophia Shaw, a general's daughter, said to be his fiancée. It is not convincing. On this dark morning, with the wind gusting sleet into his face and the southern sky lit by flashes of cannon, he will stop for nobody.

As he hurries through the mud toward Queenston, he encounters young Samuel Jarvis, a subaltern in his favourite militia unit, the York Volunteers. Jarvis, galloping so fast in the opposite direction that he cannot stop in time, finally reins his horse, wheels about, tells his general that the enemy has landed in force at the main Queenston dock. Jarvis's mission ought not to be necessary because of Brock's system of signal fires, but in the heat of battle nobody has remembered to light them.

Brock gallops on in the pre-dawn murk, past harvested grain fields, soft meadows, luxuriant orchards, the trees still heavy with fruit. The York Volunteers, stationed at Brown's Point, are already moving toward Queenston. Brock dashes past, waving them on. A few minutes later his two aides also gallop by. John Beverley Robinson, marching with his company, recognizes John Macdonell, Brock's provincial aide and his own senior in the York legal firm to which the young volunteer is articled. Brock has reason to be proud of the York militia, who answered his call to arms with alacrity, accompanied him on the embarkation to Amherstburg, were present at Detroit's downfall, and are now here on the Niagara frontier after six hundred miles of travel by boat and on foot.

A few minutes after Brock passes, Robinson and his comrades encounter groups of American prisoners staggering toward Fort George under guard. The road is lined with groaning men suffering from wounds of all descriptions, some, unable to walk, crawling toward nearby farmhouses, seeking shelter. It is the first time that these volunteers have actually witnessed the grisly by-products of battle, and the sight sickens them. But it also convinces them, wrongly, that the engagement is all but over.

Dawn is breaking, a few red streaks tinting the sullen storm clouds, a fog rising from the hissing river as Brock, spattered with mud from boots to collar, gallops through Queenston to the cheers of the men of his old regiment, the 49th. The village consists of about twenty scattered houses separated by orchards, small gardens, stone walls, snake fences. Above hangs the brooding escarpment, the margin of a prehistoric glacial lake. Brock does not slacken his pace but spurs Alfred up the incline to the redan, where eight gunners are sweating over their eighteen-pounder.

From this vantage point the General has an overview of the engagement. The panorama of Niagara stretches out below him – one of the world's natural wonders now half-obscured by black musket and cannon smoke. Directly below he can see Captain Dennis's small force pinning down the Americans crouching under the riverbank at the landing dock. Enemy shells are pouring into the village from John Lovett's battery on the Lewiston heights, but Dennis is holding. A company of light infantry occupies the crest directly above the redan. Unable to see Wool's men scaling the cliffs, Brock orders it down to reinforce Dennis. Across the swirling river, at the rear of the village of Lewiston, the General glimpses battalion upon battalion of American troops in reserve. On the American shore several regiments are preparing to embark. At last Brock realizes that this is no feint.

He instantly dispatches messages to Fort George and to Chippawa to the south asking for reinforcements. Some of the shells from the eighteen-pounder in the redan are exploding short of their target, and Brock tells one of the gunners to use a longer fuse. As he does so, the General hears a ragged cheer from the unguarded crest above and, looking up, sees Wool's men charging down upon him, bayonets glittering in the wan light of dawn. He and the gunners have time for one swift action: they hammer a ramrod into the touchhole of the eighteen-pounder and break it off, thus effectively spiking it. Then, leading Alfred by the neck reins, for he has no time to remount, the Commander-in-Chief and Administrator of Upper Canada scuttles ingloriously down the hillside with his men.

In an instant the odds have changed. Until Wool's surprise attack, the British were in charge of the battle. Dennis had taken one hundred and fifty prisoners; the gun in the redan was playing havoc with the enemy; Brock's forces controlled the heights. Now Dennis is retreating through the village and Wool's band is being reinforced by a steady stream of Americans.

Brock takes shelter at the far end of the town in the garden of the Hamilton house. It would be prudent, perhaps, to wait for the reinforcements, but Brock is not prudent, not used to waiting. As he conceives it, hesitation will lose him the battle: once the Americans consolidate their position in the village and on the heights they will be almost impossible to dislodge.

It is this that spurs him to renewed action – the conviction that he must counterattack while the enemy is still off balance, before more Americans can cross the river and scale the heights. For Brock believes that whoever controls the heights controls Upper Canada: they dominate the river, could turn it into an American waterway; they cover the road to Fort Erie; possession of the high ground and the village will slice the thin British forces in two, give the Americans warm winter quarters, allow them to build up their invading army for the spring campaign. If the heights are lost the province is lost.

He has managed to rally some two hundred men from the 49th and the militia. "Follow me, boys," he cries, as he wheels his horse back toward the foot of the ridge. He reaches a stone wall, takes cover behind it, dismounts. "Take a breath, boys," he says; "you will need it in a few moments." They give him a cheer for that.

He has stripped the village of its defenders, including Captain Dennis, bleeding from several wounds but still on his feet. He sends some men under Captain John Williams in a flanking movement to attack Wool's left. Then he vaults the stone fence and, leading Alfred by the bridle, heads up the slope at a fast pace, intent on re-taking the gun in the redan.

His men, struggling to keep up, slide and stumble on a slippery footing of wet leaves. Above him, through the trees, Wool's men can be seen reinforcing the gun emplacement. There is a confused skirmish; the battle seesaws; the Americans are driven almost to the lip of the precipice. Someone starts to wave a white handkerchief. Wool tears it away, orders a charge. The British are beaten back, and later some will remember Brock's cry, "This is the first time I have ever seen the 49th turn their backs!"

The sun, emerging briefly from the clouds, glistens on the crimson maples, on the Persian carpet of yellow leaves, on the epaulettes of the tall general, sword in hand, rallying his men for a final charge. It makes a gallant spectacle: the Saviour of Upper Canada, brilliant in his scarlet coat, buttons gleaming, plumed hat marking him unmistakably as a leader, a gap opening up between him and his gasping followers.

Does he realize that he is a target? No doubt he does – he has already been shot in the hand – but that is a matter of indifference. Leaders in Brock's army are supposed to lead. The spectacle of England's greatest hero, Horatio Nelson, standing boldly on deck in full dress uniform, is still green in British memory. The parallels are worthy of notice. The two heroes share similar strengths and flaws: disdain for the enemy, courage, vanity, ambition, tactical brilliance, innovative minds, impetuosity. Both have the common touch, are loved by their men, whom they, in turn, admire, and are idealized by the citizens of the countries they are called upon to protect. And both, by their actions, are marked for spectacular death. They seem, indeed, to court it. Brock's nemesis steps out from behind a clump of bushes and when the General is thirty paces from him draws a bead with his long border rifle and buries a bullet in his chest, the hole equidistant from the two rows of gilt buttons on the crimson tunic. George Jarvis, a fifteen-year-old gentleman volunteer in the 49th, rushes over. "Are you much hurt, sir?" he asks. There is no answer, for Brock is dead. A grisly spectacle follows as a cannonball slices another soldier in two and the severed corpse falls upon the stricken commander.

The gallant charge has been futile. Brock's men retreat down the hill, carrying their general's body, finding shelter at last under the stone wall of the Hamilton garden at the far end of the village. Here they are joined by the two companies of York Volunteers, whom Brock passed on his gallop to Queenston. These men, arriving on the dead run, catch their breath as American cannon fire pours down upon them from the artillery post on the opposite heights. A cannon-ball slices off one man's leg, skips on, cripples another in the calf. Then, led by young John Macdonell, the dead general's aide, the augmented force makes one more attempt to recapture the heights.

Impulsively, Macdonell decides to follow Brock's example. Possessed of a brilliant legal mind – he was prosecuting criminal cases at sixteen and has been acting attorney-general of the province for a year – he has little experience in soldiering. Quick of temper and a little arrogant, he reveres his dead commander and, in the words of his fellow aide Major Glegg, determines "to accompany him to the regions of eternal bliss." Macdonell calls for a second frontal attack on the redan. Seventy volunteers follow him up the heights to join the remainder of the 49th under Captain John Williams taking cover in the woods. Together, Williams and Macdonell form up their men and prepare to attack.

"Charge them home and they cannot stand you!" cries Williams. The men of the 49th, shouting "Revenge the General!" (for he was *their* general), sweep forward. Wool, reinforced by several hundred more men, is waiting for them, his followers concealed behind logs and bushes.

As Macdonell on horseback waves his men on, his steed, struck by a musket ball, rears and wheels about. Another ball strikes Macdonell in the back, and he tumbles to the ground, fatally wounded. Williams, on the right flank, also falls, half scalped by a bullet. As Captain Cameron rushes forward to assist his fallen colonel, a ball strikes him in the elbow and he too drops. Macdonell, in terrible pain, crawls toward his closest friend, Lieutenant Archibald McLean of the York Volunteers, crying, "Help me!" McLean attempts to lead him away and is hit by a ball in the thigh. Dismayed by these losses, the men fall back, bringing their wounded with them. Dennis is bleeding from five wounds. Williams, horribly mangled, survives, but Macdonell is doomed.

Everything that Brock feared has happened. The Americans occupy both the village and the heights and are sending over reinforcements, now that they have unopposed possession of the river. The British have retreated again to the outskirts of the village. All of their big guns, except for one at Vrooman's Point, have been silenced.

At ten o'clock on this dark October morning, Upper Canada lies in peril.

•

AT THIS POINT, all General Van Rensselaer's forces should be across the river, but so many of his boats have been destroyed or abandoned that he is hard put to reinforce his bridgehead. He has no more than a thousand men on the Canadian side, and of these two hundred are useless. Stunned by their first experience of warfare, the militiamen cower beneath the bank; no power, it seems, no exhortation to glory or country, no threat of punishment can move them.

The General crosses at noon with his captain of engineers, whose job it is to help the troops on the heights. Unfortunately all the entrenching tools have been left at Lewiston; conditions are such that they will never arrive. The General sends the touchy Winfield Scott to the top of the ridge to take over from the wounded Wool, then prepares to return to the American shore. As he does so, a rabble of militiamen leaps into the boat with him.

During this lull, Winfield Scott works furiously with the engineers to prepare a defence of the high ground. The Americans know that British reinforcements are on their way from both Chippawa and Fort George; an American-born militiaman has deserted with that information. Scott would like to attack the Chippawa force, cutting it off from the main army, but has not enough men for the job; nor can he get more. His little force is diminishing. Whole squads of militia slink away into the woods or the brush above the bluffs. Scott posts his remaining men along the ridge with their backs to the village, his left flank resting on the edge of the bluff, his right in a copse of trees and bushes.

He realizes his danger. Ammunition is running out. He has managed to get a six-pound gun across the river in a larger boat, but there are only a few rounds available for it. In the distance he can see a long column of red-coated regulars marching up the road from Fort George under Brock's successor, Major-General Roger Sheaffe.

Now Scott becomes aware of an odd spectacle. Dashing back and forth along the ragged line of the militia is a man in civilian clothes, waving a naked sword, swearing profusely, and exhorting the men to form and fight to the death. This is Brigadier-General William Wadsworth of the New York militia, who has the reputation of being the most eloquently profane officer in the army. He has come across the river on his own, without orders, to try to instil some fighting spirit into his citizen soldiers.

Scott is nonplussed. Wadsworth outranks him, but he is not a regular. Scott cannot – *will* not – serve under him.

"General Wadsworth," he says, "since you are in command I propose to confine my orders strictly to the regular troops here!"

To which the militia general replies, quite sensibly and amiably:

"That's all damned nonsense, sir! You are a regular officer, you know professionally what should be done! Continue your command, sir, I am here simply for the honor of my country and that of the New York Militia!"

And off he rushes to raise some volunteers for the firing line.

Scott desperately needs to get the eighteen-pound cannon at the redan into action to protect his rear and cover the landing of the reinforcements that his general has promised him. But Brock has spiked it well: Scott's men cannot drive or drill the ramrod out. The Lieutenant-Colonel scrambles down the hillside to help, but as he does so a terrifying sound pierces the air. It is the screaming war-whoop of the Mohawk Indians, led by John Norton and his Indian friend, the young chief John Brant. They come swooping out of the woods and hurtling across the fields, brandishing their tomahawks, driving in Scott's pickets and forcing the trembling troops back. Only Scott's own presence and voice prevent a general rout. The Indians retire into the woods at the first volley, then work their way around toward the American left. No American soldier has fallen during this brief attack, but the damage is done, for the cries of the Indians have carried across the river and sent a chill through the militiamen on the far side.

Almost at the same time, two British guns have opened up in the garden of the Hamilton house, effectively barring passage across the river. Scott knows that his chances of getting reinforcements before the final battle are slim. He can see the men he needs – hundreds of them, even thousands, lined up on the far bank like spectators at a prizefight. For all the good they can do him, they might as well be back at their farms, where at this moment most of them fervently wish they were.

General Van Rensselaer is helpless. He has promised reinforcements and ammunition to the defenders on the heights but can supply neither. He has sent to Brigadier-General Smyth asking for more men, but Smyth again declines. And he cannot budge the troops at the embarkation point. They have been milling about for some hours in the drizzle, watching the boats return with terribly wounded men (and sometimes with deserters), watching other boats founder in the frothing stream, and now, with the screams of the Indians echoing down from the heights, they have no stomach for battle.

The General, riding a borrowed horse, with Major Lovett at his side, moves through the sulking soldiers, urging them to enter the boats. No one budges. One of their commanders, a Lieutenant-Colonel Bloom, returns from the heights wounded, mounts his horse and, still bleeding, exhorts, swears, prays. The troops refuse to advance. A local judge, Peck by name, appears from somewhere, a large cocked hat on his head, a long sword dangling from his broad belt, preaching and praying to no avail. The troops have broken ranks and assumed the role of witnesses to the coming battle, and there is nothing, under the Constitution, that their officers can do.

Frustrated to fury and despair, Van Rensselaer starts to compose a note to General Wadsworth:

"I have passed through my camp; not a regiment, not a company is willing to join you. Save yourselves by a retreat if you can. Boats will be sent to receive you."

The promise is hollow. The terrified boatmen refuse to recross the river.

•

AT NEWARK, early that morning, Captain James Crooks of the 1st Lincoln Militia, a Canadian unit, notes the inclement weather and decides against turning out. All that summer at daybreak the militia-men have paraded on one of the village streets, protected by intervening buildings from the eyes of the enemy in order to conceal their paucity. The wind and the sleet convince Captain Crooks that for once his subordinates can handle the parade. He turns over in his blankets, is starting to doze off again when a knock comes at his window and a guard reports that the Yankees have crossed the river at Queenston. Crooks is startled; this is the first he has heard of it. Even now he cannot hear the sound of the guns because of the gale blowing off the lake.

The orders are to rendezvous at the fort. Crooks leaps from his bed, pulls on his uniform, orders his men to form up, noting with pleasure the enthusiasm with which each unit outdoes the others to see which can reach the bastion first. Once there, the men stack their arms and wait. No one knows exactly what is happening, but the word is out that General Brock has already left for Queenston.

At the fort's gate, Crooks runs into the artillery commander, Captain William Holcroft, who tells him he is about to open fire on Fort Niagara across the river but is short of men. Crooks supplies him with several including Solomon Vrooman, who is sent to man the twenty-four-pounder on a point a mile away. Vrooman's big gun, which is never out of action, does incalculable damage and is one reason for the American militia's refusal to cross the river. From this day on, the emplacement will be known as Vrooman's Point.

At the naval yards, Crooks encounters Captain James Richardson, who is thunderstruck at the news of the attack. His ship, at dock loaded with gunpowder, is within point-blank range of the American battery, nine hundred yards across the water. He makes haste to unload his explosive cargo and send it to the fort. This proves fortunate; the powder in the fort's magazine, which has not seen use since the Revolutionary War, is so old it cannot propel shot more than half-way across the river.

A deafening artillery battle follows. The Americans heat their cannonballs until they glow red, then fire them into the village and the fort, burning the courthouse, the jail, and fifteen other buildings until, at last, their batteries are reduced by British cannon.

In the meantime Brock's express has arrived from Queenston with orders for 130 militiamen to march immediately to the relief of the heights. Captain Crooks is anxious to lead his men, but an older brother in the same company is the senior of the two. Crooks manages to talk him into staying behind, assembles men from five flank companies, forms them into a reinforcement detachment, and marches them off toward the scene of battle. A mile out of Newark he is told of Brock's death, tries to keep the news from his men, fails, is surprised to find it has little immediate effect. At Brown's Point, he passes one of the York Volunteers, who asks him where he is going. When he answers, "To Queenston," the officer tells him he is mad: if he goes any farther all his people will be taken prisoner; the General is dead; his force is completely routed; his aide is mortally wounded; four hundred Yankees are on his flank, moving through the woods to attack Newark. Crooks replies that he has his orders and will keep going. He tells his men to load their muskets and marches on. Shortly afterward he encounters a second officer who repeats almost word for word what he has heard a few minutes before. Crooks ignores him.

About a mile from town he halts his men at a house owned by a farmer named Durham. It is filled with American and British wounded, including the dying Macdonell. The troops are hungry, having missed their breakfast. He sends them foraging in a nearby garden to dig potatoes. Soon every pot and kettle in the house is bubbling on the fire, but before the potatoes can be eaten General Sheaffe arrives with the remainder of the 41st Regiment and orders the militia to fall in. Off they march to battle, still hungry.

Sheaffe, a cautious commander, has no intention of repeating Brock's frontal assault, has planned instead a wide flanking movement to reach the plateau above the village, where Wool's Americans are preparing for battle. His force will veer off to the right before entering the village, make a half circle around the heights, and ascend under cover of the forest by way of an old road two miles west of Queenston. Here Sheaffe expects to be joined by the second detachment that Brock ordered from Chippawa. In this way he can keep his line of march out of range of the American battery on the heights above Lewiston while the Indians, who have preceded him, act as a screen to prevent the enemy patrols from intercepting him as he forms up for battle.

Meanwhile, Captain Holcroft of the Royal Artillery has, at great risk, managed to trundle two light guns through the village, across a ravine, and into the garden of the Hamilton house, guided by Captain Alexander Hamilton, who knows every corner of the ground. It is these guns that Winfield Scott hears, effectively blocking the river passage, as Norton and his Mohawks harass his forward positions.

The Indians, screening Sheaffe's force, continue to harry the Americans. They pour out of the woods, whooping and firing their muskets, then vanish into the trees, preventing Scott from consolidating his position, driving in the pickets and flank patrols to inhibit contact with the advancing British, and forcing the Americans into a tighter position on the heights. Their nominal chief is John Brant, the eighteen-year-old son of the late Joseph Brant, the greatest of the Mohawk chieftains, whose portrait by Romney will later grace every Canadian school book. But the real leader is the theatrical Norton, a strapping six-foot Scot who thinks of himself as an Indian and aspires to the mantle of his late mentor. He is more Indian than most Indians, has indeed convinced many British leaders (including the English parliamentarian and abolitionist William Wilberforce) that he is a Cherokee. He wears his black hair in a long tail held in place by a scarlet handkerchief into which he has stuck an ostrich feather. Now, brandishing a tomahawk, his face painted for battle, he whoops his way through the woods, terrifying the American militia and confusing the regulars.

Directly behind the woods on the brow of the heights, hidden by the scarlet foliage and protected by the Mohawks, Roger Sheaffe forms up his troops on Elijah Phelps's ploughed field. He is in no hurry. He controls the road to Chippawa and is waiting for Captain Richard Bullock to join him with another 150 men from the south. Captain Dennis of the 49th has already joined his company, his body caked with blood. Exhausted and wounded as a result of the battle at the river's edge, he refuses to leave the field until the day is won. Now he stands with the others, waiting for the order to advance, while the American gunners pour down fire from across the river. For the unblooded militia the next hour is the longest they have known, as a rain of eighteen-pound balls and smaller shot drops about them.

At about four o'clock, just as Bullock comes up on the right flank, Sheaffe orders his men to advance in line. He has close to one thousand troops in all. The enemy has almost that number – or *had* almost that number, but now many of the American militia, with the war cries of the Indians echoing in their ears, have fled into the woods or down the cliff toward the river. When Scott counts his dwindling band he is shocked to discover that it numbers fewer than three hundred. In the distance he sees the scarlet line of British regulars, marching in perfect order, the Indians on one flank, the militia slightly behind, two three-pound grasshopper guns firing.

Van Rensselaer's despairing note has just reached Wadsworth: reinforcement is not possible. The Americans call a hurried council and agree to a strategic withdrawal.

Now the battle is joined. James Crooks, advancing with his militia detachment, has been in many hailstorms but none, he thinks wryly, where the stones fly thick as the bullets on this October afternoon. Little scenes illuminate the battle and remain with him for the rest of his days: the sight of an Indian tomahawking a York militiaman in the belief that he is one of the enemy. The sight of the Americans' lone six-pounder, abandoned, with the slow match still burning (he turns it about and some of his men fire several rounds across the river). The bizarre spectacle of Captain Robert Runchey's platoon of black troops – escaped slaves who have volunteered at Newark – advancing on the flank of the Indians. The sight of a companion, his knuckles disabled by a musket ball at the very moment of pulling the trigger. Crooks seizes the weapon and fires off all its spare ammunition, saving the final round for a man in a small skiff in the river whom he takes to be an American fleeing the battle. Fortunately he misses; it is one of his own officers crossing over with a flag of truce to demand General Van Rensselaer's surrender.

Scott's regulars are attempting to cover the American withdrawal. The Colonel himself leaps up on a fallen tree and literally makes a stump speech, calling on his men to die with their muskets in their hands to redeem the shame of Hull's surrender. They cheer him and face the British, but the advance continues with all the precision of a parade-ground manoeuvre, which, of course, it is. The Americans are trapped between the cliff edge on their left and the cannon fire from Holcroft's guns in the village below them on their right.

As the Indians whoop forward once more – the British and Canadian militia advancing behind with fixed bayonets – the American line wavers, then breaks. The troops rush toward the cliffs, some tumbling down the hill, clinging to bushes and outcroppings, others, crazed with fear, leaping to their deaths on the rocks below. Scores crowd the beach under the shoulder of the mountain, waiting for boats that will never come. Others, badly mangled, drown in the roaring river.

The three ranking Americans, Scott, Wadsworth, and Chrystie, carried downward by the rush of escaping men, now decide that only a quick surrender will save the entire force from being butchered by the Indians. The problem is how to get a truce party across to the British lines. Two couriers, each carrying a white flag, have tried. The Indians have killed both.

At last Winfield Scott determines to go himself.

There are no white handkerchiefs left among the company, but Totten, the engineering officer, has a white cravat, which Scott ties to his sword point. He will rely on his formidable height and his splendid uniform to suggest authority. These attributes, however, are of little value, for Scott is almost immediately attacked and seized by young Brant and another Indian, who spring from a covert and struggle with him. The American's life is saved by the timely appearance of

248

John Beverley Robinson and his friend Samuel Jarvis of the York Volunteers, who free him and escort him to Sheaffe.

The British general accepts Scott's surrender and calls for his bugler to sound the cease-fire. The Mohawk pay no attention. Enraged at the death of two of their chiefs, they are intent on exterminating all the Americans huddled under the bluff. Scott, seeing his men's predicament, hotly demands to be returned to share their fate. Sheaffe persuades the future conqueror of Mexico to have patience. He himself is appalled at the carnage, and after the battle is over some of his men will remember their general flinging off his hat, plunging his sword into the ground in a fury, and demanding that his men halt the slaughter or he, Sheaffe, will immediately give up his command and go home. A few minutes later the firing ceases and the battle is over. It is half-past four. The struggle has raged for more than twelve hours.

Now, to Scott's mortification and despair, some five hundred militiamen appear from hiding places in the crevices along the cliffs and raise their hands in surrender.

The British have taken 925 prisoners including a brigadier-general, five lieutenant-colonels, and sixty-seven other officers. One prisoner is allowed to go free – the diminutive sextuagenarian Samuel Stubbs of Boonsboro, Kentucky. Stubbs, expecting to be killed and scalped, discovers that the British look on him as an oddity, as if he had been born with two heads. A British officer takes one look at Stubbs and lets him go. "Old daddy," he says, "your age and odd appearance induce me now to set you at liberty, return home to your family and think no more of invading us!" Stubbs promises cheerfully to give up fighting, but "I didn't mean so for I was determined I wouldn't give up the chase so, but at 'um again." And so he will be – all the way from the attack on Fort York to the final bloody battle of New Orleans, where in his sixty-sixth year, he is responsible for the deaths of several British officers.

In addition, the Americans suffer some 250 casualties. These include the badly mangled Solomon Van Rensselaer, who will eventually recover, and John Lovett, who, though not hit by ball or shrapnel, is incapacitated for life. What began as a lark has for him ended as tragedy. For Lovett, the conversationalist and wit, the world has gone silent. Placed in charge of the big guns on the heights above Lewiston, he has been rendered permanently deaf.

British casualties, by contrast, are light.

"God, man," says the staff surgeon, Dr. Thorne, to James Crooks as the battle ends, "there does not seem to be any of you killed."

"Well, Doctor," replies the Captain, "it is well it is so but go into that guard house and you'll find plenty to do for your saws...."

The British have lost only fourteen killed and seventy-seven wounded, but there is one loss that cannot be measured and by its nature evens the score at the Battle of Queenston Heights. Isaac Brock is gone. There is no one to fill his shoes.

●

ALL OF CANADA is stunned by Brock's loss. His own soldiers, the men of the 49th who were with him in Holland and at Copenhagen, are prostrated by the news. Of all the scenes of sorrow and despair that day, the most affecting is the one reported by Lieutenant Driscoll of the 100th Regiment, who had come up from Fort Erie to help direct artillery fire against the American battery at Black Rock. At two that afternoon Driscoll looks up to see a provincial dragoon gallop up, dishevelled, without sword or helmet, his horse bathed in foam, his own body spattered with mud.

One of Brock's veterans, a man named Clibborn, speaks up:

"Horse and man jaded, sir; depend upon it, he brings bad news."

Driscoll sends the veteran across to discover what message the dragoon has brought. The soldier doubles over to the rider but returns at a funereal pace, and Driscoll realizes that something dreadful has occurred. He calls out:

"What news, Clibborn? What news, man? Speak out."

Clibborn walks slowly toward the battery, which is still maintaining a brisk fire at the Americans across the river. Musket balls plough into the ground around him; he does not seem to see them. He cannot speak, can only shake his head. At last he slumps down on the gun platform, his features dead white, his face a mask of sorrow.

Driscoll cannot stand the silence, shakes Clibborn by the shoulder:

"For heaven's sake, tell us what you know."

Clibborn answers at last, almost choking:

"The General is killed; the enemy has possession of Queenston Heights."

At those words, every man in the battery becomes paralysed. The guns cease firing. These are men of the 49th, all of whom have served under Brock in Europe; they are shattered by the news. Some weep openly. Others mourn in silence. Several begin to curse in frustration. The sound of enemy cheers, drifting across the river, rouses them to their duty. In a helpless rage over the death of their general, they become demonic, loading, traversing, and firing the heavy guns as if they were light field pieces, flinging round after round across the river in an attempt to avenge their former chief.

All over the province, similar expressions of grief are manifest. Glegg, Brock's military aide, calls it "a public calamity." Young George Ridout of the York Volunteers writes to his brother that "were it not for the death of General Brock and Macdonell our victory would have been glorious...but in losing our man...is an irreparable loss." Like many others, Ridout is convinced that Brock was the only man capable of leading the divided province. Samuel Jarvis crosses the lake to bring the news of the tragedy to York where "the thrill of dismay... was something indescribable."

In Quebec, an old friend, Anne Ilbert, who once volunteered to embroider some handkerchiefs for the bachelor general so the laundresses wouldn't steal them, writes to an acquaintance that "the conquest of half the United States would not repay us for his loss...by the faces of the people here you would judge that we had lost everything, so general is the regret everyone feels for this brave man, the victory is completely swallowed up in it." She fears for the future, wonders what the troops will do under another commander, suspects that Upper Canada will fall to the Americans before winter's end. "This is the first real horror of war we have experienced. God send it may not lead to a train of others."

Prevost, when he learns of his general's death, is so badly shaken that he can scarcely hold the pen with which to report the tragedy to Sir John Sherbrooke in Halifax. Yet he mentions the matter only briefly in that letter. And later, when a dispatch reaches him quoting the Prince Regent at some length on Brock's heroism and ability, he publishes in the Quebec *Gazette* the first non-committal sentence only, omitting phrases about "an able and meritorious officer...who... displayed qualities admirably adapted to awe the disloyal, to reconcile the wavering, and animate the great mass of the inhabitants against successive attempts by the enemy to invade the province...."

Meanwhile, Sheaffe concludes an immediate armistice with the Americans, "the most ruinous policy that ever was or could have been adopted for the country," to quote a nineteen-year-old subaltern, William Hamilton Merritt, the future builder of the Welland Canal. Brock, who has been knighted for the capture of Detroit (posthumously, as it develops), would certainly have pursued Van Rensselaer's badly shaken force across the river to attack Fort Niagara and seize the northern half of New York state, but Sheaffe is a more cautious commander – Prevost's kind of general.

Brock's body, brought back to Newark, lies in state for three days. His funeral, in George Ridout's words, is "the grandest and most solemn that I have ever witnessed or that has been seen in Upper Canada." Brock's casket and Macdonell's are borne through a double line of Indians and militia – five thousand men resting on reversed arms. The twin coffins are buried in the York bastion of the fort. Guns boom every minute during the procession while across the river, at both Niagara and Lewiston, the Americans fire a salute to their old enemy. Sheaffe, on hearing the American guns, is overcome and says in a choked voice to one of his officers that "noble minded as General Brock was, he would have ordered the same had a like disaster befallen the Enemy."

Upper Canada is numb, its people drawn closer by a common tragedy that few outsiders can comprehend. In the United States, attention is quickly diverted by another naval skirmish in which the American frigate *Wasp*, having incapacitated and captured the British sloop of war *Frolic*, is herself taken by the enemy.

Europe is far more interested in the fate of Moscow, under attack by Napoleon, who at the very moment of the naval skirmish on October 18 is preparing to withdraw his army from the charred and deserted Russian capital. This bitter decision, still unknown to most of the world, marks the beginning of the end of the war with France. Had Madison foreseen it, the invasion of Canada, scarcely yet underway, would never have been attempted.

With Brock's burial, the myth takes over from the man. The following day, the Kingston *Gazette* reports "the last words of the dying Hero."

General Brock, watchful as he was brave, soon appeared in the midst of his faithful troops, ever obedient to his call, and whom [he] loved with the adoration of a father; but, alas! whilst collecting, arranging, forming, and cheering his brave followers, that great commander gloriously fell when preparing for victory – *"Push on brave York Volunteers,"* being then near him, they were the last words of the dying Hero – Inhabitants of Upper Canada, in the day of battle *remember BROCK.*

If Brock ever uttered these words it could only have been when he passed the York Volunteers on the road to Queenston. It was the 49th, his old battalion, that surrounded him at the moment of his fall. Nor do dead men utter school-book slogans. Nonetheless, the gallant injunction passes into common parlance to become almost as well known as "Don't give up the ship," uttered in the same war by an American naval commander whose men, on his death, did give up the ship. The phrase will be used in future years to support a further myth – that the Canadian militia really won the war. In December, the York *Gazette* gushes that "it must afford infinite satisfaction to every Loyal Bosom that on every occasion, the Militia of the Province has distinguished itself with an alacrity & spirit worthy of Veteran Troops." It is not an assessment with which the dead general would have agreed, but it is a fancy that will not die. John Strachan, future bishop of Toronto, leader of the Family Compact and mentor of the young officers who formed the backbone of the York Volunteers, helps to keep it green. In Strachan's belief, the militia "without the assistance of men or arms except a handful of regular troops" repelled the invasion.

The picture of Brock storming the heights at Queenston, urging on the brave York Volunteers, and saving Canada in the process is the one that will remain with the fledgling nation. He is the first Canadian war hero, an Englishman who hated the provincial confines of the Canadas, who looked with disdain on the civilian leaders, who despised democracy, the militia, and the Indians, and who could hardly wait to shake the Canadian mud from his boots and bid good-bye forever to York, Fort George, Quebec, and all the stuffy garrison towns between. None of this matters.

His monument will be erected on the ridge, not far from where he fell, by the leaders of a colonial aristocracy intent on shoring up power against republican and democratic trends seeping across the border. This Tuscan pillar, 135 feet high, becomes the symbol of that power – of the British way of life: the Loyalist way as opposed to the Yankee way. In 1840, a disaffected Irish Canadian named Benjamin Lett, one of William Lyon Mackenzie's followers in his failed rebellion against an elitist autocracy, determines on one last act of defiance and chooses the obvious site: he blows up Brock's monument. The

Family Compact cannot do without its symbol, mounts a long public campaign, raises fifty thousand dollars, builds a more splendid monument, half as high again as its predecessor – taller, it is said, than any in the world save for Wren's pillar marking London's Great Fire. John Beverley Robinson, Strachan's protégé and the Compact's chief justice, is on hand, of course, at the dedication, and so is his successor and fellow subaltern in the Brave York Volunteers, Mr. Justice Archibald McLean. Robinson's spectacular career dates from Queenston Heights when, a mere law student of twenty-one, he is named acting attorney-general of the province to replace the mortally wounded Macdonell. ("I had as much thought of being made Bey of Tunis," he recalled.) By Confederation the field on which he and McLean did battle has become, in the words of the *Canadian Monthly*, "one of Canada's sacred places" and the battle, in the description of the Canadian nationalist George Denison, is "Canada's glorious Thermopylae."

So Brock in death is as valuable to the ruling class as Brock in life. He will not be remembered for his real contribution to the country: his military prescience, his careful preparation for war during the years of peace, his astonishing bloodless capture of an American stronghold. When Canadians hear his name, as they often will over the years, the picture that will form in their minds will be of that final impetuous dash, splendidly heroic but tragically foolish, up the slippery heights of Queenston on a gloomy October morning.

7

BLACK ROCK
Opéra Bouffe on the Niagara

Hearts of War! Tomorrow will
be memorable in the annals
of the United States.

— Brigadier-General Alexander Smyth,
November 29, 1812.

BUFFALO, NEW YORK, November 17, 1812. Brigadier-General Alexander Smyth is putting the finishing touches to a proclamation, which, like Hull's, will return to haunt him.

"*Soldiers!*" he writes, underlining the word. "You are amply prepared for war. You are superior in number to the enemy. Your personal strength and activity are greater. Your weapons are longer. The regular soldiers of the enemy are generally old men, whose best years have been spent in the sickly climate of the West Indies. They will not be able to stand before you when you charge with the bayonet.

"You have seen Indians, such as those hired by the British to murder women and children, and kill and scalp the wounded. You have seen their dances and grimaces, and heard their yells. Can you fear *them*? No. You hold them in the utmost contempt."

Smyth warms to his task. Having stiffened the backs of the regular troops he will now imbue the recalcitrant militia with a fighting spirit:

"VOLUNTEERS!" he prints in large, bold capitals. "I esteem your generous and patriotic motives. You have made sacrifices on the altar of your country. You will not suffer the enemies of your fame to mislead you from the path of duty and honor, and deprive you of the esteem of a grateful country. You will shun the *eternal infamy* that awaits the man, who having come within sight of the enemy, *basely* shrinks in the moment of trial.

"SOLDIERS OF EVERY CORPS! It is in your power to retrieve the honor of your country; and to cover yourselves with glory. Every man who performs a gallant action, shall have his name made known to the nation. Rewards and honors await the brave. Infamy and contempt are reserved for cowards. Companions in arms! You came to vanquish a valiant foe. I know the choice you will make. Come on my heroes! And when you attack the enemy's batteries, let your rallying word be '*The cannon lost at Detroit—or death.*'"

Out it goes among the troops and civilians, most of whom greet it with derision. To this Smyth is absolutely oblivious, for he is a prisoner of his ego. The word "vanity" hardly does justice to his own concept of himself. He is wholly self-centred. His actions and words, which others find bizarre and ridiculous, are to him the justifiable responses of a supreme commander who sees himself as the saviour of the nation. The newspapers scoff at him as "Alexander the Great" and "Napoleon II." Smyth is the kind of general who takes that satire as a compliment.

If words were bullets and exclamation points cannonballs, Smyth might cow the enemy through the force of his verbiage. A master of the purple passage, he bombards his own countrymen with high-flown phrases:

> Men of New York: The present is the hour of renown. Have you not a wish for fame? Would you not choose to be one of those who, imitating the heroes whom Montgomery led, have in spite of the seasons, visited the tomb of the chief and conquered the country where he lies? Yes—You desire your share of fame. Then seize the present moment. If you do not, you will regret it. . . .
>
> Advance, then, to our aid. I will wait for you a few days. I cannot give you the day of my departure. But come on, come in companies, half companies, pairs or singly. I will organize you for a short tour. Ride to this place, if the distance is far, and send back your horses. But remember that every man who accompanies us places himself under my command, and shall submit to the salutary restraints of discipline.

Smyth is now in total charge of the Niagara campaign. Stephen Van Rensselaer has resigned in his favour. (He will run for governor in the spring, to be beaten by the craftier Tompkins.) His cousin Solomon is recovering from his wounds and dandling his new son on his lap; he will not fight again. Smyth, who never came face to face with either, reigns supreme.

On paper, the new commander's qualifications seem suitable

enough. He is an Irishman whose father, a parish rector, brought him to Virginia at the age of ten. A member of his state's bar, he has also been an elected representative in the lower house. As the colonel of a rifle regiment, he was ordered to Washington in 1811 "to prepare a system of discipline for the army." Within eighteen days of the declaration of war he was promoted to inspector general and ordered to the Niagara frontier.

"I must not be defeated," he declares on taking over from Van Rensselaer; and he enters into a flurry of boat building, for he intends, he says, to land more than four thousand men on the Canadian shore. This is bombast: more than half his force is in no condition to fight. The bulk of the regulars are raw recruits who have never fired a musket. The militia continue to desert – one hundred in a single night. Hundreds more clog the hospitals suffering from measles, dysentery, grippe. The cemetery behind the camp, where men are buried four to a grave, has expanded to two acres. The ill-clothed army has not yet been paid; two regular regiments and one militia company have already mutinied on this account; the captain of another volunteer company warns that his men will not cross the river until they receive pay and clothing allowances. The troops of Fort Niagara are starving for want of bread, and there is considerable doubt whether the eighteen hundred Pennsylvania volunteers due to arrive in mid-November will agree to fight on foreign soil.

Nonetheless, on November 9 the General announces that he will invade Canada in fifteen days. So loudly does he boast about his intentions that the British are well prepared for any attack; on November 17 they launch a heavy bombardment of Smyth's headquarters at Black Rock, burning the east barrack, exploding the magazine, and destroying a quantity of the furs captured from *Caledonia*. Just as the Quartermaster General, Peter B. Porter, is sitting down to dinner, a twenty-four-pound cannonball crashes through the roof of his home, a disaster not calculated to improve a digestion already thrown out of kilter by Smyth's bizarre and inconclusive orders. Another cannonade begins at dawn on the twenty-first opposite Fort Niagara. The British pour two thousand rounds of red-hot shot into the American fort, which replies in kind. Buildings burn; guns blow up; men die; nothing is settled.

On November 25, Smyth issues orders for the entire army to be ready to march "at a moment's warning." Two days later he musters forty-five hundred men at Black Rock for the impending invasion.

"Tell the brave men under your command not to be impatient," he writes to Porter, who is in charge of the New York volunteers. "See what harm impatience did at Queenston. Let them be firm, and they will succeed."

At three on the morning of the twenty-eighth, Smyth sends an advance force of some four hundred men across the river to destroy the bridge at Frenchman's Creek (thus cutting British communications between Fort Erie and Chippawa) and to silence the battery upstream. The British are waiting. Boats are lost, destroyed, driven off. In the darkness there is confusion on both sides, with men mistaking enemies for friends and friends for enemies. In spite of this the Americans seize the battery and spike its guns while a second force reaches the bridge, only to discover that they have left their axes in the boats and cannot destroy it before the British counterattack. In the end some of the advance party are captured for lack of boats in which to escape. The remainder cross to the safety of the American camp with little accomplished.

An incredible spectacle greets the British next morning. Lining their own shore in increasing numbers, they watch the American attempt at embarkation as if it were a sideshow. Smyth himself does not appear but leaves the arrangements to his subordinates. The operation moves so ponderously that the afternoon shadows are lengthening before all the troops are in the boats. Some have been forced to sit in their craft for hours, shivering in the late November weather – a light snow is falling and the river is running with ice.

The only logical explanation for an action that defies logic is that Smyth is attempting to terrify the British into surrendering through what General Sheaffe calls "an ostentatious display" of his force. If so, it does not work. When Smyth sends a message across to Lieutenant-Colonel Cecil Bisshopp, urging him to surrender to "spare the effusion of blood," Bisshopp curtly declines.

Late in the afternoon, with the entire force prepared at last to cross the river, the General finally makes an official appearance and issues an amazing order. "Disembark and dine!" he cries. At this point the troops are on the edge of rebellion. Several, reduced to impotent fury, pointedly break their muskets.

Smyth returns to his paper war:

Tomorrow at 8 o'clock, all the corps of Army will be at the Navy yards, ready to embark. Before 9 the embarkation will take place.

The General will be on board. Neither rain, snow, or frost will prevent the embarkation.

It will be made with more order and silence than yesterday; boats will be alloted to the brave volunteers....

The cavalry will scour the fields from Black Rock to the bridge & suffer no idle spectators.

While embarking the music will play martial airs. *Yankee Doodle* will be the signal to get underway....

When we pull for the opposite shore, every exertion will be made. The landing will be effected in despite of cannon, The whole army has seen that cannon is to be little dreaded.

The information brought by Captain Gibson assures us of victory....

Smyth's council of officers is aghast. Surely, with the British alerted, the General does not propose a daylight frontal assault from the identical embarkation point on a strongly fortified position! But Smyth declines to change his plans.

Next morning, however, the troops, who arrive at the navy yard promptly at eight, are sent into the nearby woods to build fires and keep warm. Smyth's staff has managed overnight to knock some sense into their commander. The departure time is changed to three the following morning. The troops will not cross directly but will slip quietly down the river, hoping to avoid the enemy cannon, and will land above Chippawa, attack its garrison and, if successful, march through Queenston to Fort George.

In the dark hours of the following morning, the wet and exhausted men are once more herded down to the boats. As before, the embarkation proceeds in fits and starts; when dawn arrives the boats are still not fully loaded. Now Smyth discovers that instead of three thousand men he has fewer than fifteen hundred in the boats, many of these so ill they cannot stand a day's march. The Pennsylvania volunteers have not even arrived on the ground; they are, it develops, perfectly prepared to fight on foreign soil but not under General Smyth. Other troops, lingering on the shore, sullenly refuse to embark.

Out in midstream, about a quarter of a mile from shore, Peter B. Porter has been waiting impatiently in a scout boat to lead the flotilla downriver to the invasion point. Hours pass. On the shore, the confusion grows. In his quarters, General Smyth is holding a council with his regular officers to which the militia commanders have not been invited. At last a message is sent out to Porter: the troops are to disembark. The invasion of Canada is to be abandoned for the present. Smyth does not intend to stir until he has three thousand men fit for action. The regulars will go into winter quarters; the volunteers are dismissed to their homes.

This intelligence provokes a scene of the wildest fury. Officers break their swords in rage; ordinary soldiers batter their muskets to pieces against tree trunks. The mass of the militia runs amok, firing off their weapons in all directions, some shouting aloud in frustration, others cheering in delight. Some of the volunteers offer to fight under Porter, promising to capture Fort Erie if Smyth will give them four cannon. The embattled commander turns the request aside.

Roused to a passion, the troops try to murder their general. Musket balls whiz through his tent, almost killing an aide who has his belt and cap shot off. Smyth doubles his guard, moves his headquarters repeatedly to protect his life.

Porter is outraged by Smyth's posturing. Some of the other officers are calling the General a traitor. Porter merely attacks him as a coward but puts that word into the public record in the Buffalo *Gazette* (which is forced, briefly, to cease publication, so great are the disturbances). A duel follows on Grand Island; shots are exchanged; both men's marksmanship is lamentable; unmarked, they shake hands, but the bitterness continues.

Smyth is the object of intense execration. Governor Tompkins's censure is blunt: "Believing that there was some courage and virtue left in the world, I did not, indeed could not, anticipate such a scene of gasconading and of subsequent imbecility and folly as Genl. Smith [*sic*] has exhibited. To compare the events of the recent campaign with those of the days of the Revolution, is almost enough to convince one, that the race of brave men and able commanders will before many years become extinct."

Smyth's career is finished. With his life in danger from both his officers and his men, he slips away to his home in Virginia where, within three months, the army drops him from its rolls.

Dearborn is aghast. He has sent four thousand troops to Niagara: how is it that not much more than a thousand were in a condition to cross the river? He himself has kept such a low profile that the firestorm of public disgust and fury with the losses of Hull, Van Rensselaer, and Smyth sweeps past him. Yet as the senior commander he is as culpable as any, and so is his fellow physician, the myopic secretary of war Dr. Eustis.

At Lake Champlain Dearborn has the largest force of all under arms, including seven regular army regiments with supporting artillery and dragoons. But these have been infected by the same virus as the others. Dearborn's overall strategy is to attack Montreal simultaneously with Smyth's invasion on the Niagara. On November 8, he informs Eustis that he is about to join the army under General Bloomfield at Plattsburg to march on Lower Canada. An attack of rheumatism delays him. On November 19, when he finally arrives, he finds Bloomfield too ill to lead his troops. Illness, indeed, has all but incapacitated his army, a third of which is unfit for duty. An epidemic of measles has raged through the camps. A neglect of proper sanitary measures has reduced one regiment from nine hundred to two hundred able-bodied men. Typhus, accompanied by pneumonia, has killed two hundred at Burlington. Fifteen per cent of Dearborn's entire force has died from one of these several afflictions.

Dearborn takes command of his depleted invasion force. Two separate and independent advance columns, numbering about 650 men, are dispatched north to surprise the British outposts at the border. They advance by different roads, run into one another in the dark, each mistaking the other for the enemy. A brisk skirmish follows until daylight, when, exhausted and dispirited by their error, they retreat with twenty casualties, a number that is shortly augmented by forty deaths from disease contracted during the expedition. Meanwhile Dearborn manages to get three thousand militia men as far as Rouse's Point at the northern end of Lake Champlain. When two-thirds refuse to cross the border, Dearborn gives up, slinks back to Plattsburg, and returns to Albany as quietly as possible. The news of Smyth's humiliation provides the final blow. Dearborn offers to surrender his command "to any gentleman whose talents and popularity will command the confidence of the Government and the country." But it will be another six months before his government, and a new and more aggressive secretary of war, get around to relieving him.

8

FRENCHTOWN
Massacre at the River Raisin

The Battle's o'er, the din is past!
Night's mantle on the field is cast,
The moon with Sad and pensive beam
Hangs sorrowing o'er the bloody Stream...
Oh! Pitying Moon! Withdraw thy light
And leave the world in murkiest night!
For I have seen too much of Death
Too much of this dark fatal heath...

— From "A Night View of the Battle of the Raisin,
January 22nd, 1813" (written on the field by
Ensign William O. Butler).

GEORGETOWN, KENTUCKY, August 16, 1812. Henry Clay is addressing two thousand eager Kentucky militiamen who have volunteered to march into Canada under the banner of William Henry Harrison to reinforce Hull's Army of the Northwest. The dark eyes flash, the sonorous voice rolls over the raw troops as he exhorts them to victory. More than most Americans, Clay is telling them, they have a twofold responsibility – to uphold the honour of their state as well as that of their country:

"Kentuckians are famed for their bravery – you have the double character of Americans and Kentuckians to support!"

This is more than posturing. Kentucky is a world unto itself, as different from Maine and New York as Scotland from Spain. No frustrated general will need to prod the Kentuckians across the Canadian border; they will, if necessary, swim the Detroit River to get at the British. When, the previous May, the Governor called for volunteers to fill Kentucky's quota of fifty-five hundred men, he found he had too many on his hands. Clay at the time wrote to the Secretary of State that he was almost alarmed at the enthusiasm displayed by his people.

Now, on the very day of Hull's defeat, Clay fires up the troops, who confidently believe that the American forces are already half-way across Canada. And why not? Kentucky has been told only what it wants to hear. The newspaper stories from the frontier have been highly optimistic. Editors and orators have bolstered the state's heroic image of itself. In these exhortations can be heard echoes of the Revolution. "Rise in the majesty of freedom," the Governor, Charles

Scott, has pleaded; "regard as enemies the enemies of your country. Remember the Spirit of '76."

The troops who are to march off through the wilderness of Michigan and into Canada expect the briefest of wars – a few weeks of adventure, a few moments of glory (swords glistening, bugles calling, drums beating, opponents fleeing), then home to the family farm with the plaudits of the nation and the cheers of their neighbours ringing in their ears.

Most have signed on for six months only, convinced that the war cannot last even that long. On this warm August day, standing in ragged, undisciplined lines, basking in Clay's oratory, they do not contemplate November. They wear light shoes and open shirts of linen and cotton: no coats, no blankets. Not one in twenty is prepared for winter. The war department has lists of goods needed for the campaign, but no one has paid much attention to that. The army is without a commissariat; private contractors, whose desire for profit often outweighs their patriotism, have been hired to handle all supplies. As for the Congress, it has not been able to screw up enough courage to adopt new taxes to finance the war; the unpopular resolution has been postponed, and Clay and his Hawks, eager to get on with the fighting, have gone along with the delay without a whimper.

Every able-bodied man in Kentucky, it seems, wants to fight. Six congressmen don uniforms. One, Samuel Hopkins, becomes a major-general; two are happy to serve as privates. Clay remains behind to fight the war in Congress, but his brother-in-law, Nathaniel Hart, goes as a captain, and so does John Allen, the second most eminent lawyer in the state. Thomas Smith, editor of the Kentucky *Gazette*, inflamed by the optimistic reports in his own newspaper, quits his desk and signs up to fight the British and the Indians. Dr. John M. Scott, a militia colonel and an old campaigner, insists on his right to command a regiment even though he is desperately ill; his friends expect (rightly) that he will not return alive. By the end of the year there will be more than eleven thousand Kentuckians in the army.

Most of these will be in the volunteer forces, for the people of Kentucky are confident that the war will be fought to a speedy conclusion by citizen soldiers enrolled for a single, decisive campaign. Regulars are sneered at as hired mercenaries who cannot compete for valour or initiative with a volunteer who has a direct interest in the outcome of the struggle.

The idea of individual initiative is deeply ingrained in the Kentucky character. They are a hardy, adventurous people, confident to the point of ebullience, optimistic to the point of naïveté – romantic, touchy, proud, often cruel. Not for them the effete pastimes of settled New England. Their main entertainments are shooting, fighting, drinking, duelling, horse racing. Every Kentucky boy is raised with a rifle. An old state law provides that every white male over sixteen must kill a certain number of crows and squirrels each year. Instead of raffles, Kentuckians hold shooting contests to pick winners. The very word "Kentuck" can cause a shiver of fear in the Mississippi River towns, where their reputation is more terrifying than that of the Indians. As scrappers they are as fearless as they are ferocious, gouging, biting, kicking, scratching. Kentuckians like to boast that they are "half horse and half alligator tipped with snapping turtle." A future congressman, Michael Taul, is elected captain of his militia company not because he has any military training – he has none – but because he has beaten his opponent, William Jones, in a particularly vicious encounter – a "hard fight," in Taul's words, "fist and skull, biting and gouging, etc."

Kentucky lies on the old Indian frontier, and though its Indian wars are history, bloody memories remain. Youths are raised on tales of British and Indian raiders killing, scalping, and ravaging during the Revolution. Tippecanoe has revived a legacy of fear and hatred. The reports of British weapons found at Prophet's Town confirm the people of the state in their belief that John Bull is again behind the Indian troubles.

Tippecanoe is seen as the real beginning of the war. "War we now have," the Kentucky *Gazette* exulted when news of the battle reached Lexington. The shedding of Kentucky blood on the banks of the Wabash fuelled the latent desire for revenge, so that when war was declared Kentucky indulged in a delirium of celebration. Towns were illuminated, cannon and muskets discharged in the villages. And in the larger towns, Senator John Pope, the one Kentucky member of the Twelfth Congress to vote against the war, was hanged in effigy.

On the Fourth of July, the state wallowed in patriotic oratory. At a public celebration in Lexington no fewer than eighteen toasts were drunk, the celebrants raising their glasses to "Our volunteers – Ready to avenge the wrongs and vindicate the right of their country – the spirit of Montgomery will lead them to victory on the Plains of

Abraham." Little wonder that a Boston merchant travelling through Kentucky a little later described its people as "the most patriotic...I have ever seen or heard of."

This yeasty nationalism springs out of Kentucky's burgeoning economy. It has become the most populous state west of the Alleghenies. In two decades its population has leaped from 73,000 to more than 406,000. Log cabins have given way to handsome brick houses. Frontier outposts have become cities. But all this prosperity depends on a sea-going trade – a trade now threatened by Great Britain's maritime strictures. The opposite side of the coin of nationalism is a consuming hatred of Great Britain. Henry Clay is its voice.

What Clay wants, Clay is determined to get; and Henry Clay wants William Henry Harrison to command the army going north to subdue the Indians and to reinforce General Hull at Detroit. The Hero of Tippecanoe is by all odds the most popular military leader in the state. Every Kentuckian, it seems, wants to serve under him; but the Secretary of War has long since chosen James Winchester of Tennessee to take command. Now an active campaign, spearheaded by Clay and orchestrated with all the cunning of a political *coup d'état*, is mounted to force the government's hand and replace Winchester with Harrison. In this enterprise, Clay has Harrison's willing cooperation. The Hero of Tippecanoe himself tours the state, rousing martial feeling, fuelling the clamour for his appointment.

Early in August a caucus of influential Kentucky politicians, including Scott, the retiring governor, Isaac Shelby, the governor-elect, and several of the War Hawks, agrees to appoint Harrison a brevet (honorary) major-general in the Kentucky militia. He accepts command of two regiments of infantry and one of mounted rifles (under Clay's young congressional colleague, Richard M. Johnson) which have already left to join General Winchester in Cincinnati. But Clay wants more. Harrison outranks Winchester, but Winchester is a regular army man. It is important that there be no ambiguity about who is in charge. Once more he puts pressure on James Monroe, the Secretary of State, rising to heights of hyperbole, which, even for Henry Clay, are more than a little florid:

"If you will carry your recollection back to the Age of the Crusades and of some of the most distinguished leaders of those expeditions, you will have a picture of the enthusiasm existing in this country for the expedition to Canada and for Harrison as the commander."

Up to this point, James Monroe has fancied himself for the post of commander-in-chief of the Army of the Northwest. The cabinet, in fact, has been seriously considering his appointment. But now, with Clay and his cronies in full cry, the Secretary's military ambitions are dashed. The pressure is too great. Harrison it will be.

●

AS THE CABINET vacillates over the choice of a commander for the new northwest army, Harrison marches to Cincinnati at the head of his troops. He is convinced that he can persuade Winchester to allow him to take command of all the forces for the relief of Detroit. On August 26, he receives the dreadful news of Hull's surrender. Two days later, he reaches Winchester's camp at Cincinnati and immediately assumes command of all the Kentucky militia, leaving Winchester in charge of the regulars. Stiff little notes pass between the generals' tents. Harrison insists that he, as a major-general, outranks Winchester. Winchester objects, points out that Harrison is only a political appointee, but when Harrison persists, Winchester at last gives in: Harrison can assume command under his own responsibility. Winchester returns to Lexington to continue recruiting.

The new commander has some twenty-one hundred men at Cincinnati; an equal number are on their way to join him. They inspire mixed feelings. The Kentuckians, in his opinion "are perhaps the best materials for forming an army the world has produced. But no equal number of men was ever collected who knew so little of military discipline." It is a shrewd assessment.

He has neither time nor personnel to instruct his raw recruits in the art of soldiering. He is, in fact, short of almost everything – of food, clothing, equipment, weapons, ammunition, flints, swords. His only ordnance piece is an ancient cast-iron four-pounder. Autumn is fast approaching with its chilling rain and sleet. He must hack new roads through forest and swamp, build blockhouses and magazines, all the time watched and harassed by the Indians on his flank.

And he must move immediately, for word has come that the British and the Indians are planning an attack on Fort Wayne, the forward outpost on the Maumee. Three hundred Indians are laying siege to the fort, a British column is moving south, houses have been burned, crops and livestock destroyed. The commander, James Rhea, has some eighty men with whom to withstand the siege but is himself nervous and frequently drunk. Harrison's first task is to relieve the fort.

That same day he dispatches all his available troops on that mission. He joins them at Dayton on September 1. Here are more cheers for Harrison and a salute of cannon, marred only by the tragic incompetence of the gunners. During the salute one man is seriously wounded, another has both hands blown off. And here Harrison receives a blow of a different kind: the government has officially confirmed his commission, but only as brigadier-general. Winchester now outranks him.

He does not give up. In another letter to Washington, he subtly advances his cause: "The backwoodsmen are a singular people.... From their affection and an attachment everything may be expected but I will venture to say that they never did nor never will perform anything brilliant under a stranger."

The message, though self-serving, is undoubtedly true. Winchester is unpopular largely because he *is* a stranger. Harrison is a known hero. All along his route of march, volunteers have flocked to his banner. At Piqua, en route to Fort Wayne, he makes from the tailboard of a camp wagon one of those tough little stump speeches for which he is famous. He is planning a forced march on half-rations, and some of the Ohio militia are hesitating. To them Harrison declares that "if there is any man under my command who lacks the patriotism to rush to the rescue, he, by paying back the money received from the government, shall receive a discharge. I do not wish to command such...." Only one man makes this choice. His comrades are given a permit to escort him part of the way home. They hoist him onto a rail and with a crowd following duck him several times in the river.

Harrison, at the head of three thousand men, reaches Fort Wayne on September 12. The fort is relieved without a shot being fired though not entirely bloodlessly, since during the march one man has been shot and killed in error by one of the guards. The bodies of two sentinels, killed by the Indians and buried within the palisade, are disinterred and brought out to be buried with full military honours. The troops, many of whom have never seen a dead man, stand by in awe. William Northcutt, a young dragoon in Captain William Garrard's company of "Bourbon Blues" (made up of men from Bourbon County, Kentucky, all uniformed in blue broadcloth), cannot help shedding tears as the corpses are brought out through the gate, even though the men are complete strangers. But before his term of service is over, Northcutt becomes so hardened that he could, if necessary, sleep on a corpse, and it occurs to him as the war grows nastier that "the man that thinks about dying in a Battle is not fit to be there and will do no good for his country...."

Harrison is determined to crush all Indian resistance. Columns of cavalry fan out to destroy all Indian villages within sixty miles. The ailing Colonel John Scott insists on leading the attack on the Elkhart River in Indiana Territory, though his officers urge him not to go. But he mounts his horse, crying out: "As long as I am able to mount you, none but myself shall lead my regiment...." It is the death of him. Exhausted, after a protracted march of three days and nights, he is scarcely able to return to camp. Shortly afterwards he is carried home in a litter where, the second day after arrival, he expires.

Harrison's policy of search and destroy makes no distinction between neutral and hostile tribes. His intention is to turn the frontier country into a wasteland, denying both food and shelter to the natives. Mounted columns, one led by Harrison himself, burn several hundred houses, ravage the corn fields, destroy crops of beans, pumpkins, potatoes, and melons, ransack the graves and scatter the bones. The Potawatomi and Miami flee to British protection at Brownstown and Amherstburg and wait for revenge.

On September 18, General Winchester arrives at Fort Wayne to take command of the Army of the Northwest. The troops are in an ugly mood. They do not wish to be commanded by a regular officer, fearing perhaps (without much evidence) that Winchester will be a greater disciplinarian than Harrison.

Winchester's ordeal has only begun. As he moves slowly north, the Kentuckians under his command refuse his orders, torment him with pranks and practical jokes, and are generally obstreperous. He cannot even visit the latrine without suffering some indignity. At one camp, they skin a porcupine and place the skin on a pole over the latrine pit; the General applies his buttocks to the hide with painful results. At another, they employ a trick that must go back to Caesar's army: sawing a pole partially through so that it fails to support the General's weight at a critical moment. The next morning, William Northcutt of the Bourbon Blues, passing Winchester's tent, notes with amusement the General's uniform, drying out, high on a pole.

What has Winchester done to deserve this? His only crime is to be less popular than Harrison. He does suffer by comparison, for Harrison at forty is vigorous, decisive, totally confident, while Winchester, at sixty, is inclined to fussiness, a little ponderous, and not entirely sure of himself. (He did not have to relinquish command to Harrison during that first encounter at Cincinnati.) Like Hull, he appears to the young recruits to be older than his years (Northcutt thinks him at least seventy) – a plump, greying figure who has to be helped to mount and dismount his horse. Worst of all, Winchester fears his own troops and places a bodyguard around his quarters day and night.

Like so many others, he is a leftover from another war, his reputation resting on the exploits of his youth – on those memorable years in the mid-seventies when America struggled for her independence and young James Winchester, at twenty-four, was promoted in the field for his gallantry, wounded in action, captured, exchanged, recaptured and exchanged again to fight as a captain at Yorktown. All that is long behind him, as are his years as an Indian fighter in North Carolina. Honours he has had: brigadier-general in the North Carolina militia; Speaker of the state senate of Tennessee; master of a vast Tennessee estate, surmounted by the great stone mansion known as Cragfont; father of fourteen children, four of them born out of wedlock but rendered legitimate by a tardy marriage. A kindly, sedentary man, fond of rich, easy living, known for his humanity. But no Harrison.

He lacks Harrison's style, has not Harrison's way with men, cannot bring himself to mingle with the troops in Harrison's easy, offhand manner. It is impossible to think of Winchester, dressed in a simple hunting shirt, making a stump speech to the Kentucky volunteers; it is equally impossible to believe that anyone would saw through a log in Harrison's latrine.

The murmurings against Winchester are not confined to the men. A group of officers, led by Henry Clay's congressional colleague Captain Sam McKee, is drawing up a petition, apparently with Harrison's blessing, urging that the command be taken from Winchester. The rebels get cold feet, temporize, delay, and are relieved at last of the charge of mutiny by a war department order authorizing Harrison to assume command of the Army of the Northwest.

●

OLD FORT DEFIANCE, OHIO, October 2, 1812. It is close to midnight when William Henry Harrison, accompanied by a strong escort, gallops into camp, summoned by a frantic note from General

Winchester warning that a combined force of British redcoats and Indians is marching south. Winchester's intelligence is accurate but out of date. The British, believing themselves outnumbered, have already withdrawn.

Now Harrison breaks the news that he is in full command of the new Army of the Northwest, charged with the task of subduing the Indians in his path, relieving Detroit, and invading Canada. Winchester is crestfallen. Convinced that Harrison has secretly connived against him, he seriously considers resigning, then thinks better of it and decides to hang on until Fort Amherstburg is captured. Harrison determines to mollify him by giving him command of the army's left flank and naming in his honour the new fort being built not far from the ruins of the old: Fort Winchester.

The troops are unaware of Harrison's presence. Half starved, inadequately clothed, they have lost the will to fight. A delegation of Kentucky officers wakes Harrison to warn him that one regiment intends to quit and go home. All attempts to dissuade them have been met with insults.

Early the next morning, Harrison acts. He orders Winchester to beat the alarm instead of the customary drum roll for reveille. The Kentuckians pour out of their tents, form a hollow square, and, as Winchester introduces them to their new commander, holler their enthusiasm.

Harrison knows exactly what to say. He tells them they can go home if they wish to, "but if my fellow soldiers from Kentucky, so famed for patriotism, refuse to bear the hardships incident to war... where shall I look for men who will go with me?"

Cheers and shouts greet these words and continue as the General reveals that two hundred wagons loaded with biscuit, flour, and bacon are on their way; some supplies, indeed, have already arrived. This kills all talk of desertion. One Kentuckian writes home that "Harrison, *with a look*, can awe and convince...where some would be refractory...All are afraid and unwilling to meet with his censure."

Harrison has been given authority to requisition funds and supplies, to protect the northwestern frontier, and after retaking Detroit to penetrate Upper Canada "as far as the force under your command will in your judgment justify." For this purpose he expects to have ten thousand troops.

His strategy is to move the army to the foot of the Rapids of the Maumee in three columns. Winchester, protecting his left flank, will

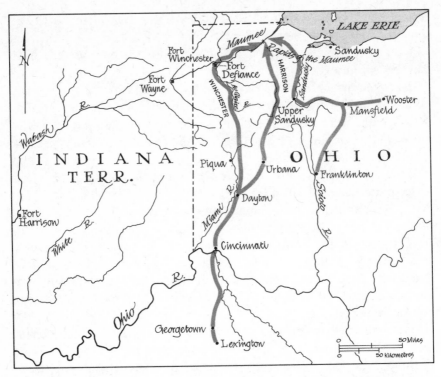

Harrison's Three-Column Drive to the Maumee Rapids

march from the new fort along the route of the Maumee. A central force of twelve hundred men will follow Hull's road to the same rendezvous. The right division, under Harrison himself, is proceeding from Wooster, Ohio, by way of the Upper Sandusky.

But Winchester is pinned down at the newly constructed fort that bears his name. He dare not move without supplies, and the promised supplies are not forthcoming. Harrison has ordered Brigadier-General Edward Tupper's mounted brigade to dash to the foot of the Rapids of the Maumee to harvest several hundred acres of corn for the famished troops. But the scalping of a ranger not two hundred yards from the camp has the men in such a panic that only a handful will follow. The mission is abandoned.

On October 8, the day after Tupper's fiasco, Frederick Jacob of the 17th Regiment is caught asleep at his post, and Winchester, faced with growing insubordination, decides to make an example of him. A court martial sentences Jacob to be shot. The following morning Winchester's entire force, reduced now to eighteen hundred, forms a

276

hollow square to witness the execution. Drums roll, the chaplain prays, the prisoner is led to the post, blindfolded, made to kneel. The troops fall silent, waiting for the volley. Then, at the last instant, a reprieve arrives. The General has judged the wretched guard "not to be of sound mind," a verdict which if unjustified at the outset may well be applicable in the days following the ordeal.

There are other punishments: "riding the wooden horse," in which the offender is placed astride a bent sapling and subjected to a series of tossings and joltings to the great amusement of the troops, or a dozen well-laid blows on the bare posterior with a wooden paddle bored full of holes to help break the skin. In spite of these salutary examples, the army is murmuring its discontent over the continued lack of supplies. Rations remain short, Harrison's promises to the contrary. There is little flour, almost no salt, and the beef—what there is of it—is deplorable.

Disdaining strict orders, men wander out of camp and waste their ammunition in search of game, many barefoot, their clothes in rags. They sleep on frozen ground, some without blankets. More than two hundred are sick at one time. By November, three or four die each day from typhus. Civilian contractors reap a harvest; the price of hogs goes sky high while clothing ordered for the troops comes in sizes so small it seems to have been designed for small boys. Materials are shoddy, delays calculated. One contractor's profit, it is said, amounts to $100,000.

Nothing seems to be going right. In late September, the new governor of Kentucky, Isaac Shelby, has ordered two thousand mounted thirty-day volunteers—"the most respectable citizens that perhaps were ever embodied from this or any other State in the Union"—to march under Major-General Samuel Hopkins, one of Clay's congressional War Hawks, against the Indians of Indiana and Illinois territories. Shelby does not wait for war department authorization or equipment. The men, whipped to a high pitch of enthusiasm, bring their own arms and blankets. The quota of volunteers is exceeded; twelve hundred disappointed Kentuckians have to be sent home.

The euphoria does not last. By October 14, after two hard weeks in the saddle, the volunteers are dispirited. They cannot find any Indians, their rations dwindle away, they become hopelessly lost. At this point, their unseen quarry fires the tall prairie grass, threatening all with a painful death.

Hopkins's choice is retreat or mutiny, a situation that leaves the

Governor aghast. What has happened to Kentucky's *élan*? "...the flower of Kentucky are now returning home deeply mortified by the disappointment." On mature consideration, Shelby decides to put the blame on "secret plotting."

There is worse to come. A note of uncertainty begins to creep into Harrison's dispatches to Washington: "If the fall should be very dry, I will retake Detroit before the winter sets in; but if we should have much rain, it will be necessary to wait at the Rapids until the Margin of the Lake is sufficiently frozen to bear the army and its baggage."

"The one bright ray amid the gloom of incompetency" (to quote John Gibson, acting governor of Illinois Territory) is the news of Captain Zachary Taylor's successful defence of Fort Harrison — a desperate struggle in which a handful of soldiers and civilians, many of them ill, withstood repeated attacks by Miami and Wea warriors until relief arrived. It is the first land victory for the United States, and it wins for Taylor the first brevet commission ever awarded by the U.S. government. Nor will the moment of glory be forgotten. One day, Brevet Major Taylor will become twelfth president of the United States.

The news from the Niagara frontier banishes this brief euphoria. Another army defeated! A third bogged down. By October 22, Harrison finds he can no longer set a firm date for the attack on Detroit. There are no supplies of any kind in Michigan Territory; the farms along the Raisin have been ravaged. He will require one million rations at the Rapids of the Maumee before he can start a campaign; but the fall rains have already begun and he cannot move his supplies, let alone his artillery. By early November, the roads are in desperate condition and horses, attempting to struggle through morass and swamp, are dying by the hundreds.

The army switches to flatboats, but just as these are launched the temperature falls and the boats are frozen fast along the Sandusky, Au Glaize, and St. Mary's rivers. By early December, Harrison despairs of reaching the rapids at all and makes plans to shelter his force in huts on the Au Glaize. He suggests that Shelby prepare the public for a postponement in the campaign by disbanding all the volunteer troops except those needed for guard and escort duty. But Washington will have none of it. The Union has suffered two mortifying failures at Detroit and Queenston; it will not accept a third.

The setbacks continue. Hopkins's failure has left Harrison's left flank open to Indian attack. He decides to forestall further Indian

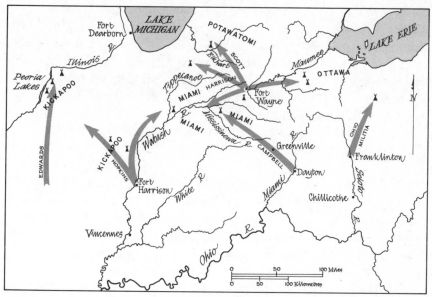

American Search and Destroy Missions against the Tribes, Autumn, 1812

raids on Winchester's line of communications by striking at the Miami villages along the Mississinewa, a tributary of the Wabash in Indiana Territory. On November 25, Lieutenant-Colonel John Campbell and six hundred cavalry and infantry set out to do the job. The result is disastrous.

In spite of Campbell's attempts at secrecy, the Miami are forewarned. They leave their villages, wait until the troops are exhausted, then launch a night attack, destroying a hundred horses, killing eight men, wounding forty-eight. A false report is spread that the dreaded Tecumseh is on the way at the head of a large force. Campbell's dejected band beats a hasty retreat.

It is bitterly cold; provisions are almost gone; the wounded are dying from gangrene, the rest suffer from frostbite. A relief party finally brings them into Greenville, where it is found that three hundred men – half of Campbell's force – are disabled. One mounted regiment is so ravaged it is disbanded. Harrison has lost the core of his cavalry without any corresponding loss among the Indians. The General decides to put a bold front on the episode: he announces that the expedition has been a complete success. He has learned something from the experience of Tippecanoe.

By December 10, Harrison has managed to get his cannon to Upper Sandusky, but at appalling cost. He has one thousand horses, hauling and pulling; most are so exhausted they must be destroyed, at a cost of half a million dollars. Wagons are often abandoned, their contents lost or destroyed. The teamsters, scraped up from frontier settlements, are utterly irresponsible. "I did not make sufficient allowance for the imbecility and inexperience of public agents and the villainy of the contractors," Harrison writes ruefully to the acting secretary of war, James Monroe, who has replaced the discredited Dr. Eustis.

Winchester's left wing is still pinned down near the junction of the Maumee and the Au Glaize, waiting for supplies. It is impossible to get them through the Black Swamp that lies between the Sandusky and the Maumee. William Atherton, a diminutive twenty-one-year-old soldier in Winchester's army who is keeping an account of his adventures, writes that he now sees "nothing but hunger and cold and nakedness staring us in the face." The troops have been out of flour for a fortnight and are existing on bad beef, pork, and hickory nuts. Sickness and death have reduced Winchester's effective force to eleven hundred. Daily funerals cast a pall over the camps, ravaged by the effects of bad sanitation and drainage (Winchester is forced to move the site five times) and the growing realization that there is no chance of invading Canada this year.

On Christmas Eve, another soldier, Elias Darnell, confides to his journal that "obstacles had emerged in the path to victory, which must have appeared insurmountable to every person endowed with common sense. The distance to Canada, the unpreparedness of the army, the scarcity of provisions, and the badness of the weather, show that Malden cannot be taken in the remaining part of our time.... Our sufferings at this place have been greater than if we had been in a severe battle. More than one hundred lives...lost owing to our bad accommodations! The sufferings of about three hundred sick at a time, who are exposed to the cold ground, and deprived of every nourishment, are sufficient proofs of our wretched condition! The camp has become a loathsome place...."

On Christmas Day, Winchester receives an order from Harrison. He is to move to the Rapids of the Maumee as soon as he receives two days' rations. There he will be joined by the right wing of the army. Two days later, a supply of salt, flour, and clothing arrives.

Winchester, eager to be off, sets about building sleds, since his boats are useless. On December 29, he is ready. The troops are exuberant – anything to be rid of this pestilential camp! But Darnell realizes what they are facing:

"We are now about commencing one of the most serious marches ever performed by the Americans. Destitute, in a measure, of clothes, shoes and provisions, the most essential articles necessary for the existence and preservation of the human species in this world and more particularly in this cold climate. Three sleds are prepared for each company, each to be pulled by a packhorse, which has been without food for two weeks except brush, and will not be better fed while in our service...."

The following day, the troops set off for the Maumee rapids. Few armies have presented such a ragtag appearance. In spite of the mid-winter weather, scarcely one possesses a greatcoat or cloak. Only a lucky few have any woollen garments. They remain dressed in the clothes they wore when they left Kentucky, their cotton shirts torn, patched, and ragged, hanging to their knees, their trousers also of cotton. Their matted hair falls uncombed over their cheeks. Their slouch hats have long since been worn bare. Those who own blankets wrap them about their bodies as protection from the blizzards, holding them in place by broad belts of leather into which are thrust axes and knives. The officers are scarcely distinguishable from the men. They carry swords or rifles instead of long guns and a dagger – often an expensive one, hand-carved – in place of a knife.

Now these men must become beasts of burden, for the horses are not fit to pull the weight. Harnessed five to a sleigh, they haul their equipment through snow and water for the next eleven days. The sleighs, it develops, are badly made – too light to carry the loads, not large enough to cross the half-frozen streams. Provisions and men are soon soaked through. But if the days are bad, the nights are a horror. Knee-deep snow must be cleared away before a camp can be made. Fire must be struck from flint on steel. The wet wood, often enough, refuses to burn. So cold that they cannot always prepare a bed for themselves, the Kentuckians topple down on piles of brush before the smoky fires and sleep in their steaming garments.

Then, on the third day, a message arrives from Harrison: *turn back!* The General has picked up another rumour that the redoubtable Tecumseh and several hundred Indians are in the area. He advises –

does not order – Winchester not to proceed. With the Indians at his rear and no certainty of provisions at the rapids, any further movement toward Canada this winter would be foolhardy.

But James Winchester is in no mood to retreat. He is a man who has suddenly been released from three months of dreadful frustration – frustration over inactivity and boredom, frustration over insubordination, frustration over sickness and starvation, and, perhaps most significant, frustration over his own changing role as the leader of his men. Now at least he is on the move; it must seem to him some sort of progress; it is action of a sort, and at the end – who knows? More action, perhaps, even glory...vindication. He has no stomach to turn in his tracks and retreat to that "loathsome place," nor do his men. And so he moves on to tragedy.

•

AT FORT AMHERSTBURG, Lieutenant-Colonel Procter has concluded that the Americans have gone into winter quarters. His Indian spies have observed no movement around Winchester's camp for several weeks, and he is convinced that Harrison has decided to hold off any attempt to recapture Detroit until spring. It is just as well, for he has only a skeleton force of soldiers and a handful of Indians.

The Indians concern Procter. He cannot control them, cannot depend on them, does not like them. One moment they are hot for battle, the next they have vanished into the forest. Nor can he be sure where their loyalties lie. Matthew Elliott's eldest son, Alexander, has been killed and scalped by one group of Indians who pretended to be defecting to the British but who were actually acting as scouts for Winchester. Brock called them "a fickle race"; Procter would certainly agree with that. Neither has been able to understand that the Indians' loyalty is not to the British or to the Americans but to their own kind. They will support the British only as long as they believe it suits their own purpose. But the British, too, can be fickle; no tribesman, be he Potawatomi, Wyandot, Shawnee, or Miami, can ever quite trust the British after the betrayal at Fallen Timbers in 1794.

Nor do the British trust them – certainly not when it comes to observing the so-called rules of warfare, which are, of course, white European rules. Tecumseh is the only chief who can restrain his followers from killing and torturing prisoners and ravaging women and children. Angered by Prevost's armistice and ailing from a wound received at Brownstown, Tecumseh has headed south to try to draw the Creeks and Choctaws to his confederacy. His brother, the Prophet, has returned to the Wabash.

Procter needs to keep the Indians active, hence his attempt to capture Fort Wayne with a combined force of natives and regulars. The attempt failed, though it helped to slow Harrison's advance. Now he is under orders from Prevost to refrain from all such offensive warfare. His only task is defence against the invader.

He must tread a line delicately, for the Indians' loyalty depends on a show of British resolution. As Brock once said, "it is of primary importance that the confidence and goodwill of the Indians should be preserved and that whatsoever can tend to produce a contrary effect should be carefully avoided." That is the rub. The only way the confidence and goodwill of the Indians can be preserved is to attack the Americans, kill as many as possible, and let the braves have their way with the rest. Procter is not unmindful of how the news of the victory at Queenston has raised native morale – or of how the armistice has lowered it.

Prevost, as usual, believes that the British have overextended themselves on the Detroit frontier. Only Brock's sturdy opposition prevented the Governor General from ordering the evacuation of all captured American territory to allow the release of troops to the Niagara frontier. But Brock understood that such a show of weakness would cause the Indians to consider making terms with the enemy.

Brock's strategy, which Procter has inherited, has been to let the Americans keep the tribes in a state of ferment. The policy has succeeded. Harrison's attempt to subdue the Indians on the northwestern frontier has delayed his advance until midwinter and caused widespread indignation among the natives. Some six thousand have been displaced, nineteen villages ravaged, seven hundred lodges burned, thousands of bushels of corn destroyed. Savagery is not the exclusive trait of the red man. The Kentuckians take scalps whenever they can, nor are women and children safe from the army. Governor Meigs had no sooner called out the Ohio militia in the early fall than they launched an unprovoked attack on an Indian village near Mansfield, burning all the houses and shooting several of the inhabitants.

The worst attacks have been against the villages on the Peoria lakes, destroyed without opposition by a force of rangers and volunteers under Governor Ninian Edwards of Illinois Territory. One specific foray will not soon be forgotten: a mounted party under a captain named Judy came upon an Indian couple on the open prairie. When the man tried to surrender, Judy shot him through the body. Chanting his death song, the Indian killed one of Judy's men and was in turn riddled with bullets. A little later the same group captured and killed a starving Indian child.

In their rage and avarice, Edwards's followers scalp and mutilate the bodies of the fallen and ransack Indian graves for plunder. Small wonder that the Potawatomi chief Black Bird, in a later discussion with Claus, the Canadian Indian superintendent, cries out in fury, "The way they treat our killed and the remains of those that are in their graves to the west make our people mad when they meet the Big Knives. Whenever they get any of our people into their hands they cut them like meat into small pieces."

All that fall the Indians continue to concern Procter. They have been devouring his provisions at an alarming rate. The white leadership is shaky. At seventy, Matthew Elliott can scarcely sit a horse, and McKee is worn down by drink. Tecumseh's restraining hand is absent. Procter has some hope of reorganizing the tribes around Amherstburg into a raiding party under Colonel William Caldwell, a veteran of Butler's Rangers during the Revolution. Caldwell possesses enormous influence among the Wyandot, whom he has persuaded to adopt the British cause.

Meanwhile, Procter solves part of his supply problem by dispatching most of the Indians under Elliott to the Rapids of the Maumee, where several hundred acres of corn are waiting to be harvested – the same corn that Harrison has been trying vainly to seize. Elliott may be old and infirm, but he has lost none of his frontier cunning. He has sent Indian spies into Ohio who report that Winchester is again advancing. Elliott dispatches couriers to the villages of the Ottawa and the Potawatomi in Michigan Territory and to the Miami at the ravaged villages of the Mississinewa in Indiana. War parties begin to trickle into Amherstburg; within a month the native force has increased from three hundred to almost eight hundred braves, all stirred to a fever by the depredations of Harrison's army.

Winchester's army, meanwhile, is advancing toward the rapids. He arrives on January 11; Procter learns of this two days later. The British commander moves swiftly, calling out the militia, assembling the Indians. It is his intention to scorch the earth (whatever is not already scorched) along the Detroit frontier to deny the Americans provisions and shelter. The following day he dispatches Major Ebenezer Reynolds of the Essex militia with two flank companies and a band of Potawatomi to the little village of Frenchtown on the River Raisin. Reynolds's orders are to destroy the village and all its supplies and to remove the French-speaking settlers – forcibly, if necessary – to Canadian soil.

It is not a pleasant task. Who wants his home destroyed, his property removed, and his cattle driven off and killed by Indians? The settlers have worked hard to improve their farms, which lie on both sides of the narrow, low-banked river. Their town, a simple row of some twenty dwelling houses, squatting on the north bank three miles from the mouth, is not designed as a fort. Its only protection is a fence made of split pickets to secure the yards and gardens. The villagers are in a panic; as Reynolds and his men move in, a delegation slips away, heading for the Rapids of the Maumee to plead with Winchester for help. They carry with them a note for Harrison from Isaac Day, a long-time Detroit citizen, who writes that "five hundred true and brave Americans can secure the District of Erie – A timely approach of our armies will secure us from being forced to prison and the whole place from being burned by savage fury." Day has scarcely sent off this letter when he is seized and jailed. If Winchester is to act at all to save the settlement, he must act at once.

●

RAPIDS OF THE MAUMEE, January 17, 1813. Winchester and his senior officers sit in council. Should they go to the relief of Frenchtown? For almost four days word has been coming back of Indian outrages and British highhandedness. Everything is being removed from the village – cattle, carrioles, sleighs, grain, foodstuffs. Citizens such as Isaac Day, suspected of pro-American feelings, have been bundled off to confinement across the river. Winchester's information is that the British force is ridiculously small: between forty and fifty militia and perhaps a hundred Indians. It is, however, building rapidly. If the Americans move quickly, Day's note has told them, they can provision themselves at Frenchtown by securing three thousand barrels of flour and much grain. That possibility must seem as tempting as the succour of the villagers.

Lieutenant-Colonel John Allen rises – a graceful, commanding presence, perhaps the most popular man in Winchester's army, certainly the most distinguished, the most eloquent. A handsome Kentuckian, tall, sandy-haired, blue-eyed, close friend and boyhood companion of the lamented Jo Daviess (Tippecanoe's victim), next to Clay the state's greatest orator, leading lawyer, state senator, one-time candidate for governor. When he speaks all listen, for Allen commands as much respect as, if not more than, his general.

He is fed up with inactivity – weary of slow movements that get nowhere, as he complains in one of his letters to his wife, Jane, herself the daughter of a general. He hungers for action; now he sees his chance.

Winchester's forces, he points out, have three choices: they can withdraw – an ignominy which, piled upon other American setbacks, is unthinkable. They can wait here at the Maumee rapids for the rest of Harrison's force, but if they do that they will give the British time to build strength. Or they can go to the aid of the beleaguered inhabitants of Frenchtown, secure the desperately needed food at the settlement, strike a decisive blow against the British, open the road to Detroit, and – certainly not least – cover themselves with glory.

The council does not need much convincing, nor does Winchester. Why wait for Harrison, who is sixty-five miles away? A victory over the British – *any* victory – can make Winchester a national hero. His men, he knows, are as eager to move as he is. The term of the six-month volunteers will end in February; they have refused to re-enlist. All want one brief taste of glory before returning home. They have just received a welcome shipment of woollen underwear, and their morale, reduced by long weeks of inactivity and hunger, has risen again. And there is *food* at Frenchtown! Winchester, who has already written to General Perkins at Lower Sandusky asking for reinforcements for a proposed advance, now dispatches a second letter to Harrison announcing his intention to send a detachment to relieve Frenchtown and hold it.

One of Harrison's many frustrations during this exhausting fall and winter has been a collapse of communications. His letter to Winchester, urging him to abandon his march to the rapids, arrived too late. Winchester's reply, announcing his intention to move ahead to the rapids, does not reach him until the force is actually at its destination. It is carried by an eighteen-year-old Kentucky volunteer named Leslie Combs, who, with a single guide, crosses one hundred miles of trackless forest through snow so deep that the two men dare not lie down for fear of suffocation and are forced to sleep standing up. Exhausted, ill, and starving, the pair reach Fort McArthur on January 9. Harrison, at Upper Sandusky, gets Winchester's letter two days later.

Five days pass during which time Harrison has no idea of Winchester's position or intentions. Then on the night of the sixteenth he hears from Perkins at Lower Sandusky that Winchester has reached the rapids and wants reinforcements, apparently contemplating an attack.

The news alarms him – if it were in his power he would call Winchester off. He sets off at once for Lower Sandusky, travelling so swiftly that his aide's horse drops dead of exhaustion. There he immediately dispatches a detachment of artillery, guarded by three hundred infantrymen, to Winchester's aid. The camp at the rapids is only thirty-six miles away, but the roads are choked with drifting snow, and the party moves slowly.

Two days later, on January 18, he receives confirmation of Winchester's intention to send a detachment to relieve Frenchtown. Now Harrison is thoroughly alarmed. The proposed move is "opposed to a principle by which I have ever been governed in Indian warfare, i.e. never to make a detachment but under the most urgent circumstances." He orders two more regiments to march to the rapids and sets off himself, with General Perkins, in a sleigh. Its slowness annoys him. He seizes his servant's horse, rides on alone. Darkness falls; the horse stumbles into a frozen swamp; the ice gives way; Harrison manages to free himself and pushes on through the night on foot.

Winchester, meanwhile, has already ordered Lieutenant-Colonel William Lewis and 450 troops to attack the enemy at Frenchtown on the Raisin. Off goes Lewis, with three days' provisions, followed a few hours later by a second force of one hundred Kentuckians under the eager Lieutenant-Colonel Allen. They rendezvous at Presqu'Isle, a French-Canadian village on the south side of the Maumee, twenty miles from the rapids, eighteen from the Raisin. Elias Darnell is overwhelmed, as are his comrades, by this first contact with anything remotely resembling civilization:

"The sight of this village filled each heart with emotions of cheerfulness and joy; for we had been nearly five months in the wilderness, exposed to every inconvenience, and excluded from everything that had the appearance of a civilized country."

The inhabitants pour out of their homes, waving white flags, shouting greetings. The troops are in high spirits; they know that some will be corpses on the morrow, but with the eternal optimism of all soldiers, most hew to the conviction that they will survive. Nonetheless, those who can write have sent letters home to wives, parents, or friends. One such is Captain James Price, commander of the Jessamine Blues, who writes rather formally to his wife, Susan, at Nicholasville, Kentucky, that "on the event of battle I have believed it proper to address you these lines."

It is his two-year-old son that concerns Captain Price rather than his three daughters who, he feels, are his wife's responsibility: "Teach my boy to love truth," he writes, "to speak truth at all times.... He must be taught to bear in mind that 'an honest man is the noblest work of God'; he must be rigidly honest in his dealings.... Never allow him to run about on Sabbath days, fishing. Teach my son the habits of industry.... Industry leads to virtue.... Not a day must be lost in teaching him how to work.... It may be possible I may fall in battle and my only boy must know that his father, next to God, loves his country, and is now risking his life in defending that country against a barbarous and cruel enemy.... Pray for me that you may be with me once more."

The following morning, January 18, as the Kentucky soldiers march along the frozen lake toward their objective, they meet refugees from Frenchtown. What kind of artillery do the British have, the troops want to know. "Two pieces about large enough to kill a mouse," is the reply. From Frenchtown comes word that the British are waiting. Lewis forms up his troops on the ice, and as they come in sight of the settlement, the lone British howitzer opens up. "Fire away with your mouse cannon!" some of the men cry, and as the long drum roll sounds the charge, they cross the slippery Raisin, clamber up the bank, leap the village pickets, and drive the British back toward the forest.

Later, one of the French residents tells Elias Darnell that he has watched an old Wyandot—one of those who took part in the rout of Tupper's Ohio militia at the rapids—smoking his pipe as the Americans come into sight. "I suppose Ohio men come," he says. "We give them another chase." Then as the American line stampedes through the village he cries, "Kentuck, by God!" and joins in the general retreat.

The battle rages from 3 P.M. to dark. John Allen forces the British left wing back into the forest. The British make a stand behind a chain of enclosed lots and small clusters of houses, where piles of brush and deadfalls bar the way. The American centre under Major George Madison (a future governor of Kentucky) and the left under Major Benjamin Graves now go into action, and the British and Indians fall back, contesting every foot. When dusk falls they have been driven two miles from the village, and the Americans are in firm possession.

Lewis's triumphant account of the victory is sent immediately by express rider to Winchester, who receives it at dawn. The camp at the rapids is ecstatic. Harking back to Henry Clay's speech of August 16, Lewis reports that "both officers and soldiers supported the double character of Americans and Kentuckyans." The state's honour has been vindicated. The soldiers at both Frenchtown and the rapids now feel they are unbeatable, that they will roll right on to Detroit, cross the river, capture Amherstburg. General Simon Perkins, after the fact, will write dryly: "I fancy they were too much impressed with the opinion that Kentucky bravery could not fall before [such] a foe as Indians and Canadians."

The troops on the Raisin are dangerously exposed. Yet their eagerness for battle is such that Winchester would be hard put to withdraw them even if he wished to – even Harrison will admit that. But Winchester does not wish to. Caught up in the general intoxication of victory, seeing himself and his army as the saviours of his country's honour, he takes what troops he can spare – fewer than three hundred – and marches off to Frenchtown.

There is another force drawing him and his men toward the little village – an attraction quite as powerful as the prospect of fame and glory: Frenchtown, at this moment, is close to paradise. Here on the vine-clad banks of *la Rivière au Raisin* is luxury: fresh apples, cider by the barrel, sugar, butter, whiskey, and more – houses with roofs, warm beds, hearthsides with crackling fires, the soft presence of women. When Winchester arrives late on the twentieth, Lewis's men have already sampled these delights. Billeted in no particular order in the homes of the enthusiastic settlers, they are already drunk and quarrelsome, wandering about town late into the night. There is some vague talk of entrenching the position, but it is only talk. The men are weary from fighting, unruly from drink, and in no mood to take orders.

The village is surrounded on three sides by a palisade constructed of eight-foot logs, split and sharpened at the ends. These pickets, which do not come all the way down to the river bank, enclose a compact community of log and shingle houses, interspersed with orchards, gardens, barns, and outbuildings. The whole space forms a rectangle two hundred yards along the river and three hundred deep.

On the right of the village, downriver, lies an open meadow with a number of detached houses. Here Lieutenant-Colonel Samuel Wells, brother to the slain scout Billy Wells and a veteran of Tippecanoe, encamps his regulars. Winchester demurs: the regulars would be better placed within the palisade. But Wells insists on his prerogatives: military etiquette determines that the regular troops should *always* be on the right of the militia. Winchester does not argue. Wells's men are exposed, but he expects to find a better campground for them on the following day.

Leaving Wells in charge of the main camp, the General and his staff, including his teen-aged son, take up quarters on the south side of the river in the home of Colonel Francis Navarre, a local trader. It is a handsome building, the logs covered with clapboard, the whole shaded by pear trees originally brought from Normandy. Winchester is given a spacious guest-room at the front of the house, warmed by a fireplace. It is now Wells's turn to demur. He believes the General and his officers should be as close as possible to the troops on the far side of the river in case of sudden attack. The British fort is only eighteen miles away.

But James Winchester has made up his mind. For twenty years as a wealthy plantation owner he has enjoyed the creature comforts of a sedentary life. For five months without complaint he has slept out in the elements, enduring the privations with his troops, existing on dreadful food – when there was food at all – drinking, sometimes, stagnant water scooped out of wagon tracks. Later, he will argue that there was no house in Frenchtown; he would have had to move some of the wounded. But this is palpably false.

A strange lassitude has fallen over the General and his troops. The sudden euphoric victory, the almost magical appearance of food, drink, warmth, and shelter – the stuff of their dreams for these past weeks – has given them a dreamlike confidence. There is talk of moving the camp to a better position, and on the following day the General and some of his officers ride out to look over the ground. Nothing comes of it. It does not apparently occur to them that it might be a good idea to put the river between themselves and the British.

Wells leaves camp that morning claiming that he has baggage to collect at the rapids. Winchester, who believes that Wells has lost faith in him, sends a note with him to Harrison, detailing his situation. It reflects his sense of security: his patrols have detected no British in the vicinity; he does not believe any attack will take place for several days. His own intentions are far from clear. Later that night, Captain Nathaniel Hart, Harrison's emissary, rides in with the news that Harrison has arrived at the Maumee rapids and that reinforcements are on the way. This adds to the general complacency.

It is an axiom of war that from time to time even the best of generals suffer from a common failing—a refusal to believe their own intelligence reports. Psychological blinkers narrow their vision; they decline to accept any evidence that fails to support their own appreciation of the situation. Winchester seems deaf to all suggestions that the British are massing for an attack. On the morning of the twenty-first, he sends Navarre's son Peter and four of his brothers to scout toward the mouth of the Detroit River. En route, they intercept Joseph Bordeau, Peter's future father-in-law, crossing on the ice from the British side. Bordeau, who has escaped from Amherstburg, brings positive news that the British, with a large body of Indians, will be at the Raisin some time after dark. But "Jocko" La Salle, a voluble and genial French Canadian—and a possible British plant—convinces Winchester that this news must be in error. Winchester and his officers, "regaling themselves with whiskey and loaf sugar" as Elias Darnell believes, dismiss Peter Navarre with a laugh.

That afternoon, a second scout confirms the story, but again Winchester is deaf. Later in the evening, one of Lewis's ensigns learns from a tavern keeper that he has been talking to two British officers about an impending attack. But Lewis does not take the report seriously.

Some of Winchester's field officers expect that a council will be called that night, but no word comes from the General. Though Winchester has issued vague orders about strengthening the camp, little has been done. Nor does he issue the ammunition, stored at Navarre's house. Wells's detachment is down to ten rounds per man.

It is bitterly cold. The snow lies deep. Nobody has the heart to send pickets out onto the roads leading into the settlement. William Atherton notices that most of the men act as if they were perfectly secure, some wandering about town until late into the night. Atherton himself feels little anxiety, although he has reason to believe the situation is perilous. He sleeps soundly until awakened by the cry "To arms! to arms!" the thundering of cannon, the roar of muskets, and the discordant yells of attacking Indians.

AMHERSTBURG, UPPER CANADA, January 19, 1813. It is long past midnight. From the windows of Draper's tavern comes the sound of music and merriment, laughter and dancing. The young people of the town and the officers of the garrison have combined to hold a ball to celebrate the birthday of Queen Charlotte, the consort of the mad old king of England. Suddenly the music stops and in walks Procter's deputy, Lieutenant-Colonel St. George, equipped for the field. His voice, long accustomed to command, drowns the chatter.

"My boys," says the Colonel, "you must prepare to dance to a different tune; the enemy is upon us and we are going to surprise them. We shall take the route about four in the morning, so get ready at once."

Procter has just received word of the British defeat at the Raisin. The Americans, he knows, are in an exposed position and their numbers are not large. He determines to scrape up as many men as possible and attack at once. This swift and aggressive decision is not characteristic of Procter, a methodical, cautious officer who tends to follow the book. It was Procter, after all, who strongly opposed Brock's sally against Detroit. Now Brock's example – or perhaps Brock's ghost – impels him to precipitate action. The moves are Procter's, but the spirit behind them is that of his late commander.

He plans swiftly. He will send a detachment under Captain James Askin to garrison Detroit. He will leave Fort Amherstburg virtually defenceless, manned only by the sick and least effective members of the militia under Lieutenant-Colonel Jean-Baptiste Bâby. The remainder – every possible man who can be called into service, including provincial seamen from the gunboats – will be sent across the river. In all, he counts 597 able men and more than five hundred Indians – Potawatomi displaced from their homes by Harrison, with bitter memories of Tippecanoe; Miami, victims of the recent attacks at Mississinewa; and Chief Roundhead's Wyandot, formerly of Brownstown.

The first detachment leaves immediately, dragging three three-pound cannon and three small howitzers on sleighs. John Richardson, the future novelist, is young enough at fifteen to find the scene romantic – the troops moving in a thin line across the frozen river under cliffs of rugged ice, their weapons, polished to a high gloss, glittering in the winter sunlight.

Lieutenant Frederic Rolette, back in action again after the prisoner exchange that followed the battle of Queenston Heights and fresh from his losing struggle to regain the gunboat *Detroit* from the Americans, has charge of one of the guns. He is suffering from such a splitting headache that Major Reynolds urges him to go back. Rolette looks insulted, produces a heavy bandanna. "Look here," he says, "tie this tight around my head." Reynolds rolls it into a thick band and does so. "I am better already," says Rolette and pushes on.

The following day the rest of Procter's forces cross the river, rest that night at Brownstown, and prepare to move early next morning. As darkness falls, John Richardson's favourite brother, Robert, aged fourteen, a midshipman in the Provincial Marine, sneaks into camp. His father, an army surgeon, has given him strict orders to stay out of trouble on the Canadian side, but he is determined to see action and attaches himself to one of the gun crews.

In the morning, Procter moves his force of one thousand to Rocky River, twelve miles from Brownstown, six miles from the American camp. Two hours before dawn on the following day they rise, march the intervening distance, and silently descend upon the enemy.

The camp at Frenchtown is asleep, the drum roll just sounding reveille. This, surely, is the moment for attack, while the men are still in their blankets, drowsy, brushing the slumber from their eyes, without weapons in their hands. But the ghost of Isaac Brock has departed. Procter goes by the book, which insists that an infantry charge be supported by cannon. Precious moments slip by, and the army's momentum slows as he places his pieces. A sharp-eyed Kentucky guard spots the movement. A rifle explodes, and the leading grenadier of the 41st, a man named Gates, drops dead: a bullet has literally gone in one ear and out the other. Surprise is lost. The battle begins. Procter's caution will cost the lives of scores of good men.

It is still dark. The British and Canadians can see flashes of musketry several hundred yards to the front but nothing else. Slowly, in the pre-dawn murk, a blurred line of figures takes shape, standing out in front of the village. They fire a volley at this welcome target, but the line stands fast. They fire again without effect. Who are these supermen who do not fall when the muskets roar? Dawn provides the answer: they have been aiming, not at their enemies, but at a line of wooden pickets that protects them.

A second problem frustrates them. Procter has placed one of his three-pounders directly in front of his centre, so that the American

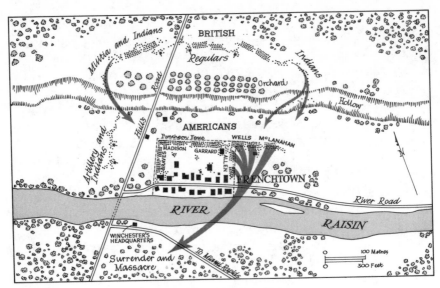

The Battle of Frenchtown

fire aimed at the gun plays upon the men behind it while the gunners themselves are in jeopardy from their own men in the rear.

A British musket ball strikes Frederic Rolette in the head. The tightly rolled silk bandanna saves his life. The ball is caught in the fold and flattens against his skull, increasing his headache and causing a goose egg but no further damage.

The fire grows hotter. Behind the palisades the Americans can easily pick out targets against the lightening sky. When the British abandon a three-pounder twenty yards from the fence, the Kentuckians leap over the puncheons to capture it. But Rolette's mate, Second-Lieutenant Robert Irvine, the same man who tried to beat off the attack on *Caledonia*, seizes the drag rope and hauls it back to the British line just as a musket ball shreds his heel.

Private Shadrach Byfield, whose name was left off the list for prize money after the fall of Detroit, is fighting in Adam Muir's company of the 41st when the man on his left falls dead. It is light enough now to see the enemy, and he spots a Kentuckian coming through the palisades. "There's a man!" cries Byfield to a friend. "I'll have a shot at him." As he pulls the trigger, a ball strikes him under the left ear and he topples to the ground, cutting his friend's leg with his bayonet in the process. He is only twenty-three, a Wiltshire man who joined the

British army at eighteen – the third in his family to enlist – an action that caused his poor mother to fall into a speechless fit from which she never recovered. Now he believes his last moment has come. "Byfield is dead!" his friend cries out, and Shadrach Byfield replies, in some wonder, "I believe I be." An age-old question flashes across his mind, a question that must occur to every soldier the instant he falls in battle. "Is this death?" he asks himself. *Is this how men die?*

But he is not dead. He raises his head and begins to creep off on his hands and knees. "Byfield," calls a sergeant, "shall I take you to the doctor?" But Shadrach Byfield at twenty-three is an old soldier. "Never mind me, go and help the men," he says, and makes his way to a barn to have his wound dressed. Here he encounters a spectacle so affecting that he can never forget it – a young midshipman, wounded in the knee, crying in pain for his mother, convinced he is going to die.

At the palisade, John Richardson feels as if he were sleep-walking. The early call and the six-mile march have exhausted him. Even as the balls begin to whistle about his head he continues to feel drowsy. He tries to fire his musket, finds it will not respond; someone the night before has stolen his flintlock and replaced it with a damaged part. The infantry manual lists twelve separate drill movements for firing a Brown Bess musket and Richardson goes through all of them without effect, but all he gets is a flash in the pan. He finds a bit of wire, tries to fix his weapon, fires again, gets another flash. He feels more frustration than fear at being fired upon by an unseen foe and not being able to fire back, even though he later comes to realize that if he had fired fifty rounds not one of them would have had any effect on the pickets (and probably not on the enemy, either, for the musket is a wretchedly inaccurate weapon).

To his horror, Richardson notes that the American sharpshooters are picking off the wounded British and Canadians as they try to crawl to safety and that some are making use of the tomahawk and scalping knife. He is still struggling vainly with his useless weapon when he hears his name called. Somebody shouts that his brother has been wounded – young Robert's right leg was shattered as he applied a match to a gun. Now, in great pain, Robert begs to be carried off, not to the staff section where his father is caring for the wounded, but to another part of the field so that he may escape his parent's wrath. And there Shadrach Byfield is witness to his suffering.

On the left of the British line, Richardson can hear the war-whoops of the Indians who, with the help of the Canadian militia, are driving directly through the open field in which Lieutenant-Colonel Wells insisted on placing the regulars of the 17th U.S. Infantry. Wells is still at the Maumee. His second-in-command, Major McClanahan, cannot hold his unprotected position. The troops fall back to the frozen Raisin, and the American right flank is turned.

The Americans are in full flight across the river with Caldwell and his Indians under Roundhead, Split Log, and Walk-in-the-Water in hot pursuit. One of the Wyandot overtakes an American officer and is about to tomahawk him when Caldwell intercedes, makes him prisoner, takes him to the rear. The Kentuckian, catching him off guard, draws his knife and slits Caldwell's throat from ear to ear, but the wound is shallow and Caldwell, who is as tough as his Indian followers, catches his assailant's arm, pulls the dagger from his throat, and plunges it again and again into his prisoner's body until he is dead. Caldwell survives.

But where, when all this is going on, is the General?

Winchester has awakened to the sound of musket fire and howitzer bombs exploding. He runs to the barn, borrows a horse from his host (who, fearing British retribution, is glad to be rid of him), dashes into action. His two battalion commanders, Lewis and Allen, join him, and the three attempt to rally the fleeing men under the bank of the Raisin. It is too late; the troops, pursued by the Indians, are in a panic. Lewis has sent two companies to the right flank to reinforce the regulars, but these too are in retreat.

The three officers withdraw across the river and attempt a second rally behind the fences on the south side. It is futile. The men dash past into a narrow lane leading to the main road. This is suicide, for the Indians are ahead of them and behind them, on both sides of the lane. One hundred men are shot, tomahawked, scalped. Winchester attempts a third rally in an orchard about a mile and a half from the village. It also fails.

The right flank is in full retreat, the men throwing away their weapons in panic. The Potawatomi are in no mood to offer quarter. Lieutenant Ashton Garrett tries to form up a group of fifteen men but finding some sixty Indians running along both sides and in front with their arms at the trail decides instead to surrender. The Indians order Garrett and his men to ground their arms; then, securing all the weapons, they coolly shoot and scalp every one except Garrett himself.

John Allen, shot in the thigh during his attempts to stem the retreat, limps on for two miles until he can go no farther. Exhausted and in pain, he slumps onto a log, resigned to his fate. One of the Potawatomi chiefs, seeing his officer's uniform, determines to capture and ransom him, but just as he signals that intention a second Indian moves in. Allen dispatches him with a swipe of his sword. The other shoots the Colonel dead and scalps him.

Winchester and Lewis are more fortunate. They fall into the hands of Roundhead, the principal chief of the Wyandot, who, after stripping the General of his cocked hat, coat, and epaulettes, takes the two officers and Winchester's seventeen-year-old son by a circuitous route back behind the British lines. The battle for the village is still raging, but Winchester, noting Procter's artillery, dazed by the rout and despairing of any reinforcements from Harrison, has given up hope. As the Indians return with as many as eight or nine scalps hanging from their belts, he asks to see Procter. The British commander is blunt:

"Some of your troops, sir, are defending themselves from the fort in a state of desperation – had you not better surrender them?"

"I have no authority to do so," replies Winchester, shivering in the cold in his silk shirt. "My command has devolved upon the senior officer in the fort, as you are pleased to call it."

Procter now makes the classic answer – Brock's threat at Detroit, Roberts's at Mackinac: if there is no surrender he will be forced to set the town on fire; if he is forced to attack, he cannot be responsible for the conduct of the Indians or the lives of the Americans; if Winchester will surrender, he will be responsible for both. Winchester repeats that he is no longer in command but will recommend surrender to his people.

The command of the American forces still fighting inside the palisade has devolved on Major George Madison, a forty-nine-year-old veteran of the Revolution and of St. Clair's defeat at the hands of the Indians in 1791 and for twenty years keeper of public accounts for the state of Kentucky. At this moment he is concerned about the possession of an empty barn 150 yards from the palisade. If the enemy seizes that building, they will hold a commanding position overlooking the defenders. Madison calls for a volunteer to fire the barn, and a young ensign, William O. Butler, steps forward, seizes a blazing stick of firewood, vaults the fence, and dashes toward the barn under direct fire from the British and Indians on both sides.

Butler reaches the barn, flings the burning brand into a pile of hay, races back through a hail of musket balls, has almost reached the safety of his own lines when he realizes that the hay has not caught. Back he goes, re-enters the barn, fans the hay into a roaring blaze, outstrips the Indians trying to head him off, and with his clothes ripped by passing musket balls tumbles across the pickets and comes to a full stop, standing upright, trying to catch his breath. It is then that a musket ball strikes him full in the chest. Fortunately, it is spent, and Butler survives. Like his commander, George Madison, he will one day run for governor of Kentucky.

Now comes a lull in the fighting. Of the sixteen British gunners, thirteen are casualties; the remainder are too numb with cold to fire their weapons. Moreover, their ammunition is low; a wagon bearing additional rounds has been shot up and its driver killed by Kentucky riflemen. Procter has withdrawn his forces into the woods, waiting for the Indians to return from the chase before resuming the attack. The defenders seize this interlude to devour some breakfast. This is the moment when Winchester agrees to attempt a surrender.

The Americans, seeing a flag of truce, believe that Procter is asking for a respite to bury his dead. It does not occur to any that surrender is being proposed. When he learns the truth, George Madison is mortified; yet he knows his position is hopeless, for he has only a third of a keg of cartridges left. The reserve supply remains at the Navarre house across the river. He insists, however, on conditions.

"It has been customary for the Indians to massacre the wounded and prisoners after a surrender," he tells Procter. "I shall therefore not agree to any capitulation which General Winchester may direct, unless the safety and protection of all the prisoners shall be stipulated."

Procter stamps his foot:

"Sir, do *you* mean to dictate for *me*?"

"I mean to dictate for myself," Madison coolly replies. "We prefer to sell our lives as dearly as possible rather than be massacred in cold blood."

Procter agrees, but not in writing. Private property, he promises, will be respected; sleighs will be sent the following morning for the American sick and wounded; the disabled will be protected by a proper guard.

Thus the battle ends. Some of the troops plead with their officers not to surrender, saying they would rather die in action. Many are reduced to tears. Others, in a rage, throw down their guns with such force as to shiver the stocks from the barrels. Some joke and laugh. One stands on a stile block and shouts to the English, "You have taken the greatest set of game cocks that ever came from Kentuck." But the general feeling is one of despair. Atherton notes that news of the surrender is "like a shock of lightning from one end of the lines to the other." To Thomas P. Dudley, another Lexington volunteer, "the mortification at the thought of surrender, the Spartan band who fought like heroes, the tears shed, the wringing of hands, the swelling of hearts, indeed, the scene beggars description."

Only thirty-three men have managed to escape. McClanahan, Wells's second-in-command is one. Private John J. Brice is another; he gets away by pulling off his shoes and running through the snow in his stocking feet in order to leave tracks resembling those of an Indian in moccasins and so becomes the first man to report the defeat and surrender to Harrison.

Winchester's loss is appalling. Two hundred Kentuckians are dead or wounded, another seven hundred are prisoners of the British, and the worst is yet to come. The blow to American morale, already bruised by the losses at Mackinac, Detroit, and Queenston, is overwhelming. As for Harrison, the Battle of Frenchtown has wrecked his plans. His left wing has been shattered, his advance on Detroit halted indefinitely. He must now withdraw up the Maumee, out of reach of the enemy. The idea of a swift victory over Canada is gone forever.

●

FRENCHTOWN, MICHIGAN TERRITORY, January 23, 1813. William Atherton wakes at dawn, the wound in his shoulder throbbing. He cannot escape a feeling of dread that has tormented his sleep. An ominous stillness hangs over the village where the American wounded are still hived. Procter, fearing an imminent attack from Harrison, has long since dragged his own wounded off on sleds, and since there are not enough of these for the Americans, he has promised to return early in the morning to take them all to Amherstburg.

No one points to the illogic of this. If Procter fears Harrison's early arrival, why would he return for the wounded? If he doesn't fear it, why has he departed, taking everybody with him except one officer, Major Reynolds, and three interpreters? Actually, Harrison, learning of the disaster, has withdrawn his relief force. In the chorus of recriminations that will follow, nobody apparently bothers to ask why. With Procter's forces off balance and Fort Amherstburg virtually defenceless, he might easily have snatched victory from defeat. But he contents himself with putting all the blame on Winchester.

The camp at Frenchtown is uneasy. Some time in the dark hours of the night, Reynolds and the interpreters have slipped away. Atherton's fears have been further aroused by an Indian, apparently a chief, who speaks fluent English and who came into his quarters the evening before, seemingly trying to gain information about Harrison's movements. Just as he left, the Indian made an oddly chilling remark: "I am afraid," he said, "some of the mischievous boys will do some mischief before morning."

The sun has been up for no more than an hour when Atherton's fears are realized. Without warning, the door of the house in which he and some of the wounded are being cared for is forced open, and an Indian, his face smeared with red and black paint, appears waving a tomahawk, followed by several others. Their purpose is loot: they begin to strip the clothing and blankets from the wounded, groaning on the floor. Atherton, near the door, manages to slip out of the room, only to come face to face with one of the most savage-looking natives he has ever seen. This creature's face is painted jet black. Half a bushel of feathers are fastened to his scalp lock, an immense tomahawk gleams in his right hand, a scalping knife hangs from his belt. He seizes Atherton by the collar, propels him out the front door, leads him through the gate and down the river for a hundred yards to the home of Jean-Baptiste Jerome, where several wounded officers have spent the night. The building has also done duty as a tavern, and the Indians are ransacking the cellars for whiskey.

In front of the house Atherton sees a scarecrow figure, bleeding, barefoot, clad only in a shirt and drawers. This is Captain Nathaniel Hart, commander of the Lexington Light Infantry, inspector of the North West Army, the emissary whom Harrison sent to Winchester the night before the battle. He is twenty-eight and wealthy, having made a fortune in hemp. Now he is pleading for his life. The previous night, Hart, badly wounded in the knee, was visited by an old friend, Matthew Elliott's son William, a militia captain who was once cared for in the Hart home in Lexington during a bout of illness. Hart has Elliott's assurance that he will send his personal sleigh for him in the morning and convey him to his home in Amherstburg. In fact, Elliott has assured all the wounded in Jerome's house that they are in no danger. The promise is hollow; they are all in deadly peril. Some are already dying under the tomahawk blows of the Indians.

Hart turns to an Indian he recognizes – the same English-speaking chief whom Atherton encountered the evening before – and reminds him of Elliott's promise.

"Elliott has deceived you," the Indian replies. "He does not intend to fulfill his promise."

"If you will agree to take me, I will give you a horse or a hundred dollars," Hart declares. "You shall have it on our arrival at Malden."

"I cannot take you."

"Why?"

"You are too badly wounded."

"Then," asks Captain Hart, "what do you intend to do with us?"

"Boys," says the Indian, "you are all to be killed."

Hart maintains his composure, utters a brief prayer. Atherton expects at any moment to feel the blow of a tomahawk. Now follows a scene of pure horror: Captain Paschal Hickman, General William Hull's son-in-law, emerges from Jerome's house, dragged by an Indian who throws him face down into the snow. Hickman, who has already been tomahawked, chokes to death in his own blood as Atherton watches in terror, then, taking advantage of the confusion, turns from the spectacle and begins to edge slowly away, hoping not to be seen.

Albert Ammerman, another unwilling witness to the butchery, crouches on a log, guarded by his Indian captor. A private in the 1st Regiment of Kentucky Volunteers, he has been wounded in the thigh but is doing his best to conceal his injury, for he knows it is the Indians' practice to kill all who cannot walk. Now he watches helplessly while the Indians loot the houses, strip the clothes from the wounded, tomahawk and scalp their prey, and set fire to the buildings. Some, still alive, force their heads out of the windows, half-enveloped in smoke and flames, seeking rescue. But there is no rescue.

Ammerman is marched off at last toward Brownstown with some other prisoners. After limping about half a mile, they are overtaken. One Indian has Captain Hart in custody and is engaged in a violent argument with another, apparently over the reward that Hart has offered for his safe conduct to Amherstburg. As Ammerman watches, the two take aim at each other as if to end the quarrel. But they do not fire. Instead they turn upon their prisoner, pull him from his horse, knock him down with a war-club, tomahawk him, scalp him, strip him of his remaining clothing, money, and effects. Ammerman (who will shortly be ransomed in Detroit) notes that Hart, during these final moments, refrains from making any pleas and appears, to the end, perfectly calm. The news of his death, when it finally filters through to Lexington three months later, will cause a particular shiver of despair and fury in Kentucky. For this mangled and naked corpse, thrown like carrion onto the side of the road, was once the brother-in-law of Speaker Henry Clay.

Back at Frenchtown, little William Atherton (he is only five foot five) is trying to reach a small log building some distance from the scene of horror. He edges toward it, is a few steps from it, when a Potawatomi seizes him and asks where he is wounded. Atherton places a hand on his shoulder. The Indian feels it, finds it is not serious, determines that Atherton shall be his prize, perhaps for later ransom. He wraps his new possession in a blanket, gives him a hat, takes him to the back door of one of the houses, and puts the wounded Kentuckian in charge of all his plunder.

Atherton is flabbergasted. For almost an hour he has expected certain death. Now he lives in the faint hope that his life may be spared. He experiences "one of those sudden transitions of mind impossible to be either conceived or expressed, except by those whose unhappy lot it has been, to be placed in like circumstances."

As the house blazes behind him, Atherton watches his fellow prisoners being dragged away to Brownstown. For the first time, perhaps, he has been made aware of the value a man places on his own life. He sees members of his own company, old acquaintances, so badly wounded they can scarcely be moved in their beds, suddenly leap up, hearing that the Indians will tomahawk all who cannot depart on foot. They hobble past him on sticks but, being unable to keep up, are soon butchered.

After two hours, Atherton's captor returns with an army pack horse and a great deal of plunder. The Potawatomi hands his prisoner the bridle, and the two set off on the road to Brownstown, bordered now by a ghastly hedgerow of mutilated corpses.

They halt for the night at Sandy Creek, where a number of Potawatomi are encamped. Here, around a roaring fire of fence rails, the Indians feed their captives gruel. And here another grisly scene takes place. An Indian walks up to Private Charles Searls and proposes to exchange his moccasins for the soldier's shoes. The exchange effected, a brief conversation follows, the Indian asking how many men Harrison has with him. The name of the Hero of Tippecanoe seems to drive him into a sudden rage. His anger rising, he calls Searls a "Madison," raises his tomahawk, strikes him a deep blow on the shoulder.

Searls, bleeding profusely, clutches the weapon embedded in his flesh and tries to resist, whereupon a surgeon's mate, Gustavus Bower, tells him his fate is inevitable. Searls closes his eyes, the blow falls again, and Bower is drenched with brains and blood. Not long after, three more men are indiscriminately dispatched.

When Atherton asks his captor if the Indians intend to kill all the prisoners, the Indian nods. Atherton tries to eat, has no stomach for it, even though he has had little nourishment for three days. Then he realizes his captor does not understand English and hope returns.

The march resumes with many alarms. Atherton is in daily fear of his life, sleeping with a kerchief tied around his head in the belief that the Indians will want to steal it before tomahawking him in his sleep, thus giving him some warning. But they do not kill him. His captor, whose brother has been killed at the River Raisin, has other plans. It is the custom of the Potawatomi, among others, to adopt healthy captives into the families of those who have lost sons in the same engagement. It is some time before Atherton realizes that his enemies do not intend to kill or ransom him. On the contrary, they are determined to turn him into an Indian. For the rest of his life, if they have their way, he will live as a savage in the forest.

From Frenchtown, Dr. John Todd, surgeon for the 5th Regiment of Kentucky Volunteers who has been left in charge of the wounded, is conveyed to the British camp where he again encounters Captain William Elliott. The two met the previous evening when Todd was a witness to the discussions between Elliott and Hart. Now Todd urges Elliott to send his sleigh back to the Raisin where some of the badly wounded, including his friend Hart, may yet be saved. But Elliott, who has lived all his life with the Indians and is half Shawnee, knows it is too late and says so. When Todd presses the case, Elliott remarks that charity begins at home, that the British and Canadian wounded must be cared for first, that when sleighs are available they will be sent to Frenchtown. He adds, in some exasperation, that it is impossible to restrain the Indians and tries to explain that they are simply seeking revenge for their own losses. Tippecanoe is only fourteen months in the past, Mississinewa less than two.

Along the frozen shores of the River Raisin a great stillness has fallen. The cold is numbing; nothing moves. Those few settlers who still remain in Frenchtown do not venture outside their doors.

In the little orchard across the river, along the narrow lane that leads from the Navarre home and beside the Detroit River road, the bodies of the Americans lie, unshriven and unburied. The Potawatomi have made it known that any white man who dares to touch the remains of any of the hated Harrison men will meet a similar fate.

The naked corpses lie strewn for miles along the roadside in the grotesque attitudes of men who, in a sudden flash, realize their last moment has come. In death they bear a gruesome similarity, for each skull is disfigured by a frozen smear of fleshy pulp where the scalp has been.

Here, contorted in death, lies the flower of Kentucky: Captain Hart and Captain Hickman; Lieutenant-Colonel John Allen; Captain John Woolfolk, Winchester's aide-de-camp, who offered one thousand dollars to anyone who would purchase him but was tomahawked in spite of it; Captain John Simpson, Henry Clay's fellow congressman and supporter; Ensign Levi Wells, the son of Lieutenant-Colonel Sam Wells of the 4th Infantry; Allen Darnell, whose brother looks helplessly on as he is shot and scalped because he cannot keep up with the others; and Ebenezer Blythe, a surgeon's mate, tomahawked in the act of offering ransom. And here, like a discarded doll, is the cadaver of young Captain Price of the Jessamine Blues whose last letter home gave instructions for the upbringing of his two-year-old son.

A few days after the battle, the French inhabitants, emerging at last from their homes, are treated to a ghastly spectacle. Trotting along the roadway come droves of hogs that have been feeding off the corpses and are now carrying off the remains – whole arms and legs, skulls, bits of torso and entrails clamped between their greedy jaws. The hogs, too, are victims of the war, for they seem now to be as demented as the men who fight it, "rendered mad," according to one opinion, "by so profuse a diet of Christian flesh."

The war, which began so gently, has turned ugly, as all wars must. The mannerly days are over. New emotions – hatred, fury, a thirst for revenge, a nagging sense of guilt – distort the tempers of the neighbours who live on both sides of the embattled border. And it is not over. Peace is still two years away. The blood has only begun to flow.

AFTERVIEW
The New War

WITH THE BATTLE OF FRENCHTOWN, the campaign of
1812 ended. It was too cold to fight. The war was postponed until
spring, when it would become a new war with new leaders and
new followers. The six-month volunteers from Kentucky, Ohio,
Pennsylvania and other states went back to their farms, refusing to
enlist for another term of service. Harrison withdrew up the Maumee
to start work on a new outpost, Fort Meigs. Along the Niagara River
the American regulars moved back ten miles while others went into
winter quarters at Sackets Harbor, Burlington, and Greenville. The
only American fighting men in Canada were the prisoners of war at
Quebec.

It was as if both Canada and the United States were starting from
scratch. America had a new secretary of war, John Armstrong. Most
of the old commanders – Brock, Hull, Van Rensselaer, Smyth,
Winchester – were gone. Dearborn's days were numbered as were
Sheaffe's. Only two major leaders remained from the early days of
1812, Tecumseh and Harrison, old adversaries fated to meet face to
face at the Thames in the autumn of 1813.

Now Canada had time to breathe. With Napoleon's army fleeing
Russia, some of the pressure was off Great Britain. A detachment of
reinforcements was dispatched to Bermuda, there to wait until the ice
cleared in the St. Lawrence. The United States, too, had time to rethink
its strategy – or lack of it – and to plan more carefully for the future.

It was not the war that the Americans, inspired and goaded by the eloquence of Henry Clay and his colleagues, had set out to fight and certainly not the glamorous adventure that Harrison's volunteers expected. The post-Revolutionary euphoria, which envisaged the citizen soldiers of a democratic nation marching off to sure victory over a handful of robot-like mercenaries and enslaved farmers, had dissipated. America had learned the lessons that most nations relearn at the start of every war – that valour is ephemeral, that the heroes of one war are the scapegoats of the next, that command is for the young, the vigorous, the imaginative, the professional. Nor does enthusiasm and patriotism alone win battles: untrained volunteers, no matter how fervent, cannot stand up to seasoned regulars, drilled to stand fast in moments of panic and to follow orders without question. It was time for the United States to drop its amateur standing now that it intended to do what its founding fathers had not prepared for – aggressive warfare.

It was clear that possession of the water held the key to victory. Britain, by seizing Michilimackinac and Detroit, both commanding narrow channels, effectively controlled all easy transit to the northwest and thus to the fur trade. Two other strong points, Kingston and Montreal, commanded the entrance to Lake Ontario and the St. Lawrence lifeline to the sea. And so, as winter gave way to spring, the ring of hammers on the Lakes announced a different kind of contest as both sides engaged in a shipbuilding race.

Immediately after Hull's defeat, Madison and Eustis had awoken to the fact that the disgraced commander's original proposals had been right. And so to Sackets Harbor that winter – the only available harbour at the eastern end of Lake Ontario – a new commander, Captain Isaac Chauncey, quickly dubbed a commodore, was dispatched with 700 seamen and marines and 140 ships' carpenters to help construct two fighting ships, each of thirty-two guns. Jesse Elliott, hero of the previous summer's attack, had added the captured *Caledonia* to the vessels he was already building. Brock had rightly seen that event as a serious and significant loss. At Erie, Pennsylvania, two twenty-gun brigs and several gunboats were also under construction. With Elliott's warships these formed the backbone of the fleet with which Oliver Hazard Perry would in the summer of 1813 seize control of the lake from the British, thus opening up Amherstburg and the valley of the Thames to American attack.

The British were also building ships – one big vessel at the protected harbour of Kingston, another at York, wide open to attack, a split decision that proved costly when Chauncey's fleet appeared off the capital in April. At Amherstburg a smaller vessel was under construction. But the British suffered from a lack of supplies, of mechanics, and, most important, of trained seamen. Already, following some skirmishing outside Kingston Harbour in November, control of Lake Ontario was in doubt. Was it possible that the upstart Americans could outsail, outmanoeuvre, and outfight the greatest maritime power in the world? On the Atlantic, in single engagements – the *United States* versus the *Macedonian* in October, the *Constitution* versus the *Java* in December – the Americans were the winners. After a season of reverses on land, these victories, though not significant in military terms, gave the country hope.

British strategy remained the same: to stay on the defensive. An attempt would be made to dislodge Harrison from his threatening position at Fort Meigs on the Maumee, but with Brock gone there was no hint of offensive warfare. The Americans planned to open the campaign with attacks on both Kingston and York to destroy the new warships, then to seize Fort George at the mouth of the Niagara and march on Fort Erie. By spring Dearborn had watered down this plan, eliminating Kingston, which was held to be too strong for an attack.

The United States remained deeply divided over the war. Following Napoleon's disastrous retreat from Moscow, the Russian minister in Washington proposed to Madison (now serving his second term as the result of the November election) that his emperor, Alexander I, mediate between the two belligerents. After all, with the Orders in Council out of the way the only real impediment to peace was the matter of impressment, and with the war in Europe apparently winding down, that would soon be of academic interest. Madison agreed, but before the issue could be negotiated, Alexander, to England's fury, made a separate peace with Napoleon. Russia, the British felt, like America before her had stabbed them in the back. And so the war went on.

The New England states continued, in effect, to be at peace with their neighbours in Britain's Atlantic colonies. But across the nation a new and savage emotion, which since the beginning of history has acted as a unifying force among peoples, was beginning to be felt. The contempt and disdain once felt for the British had been transformed into rage. Procter was the villain; his officers were seen as monsters. Harrison's troops, especially, thirsted for revenge and would get it finally when autumn reddened the leaves in the valley of the Thames.

In Kentucky, the failure at the Raisin cut deep. When the news reached Lexington, Governor Shelby was attending a theatrical performance. He hurried out as whispers of the defeat rippled from row to row. People began to leave, some in tears, all distressed, until by the play's third act the house was empty. Scarcely a family in the state was not touched in some way by the tragedy at Frenchtown. The idea of a swift victory was shattered. For hundreds of families, weeping over lost sons and lost illusions, the war that at the outset seemed almost like a sporting event had become a horror. Some did not learn for months whether their men were alive, dead, or in prison. Some never knew.

Captain Paschal Hickman's mother did not recover from the blow. "Sorely distressed about the massacre," in the words of her husband, "...she pined away and died on June 9, 1813."

Captain Hart's widow, Anna, suffered a similar end. Prostrated over her husband's fate, she was sent by relatives to New Orleans and then to New York in the hope that a change of scene would lighten her grief. It failed. She set out again for Lexington but could go no farther than Philadelphia, where she died at twenty-seven.

Lieutenant-Colonel Allen's widow, Jane, hoped against hope that her husband was not dead but a captive of the Indians. For eight years she watched and waited at her home on the Lexington-Louisville road, keeping the shutters open each night that he might see the candle she kept burning there. At last, with all hope extinguished, she, too, wasted away from grief. In February, 1821, she died.

It was not only in Kentucky that the tragedy struck home. All of America was dumbfounded. In the town of Erie, Pennsylvania, the citizens at a public meeting resolved to wear black crêpe on their arms and in their hats for ninety days out of respect for those who "gloriously fell in the field defending the only free government on earth." In Kentucky, a new slogan arose and was used to stimulate recruiting: *Remember the Raisin!* Nine counties were named in honour of nine officers slain on its frozen banks. Now the government's war loan, only two-thirds subscribed, was taken up in a new wave of patriotic fervour, partly as a result of the efforts of John Jacob Astor, whose own patriotism had been called in question as the result of his actions of the previous summer.

Lieutenant-Colonel Procter, the subject of almost universal excoriation in America, brushed off the massacre at the Raisin as he would an annoying insect. In his dispatch to Sheaffe he simply wrote that "the zeal and courage of the Indian Department never were more conspicuous than on this occasion, the Indian warriors fought with their usual courage." In a later report he referred to the massacre briefly and with regret but stated that the Kentucky soldiers too killed the wounded and took scalps; all perfectly true. That, however, scarcely justified the General Order issued at Quebec on February 8, which was enough to make the American prisoners grind their teeth:

> On this occasion, the Gallantry of Colonel Procter was most nobly displayed in his humane and unwearied exertions in securing the vanquished from the revenge of the Indian warriors.

That was not the view of some of Procter's people. Dr. Robert Richardson, two of whose sons fought at the Raisin, was outraged by the massacre and wrote to his father-in-law, John Askin, "We have not heard the last of this shameful transaction. I wish to god it could be contradicted."

Crowded into a small wood yard at Amherstburg, without tents, blankets, or fires, unprotected from rain and snow, Procter's prisoners shivered in their thin clothing for almost two days before being moved to a chilly warehouse. Eventually, they were marched five hundred miles by a roundabout route through the back country to Fort George, where the regulars were sent to Quebec City and the volunteers paroled to their homes under the guarantee that they would not take up arms against Great Britain or her allies until exchanged in the regular way.

Allies? When one Kentuckian sarcastically asked a British officer who Great Britain's allies were, the reply was evasive and shamefaced: Britain's allies, said the officer, were well known; he did not wish to continue the discussion. Nor did Henry Procter want to talk about the massacre, half convincing himself that it had never happened. In Detroit, when a group of citizens asked for an inquiry into the killing of the prisoners, he flew into a rage and demanded firm evidence that any such atrocity had occurred. Like Brock before him, Procter was a virtual prisoner of the Indians, whose American captives languished that spring in the villages of the Potawatomi. His own force, badly mauled at Frenchtown, was smaller than Harrison's on the Maumee. Indian support was essential to even the odds, and he knew that he would not get it if he tried to interfere with time-honoured rituals. He refused to bow to demands that the Indians release all their captives to him, agreeing to ransom them but for no more than five dollars a head – an empty gesture when the going rate in Detroit started at ten dollars and ran as high as eighty.

The Indians scattered that spring to their hunting-grounds. Tecumseh was still in the south, pursuing his proposal to weld the tribes into a new confederacy. The British saw eye to eye with his plan for an Indian state north of the Ohio; it would act as a buffer between the two English-speaking nations on the North American continent and make future wars unattractive. The idea had long been at the core of British Indian policy.

But the Indians were soon ignored. In the official dispatches they got short shrift. The names of white officers who acted with conspicuous gallantry were invariably recorded, those of the Indian chieftains never. Even the name of Tecumseh, after Brock's initial report, vanishes from the record. Yet these painted tribesmen helped save Canada's hide in 1812:

At Michilimackinac and Detroit, their presence was decisive. In each case the threat of an Indian attack broke the morale of the defenders and brought about unconditional surrender.

At the River aux Canards and Turkey Creek, Tecumseh's warriors, acting as a screen, contributed to Hull's decision not to attack Fort Amherstburg. At Brownstown and Maguaga, the same mixed group of tribesmen was essential to the British success in preventing Captain Brush's supply train from getting through to Detroit.

At Queenston Heights, the Mohawk advance guard so terrified Scott's militiamen that hundreds fled to the woods before the battle was joined, while the forward American scouts were prevented from probing the strength and position of Sheaffe's forces. The war-whoops of

Norton's followers, echoing across the gorge, sent a chill through thousands more, confirming them in their refusal to cross the river.

And at Frenchtown, the Wyandot and Potawatomi turned Winchester's right flank and caused the surrender of his entire force.

Perhaps if Brock and Tecumseh had lived, the Indian claims might have received greater consideration. Brock's attitude to the tribes was ambivalent, but he believed in keeping his promises; his dispatches to Prevost underline his concern for the Indian position. But with Brock gone, Tecumseh's death at the Thames in the fall of 1813 (the Indians fighting on after Procter and the British fled) meant an end to Shawnee aspirations for a native confederacy.

It was among the white settlers in Upper Canada that a new confederacy was taking shape. There the war was no longer looked on with indifference. In the muddy capital of York a new leader was about to emerge in the person of the Reverend Dr. John Strachan, perhaps the most significant and influential Canadian of his time, a product of the War of 1812. In December of that first war year Strachan presided over the formation of the Loyal and Patriotic Society of Upper Canada, organized to provide winter clothing for the militia and, later, to help their families and others who had suffered from the war. The directors of the Loyal and Patriotic Society included Strachan's protégés and the elite of York – the tight ruling group that would soon be known as the Family Compact.

Thus the key words in Upper Canada were "loyalty" and "patriotism" – loyalty to the British way of life as opposed to American "radical" democracy and republicanism. Brock – the man who wanted to establish martial law and abandon habeas corpus – represented these virtues. Canonized by the same caste that organized the Loyal and Patriotic Society, he came to represent Canadian order as opposed to American anarchy – "peace, order and good government" rather than the more hedonistic "life, liberty and the pursuit of happiness." Had not Upper Canada been saved from the invader by appointed leaders who ruled autocratically? In America, the politicians became generals; in British North America, the opposite held true.

This attitude – that the British way is preferable to the American; that certain sensitive positions are better filled by appointment than by election; that order imposed from above has advantages over grass-roots democracy (for which read "licence" or "anarchy"); that a ruling elite often knows better than the body politic – flourished as a result of an invasion repelled. Out of it, shaped by an emerging nationalism and tempered by rebellion, grew that special form of state paternalism that makes the Canadian way of life significantly different from the more individualistic American way. Thus, in a psychological as well as in a political sense, we are Canadians and not Americans because of a foolish war that scarcely anyone wanted or needed, but which, once launched, none knew how to stop.

CODA: *William Atherton's War*

MICHIGAN TERRITORY, April, 1813. To William Atherton, captive of the Potawatomi, home seems to be on another planet. Adopted into a Potawatomi family to replace a son killed at Frenchtown, he now lives as an Indian, wears Indian buckskin, hews to Indian customs. He hunts with bow and arrow, engages in the corn dance, sleeps in a wigwam, exists on boiled corn and bristly hogmeat. He neither hears nor speaks English.

His one contact with civilization is a tattered Lexington newspaper, found among the Indians' effects. This is his sole comfort: he reads and re-reads it, clinging to the brittle pages as a reminder that somewhere beyond the brooding, snow-covered forests there really is another world — a world he once took for granted but which comes back to him now as if in a dream. Will he ever see it again? As winter gives way to spring, Atherton gives way to despair, stealing out of camp for moments of solitude when he can think of home and weep without being discovered.

In May, the Indians head for Detroit. On the way, they encounter another band which has just captured a young American surgeon in battle. What battle? Atherton has no way of knowing that an American fleet has captured York and that the British have badly mauled Harrison's army during the siege of Fort Meigs on the Maumee. The two men converse eagerly in the first English that Atherton has heard in three months; then the other departs, Atherton believes to his death.

They reach Amherstburg, but Atherton has no hope of escape. With his long swarthy face and his matted brown hair, uncut for months, he is just another Indian to the British, who fail to notice his blue eyes. When the band moves across to Spring Wells to draw rations at the British commissary, Atherton's Indian father learns, with delight, that his new son can write. He has him double the original number of family members on the chit, thus increasing the handout of provisions. Again, the British do not realize that Atherton is white.

He loses track of time. Crawling with vermin, half-starved, with no hope of escape from the family that nurtures but also guards him, he throws himself on their mercy and pleads to be ransomed. To his surprise, his Indian father agrees, albeit reluctantly. It is clear that Atherton has become part of the family, more a son than a captive. They cannot refuse him, even though it means losing him. Eventually, in Detroit, they find a man who will give a pony for him. Atherton bids his Indian parents goodbye — not without sorrow, for they have, in their fashion, been kind — and becomes a prisoner of war. All that summer he is lodged in a British guardhouse, almost naked, sleeping on the floor with a log for a pillow, wondering about the course of the war.

Fort George is assaulted and taken by the Americans. At Stoney Creek, a British force captures two American generals who mistake them for friends in the darkness. The Caughnawagas trounce the Americans at Beaver Dams, the battle that makes a heroine of Laura Secord. Of these triumphs and defeats Atherton knows nothing. Only when his captors return from the unsuccessful British siege of Fort Stephenson at Lower Sandusky, their faces peppered with small shot, does he have an inkling that beyond the guardhouse walls, all along the border, men are still fighting and dying.

Summer gives way to fall. On September 10, Atherton and his fellow prisoners can hear the rumble of heavy guns reverberating across Lake Erie. Clearly, a naval battle is raging, but his captors refuse details. At last a private soldier whispers the truth: Oliver Hazard Perry has met the enemy and they are his. The British fleet is obliterated. Erie is an American lake.

The victory touches off a major retreat. The British pack up hastily in the face of Harrison's advancing army. Atherton can hardly wait for the Kentucky forces to arrive and free him, but that is not to be. The prisoners are hurried across to the Canadian shore and herded up the Thames Valley to Burlington, then on to York, Kingston, Montreal.

It seems as if the entire city has turned out to stare at them — verminous, shaggy, half-starved after a journey of nine hundred miles. As Atherton trudges down the cobbled streets he notices the doors and windows crammed with curious women. In the jail they are given a little "Yankee beef," taunted with the fact that it has been purchased by the British from Americans trading with the enemy.

Two weeks later they are sent to Quebec City. Here, for the first time, Atherton learns that Harrison has captured Fort Amherstburg, rolled up the Thames, won the Battle of Moravian Town, and presided over the death of his enemy, Tecumseh.

The Kentuckians' reputation has preceded them. The Quebeckers think of them as a species of wildman — savage forest creatures, half-human, half-beast. They crowd to the jail, peering at the captives as they would at animals in a zoo, astonished, even disappointed, to find they do not live up to their billing. One man gazes at them for some minutes, then delivers the general verdict: "Why, they look just like other people."

Beyond the prison, the war rages on. The two-pronged American attack designed to seize Montreal fizzles out at Châteauguay and Crysler's Farm, but Atherton is only dimly aware of it. Fall turns to winter, with both sides once again deadlocked along the border. As the spring campaign opens, a more cheerful piece of news reaches Quebec: there is to be a general prisoner exchange. Eventually Atherton is released and sent back across the border, only a few weeks before the war's bloodiest battle at Lundy's Lane. In Pittsburgh he encounters a group of vaguely familiar men — British prisoners of war. Who are they? Where has he seen them before? He remembers: these are the soldiers who were once his guards when he was a captive in Detroit. It all seems a long time ago.

Atherton reaches his home at Shelbyville, Kentucky, on June 20, 1814, almost two years to the day since war was first declared. The invasion goes on. The battles of Chippawa and Lundy's Lane, the long siege of Fort Erie, and the naval encounter on Lake Champlain all lie ahead. But Atherton is out of it. He has had enough, will not fight again.

His story is not unique. Eighty or ninety Kentuckians have been captured by the Potawatomi braves, and of these a good number have been adopted into Indian families. Timothy Mallory has all his hair shaved off except for a scalp lock, his face painted half black, half red, his ears pierced for rings. John Davenport is painted, adorned with earrings, bracelets, and a silver band wound round his shaved skull. "We make an Indian out of you," one of his captors promises, "and by'n by you have squaw, by'n by you have a gun and horse and go hunting."

Both these men live as Indians for several months and like Atherton, who prefers his treatment by the Indians to that of the British (he finds them "brave, generous, hospitable, kind and...honest"), are surprised to discover that their Indian families are genuinely fond of them, that the women go out of their way to protect them when the braves indulge in drinking bouts, and that when at last they are ransomed, the Indians are clearly reluctant to part with them.

No one knows exactly how many Kentucky volunteers are held captive by the natives, adopted into families that have lost sons in the battle. No one knows exactly how many have escaped or been ransomed. It is possible, even probable, that as the war rolls on there are some Kentuckians who have gone entirely native, taken Indian wives and removed themselves from white society.

There is irony in this; but then it has been a war of irony and paradox — a war fought over a grievance that was removed before the fighting began; a war that all claimed to have won except the real victors, who, being Indians, were really losers; a war designed to seize by force a nation that could have been attached by stealth. Are there in the forests of Michigan among the Potawatomi – those veterans of Tippecanoe – certain warriors of lighter skin and alien background? If so, that is the final irony. Ever since Jefferson's day it has been official American policy to try to turn the Indians into white men. Who can blame the Indians if, in their last, desperate, doomed resistance, they should manage in some measure to turn the tables?

Sources and Acknowledgements
Notes
Select Bibliography
Index

Sources and Acknowledgements

This work is based largely on primary sources – official documents and correspondence, military reports and records, public speeches, private letters, diaries, journals, memoirs, and contemporary newspaper accounts. I have as well made a reconnaissance of those battlefields whose sites have not been obliterated by the advance of civilization.

As every lawyer knows, witnesses to any event rarely agree; thus it has often been necessary to compare various conflicting reports to arrive at an approximation of the truth. Confused recollections of even minor skirmishes are not easy to untangle. Each participant sees the engagement from his own point of view. Opposing generals invariably underestimate their own strength and overestimate that of the enemy, seeking in a variety of ways to shape their reports to make themselves seem brilliant. The memories of junior officers and common soldiers are distorted by the heat of the moment and often clouded by the passage of time. Fortunately, in almost every case there is such a richness of material available on the events of 1812–13 (much of the human detail ignored by historians) that it is possible to arrive at a reasonably clear and accurate account of what occurred, not only tactically and politically but also in the hearts and minds of the participants.

For each incident I have had to ask myself these questions: was the narrator – diarist, officer, soldier, correspondent, memoirist – present at the event described? How soon after the event did he set down his account of what happened? How competent was he as a witness? Can some of his statements be cross-checked against those of others to assess his credibility? A memoir written thirty years after the events, obviously, cannot be considered as reliable as one scribbled down on the spot.

Students of the war may be surprised that I have set aside John Richardson's famous account of the death of the young American captive after the battle of Brownstown (page 149) in favour of a less well known description by Thomas Verchères de Boucherville. Richardson, after all, belongs to the pantheon of early Canadian novelists; de Boucherville was only a fur trader and storekeeper. The two versions were both set down many years after the event and differ considerably in detail, Richardson's being the more dramatic. But a close reading of his account reveals that the future novelist, who was only fifteen at the time, was not actually present at the scene he describes while de Boucherville was. De Boucherville was also twelve years older and experienced in Indian customs. There can be no doubt that his version is the more reliable.

For the leading British, American, and Canadian figures in the war, a wealth of easily authenticated biographical and background material is available. But for the Indians, with two exceptions, there is very little. This was really their war; for them the stakes were higher, the victories more significant, the defeats more devastating. One would have liked to know more about Roundhead, Walk-in-the-Water, Black Bird, Little Turtle, and all the other shadowy tribesmen who appear briefly and often violently on the stage. History, alas, ignores them. They have come down to us as faceless "savages," brandishing their tomahawks, shouting their war cries, scalping their victims, melting into the forests.

Only Tecumseh and to some degree his brother, the Prophet, stand out as individuals—flesh-and-blood figures with human strengths, human weaknesses, and human emotions. Here, nevertheless, one must tread cautiously, for so much of their story—especially that of their early years—is overlaid with legend. It was Charles Goltz who recently revealed in his superb doctoral dissertation on the Shawnee brothers that one widely accepted tale of Tecumseh's early years was pure myth.

Most of his biographers have tried to explain Tecumseh's hatred of the white man with an anecdote about his father's death. As the story goes, the father was killed by a group of white hunters when he refused to act as their guide and died in the arms of his son, denouncing the faithlessness of white men. There is much detail: the mother at the graveside urging the young Shawnee to seek eternal revenge; Tecumseh's yearly visits to the scene to renew his pledge; and so on. But, as Goltz discovered, this web of convincing evidence was the invention of an Indiana woman who, in 1823, entered it in a fiction contest sponsored by the *New York Mirror*. The following year a Canadian magazine reprinted the tale, and it became accepted as history.

In compiling and sifting all this mountain of material I have again depended upon the extraordinary energy and wise counsel of the indefatigable Barbara Sears, for whom the term "research assistant" is scarcely adequate. I cannot praise her labours too highly. She and I wish to thank a number of people and institutions who helped make this work possible.

First, the Metropolitan Library of Toronto, with special thanks to Edith Firth and her staff at the Canadian History Department, to Michael Pearson and the staff of the History Department, and to Norma Dainard, Keith Alcock, and the staff of the newspaper section. Thanks also to Robert Fraser of the editorial staff of the *Dictionary of Canadian Biography*.

Second, the Public Archives of Canada, with special thanks to the staff of the manuscript division, to Patricia Kennedy of the Pre-Confederation Archives, to Peter Bower, Gordon Dodds, Bruce Wilson, and Brian Driscoll of British Archives, and to Glenn T. Wright and Grace Campbell of the Public Records Division; the Ontario Archives; the Library of Congress Manuscript Division; the Filson Club of Kentucky; and Peter Burroughs of Dalhousie University.

Third, the U.S. National Archives, Washington; the Buffalo Historical Society (Art Detmers); the Chatham Kent Museum (Mary Creasey); the Historical Society of Pennsylvania; the Indiana State Library; the Kentucky Historical Society; the Wisconsin Historical Society; the Lundy's Lane Historical Society; the Niagara Historical Society; the Niagara Parks Commission's Fort Erie staff; Parks Canada's staff at Fort George and Fort Malden; Robert S. Allen and Elizabeth Vincent at Parks Canada, Ottawa; the Public Record Office, London, England; the Tennessee State Museum; Esther Summers; Bob Green; Paul Romney; and Professor H.N. Muller.

I am especially grateful for the useful comments and suggestions made by Janice Tyrwhitt, Charles Templeton, Roger Hall, Elsa Franklin, Janet Berton, and Leslie Hannon, who read the manuscript at various stages. The several versions were typed by Ennis Armstrong, Catherine Black, and Lynne McCartney. I was rescued from certain grammatical imbecilities by my wife, Janet, and from various textual inconsistencies by my editor Janet Craig, for whose unsparing eye and great common sense I am specially grateful. The errors that remain are mine.

Kleinburg, Ontario
March, 1980

Notes

Abbreviations used:

ASPFR   American State Papers, Foreign Relations
ASPIA   American State Papers, Indian Affairs
ASPMA   American State Papers, Military Affairs
LC   Library of Congress
MTPL   Metropolitan Toronto Public Library
PAC   Public Archives of Canada
PAO   Public Archives of Ontario
SN   Secretary of the Navy
SW   Secretary of War
USNA   United States National Archives

Preview: Porter Hanks's War

page	line	
13	31	Brannan, pp. 34–35, Hanks to SW, 4 Aug. 1812.
14	11	Ibid.; May, p. 14.
14	35	Brannan, pp. 34–35, Hanks to SW, 4 Aug. 1812.
14	38	Ibid.
15	10	Jefferson, VI: 75–76, Jefferson to Duane, 4 Aug. 1812.

Overview

page	line	
20	36	Bonney, p. 269, Sheaffe to Stephen Van Rensselaer, 16 Oct. 1812.
21	3	Kirby, p. 157.
23	18	PAC, RG 8, vol. 1219, p. 274, Prevost to Bathurst, 27 Aug. 1814.
23	23	PAC, MG 24 A57, vol. 19, Sherbrooke proclamation, 3 July 1812.
24	9	Quaife, *Askin Papers*, p. 709, [Askin] to McGill, 17 July 1812; p. 729, Brush to Askin, 11 Aug. 1812; p. 729, Brush to Askin, 24 Aug. 1812.
24	20	Quoted in Perkins, *Prologue*, p. 415.
25	8	Perkins, *Prologue*, pp. 90–93.
28	12	PAO, Register of persons connected with high treason during the War of 1812 with the U.S.A.

page	line	
28	24	PAC, RG 19 E5(a), vol. 3739, file 2, n.d. General abstract, claims for damages; *Upper Canada Gazette*, supplement, 3 June 1824.

Prelude to Invasion: 1807–1811

page	line	
35	21	U.S. Congress, ASPFR, III: 17, Barron to SN, 7 April 1807.
37	2	Ibid., 18, Barron to SN, 23 June 1807, and enclosures; p. 19, return of dead and wounded; p. 19, Hunt to Gordon, 23 June 1807; p. 19, Smith, Smith and Brooker to Gordon, 23 June 1807; p. 21, L.W. Tazewell, report of court of inquiry; Steel, pp. 245–49.
37	9	Steel, pp. 250–52.
37	12	Quoted in Perkins, *Prologue*, p. 428.
38	3	Cruikshank, "Some Unpublished Letters," p. 19, Brock to Dunn, 17 July 1807.
38	12	Quoted in Burt, p. 243.
38	30	Burt, pp. 242–46.
39	1	Tupper, p. 64, Brock to Gordon, 6 Sept. 1807.
39	11	Harrison, I: 235, Harrison speech, 17 Aug. 1807.
39	20	Ibid., p. 236.

page line
40 19 Ibid., p. 234.
40 40 Jefferson, IV: 472, Jefferson to Harrison, 27 Feb. 1803.
41 12 Harrison, I: 251, Harrison to the Shawanese, Aug. 1807.
41 32 Ibid., pp. 183–84, Harrison to the Delawares, early 1806.
42 10 Ibid., p. 251, Harrison to the Shawanese, Aug. 1807.
43 17 Randall, pp. 462–63.
43 28 LC, Foster MSS, Foster to his mother, 31 July 1807.
43 32 Ibid., Foster to his mother, 20 Sept. 1806.
43 33 Foster, *Two Duchesses*, p. 228, Foster to his mother, 30 June 1805.
44 4 LC, Foster MSS, Foster to his mother, 16 July 1807.
44 9 Foster, *Two Duchesses*, p. 233, Foster to his mother, 30 July 1805.
44 10 Ibid., p. 240, Foster to his mother, 22 Feb. 1805.
44 10 Ibid., p. 233, Foster to his mother, 30 July 1805.
44 12 Ibid., p. 247, Foster to his mother, Nov. 1805.
45 2 LC, Foster MSS, Journal.
45 36 Quoted in Perkins, *Prologue*, p. 7.
45 40 Quoted in Perkins, *Prologue*, p. 187.
46 34 PAC, RG 10, vol. 11, Gore's speech, 11 July 1808.
47 18 PAC, RG 10, vol. 11, Indian reply, 13 July 1808.
48 1 Horsman, *Expansion*, p. 146.
48 4 Ibid.
48 17 Allen, p. 63.
48 28 Horsman, "British Indian Policy," pp. 53, 56.
49 23 PAC, RG 10, vol. 11, Gore to Craig, 27 July 1808.
50 13 Goltz.
50 24 Harrison, I: 365, Journal, 4 Oct. 1809.
51 18 Ibid., p. 367.
51 30 Ibid., p. 368.
51 35 Ibid., p. 389, Harrison to SW, 3 Nov. 1809.

51 36 Ibid., p. 376, Journal, 22 Sept. 1809.
52 2 Ibid., p. 389, Harrison to SW, 3 Nov. 1809.
52 12 Cleaves, p. 68.
52 25 Harrison, I: 419, Harrison to SW, 25 April 1810.
52 28 Ibid., p. 450, Harrison to SW, 25 July 1810.
52 41 Ibid., p. 448, Harrison to the Prophet, 19 July 1810.
53 4 Ibid., pp. 448–49.
53 22 Ibid., p. 456, Harrison to SW, 6 Aug. 1810.
53 23 Ibid.
54 10 Tucker, *Tecumseh*, p. 159.
54 15 Hatch, p. 113.
54 27 Tucker, *Tecumseh*, p. 160; Drake, pp. 125–26.
54 38 Tucker, *Tecumseh*, pp. 161, 348.
55 6 Harrison, I: 460, Harrison to SW, 22 Aug. 1810.
55 22 Hatch, pp. 99–100.
55 40 Klinck, p. 73.
56 3 Tucker, *Tecumseh*, pp. 163, 348.
56 12 Harrison, I: 466, Tecumseh's speech, 20 Aug. 1810.
56 17 Ibid., p. 463.
56 28 Ibid., p. 459, Harrison to SW, 22 Aug. 1810.
57 3 Cleaves, p. 74.
57 10 Harrison, I: 461, Harrison to SW, 22 Aug. 1810.
57 12 Ibid., pp. 461, 468.
57 29 Tucker, *Tecumseh*, pp. 166, 349.
57 36 Harrison, I: 469, Tecumseh's speech, 21 Aug. 1810.
60 20 Draper MSS, Tecumseh Papers, 2YY, p. 120, Ruddell's account of Tecumseh.
60 35 Ibid., 12YY, 1821, Drake's notes on conversation with Anthony Shane.
61 4 Ibid.
61 12 Ibid.
61 25 Tucker, *Tecumseh*, pp. 77–80; Randall, p. 455.
61 29 Draper MSS, Tecumseh Papers, 12YY, 1821, Drake's notes on conversation with Anthony Shane.

page line

62 35 Harrison, I: 239, Wells to Harrison, 20 Aug. 1807.

64 3 PAC, CO 42/351/42, Elliott to Claus, 16 Nov. 1810, encl. Tecumseh's speech, 15 Nov. 1810.

64 22 Harrison, I: 447, Harrison to SW, 18 June 1810.

65 13 PAC, CO 42/351/ Elliott to Claus, 16 Nov. 1810.

65 22 Quoted in Goltz, Craig to Moirier, 25 Nov. 1811.

66 3 Weld, pp. 192–96.

66 14 Tupper, pp. 94–96, Brock to Craig, 27 Feb. 1811.

66 19 "Collections of Papers," pp. 280–81, Craig to Gore, 2 Feb. 1811.

67 15 Harrison, I: 546, Harrison to SW, 6 Aug. 1811.

68 2 Dawson, p. 184.

68 19 Drake, pp. 142–43.

68 33 Harrison, I: 549, Harrison to SW, 7 Aug. 1811.

69 6 Ibid.

69 28 Harrison, I: 527, Harrison to SW, 2 July 1811.

69 37 Ibid., p. 536, SW to Harrison, 20 July 1811.

70 13 Ibid., p. 550, Harrison to SW, 7 Aug. 1811.

70 29 Ibid., p. 558, Daviess to Harrison, 24 Aug. 1811.

70 36 " Jo Daviess," p. 355.

72 1 Harrison, I: 620, Harrison to SW, 18 Nov. 1811.

73 2 Ibid., p. 703, statement of William Brigham.

73 10 Ibid., p. 702, statement of Sergeant Orr.

73 25 Ibid., pp. 691–92, Harrison to Dr. John Scott, Dec. 1811.

74 21 Cleaves, pp. 100–101.

74 30 Ibid., p. 101.

74 36 Ibid.

75 4 Lossing, *Field-book*, p. 205.

75 10 Harrison, I: 703, statement of William Brigham.

75 15 Ibid., p. 624, Harrison to SW, 18 Nov. 1811.

75 22 Ibid., p. 702; Walker, pp. 24–25.

page line

76 10 Cruikshank, *Documents Relating to the Invasion*, p. 6, Elliott to Brock, 12 Jan. 1812.

76 30 U.S. Congress, ASPIA, I: 808, opinions of Gov. Howard and Gen. Clark, 3 March 1812.

76 38 Tucker, *Tecumseh*, p. 230.

Prelude to Invasion: 1812

82 29 Tupper, p. 151, Brock to Prevost, 12 Feb. 1812.

83 5 Nursey, p. 82.

83 19 Tupper, p. 153, Brock to Prevost, Feb. 1812.

83 25 Ibid., p. 153.

84 2 Ibid., p. 125, Brock to Prevost, 2 Dec. 1811.

84 15 Ibid., p. 95, Brock to Craig, 27 Feb. 1811.

84 16 Ibid., p. 195, Brock to Prevost, 3 July 1812.

84 34 Ibid., pp. 123–30, Brock to Prevost, 2 Dec. 1811.

85 24 Wood, I: 423, ? to Dickson, 27 Feb. 1812.

85 35 Caffrey, p. 142.

86 6 Ibid.

86 23 Quoted in Perkins, *Prologue*, p. 275.

86 29 LC, Foster MSS, Foster to his mother, 2 Jan. 1812.

86 33 Ibid., Journal, 15 April 1812.

87 13 Quoted in Brown, p. 55.

87 17 LC, Foster MSS, Journal, 29 and 30 Jan. 1812.

87 18 Ibid., Journal, 31 Jan. 1812.

87 28 U.S. Congress, ASPFR, III: 546–47, Craig to Henry, 6 Feb. 1809.

87 34 Morison, pp. 271–72.

88 4 Quoted in Cruikshank, *Political Adventures*, p. 126.

88 15 LC, Foster MSS, Journal, 19 Feb. 1812.

88 22 Ibid.

88 26 Ibid., Journal, 20 Jan. 1812, 5 Feb. 1812.

89 20 Cruikshank, *Documents Relating to the Invasion*, p. 22, Hull to SW, 6 March 1812.

90 3 Mahon, p. 44.

page line
90 17 USNA, M221/43, Dearborn to SW, 28 July 1812.

90 34 LC, Foster MSS, Journal, 15 April 1812.

90 37 Foster, *Two Duchesses*, p. 360, Foster to his mother, 18 April 1812.

91 1 PAC, CO 42/146/120, Prevost to Liverpool, 3 April 1812.

91 4 LC, Foster MSS, Journal, 15 April 1812.

91 19 Quoted in Cramer, p. 128.

91 31 Ibid.

92 28 Hull, *Memoirs*, p. 34.

93 4 McAfee, p. 51.

93 16 Cramer, p. 130.

93 23 Ibid.

93 28 Cruikshank, "General Hull's Invasion," p. 216.

93 38 Hull, *Report*, p. 136.

94 8 Ibid., Hull's defence, p. 57.

94 13 USNA, M221/47/M341, McArthur, Cass, Findley to SW, 18 July 1812; M221/45/H271, Miller to SW, 12 June 1812.

94 33 Hull, *Report*, pp. 124–25; USNA, M221/44/H275, Hull to SW, 18 June 1812.

94 40 Quaife, *War*, pp. 187–88.

95 14 Ibid., pp. 208–9; Walker, pp. 46–47.

96 13 Hull, *Memoirs*, p. 35.

96 23 Quoted in Perkins, *Prologue*, p. 434.

96 37 Quoted in Perkins, *Prologue*, pp. 433–34.

97 26 Brown, p. 52.

97 40 Tucker, *Tecumseh*, p. 114.

98 11 Quoted in Perkins, *Prologue*, p. 433.

99 9 Green, *Washington*, p. 56.

99 37 Quoted in Perkins, *Prologue*, p. 427.

100 3 Quoted in Pratt, *Expansionists*, pp. 51, 140.

100 8 Ibid., p. 153.

100 13 *Kentucky Gazette*, 3 Sept. 1811.

Michilimackinac

103 10 Quoted in Cruikshank, "General Hull's Invasion," p. 247.

page line
103 20 Wood, I: 424, Dickson to ?, 18 June 1812.

104 6 Ibid., p. 425, speech of Wabasha.

105 3 Ibid., pp. 426–27, statement of Robert Dickson.

105 15 Pike, I: 64–65.

105 17 Powell, p. 157.

106 14 Quoted in Chalou, p. 72, *Louisiana Gazette*, 6 June 1812.

106 23 Vincent.

106 39 Ibid.

107 8 Wood, I: 440, Roberts to Clegg, 29 July 1812.

107 12 PAC, RG 8, vol. 789, p. 109, D. Mitchell note, 13 June 1813.

107 26 Quaife, *Askin Papers*, p. 569, John Askin Jr. to his father, 1 Sept. 1807.

107 36 Porter, p. 258.

108 7 Quoted in Porter, p. 249.

108 23 Ibid., p. 258.

108 30 Wood, I: 448, observations of Toussaint Pothier.

108 32 Ibid., p. 430, Roberts to Brock, 12 July 1812.

108 35 Ibid.

109 2 Ibid., p. 429, Roberts to Brock, 12 July 1812.

109 17 PAC, RG 8, vol. 676, p. 183, Roberts to Adjutant General, 17 July 1812; Wood, I: 433, Roberts to Brock, 17 July 1812.

109 33 Wood, I: pp. 432–34, Roberts to Baynes, 17 July 1812; pp. 436–37, John Askin Jr. to Claus, 18 July 1812; pp. 450–51, observations of Toussaint Pothier; Kellogg, pp. 135–36; Grignon, pp. 268–69.

110 14 Kellogg, pp. 138–39.

110 35 Wood, I: 434, Roberts to Brock, 17 July 1812.

111 3 Ibid., pp. 436–37, John Askin Jr. to Claus, 18 July 1812.

111 9 Dobbins, p. 303.

112 2 Wood, I: 442, return of provisions, 30 July 1812; Quaife, *Askin Papers*, p. 730, John Askin Jr. to his father, 16 Sept. 1812.

112 8 Wood, III, part I, p. 7, General Order, Montreal, 29 May 1814.

112 29 PAC, RG 8, vol. 91, 15 Jan.

page	line	
139	*38*	Ibid., p. 45.
140	*12*	Cruikshank, *Documents Relating to the Invasion*, p. 76.
140	*15*	Richardson, *Richardson's War*, p. 32.
140	*30*	Beall, p. 799.
141	*3*	Ibid., p. 800.
141	*7*	Ibid., p. 802.
141	*16*	Hull, *Report*, p. 135.
141	*18*	Cruikshank, *Documents Relating to the Invasion*, pp. 185–86, Hull to SW, 26 Aug. 1812.
141	*36*	Beall, p. 805.
142	*10*	Cruikshank, *Documents Relating to the Invasion*, pp. 195–96, Brock, speech on opening legislature.
142	*13*	Ibid., p. 75, Brock to Prevost, 20 July 1812.
142	*21*	Ibid., p. 93, Talbot to Brock, 27 July 1812.
142	*28*	Quoted in Hamil, p. 46.
142	*32*	Cruikshank, *Documents Relating to the Invasion*, p. 196, Brock, speech on opening the legislature.
143	*2*	Cruikshank, *Documentary History*, III: 152, Brock to Baynes, 29 July 1812.
143	*8*	Ibid., p. 146, Brock to Prevost, 26 July 1812.
143	*12*	Ibid.
143	*19*	Cruikshank, *Documents Relating to the Invasion*, p. 196, Brock, speech on opening the legislature.
143	*24*	Ibid., pp. 119–20, Brock to Baynes, 4 Aug. 1812.
144	*20*	Ibid., p. 119.
144	*25*	Cruikshank, *Documentary History*, III: 152, Brock to Baynes, 29 July 1812.
145	*21*	Cruikshank, *Documents Relating to the Invasion*, p. 82, Brock, proclamation, 22 July 1812.
145	*30*	Ibid., p. 120, Brock to Baynes, 4 Aug. 1812.
145	*37*	Ibid., p. 197, Brock, speech on opening the legislature.
148	*25*	Lucas, *Journal*, pp. 46–51.
149	*34*	Quaife, *War*, pp. 92–93.
150	*17*	Hull, *Report*, p. 57.
150	*20*	Lucas, *Journal*, p. 52.
150	*22*	Quaife, *War*, p. 277.
150	*26*	Ibid.
151	*2*	Hull, *Memoirs*, p. 61.
151	*33*	Hull, *Report*, p. 58.
151	*36*	Hull, *Memoirs*, p. 64.
152	*2*	Cruikshank, *Documents Relating to the Invasion*, p. 219, Cass to SW, 10 Sept. 1812.
152	*5*	Hatch, p. 35.
152	*7*	Lucas, *Journal*, p. 105.
152	*19*	PAC, CO 42/147/80, Prevost to Liverpool, 5 Aug. 1812.
152	*23*	Ibid.
152	*34*	Ibid.
153	*40*	U.S. Congress, ASPMA, I: 323, Strong to Eustis, 5 Aug. 1812.
154	*7*	Ibid., pp. 325–26, Smith to Eustis, 2 July 1812.
154	*13*	Cruikshank, *Documents Relating to the Invasion*, p. 40, SW to Dearborn, 26 June 1812.
154	*21*	USNA, M221/43, Dearborn to SW, 13 July 1812.
154	*25*	Quoted in Adams, VI: 308, Eustis to Dearborn, 9 July 1812.
154	*30*	USNA, M221/43, Dearborn to SW, 13 July 1812.
154	*36*	Ibid., Dearborn to SW, 28 July 1812.
155	*31*	PAC, RG 8, vol. 677, pp. 31–32, Baynes to Prevost, 12 Aug. 1812, encl. report.
155	*39*	Ibid., p. 30.
156	*11*	Cruikshank, *Documents Relating to the Invasion*, p. 128, Dearborn to SW, 9 Aug. 1812.
156	*15*	Ibid., p. 127.
157	*23*	PAC, RG 8, vol. 677, pp. 33–34, Baynes to Prevost, 12 Aug. 1812, encl. report.
157	*33*	Ibid., p. 35.
158	*13*	Ibid., p. 37.
158	*22*	Cruikshank, *Documents Relating to the Invasion*, p. 129, Dearborn to Hull, 9 Aug. 1812.
159	*3*	Quaife, *War*, p. 94.
159	*26*	Quaife, "Brownstown," p. 74.
160	*5*	Richardson, *Richardson's War*, p. 34.
160	*17*	Quaife, *War*, p. 96.
160	*19*	Ibid.

page line

160 37 Ibid., p. 97.
161 3 Richardson, *Richardson's War*, p. 37.
161 5 Ibid.
161 12 Quaife, *War*, p. 97.
161 20 Ibid.; Quaife, "Brownstown," p. 75.
161 33 Quaife, "Brownstown," p. 77.
162 35 Quaife, *War*, pp. 103–5.
162 37 Cruikshank, *Documents Relating to the Invasion*, pp. 139–41, Hull to SW, 13 Aug. 1812.
163 8 Hull, *Report*, pp. 107–8.
163 10 Pearkes, p. 459.
163 21 Cruikshank, *Documents Relating to the Invasion*, p. 136, Procter to Brock, 11 Aug. 1812; p. 141, return of killed and wounded at Maguaga; p. 140, Hull to SW, 13 Aug. 1812.
163 24 Ibid., p. 195, Brock to Liverpool, 29 Aug. 1812, enclosure A.
163 32 Ibid., p. 192.
164 9 Ibid., pp. 130–31, Macdonald to Cameron, 10 Aug. 1812; Wood, I: 533, Askin Journal.
164 16 Wood, I: 535, Askin Journal; Pearkes, p. 459.
164 24 Cruikshank, *Documents Relating to the Invasion*, p. 193, Brock to Liverpool, 29 Aug. 1812.
164 31 Tupper, p. 259.
165 4 Wood, I: 534–35, Askin Journal; p. 548, McCay Diary.
165 14 Tupper, p. 243.
166 2 Ibid.
166 11 Cruikshank, *Documents Relating to the Invasion*, p. 192, Brock to Liverpool, 29 Aug. 1812.
166 12 Tupper, p. 262.
166 19 Tucker, *Tecumseh*, p. 264.
166 37 Tupper, pp. 260–61.
167 5 Nursey, p. 118; Tupper, p. 244.
167 18 Tucker, *Tecumseh*, p. 265; Nursey, pp. 118–19.
167 27 Tupper, p. 245.
167 37 Cruikshank, *Documents Relating to the Invasion*, p. 142, District General Order, 14 Aug. 1812.
168 10 Hull, *Report*, p. 135.
169 12 Lucas, *Journal*, pp. 59–60.
169 21 Cramer, p. 132; Van Deusen, p. 579.

169 33 Cruikshank, *Documents Relating to the Invasion*, p. 137, Cass to Meigs, 12 Aug. 1812; p. 219, Cass to SW, 10 Sept. 1812.
169 34 Ibid., p. 138.
170 18 Lossing, *Field-book*, p. 285.
170 21 Quaife, *Askin Papers*, p. 730, John Askin Jr. to John Askin Sr., 16 Sept. 1812.
170 25 Hull, *Report*, Hull's defence, p. 85.
171 2 Richardson, *Richardson's War*, pp. 49–51; Hull, *Report*, p. 82.
171 8 Lucas, *Journal*, p. 62.
171 31 Cruikshank, *Documents Relating to the Invasion*, p. 144, Brock to Hull, 15 Aug. 1812.
172 18 Ibid., pp. 144–45, Hull to Brock, 15 Aug. 1812.
172 27 Hull, *Report*, pp. 35–36.
172 30 Ibid., p. 150.
173 2 Lossing, *Field-book*, p. 287.
173 9 Ibid.
173 17 Witherell, p. 304.
173 24 Ibid., p. 303.
173 28 Hull, *Report*, p. 89.
173 32 Ibid., pp. 36–37.
173 33 Ibid., p. 89.
174 8 Lossing, *Field-book*, p. 285; Byfield, p. 65.
174 20 Quaife, *War*, p. 108.
174 28 Wood, I: 536.
175 4 Cruikshank, *Documents Relating to the Invasion*, p. 158, Brock to Prevost, 17 Aug. 1812; p. 187, Hull to SW, 26 Aug. 1812; pp. 219–20, Cass to SW, 10 Sept. 1812.
175 13 Wood, I: 536.
176 4 Ibid., p. 550, McCay Diary, 16 Aug. 1812.
176 7 Richardson, *Richardson's War*, p. 55.
176 17 Tupper, p. 260.
176 20 Clarke, p. 455.
176 23 Ibid., p. 456.
176 26 Richardson, *Richardson's War*, p. 55.
177 10 Cruikshank, "General Hull's Invasion," p. 281.
177 21 Hull, *Report*, pp. 90–91; Clarke, p. 450.

Chicago

Queenston Heights

page	line	
204	*28*	Ibid., p. 211.
204	*37*	Ibid., p. 209.
205	*8*	Ibid., p. 247, Solomon Van Rensselaer to his wife, 10 Oct. 1812.
205	*11*	Ibid., p. 207, Lovett to Alexander, 16 Aug. 1812.
205	*18*	Ibid., p. 200, Lovett to Alexander, 23 July 1812.
205	*18*	Ibid., p. 230, Lovett to Alexander, 8 Sept. 1812.
205	*20*	Ibid., p. 229, Lovett to Alexander, 6 Sept. 1812.
205	*38*	Ibid., pp. 202–3, Lovett to Alexander, 29 July 1812.
206	*1*	Ibid., p. 202, Lovett to Alexander, 29 July 1812.
206	*4*	Ibid., p. 200, Lovett to Alexander, 23 July 1812.
206	*9*	Ibid., p. 203, Lovett to Alexander, 29 July 1812.
206	*11*	Ibid., p. 206, Lovett to Alexander, 14 Aug. 1812.
206	*20*	Ibid., p. 196.
206	*29*	Ibid., p. 196, Lovett to Alexander, 20 July 1812.
206	*34*	Ibid., p. 201.
207	*6*	Ibid., p. 208, Lovett to Alexander, 16 Aug. 1812.
207	*17*	Ibid., p. 208, Lovett to Alexander, 16 Aug. 1812.
207	*22*	Ibid., p. 209, Lovett to [Alexander], 17 Aug. 1812.
207	*24*	Ibid., p. 209.
209	*15*	Irwin, p. 149.
209	*17*	Quoted in Irwin, p. 149, Hall to Tompkins, 9 July 1812.
209	*19*	Ibid., p. 149, Brown to Tompkins, 25 June 1812.
209	*21*	Cruikshank, *Documentary History*, III: 223–24, Porter to Tompkins, 30 Aug. 1812.
210	*6*	Bonney, p. 210.
210	*29*	Ibid., pp. 210–11.
211	*2*	Wood, I: 587, Brock to Prevost, 7 Sept. 1812.
211	*3*	Bonney, p. 229, Lovett to Alexander, 6 Sept. 1812.
211	*16*	Wood, I: 598, Evans report, 19 Aug. 1812.
211	*30*	Bonney, pp. 224–25, Solomon Van Rensselaer to his wife, 1 Sept. 1812; p. 228, Harriet Van Rensselaer to her husband, 6 Sept. 1812.
211	*39*	Ibid., p. 211, Solomon Van Rensselaer to his wife, 21 Aug. 1812; p. 227, Solomon Van Rensselaer to Van Vechten, 5 Sept. 1812.
212	*4*	Ibid., p. 247, Solomon Van Rensselaer to his wife, 10 Oct. 1812.
212	*8*	Ibid., p. 231, Solomon Van Rensselaer to Lewis, 11 Sept. 1812.
212	*11*	Ibid.
212	*13*	Ibid., p. 227, Solomon Van Rensselaer to Van Vechten, 5 Sept. 1812.
212	*17*	Ibid., p. 231, Solomon Van Rensselaer to Lewis, 11 Sept. 1812.
212	*22*	Ibid.
212	*30*	Tupper, p. 293.
212	*32*	Ibid.
213	*11*	Ibid., p. 280, Brock to his brothers, 16 Aug. 1812.
213	*22*	Ibid., pp. 110–11, Brock to Savery Brock, 7 Oct. 1811; pp. 112–13, Brock to Irving Brock, 30 Oct. 1811.
213	*24*	Ibid., p. 113, Brock to Irving Brock, 30 Oct. 1811.
213	*33*	Ibid., pp. 284–85, Brock to his brothers, 3 Sept. 1812.
214	*13*	Ibid.
214	*18*	Ibid., p. 286, Brock to his brothers, 3 Sept. 1812.
214	*22*	Ibid., p. 287, Sewell to Brock, 3 Sept. 1812.
214	*24*	Ibid., p. 287, Maitland to Brock, 8 Oct. 1812.
214	*29*	Ibid., p. 285, Powell to Brock, 27 Aug. 1812.
214	*37*	Ibid., p. 284, Brock to his brothers, 3 Sept. 1812.
215	*6*	Ibid., p. 301.
215	*8*	Ibid., p. 285, Brock to his brothers, 3 Sept. 1812.
215	*17*	Ibid., p. 300, Baynes to Brock, 13 Aug. 1812.
215	*19*	Ibid., p. 299.

215 25 Wood, I: 587, Brock to Prevost, 7 Sept. 1812.

215 26 Ibid., pp. 586–87.

215 40 Ibid., p. 587.

216 5 Ibid.

216 22 Cruikshank, *Documentary History*, III: 271–73, Brock to Procter, 17 Sept. 1812; Wood, I: 593, Brock to Prevost, 18 Sept. 1812.

216 27 Wood, I: 593, Brock to Prevost, 18 Sept. 1812.

216 31 Ibid., p. 593; Cruikshank, *Documentary History*, IV: 36–37, Prevost to Bathurst, 5 Oct. 1812.

216 40 Wood, I: 596, Brock to Prevost, 28 Sept. 1812.

217 6 Tupper, p. 316, Brock to Savery Brock, 18 Sept. 1812.

217 25 Ibid., p. 325, Prevost to Brock, 25 Sept. 1812.

217 31 Ibid.

217 38 Ibid., p. 314, Brock to Prevost, 18 Sept. 1812.

218 5 Ibid., pp. 315–16, Brock to Savery Brock, 18 Sept. 1812.

218 10 Ibid., p. 316.

218 16 Wood, I: 588–89, Brock to Prevost, 13 Sept. 1812.

218 18 Tupper, p. 316, Brock to Savery Brock, 18 Sept. 1812.

218 26 PAC, RG 8, vol. 677, p. 131, note signed "Winfield Scott," Nov. 1863.

218 32 Wood, I: 588–89, Brock to Prevost, 18 Sept. 1812.

218 40 Tupper, p. 317, Brock to Savery Brock, 18 Sept. 1812.

219 12 Ibid., pp. 316–17.

219 29 Bonney, p. 221, Lovett to Van Vechten, 28 Aug. 1812.

219 36 Cruikshank, *Documentary History*, III: 227, Stephen Van Rensselaer to Tompkins, 31 Aug. 1812.

220 3 Tompkins, III: 105, Tompkins to Porter, 9 Sept. 1812.

220 23 Cruikshank, *Documentary History*, III: 223–24, Porter to Tompkins, 30 Aug. 1812.

220 27 Bonney, p. 228, Lovett to Alexander, 6 Sept. 1812.

220 30 Ibid., p. 239, Lovett to Van Vechten, 8 Sept. 1812.

221 2 USNA, M221/43/D130, Dearborn to SW, 15 Aug. 1812.

221 6 USNA, M221/43/D154, Dearborn to SW, 22 Aug. 1812.

221 10 USNA, M221/43, Dearborn to SW, 14 Sept. 1812.

221 13 USNA, M221/43/D145, encl. Wadsworth, 26 Aug. 1812 (extract).

221 18 USNA, M221/43/D146, Dearborn to SW, 4 Sept. 1812.

221 21 USNA, M221/43/D158, Dearborn to SW, 8 Sept. 1812.

221 26 USNA, M221/43, Dearborn to SW, 14 Sept. 1812.

221 35 Bonney, p. 231, Solomon Van Rensselaer to Lewis, 11 Sept. 1812.

221 39 Ibid.

222 9 Cruikshank, *Documentary History*, III: 264–65, Stephen Van Rensselaer to Tompkins, 15 Sept. 1812.

222 17 Bonney, p. 233, Stephen Van Rensselaer to Dearborn, 17 Sept. 1812; p. 236, Stephen Van Rensselaer to Tompkins, 17 Sept. 1812.

222 24 Ibid., p. 237, Lovett to Alexander, 22 Sept. 1812; p. 242, Lovett to Alexander, 6 Oct. 1812.

222 30 Ibid., pp. 242–43, Lovett to Alexander, 6 Oct. 1812.

222 32 Ibid., p. 228, Lovett to Alexander, 6 Sept. 1812.

222 38 Ibid., p. 243, Lovett to Alexander, 6 Oct. 1812.

223 1 Cruikshank, *Documentary History*, III: 295–96, Dearborn to Stephen Van Rensselaer, 26 Sept. 1812.

223 7 Ibid., p. 296.

223 12 Ibid.

223 26 Ibid., p. 300, Smyth to Stephen Van Rensselaer, 29 Sept. 1812.

223 29 Van Rensselaer, p. 18.

224 6 Cruikshank, *Documentary History*, IV: 41, Stephen Van Rensselaer to Dearborn, 8 Oct. 1812.

page line
224   14   Ibid.
224   23   Ibid.
224   36   Ibid., p. 42.
224   40   Bonney, p. 242, Stephen Van
           Rensselaer to Smyth, 5 Oct.
           1812.
225   1   Ibid., p. 242, Stephen Van
           Rensselaer to Smyth, 6 Oct.
           1812.
225   4   Cruikshank, *Documentary His-
           tory*, IV: 79, Stephen Van
           Rensselaer to Eustis, 14 Oct.
           1812.
225   5   Severance, p. 218.
225   11   Cruikshank, *Documentary His-
           tory*, IV: 41, Stephen Van
           Rensselaer to Dearborn, 8 Oct.
           1812.
225   31   Cruikshank, *Documentary His-
           tory*, IV: 45, Elliott to SN, 9 Oct.
           1812.
225   37   Roach, p. 132.
226   3   Ibid., pp. 132–33.
226   11   Ibid., p. 134.
226   29   Ibid., pp. 134–35; Cruikshank,
           Documentary History, IV: 52,
           Hall to Stephen Van Rensselaer,
           10 Oct. 1812; p. 54, inquiry on
           loss of Detroit.
227   3   Richardson, *Richardson's War*,
           pp. 50–51.
227   9   Wood, I: 601–3, Brock to
           Prevost, 11 Oct. 1812; Cruik-
           shank, *Documentary History*, IV:
           60–62, quoting *Buffalo Gazette*,
           13 Oct. 1812.
227   17   Cruikshank, *Documentary His-
           tory*, IV: 60–62, quoting *Buffalo
           Gazette*, 13 Oct. 1812; pp. 45–
           47, Elliott to SN, 9 Oct. 1812, 10
           Oct. 1812; Elliott, pp. 51–53.
227   27   Wood, I: 601–3, Brock to
           Prevost, 11 Oct. 1812.
227   32   Ibid.
228   22   Cruikshank, *Documentary His-
           tory*, IV: 80–81, Stephen Van
           Rensselaer to Eustis, 14 Oct.
           1812; Van Rensselaer, pp. 21–23.
228   28   Bonney, p. 249
228   31   Cruikshank, *Documentary His-
           tory*, IV: 60, Fenwick to Stephen
           Van Rensselaer, undated.

page line
228   32   Ibid., p. 81, Stephen Van
           Rensselaer to Eustis, 14 Oct.
           1812.
228   38   Bonney, p. 251, Van Vechten to
           Solomon Van Rensselaer, 12 Oct.
           1812.
228   41   Cruikshank, *Documentary His-
           tory*, IV: 81, Stephen Van Rens-
           selaer to Eustis, 14 Oct. 1812.
229   4   Bonney, p. 271, Lovett to Van
           Vechten, 21 Oct. 1812.
229   14   PAC, MG 24 F70, Thomas
           Evans to ?, 15 Oct. 1812.
232   3   Ibid.
232   9   Scott, pp. 56–57.
232   10   Cruikshank, *Documentary His-
           tory*, IV: 96, Chrystie to
           Cushing, 22 Feb. 1813.
232   11   Ibid., p. 96; p. 81, Stephen Van
           Rensselaer to Eustis, 14 Oct.
           1812.
232   17   Scott, pp. 56–57; Elliott, p. 57;
           Cruikshank, *Documentary His-
           tory*, IV: 96, Chrystie to
           Cushing, 22 Feb. 1813.
232   27   Bonney, p. 279, Lovett to
           Alexander, 4 Nov. 1812; Cruik-
           shank, *Documentary History*, IV:
           93, Col. Meade's statement, 18
           Nov. 1812.
233   12   Bonney, p. 266, Lovett to
           Alexander, 14 Oct. 1812.
233   22   Cruikshank, *Documentary His-
           tory*, IV: 103, [J.B. Robinson] to
           ?, 14 Oct. 1812.
233   33   Stubbs, pp. 24–25.
234   7   Bonney, p. 266, Lovett to
           Alexander, 14 Oct. 1812.
234   17   Cruikshank, *Documentary His-
           tory*, IV: 96–97, Chrystie to
           Cushing, 22 Feb. 1813.
234   20   Van Rensselaer, pp. 28–29.
234   25   Ibid., p. 29.
234   32   Cruikshank, *Documentary His-
           tory*, IV: 98, Chrystie to
           Cushing, 22 Feb. 1813.
234   38   Cruikshank, "Letters of 1812,"
           pp. 45–47, C. Askin to J. Askin,
           14 Oct. 1812.
235   4   Cruikshank, *Documentary His-
           tory*, IV: 98, Chrystie to
           Cushing, 22 Feb. 1813.

page line

270　7　*Niles Register*, 30 Nov. 1811;
　　　　Mason, p. 79.

270　27　Harrison, II: 91, Gibson to
　　　　Hargrove, 20 Aug. 1812.

270　39　Clay, p. 720, Clay to Monroe,
　　　　25 Aug. 1812.

271　2　Cruikshank, "Harrison and
　　　　Procter," p. 130.

271　10　Harrison, II: 99, Harrison to
　　　　SW, 28 Aug. 1812.

271　13　Cleaves, p. 117; Harrison, II:
　　　　98–99, Harrison to SW, 28 Aug.
　　　　1812.

271　15　Winchester, *Historical Details*,
　　　　pp. 9–10; DeWitt, p. 90.

271　16　Ibid.

271　17　Ibid.

271　24　Harrison, II: 100, Harrison to
　　　　SW, 28 Aug. 1812.

271　28　Ibid.; ibid., pp. 103–4, Harrison
　　　　to SW, 29 Aug. 1812.

271　34　Ibid., pp. 103–4.

272　8　Darnell, 1 Sept. 1812.

272　10　Harrison, II: 92, SW to Har-
　　　　rison, 22 Aug. 1812; DeWitt,
　　　　p. 90.

272　16　Harrison, II: 110, Harrison to
　　　　SW, 3 Sept. 1812.

272　27　Cleaves, p. 119.

272　29　Darnell, 5 Sept. 1812.

273　5　Northcutt, p. 170.

273　7　Harrison, II: 143–47, Harrison
　　　　to SW, 21 Sept. 1812.

273　11　Ibid., pp. 143–44.

273　20　Ibid., pp. 143–47.

273　27　DeWitt, p. 401.

273　33　Northcutt, p. 176.

273　38　Ibid.

274　6　Ibid., p. 177.

274　31　Winchester, *Historical Details*,
　　　　pp. 71–72, Eve to Garrard, 22
　　　　Nov. 1814.

274　34　Ibid.; Harrison, II: 136–37, SW
　　　　to Harrison, 17 Sept. 1812.

275　2　Cruikshank, "Harrison and
　　　　Procter," pp. 133–34.

275　4　Ibid.

275　10　Winchester, *Historical Details*,
　　　　p. 13.

275　13　Cruikshank, "Harrison and
　　　　Procter," p. 134; Harrison, II:

page line

　　　　160–61, Harrison to Winchester,
　　　　4 Oct. 1812

275　17　Cruikshank, "Harrison and
　　　　Procter," p. 134.

275　27　Quoted in Cleaves, p. 126.

275　33　Ibid.

275　37　Harrison, II: 136–37, SW to
　　　　Harrison, 17 Sept. 1812.

276　4　Ibid., pp. 156–57, Harrison to
　　　　SW, 27 Sept. 1812.

276　12　Ibid., pp. 167–72, Tupper to
　　　　Harrison, 12 Oct. 1812.

277　6　Darnell, pp. 27–28, 9 Oct. 1812.

277　22　Lossing, *Field-book*, p. 348;
　　　　Cleaves, p. 127.

277　24　Harrison, II: 184, Harrison to
　　　　Eustis, 22 Oct. 1814.

277　28　Ibid., pp. 153–54, Shelby to
　　　　Harrison, 26 Sept. 1812.

277　39　Ibid., pp. 192–93, Shelby to
　　　　Harrison, 1 Nov. 1812.

278　3　Ibid., p. 192.

278　4　Ibid., p. 201, Shelby to Harrison,
　　　　7 Nov. 1812.

278　9　Ibid., p. 177, Harrison to SW,
　　　　13 Oct. 1812.

278　10　Ibid., p. 133, Gibson to
　　　　Hargrove, 12 Sept. 1812.

278　15　Ibid., pp. 124–28, Taylor to
　　　　Harrison, 10 Sept. 1812.

278　25　Ibid., p. 242, Harrison to SW,
　　　　12 Dec. 1812; pp. 182–84, Har-
　　　　rison to SW, 22 Oct. 1812.

278　29　Ibid., p. 241, Harrison to SW,
　　　　12 Dec. 1812.

278　32　Ibid., p. 238, Bodley to Harrison,
　　　　11 Dec. 1812; p. 241, Harrison
　　　　to SW, 12 Dec. 1812.

278　36　Cruikshank, "Harrison and
　　　　Procter," p. 134.

279　9　Harrison, II: 228, Harrison to
　　　　Campbell, 25 Nov. 1812; pp.
　　　　253–65, Campbell to Harrison,
　　　　25 Dec. 1812.

279　15　Ibid., p. 261, Campbell to Harri-
　　　　son, 25 Dec. 1812.

279　19　Ibid., pp. 288–90, General
　　　　Orders, 2 Jan. 1813.

280　8　Ibid., p. 243, Harrison to SW,
　　　　12 Dec. 1812.

280　17　Atherton, p. 19.

page	line	
280	35	Darnell, p. 40.
280	39	Winchester, *Historical Details*, p. 21.
281	12	Darnell, p. 41, 29 Dec. 1812.
281	25	Richardson, *Richardson's War*, p. 140.
281	28	Atherton, p. 27.
281	38	Winchester, *Historical Details*, p. 23.
282	18	Cruikshank, "Harrison and Procter," p. 152.
282	26	Cruikshank, "Harrison and Procter," p. 140.
283	13	Cruikshank, *Documentary History*, III: 272, Brock to Procter, 17 Sept. 1812.
283	32	Chalou, p. 163.
283	37	Cruikshank, "Harrison and Procter," p. 143.
284	6	Ibid., p. 141.
284	14	Cruikshank, *Documentary History*, VI: 242, Black Bird to Claus, 15 July 1813.
284	18	PAC, RG 8, vol. 677, pp. 163–65, Procter to Sheaffe, 30 Oct. 1812.
284	27	PAC, RG 8, vol. 677, pp. 176–77, Elliott to Claus, 28 Oct. 1812.
284	32	PAC, RG 8, vol. 677, p. 181, Elliott to St. George, 11 Nov. 1812; Chalou, pp. 207–8.
284	35	PAC, RG 8, vol. 677, p. 182, Ironside to Claus, 13 Nov. 1812; Chalou, pp. 207–8.
284	37	Wood, II: 5, Procter to Sheaffe, 13 Jan. 1813.
285	6	Cruikshank, "Harrison and Procter," p. 153.
285	20	Harrison, II: 308, Day to Harrison, 12 Jan. 1813.
285	21	Ibid., p. 314, Winchester to Harrison, 17 Jan. 1813.
286	10	Mason, p. 89.
286	29	DeWitt, p. 95; Harrison, II: 336, Harrison to SW, 26 Jan. 1813.
286	31	Harrison, II: 314, Winchester to Harrison, 17 Jan. 1813.
287	2	Lossing, *Field-book*, p. 350.
287	8	Harrison, II: 335, Harrison to SW, 26 Jan. 1813.
287	11	Ibid., p. 336; Cruikshank, "Harrison and Procter," p. 155.
287	13	Cruikshank, "Harrison and Procter," p. 155; Harrison, II: 331–32, Harrison to SW, 18 Jan. 1813.
287	17	Harrison, II: 314, Winchester to Harrison, 17 Jan. 1813; p. 336, Harrison to SW, 26 Jan. 1813.
287	21	Ibid., p. 337, Harrison to SW, 26 Jan. 1813.
287	25	Cleaves, p. 139.
287	28	Harrison, II: 314, Winchester to Harrison, 17 Jan. 1813.
287	38	Darnell, p. 46.
288	19	Quoted in Clift, p. 160, Price to his wife, 16 Jan. 1813.
288	27	Dudley, p. 1.
288	37	Darnell, p. 47.
289	7	Cruikshank, "Harrison and Procter," p. 154.
289	10	Harrison, II: 319, Lewis to Winchester, 20 Jan. 1813.
289	16	"Correspondence," Perkins to Meigs, 28 Jan. 1813.
289	19	Harrison, II: 330, Harrison to Meigs, 24 Jan. 1813.
289	33	Atherton, pp. 40, 42; Darnell, p. 50; Cruikshank, "Harrison and Procter," p. 156; "Correspondence," p. 102, Whittlesey to his wife, 25 Jan. 1813.
290	9	Lossing, *Field-book*, p. 353; DeWitt, p. 98.
290	20	Lossing, *Field-book*, pp. 353–54.
290	29	DeWitt, pp. 98–99.
290	35	Harrison, II: 339, McClanahan to Harrison, 26 Jan. 1813.
290	39	Winchester, *Historical Details*, pp. 32–33.
290	40	Ibid.
291	20	Lossing, *Field-book*, p. 354; Harrison, II: 340, McClanahan to Harrison, 26 Jan. 1813.
291	21	Darnell, pp. 50–51.
291	24	Ibid., p. 51; Lossing, *Field-book*, p. 354.
291	27	Darnell, pp. 51–52.
291	32	Harrison, II: 339, McClanahan to Harrison, 26 Jan. 1813.
291	40	Atherton, p. 42.

page	line	
page	*line*	
311	12	PAC RG 8, vol. 678, pp. 61–63, Procter to Sheaffe, 1 Feb. 1813.
311	17	PAC RG 8, vol. 1170, General Order, 8 Feb. 1813.
311	22	Quaife, *Askin Papers*, p. 570, Richardson to J. Askin, 7 Feb. 1813.
311	26	McAfee, p. 222; Witherell,

page	*line*	
		p. 307; Winchester, *Historical Details*, p. 45.
311	35	McAfee, p. 223.
312	2	Ibid., p. 225.
312	10	Beal, p. 338.

Coda: William Atherton's War

| *318* | 8 | Atherton, pp. 77–146, *passim*. |

Select Bibliography

Unpublished manuscript material

Public Archives of Canada:
RG 8, "C" series *passim*., British Military Records
RG 10, vol. 11, Indian Affairs
CO 42, vols. 143–149 (Lower Canada); vols. 351–354 (Upper Canada). Colonial Office, original correspondence, Secretary of State.
RG 19 E5(a), Department of Finance, War of 1812 Losses, vols. 3728–3768 *passim*.
FO 5, vols. 84–86. Foreign Office, General Correspondence, United States of America, series II.
MG 24 A9 Prevost Papers
MG 24 A57 Sherbrooke Papers
MG 24 B15 Cochran Papers
MG 24 F70 Evans Papers

Library of Congress:
Harrison Papers
Augustus Foster Papers

U.S. National Archives:
RG 107 Records of the office of the Secretary of War
   M6, reel 5, Letters sent by the Secretary of War
   M221, reels 42–49, Letters received by the Secretary of War

Wisconsin Historical Society:
Draper MSS, Tecumseh Papers

Public Archives of Ontario:
Tupper Papers
Hiram Walker Museum Collection

Metropolitan Toronto Public Library:
Alfred Sandham Collection

Published primary sources

Armstrong, John. *Notices of the War of 1812*, 2 vols., vol. I. New York: G. Dearborn, 1836.

Atherton, William. *Narrative of the Suffering & Defeat of the North-western Army under General Winchester....* Frankfort, Ky., 1842.

Beall, William K. "Journal of William K. Beall," *American Historical Review*, vol. 17 (1912).

Bonney, Catharina V.R. *A Legacy of Historical Gleanings....* 2nd ed., vol. I. Albany, N.Y., 1875.

Boylen, J.C. (ed.). "Strategy of Brock Saved Upper Canada: Candid Comments of a U.S. Officer Who Crossed at Queenston," *Ontario History*, vol. 58 (1966).

Brannan, John (ed.). *Official Letters of the Military and Naval Officers of the United States, during the War with Great Britain in the Years 1812, 13, 14, & 15.* Washington: Way and Gideon, 1823.

[Brenton, E.B.] *Some Account of the Public Life of the Late Lieutenant-General Sir George Prevost, Bart., Particularly of His Services in the Canadas....* London: Cadell, 1823.

Byfield, Shadrach. "Narrative," *Magazine of History*, extra no. 11, 1910.

Claus, William. "Diary," *Michigan Pioneer and Historical Collections*, vol. 23, 1895.

"Collections of Papers on File in the Dominion Archives at Ottawa, Canada, Pertaining to Michigan As Found in the Colonial Office Records," *Michigan Pioneer and Historical Collections*, vol. 25, 1896.

"Correspondence Relating to the War of 1812," *Western Reserve Historical Society*, Tract no. 92.

[Clay, Henry.] *The Papers of Henry Clay*, vol. I, edited by James Hopkins. Lexington, Ky.: University of Kentucky Press, 1959.

Coyne, James H. (ed.). "The Talbot Papers," *Royal Society of Canada Transactions*, ser. 3, sect. 2, vols. I and III, 1909.

Crooks, James. "Recollections of the War of 1812," *Women's Canadian Historical Society of Toronto*, Transaction no. 13 (1913/14).

Cruikshank, E.A. (ed.). "Campaigns of 1812–14: Contemporary Narratives...," *Niagara Historical Society Publications*, no. 9 (1902).

———— (ed.). *The Documentary History of the Campaign upon the Niagara Frontier 1812–1814.* 9 vols. Welland: Lundy's Lane Historical Society, 1902–1908.

———— (ed.). *Documents Relating to the Invasion of Canada and the Surrender of Detroit*, Canadian Archives Publications, no. 7. Ottawa: Government Printing Bureau, 1912.

———— (ed.). "Letters of 1812 from the Dominion Archives," *Niagara Historical Society Publications*, no. 23 (n.d.).

———— (ed.). "Some Unpublished Letters of General Brock," *Ontario Historical Society Papers and Records*, vol. 13 (1915).

Darnell, Elias. *A Journal Containing an Accurate and Interesting Account of the Hardships...of...Kentucky Volunteers and Regulars Commanded by General Winchester in the Years 1812–1813....* Philadelphia: Lippincott, Grambo, 1854.

Dobbins, Daniel and Dobbins, William. "The Dobbins Papers," *Buffalo Historical Society Publications*, vol. 8 (1905).

Douglas, John. *Medical Topography of Upper Canada*. London: Burgess and Hill, 1819.

Dudley, Thomas. "Battle and Massacre at Frenchtown, Michigan, January 1813," *Western Reserve Historical Society*, Tract no. 1, 1870.

Edgar, Matilda. *Ten Years of Upper Canada in Peace and War, 1805–1815; Being the Ridout Letters....* Toronto: W. Briggs, 1890.

Foster, Vere (ed.). *The Two Duchesses*. London: Blackie, 1898.

[Harrison, William Henry.] *Messages and Letters*, 2 vols., edited by Logan Esarey. Indiana Historical Collections, vols. 8 and 9. Indianapolis: Indiana Historical Commission, 1922.

Grignon, Augustin. "Seventy-two Years' Recollections of Wisconsin," *State Historical Society of Wisconsin Collections*, vol. 3 (1856).

Hatch, William S. *A Chapter in the History of the War of 1812 in the Northwest....* Cincinnati: Miami Printing & Publishing, 1872.

Heriot, George. *Travels through the Canadas....* London: Richard Phillips, 1807; reprinted, Toronto: Coles, 1971.

Hull, William. *Memoirs of the Campaign of the North Western Army of the United States, A.D. 1812....* Boston: True and Greene, 1824.

[Hull, William.] *Report of the Trial of Brigadier-General William Hull....* New York: Eastburn, Kirk, 1814.

[Jefferson, Thomas.] *The Writings of Thomas Jefferson*, vols. IV and VI, edited by H.A. Washington. New York: Riker, Thorne, 1854.

Kingston Gazette, 1812.

[Kinzie, John.] "John Kinzie's Narrative of the Fort Dearborn Massacre," edited by Mentor L. Williams, *Journal of the Illinois State Historical Society*, vol. 46 (1953).

Klinck, Carl F. (ed.). *Tecumseh: Fact and Fiction in Early Records*. Englewood Cliffs, N.J.: Prentice-Hall, 1961.

Lajeunesse, Ernest J. (ed.). *The Windsor Border Region*. Toronto: University of Toronto Press, 1960.

[Larrabee, Charles.] "Lt. Charles Larrabee's Account of the Battle of Tippecanoe," edited by Florence G. Watts, *Indiana Magazine of History*, vol. 57 (1961).

Loyal and Patriotic Society of Upper Canada. *The Report of the...Society...with an Appendix, and a List of Subscribers and Benefactors*. Montreal: W. Gray, 1817.

[Lucas, Robert.] *The Robert Lucas Journal of the War of 1812 during the Campaign under General William Hull*, edited by John C. Parish. Iowa City: Iowa State Historical Society, 1906.

Mann, James. *Medical Sketches of the Campaigns of 1812, 13, 14*. Dedham, Mass., 1816.

Melish, John. *Travels through the United States of America....* Philadelphia: T. & G. Palmer, 1812.

Montreal Herald, 1812.

Niles Weekly Register, 1811–12.

[Northcutt, William B.] "War of 1812 Diary of William B. Northcutt," edited by G. Glenn Clift, *Register of the Kentucky Historical Society*, April, 1958.

[Norton, John.] *The Journal of Major John Norton*, edited by Carl Klinck and James J. Talman. Toronto: Champlain Society, 1970.

Palmer, T.H. (ed.). *The Historical Register of the United States*, 4 vols., vol. I. Philadelphia: G. Palmer, 1814.

[Pike, Zebulon.] *The Journals of Zebulon Montgomery Pike*, edited by Donald Jackson. Norman, Okla.: University of Oklahoma Press, 1966.

[Powell, William.] "William Powell's Recollections," intro. by Lyman C. Draper, *State Historical Society of Wisconsin Proceedings*, 1912.

Quaife, Milo M. *Chicago and the Old Northwest 1673–1835, A Study of the Evolution of the Northwestern Frontier together with a History of Fort Dearborn*. Chicago: University of Chicago Press, 1913.

——— (ed.). *The John Askin Papers, 1796–1820*, 2 vols., vol. II. Detroit: Detroit Library Commission, 1931.

——— (ed.). *War on the Detroit: The Chronicles of Thomas Verchères de Boucherville, and The Capitulation by an Ohio Volunteer*. Chicago: Lakeside Press, 1940.

Richardson, John. *Eight Years in Canada*. Montreal: H.H. Cunningham, 1847.

[Richardson, John.] *Richardson's War of 1812...*, edited by Alexander C. Casselman. Toronto: Historical Publishing, 1902.

[Richardson, John.] *The Letters Veritas....* Montreal: W. Gray, 1815.

Roach, Isaac. "Journal of Major Isaac Roach, 1812–1824," *Pennsylvania Magazine of History and Biography*, vol. 17 (1893).

Schultz, Christian. *Travels on an Inland Voyage through the States....* New York: I. Riley, 1810.

Scott, Winfield. *Memoirs of Lieut.-General Scott, Written by Himself*, 2 vols., vol. I. New York: Sheldon, 1864.

Severance, Frank H. "The Case of Brig.-Gen. Alexander Smyth, As Shown by His Own Writings...," *Buffalo Historical Society Publications*, vol. 18 (1914).

[Sheaffe, Roger Hale.] "Documents Relating to the War of 1812: the Letterbook of Gen. Sir Roger Hale Sheaffe," *Buffalo Historical Society Publications*, vol. 17 (1913).

Smith, Michael. *A Geographical View of the Province of Upper Canada...*, 3rd. ed. rev. Trenton, N.J.: Moore & Lake, 1813.

Stubbs, Samuel. *A Compendious Account of the Late War, to Which Is Added, The Curious Adventures of Corporal Samuel Stubbs....* Boston: 1817; reprinted, *Magazine of History*, extra no. 152, 1929.

[Tompkins, Daniel D.] *Public Papers of Daniel D. Tompkins...*, 3 vols., edited by Hugh Hastings. Albany: J.B. Lyon, 1898–1902.

Tupper, Ferdinand Brock. *The Life and Correspondence of Major-General Sir Isaac Brock, K.B....*, 2nd ed. rev. London: Simpkin, Marshall, 1847.

United States Congress. *American State Papers: Military Affairs*, vol. I. Washington: Gales and Seaton, 1832.

——— *American State Papers: Indian Affairs*, vol. I. Washington: Gales and Seaton, 1832.

——— *American State Papers: Foreign Relations*, vol. 3. Washington: Gales and Seaton, 1832.

United States Congress, House of Representatives. *Barbarities of the Enemy Exposed in a Report....* Troy, N.Y.: Francis Adancourt, 1813.

Van Horne, James. *Narrative of the Captivity and Sufferings of James Van Horne.* Middlebury, Conn.: 1817.

Van Rensselaer, Solomon. *A Narrative of the Affair of Queenstown, in the War of 1812.* New York: Leavitt, Lord, 1836.

Verchères de Boucherville, Thomas, *see* Quaife, Milo M., *War on the Detroit.*

Walker, Adam. *A Journal of Two Campaigns of the 4th Regiment of U.S. Infantry....* Keene, N.H.: Sentinal Press, 1816.

Weld, Isaac. *Travels through the States of North America and the Provinces of Upper and Lower Canada during the Years 1795, 1796 and 1797,* 3rd. ed. London: 1800.

Whickar, J. Wesley (ed.). "Shabonee's Account of Tippecanoe," *Indiana Magazine of History,* vol. 17 (1921).

Williams, Samuel. "Expedition of Captain Henry Brush with Supplies for General Hull 1812," *Ohio Valley Historical Series,* no. 2 (1870).

[Winchester, James.] *Historical Details Having Relation to the Campaign of the North-Western Army under Generals Harrison and Winchester....* Lexington, Ky.: Worsley and Smith, 1818.

Winchester, James. "Papers and Orderly Book of Brigadier General James Winchester," *Michigan Pioneer and Historical Society Collections,* vol. 31 (1902).

Witherell, B.F. "Reminiscences of the North-west," *State Historical Society of Wisconsin Collections,* vol. 3 (1856).

Wood, William C.H. (ed.). *Select British Documents of the Canadian War of 1812,* Champlain Society, vols. 13–15, 17. Toronto: The Society, 1920–28.

York [Upper Canada] *Gazette,* 1811–12.

Secondary sources

Adams, Henry. *A History of the United States of America during the Administrations of Thomas Jefferson and James Madison.* New York: Charles Scribner's Sons, 1889–91.

Allen, Robert S. "The British Indian Department and the Frontier in North America, 1755–1830," *Canadian Historic Sites: Occasional Papers in Archeology and History,* no. 14 (1975).

Babcock, Louis L. *The War of 1812 on the Niagara Frontier.* Buffalo: Buffalo Historical Society, 1927.

Bailey, John R. *Mackinac, Formerly Michilimackinac.* Lansing, Mich.: 1895.

Bayles, G.H. "Tecumseh and the Bayles Family Tradition," *Register of the Kentucky Historical Society,* October, 1948.

Bayliss, Joseph and Estelle. *Historic St. Joseph Island.* Cedar Rapids, Ia.: Torch Press, 1938.

Beal, Vernon L. "John McDonnell and the Ransoming of American Captives after the River Raisin Massacre, *Michigan History*, vol. 35 (1951).

Beard, Reed. *The Battle of Tippecanoe*, 4th ed. Chicago: Hammond Press, 1911.

Beasley, David R. *The Canadian Don Quixote: The Life and Works of Major John Richardson, Canada's First Novelist*. Erin, Ont.: Porcupine's Quill, 1977.

Beirne, Francis F. *The War of 1812*. New York: Dutton, 1949.

Berger, Carl. *The Sense of Power: Studies in the Ideas of Canadian Imperialism, 1867–1914*. Toronto: University of Toronto Press, 1970.

Bishop, Levi. "The Battle of Brownstown," *Michigan Pioneer and Historical Collections*, vol. 6 (1884).

———— "The Battle of Monguagon," *Michigan Pioneer and Historical Collections*, vol. 6 (1884).

Botsford, David P. "The History of Bois Blanc Island," *Ontario Historical Society Papers and Records*, vol. 47 (1955).

Brett-James, Anthony. *Life in Wellington's Army*. London: Allen and Unwin, 1972.

Brown, Roger Hamilton. *The Republic in Peril: 1812*. New York: Columbia University Press, 1964.

Burt, Alfred L. *The United States, Great Britain, and British North America from the Revolution to the Establishment of Peace after the War of 1812*. New Haven: Yale University Press, 1940.

Caffrey, Kate. *The Twilight's Last Gleaming: The British against America, 1812–1815*. New York: Stein and Day, 1977.

Calder-Marshall, Arthur. *The Two Duchesses*. London: Hutchinson, 1978.

Campbell, Maria. *Revolutionary Services and Civil Life of General William Hull....* New York: D. Appleton, 1848.

Carnochan, Janet. "Sir Isaac Brock," *Niagara Historical Society Publications*, no. 15 (1907).

Chalou, George C. "The Red Pawns Go to War: British-American Indian Relations, 1810–1815." Ph.D. dissertation, University of Indiana, 1971.

Clark, Jerry E. *The Shawnee*. Lexington, Ky.: University Press of Kentucky, 1978.

Clark, S.D. *The Social Development of Canada: An Introductory Study with Select Documents*. Toronto: University of Toronto Press, 1942.

Clarke, James F. "History of the Campaign of 1812, and Surrender of the Post of Detroit," in Maria Campbell, *Revolutionary Services and Civil Life of General William Hull....* New York: D. Appleton, 1848.

Cleary, Francis. "Defence of Essex during the War of 1812," *Ontario Historical Society Papers and Records*, vol. 10 (1913).

Cleaves, Freeman. *Old Tippecanoe: William Henry Harrison and His Time*. New York: Charles Scribner's Sons, 1939; reprinted, New York: Kennikat Press, 1969.

Clift, G. Glenn. *Remember the Raisin! Kentucky and Kentuckians in the Battles and Massacre at Frenchtown, Michigan Territory*. Frankfort, Ky.: Kentucky Historical Society, 1961.

Coffin, William F. *1812: The War, and Its Moral: A Canadian Chronicle*. Montreal: J. Lovell, 1864.

348

Coleman, Christopher. "The Ohio Valley in the Preliminaries of the War of 1812," *Mississippi Valley Historical Review*, vol. 7 (1920).

Coles, Harry L. *The War of 1812*. Chicago: University of Chicago Press, 1965.

Cook, Samuel F. *Mackinaw in History*. Lansing, Mich.: R. Smith, 1895.

Craick, W.A. "The Story of Brock's Monument," unpublished manuscript, Baldwin Room, Metropolitan Toronto Public Library.

Craig, G.M. *Upper Canada: The Formative Years, 1784–1841*. Toronto: McClelland and Stewart, 1963.

Cramer, C.H. "Duncan McArthur: The Military Phase," *Ohio State Archeological and Historical Quarterly*, vol. 46 (1937).

Cruikshank, E.A. *The Battle of Queenston Heights*, 3rd ed. rev. Welland: Tribune, 1904.

———— "The 'Chesapeake' Crisis As It Affected Upper Canada," *Ontario Historical Society Papers and Records*, vol. 24 (1927).

———— "The Contest for the Command of Lake Erie in 1812–13," *Royal Canadian Institute Transactions*, vol. 6 (1899).

———— "The Contest for the Command of Lake Ontario in 1812 and 1813," *Royal Society of Canada Transactions*, ser. 3, sect. 2, vol. 10 (1916).

———— "From Isle aux Noix to Chateauguay," *Royal Society of Canada Transactions*, ser. 3, sect. 2, vol. 7 (1913).

———— "Harrison and Procter: the River Raisin," *Royal Society of Canada Transactions*, ser. 3, sect. 2, vol. 4 (1910).

———— "General Hull's Invasion of Canada in 1812," *Royal Society of Canada Transactions*, ser. 3, sect. 2, vol. 1 (1907).

———— *The Political Adventures of John Henry*. Toronto: Macmillan, 1936.

———— "Robert Dickson, the Indian Trader," *State Historical Society of Wisconsin Collections*, vol. 12 (1892).

Currie, J.G. "The Battle of Queenston Heights," *Niagara Historical Society Publications*, no. 4 (1898).

Dawson, Moses. *A Historical Narrative of the Civil and Military Services of Major-General William H. Harrison....* Cincinnati, 1824.

Dewitt, John H. "General James Winchester, 1752–1826," *Tennessee Historical Magazine*, vol. 1 (1915).

Dictionary of American Biography, 22 vols. New York: Charles Scribner's Sons, 1928–58.

Dictionary of Canadian Biography, vol. IX: *1861–70*. Toronto: University of Toronto Press, 1976.

Dictionary of National Biography, 22 vols. Oxford: Oxford University Press, 1885–1900.

Douglas, R. Alan. "Weapons of the War of 1812," *Michigan History*, vol. 47 (1963).

Drake, Benjamin. *Life of Tecumseh, and of His Brother the Prophet, with a Historical Sketch of the Shawanoe Indians*. Cincinnati: E. Morgan, 1841.

Dunn, C. Frank. "Captain Nathaniel G.S. Hart," *Filson Club Quarterly*, vol. 24 (1950).

Eaton, Clement. *Henry Clay and the Art of American Politics*. Boston: Little, Brown, 1957.

Edgar, Matilda. *General Brock*. Toronto: Morang, 1904.

Egan, Clifford L. "The Origins of the War of 1812: Three Decades of Historical Writing," *Military Affairs*, vol. 38 (1974).

Elliott, Charles W. *Winfield Scott: The Soldier and the Man*. New York: Macmillan, 1937.

Ermatinger, Charles O. *The Talbot Regime, or, The First Half Century of the Talbot Settlement*. St. Thomas: Municipal World, 1904.

Erney, Richard A. "The Public Life of Henry Dearborn." Ph.D. dissertation, Columbia University, 1957.

Farmer, Silas. *The History of Detroit and Michigan....* Detroit: Silas Farmer, 1884.

Farr, Finis. *Chicago: A Personal History of America's Most American City*. New York: Arlington House, 1973.

Forester, C.S. *The Age of Fighting Sail: The Story of the Naval War of 1812*. Garden City, N.Y.: Doubleday, 1956.

Fortescue, Sir John W. *A History of the British Army*, 13 vols., vol. VIII. London: Macmillan, 1917.

Gilpin, Alec. *The War of 1812 in the Old Northwest*. Toronto: Ryerson Press; East Lansing, Mich.: Michigan State University Press, 1958.

Glover, Richard. *Peninsula Preparation: The Reform of the British Army, 1795–1809*. Cambridge: Cambridge University Press, 1963.

Goltz, Charles H. "Tecumseh and the Northwest Indian Confederacy." Ph.D. dissertation, University of Western Ontario, 1973.

Goodman, Warren H. "The Origins of the War of 1812: A Survey of Changing Interpretations," *Mississippi Valley Historical Review*, vol. 28 (1941).

Green, Constance McLaughlin. *Washington*, vol. I, *Village and Capital, 1800–1878*. Princeton: Princeton University Press, 1962.

Green, Thomas Marshall. *Historic Families of Kentucky....* Cincinnati: Robert Clarke, 1889.

Gurd, Norman S. *The Story of Tecumseh*. Toronto: W. Briggs, 1912.

Hacker, Louis M. "Western Land Hunger and the War of 1812...," *Mississippi Valley Historical Review*, vol. 10 (1924).

Hall, Ellery L. "Canadian Annexation Sentiment in Kentucky Prior to the War of 1812," *Register of the Kentucky Historical Society*, October, 1930.

Hamil, Fred Coyne. *Lake Erie Baron*. Toronto: Macmillan, 1955.

Hammack, James W., Jr. *Kentucky and the Second American Revolution: The War of 1812*. Lexington, Ky.: University of Kentucky Press, 1976.

Hare, John S. "Military Punishments in the War of 1812," *Journal of the American Military Institute*, vol. 4 (1940).

Hatzenbuehler, Ronald L. "The War Hawks and the Question of Congressional Leadership in 1812," *Pacific Historical Review*, vol. 45 (1976).

———— "Party Unity and the Decision for War in the House of Representatives, 1812," *William and Mary Quarterly*, 3rd ser., vol. 29 (1972).

Havighurst, Walter. *Three Flags at the Straits: The Forts of Mackinac*. Englewood Cliffs, N.J.: Prentice-Hall, 1966.

Heaton, Herbert. "Non-importation, 1806–1812," *Journal of Economic History*, vol. 1 (1941).

Higginson, T.B. (ed.). *Major Richardson's Major General Sir Isaac Brock and the 41st Regiment*. Burks Falls: Old Rectory Press, 1976.

History of Pike County, Missouri. Des Moines, Ia.: Mills & Co., 1883.

Hitsman, J. Mackay. *The Incredible War of 1812: A Military History*. Toronto: University of Toronto Press, 1965.

———— "Sir George Prevost's Conduct of the Canadian War of 1812," *Canadian Historical Association Report*, 1962.

———— "Spying at Sackets Harbor, 1813," *Inland Seas*, vol. 15 (1959).

Hodge, Frederick W. (ed.). *Handbook of American Indians North of Mexico*, 2 vols. Washington: Smithsonian Institution, Bureau of American Ethnology, Bulletin no. 30, 1906; reprinted, New York: Pageant Books, 1959.

Horsman, Reginald. "British Indian Policy in the Northwest, 1807–1812," *Mississippi Valley Historical Review*, vol. 45 (1958).

———— *The Causes of the War of 1812*. Philadelphia: University of Pennsylvania Press, 1962.

———— *Expansion and American Indian Policy, 1783–1812*. East Lansing, Mich.: Michigan State University Press, 1967.

———— *Matthew Elliott, British Indian Agent*. Detroit: Wayne State University Press, 1964.

———— *The War of 1812*. New York: Knopf, 1969.

———— "Western War Aims, 1811–12," *Indiana Magazine of History*, vol. 53 (1957).

Irving, L. Homfray. *Officers of the British Forces in Canada during the War of 1812–15*. Welland: Tribune Print. for Canadian Military Institute, 1908.

Irwin, Ray. *Daniel D. Tompkins: Governor of New York and Vice President of the United States*. New York: New York Historical Society, 1968.

Jacobs, James R. *The Beginning of the U.S. Army, 1783–1812*. Princeton: Princeton University Press, 1947.

James, William. *A Full and Correct Account of the Military Occurrences of the Late War between Great Britain and the United States of America*, vol. I, London, 1818.

"Jo Daviess of Kentucky," *Harper's New Monthly Magazine*, vol. 21, August, 1860.

Johnston, C.M. "William Claus and John Norton: A Struggle for Power in Old Ontario," *Ontario History*, vol. 57 (1965).

Jones, Robert Leslie. *A History of Agriculture in Ontario, 1613–1880*. Toronto: University of Toronto Press, 1946.

Keegan, John. *The Face of Battle*. London: Jonathan Cape, 1976.

Kellogg, Louise P. "The Capture of Mackinac in 1812," *State Historical Society of Wisconsin Proceedings*, 1912.

Kelton, Dwight H. *Annals of Fort Mackinac*. Detroit: Detroit Free Press, 1888.

Ketchum, William. *An Authentic and Comprehensive History of Buffalo...*, vol. II. Buffalo: Rockwell, Baker & Hill, 1864–65.

Kirby, William. *Annals of Niagara*. Welland: Lundy's Lane Historical Society Publications, 1896.

Kirkland, Joseph. *The Story of Chicago*. Chicago: Dibble, 1892.

Koke, Richard J. "The Britons Who Fought on the Canadian Frontier: Uniforms of the War of 1812," *New York Historical Society Quarterly*, vol. 45 (1961).

Kosche, Ludwig. "Relics of Brock: An Investigation," *Archivaria*, no. 9, Winter 1979–80.

Lamb, W. Kaye. *The Hero of Upper Canada*. Toronto: Rous and Mann, 1962.

Lossing, Benson J. *The Pictorial Field-book of the War of 1812....* New York: Harper and Brothers, 1868.

———— "Hull's Surrender of Detroit," *Potter's American Monthly*, August, 1875.

Lower, Arthur R.M. *Canadians in the Making: A Social History of Canada*. Toronto: Longmans, Green, 1958.

Lucas, Sir Charles P. *The Canadian War of 1812*. Oxford: Clarendon Press, 1906.

McAfee, Robert. *History of the Late War in the Western Country....* Lexington, Ky.: Worsley and Smith, 1816.

Macmillan Dictionary of Canadian Biography, 4th ed., edited by W. Stewart Wallace and W.A. McKay. Toronto: Macmillan, 1978.

Mahan, Alfred T. *Sea Power in Its Relations to the War of 1812*, 2 vols., vol. I. Boston: Little, Brown, 1905.

Mahon, John K. *The War of 1812*. Gainesville: University of Florida Press, 1972.

Marshall, Humphrey. *The History of Kentucky....* Frankfort, Ky.: G.S. Robinson, 1824.

Mason, Philip P. (ed.). *After Tippecanoe: Some Aspects of the War of 1812*. Toronto: Ryerson; East Lansing, Mich.: Michigan State University Press, 1963.

May, George S. *War 1812*. [Lansing?]: Mackinac Island State Park Commission, 1962.

Mayo, Bernard. *Henry Clay, Spokesman of the New West*. Boston: Houghton Mifflin, 1937.

Morgan, Henry J. *Sketches of Celebrated Canadians....* Quebec: Hunter, Rose, 1862.

Morison, Samuel Eliot. *By Land and Sea*. New York: Knopf, 1954.

Muller, H.N. "A 'Traitorous and Diabolic Traffic': The Commerce of the Champlain-Richelieu Corridor during the War of 1812," *Vermont History*, vol. 44 (1976).

———— "Smuggling into Canada: How the Champlain Valley Defied Jefferson's Embargo," *Vermont History*, vol. 38 (1970).

Murray, John M. "John Norton," *Ontario Historical Society Papers and Records*, vol. 37 (1945).

Naylor, Isaac. "The Battle of Tippecanoe," *Indiana Magazine of History*, vol. 2 (1906).

Nursey, Walter R. *The Story of Sir Isaac Brock*, 4th ed. rev. Toronto: McClelland and Stewart, 1923.

Oman, Sir Charles. *Wellington's Army, 1809–1814*. London: Edward and Arnold, 1913.

Pearkes, G.R. "Detroit and Miami," *Canadian Defence Quarterly*, vol. 11 (1934).

Perkins, Bradford. *Castlereagh and Adams: England and the United States, 1812–1823*. Berkeley: University of California Press, 1964.

——— *Prologue to War: England and the United States, 1805–1812*. Berkeley: University of California Press, 1961.

Petersen, Eugene T. *Mackinac Island: Its History in Pictures*. Mackinac Island, Mich.: Mackinac Island State Park Commission, 1973.

Pirtle, Alfred. *The Battle of Tippecanoe*. Louisville: J.P. Morton, 1900.

Porter, Kenneth W. *John Jacob Astor, Businessman*. Cambridge, Mass.: Harvard University Press, 1931.

Pratt, Julius. *Expansionists of 1812*. New York: Macmillan, 1925.

——— "Western Aims in the War of 1812," *Mississippi Valley Historical Review*, vol. 12 (1925).

Quaife, Milo M. "The Story of Brownstown," *Burton Historical Collection Leaflets*, vol. 4 (1926).

Randall, E.O. "Tecumseh the Shawnee Chief," *Ohio Archeological and Historical Society Publications*, vol. 15 (1906).

Read, David B. *Life and Times of Major-General Sir Isaac Brock, K.B.* Toronto: W. Briggs, 1894.

Redway, Jacques W. "General Van Rensselaer and the Niagara Frontier," *New York State Historical Association Proceedings*, vol. 8 (1909).

Richardson, John. *Wau-nan-gee, or the Massacre at Chicago*. New York: H. Long, 1852.

Risjord, Norman K. "1812: Conservatives, War Hawks and the Nation's Honor," *William and Mary Quarterly*, 3rd ser., vol. 18 (1961).

Robinson, Sir Charles W. *Life of Sir John Beverley Robinson, Bart., C.B., D.C.L....* Toronto: Morang, 1904.

Ryerson, Adolphus Egerton. *The Loyalists of America and Their Times, from 1620 to 1816*, 2 vols., 2nd ed. Toronto: W. Briggs, 1880.

Sapio, Victor A. *Pennsylvania and the War of 1812*. Lexington, Ky.: University Press of Kentucky, 1970.

Shortt, Adam. "The Economic Effect of the War of 1812 on Upper Canada," *Ontario Historical Society Papers and Records*, vol. 10 (1913).

——— "Life of the Settler in Western Canada before the War of 1812," Dept. of History and Political and Economic Science, Queen's University, *Bulletin*, no. 12 (1914).

Slocum, Charles E. "The Origin, Description and Service of Fort Winchester," *Ohio Archeological and Historical Society Publications*, vol. 9 (1901).

Smelser, Marshall. "Tecumseh, Harrison and the War of 1812," *Indiana Magazine of History*, vol. 65 (1969).

Stagg, J.C.A. "James Madison and the Malcontents: The Political Origins of the War of 1812," *William and Mary Quarterly*, 3rd ser., vol. 33 (1976).

Stanley, George F.G. "The Indians in the War of 1812," *Canadian Historical Review*, vol. 31 (1950).

——— "The Significance of the Six Nations Participation in the War of 1812," *Ontario History*, vol. 55 (1963).

Steel, Anthony. "More Light on the Chesapeake," *Mariner's Mirror*, vol. 39 (1953).

Taylor, George R. "Agrarian Discontent in the Mississippi Valley Preceding the War of 1812," *Journal of Political Economy*, vol. 39 (1931).

———— "Prices in the Mississippi Valley Preceding the War of 1812," *Journal of Economic and Business History*, vol. 3 (1930).

Tohill, Louis A. "Robert Dickson, Fur Trader on the Upper Mississippi," *North Dakota Historical Quarterly*, vol. 3 (1928).

Tucker, Glenn. *Poltroons and Patriots: A Popular Account of the War of 1812*, 2 vols., vol. I. Indianapolis: Bobbs-Merrill, 1954.

———— *Tecumseh: Vision of Glory*. Indianapolis: Bobbs-Merrill, 1956.

Turner, Wesley B. "The Career of Isaac Brock in Canada." Ph.D. dissertation, University of Toronto, 1961.

Upton, Emory. *The Military Policy of the United States*. Washington: Government Printing Office, 1907.

Van Deusen, John G. "Court Martial of General William Hull," *Michigan History Magazine*, vol. 12 (1928).

———— "Detroit Campaign of General William Hull," *Michigan History Magazine*, vol. 12 (1928).

Vincent, Elizabeth. "Fort St. Joseph: A History." Unpublished manuscript, Parks Canada, Ottawa.

Walden, Keith. "Isaac Brock: Man and Myth; A Study of the Militia of the War of 1812 in Upper Canada." M.A. thesis, Carleton University, Ottawa, 1972.

Widder, Keith R. *Reveille till Taps: Soldier Life at Fort Mackinac, 1780–1895*. N.p.: Mackinac Island State Park Commission, 1972.

Wilkinson-Latham, Robert. *British Artillery on Land and Sea, 1790–1820*. Newton Abott: David and Charles, 1973.

Wilson, Bruce. "The Enterprises of Robert Hamilton." Ph.D. dissertation, University of Toronto, 1978.

Wilson, Samuel M. "Kentucky's Part in the War of 1812," *Register of the Kentucky Historical Society*, vol. 29.

Wiltse, Charles. *John C. Calhoun, Nationalist*. Indianapolis: Bobbs-Merrill, 1944.

Wise, S.F. and Brown, R. Craig. *Canada Views the United States: Nineteenth Century Political Attitudes*. Toronto: Macmillan, 1967.

Woodford, Frank B. *Lewis Cass, the Last Jeffersonian*. 1950. Reprinted New York: Octagon Books, 1973.

Young, James S. *The Washington Community, 1800–1828*. New York: Columbia University Press, 1966.

Zaslow, Morris and Turner, Wesley B. (eds.). *The Defended Border: Upper Canada and the War of 1812*. Toronto: Macmillan, 1964.

Index

icy toward, 39–40, 46–49, 63–66, 312; and captives, 149, 194–96, 317–18; and capture of Detroit, 174
Ironsides, George, 63
Iroquois Indians, 58, 141, 142, 145, 166. *See also* Mohawks
Irvine, 2d Lt. Robert, 226, 294

Jacob, Frederick, 276–77
Jackson, Stonewall, 178
Jarvis, George, 240
Jarvis, Samuel Peters, 181, 237, 249, 251
Java, 309
Jefferson, Thomas, 24, 28, 100; quoted, 15, 40
Jerome, Jean-Baptiste, 300
Jennings, Lt. Jesse, 56–57
Jessamine Blues, 288
Jesup, Maj. Thomas, 173, 178, 179
Johnson, Richard M., 270
Johnson, Samuel (quoted), 37
Jordan, Walter, 193–94
Judy, Capt., 284

Kentuckians, 275, 289, 316, 317; character of, 268–70, 271
Kentucky, 25, 267, 270, 310; volunteers, 70, 267–68, 277, 307
Kingsbury, Col. Jacob, 89
Kingston, 214, 308, 309
Kinzie, John, 193

Lachine, 131–32
Lady Prevost, 212
Lake Champlain, 157, 263, 317; invasion route of, 90, 131
Lake Erie, 117, 225–26, 308; and American strategy, 89–90; Battle of, 316
Lake Ontario, 209, 211, 223, 308, 309
Langdon, Augustus, 173
La Salle, "Jocko," 291
Lauewausika, *see* The Prophet
Lee, Mrs., 195
Leopard, 36
Lett, Benjamin, 253

Lewis, Morgan, 221
Lewis, Lt.-Col. William, 287, 288–89, 291, 296, 297
Lewiston, N.Y., 201, 202, 207, 223, 238
Little Turtle, 43, 48, 191, 192
Long Point, 142
Lower Sandusky, O., 287
Loyal and Patriotic Society of Upper Canada, 313
Lovett, Maj. John, 201, 202, 204–6, 207, 210, 219, 220, 222, 229, 230, 233, 249; described, 206
Lovett, Nancy, 205
Loyalists, 28, 144
Lucas, Robert, 135–36, 137, 138, 146, 150, 152, 169, 184; at Brownstown, 147–48
Lundy's Lane, Battle of, 317

MacArthur, Douglas, 178
McArthur, Col. Duncan, 91, 93–95, 135, 136–37, 150, 151, 163, 169, 170, 172, 177, 183, 187; described, 93
McCay, William, 176
McClanahan, Maj., 296, 299
McCullough, Capt. William, 140, 146, 147, 159
Macdonell, Lt.-Col. John, 171, 180, 181, 238, 241, 246
Macedonian, 309
McGregor, John, 136
Mackinac Island, *see* Michilimackinac
McKee, Alexander, 48–49, 64
McKee, Capt. Sam, 274
McKee, Thomas, 39, 48, 140, 216, 284
McKee's Point, 174
McLean, Lt. Archibald, 241, 254
McLean, Capt. Hector, 48
Madison, Dolley, 88, 91
Madison, Maj. George, 289, 297, 298
Madison, James, 24, 28, 50, 98, 99, 152, 210, 252, 308, 309
Maguaga, 147, 159; Battle of, 160–61, 312

Port Talbot, 164

Porter, Peter B., 86–87, 204–5, 209, 212, 220, 221, 259, 261–62

Potawatomi Indians, 50, 51, 56, 63, 72, 193–94, 273, 284, 292, 296, 302–3, 304, 312, 313, 315–16, 318

Pothier, Toussaint, 108

Powell, William, 105

Powell, William Dummer, 146, 214

Prescott, 203

Presqu'Isle, O., 287

Prevost, Sir George, 82, 84, 90, 109, 131, 151, 187, 251, 283; described, 132, 133; policy of, 132–33, 134, 152, 216–17, 227

Price, Capt. James, 288, 304

Prince Regent, 143, 251

Procter, Lt.-Col. Henry, 144, 161, 165, 166, 170, 182, 184–85, 214, 215, 216; and Indians, 282–83, 284, 312; and Battle of Frenchtown, 292–93, 297, 298, 299; and massacre, 310, 311–12

Prophet, the, 41–42, 43, 62–63, 69–70, 76, 184, 283; land policy of, 42, 52–53, 58; philosophy of, 62

Prophet's Town, Indiana Terr., 52–53, 72, 75

Quebec, 38–39, 82, 187, 311, 316

Queen Charlotte, 173, 175

Queenston (village), 209, 229, 233, 237, 238; attack on, 233–35

Queenston Heights, Battle of, 19, 237, 238–43, 246–50, 253, 254, 312–13

Randolph, Thomas, 74

Ratford, Jenkin, 36–37

Red-haired Man, *see* Dickson, Robert

Rensselaerwyck, 204

Republicans, 46, 96–97, 98, 203, 212

Reynolds, Maj. Ebenezer, 285, 293, 299, 300

Reynolds, Dr. James, 177

Rhea, James, 271–72

Rheaume, Francis, 103

Richard, Father Gabriel, 184–85

Richardson, Capt. James, 245

Richardson, John, 159, 176, 181, 182, 292, 295; and Indians, 159–60

Richardson, Robert, 293, 295

Richardson, Dr. Robert, 311

Ridout, George, 251

River aux Canards, 137–38, 140, 312

River Raisin, 158, 163, 170, 185, 278, 285, 288, 289, 296, 303–4. *See also* Frenchtown

Roach, 2d Lt. Isaac, 225–27

Roberts, Capt. Charles, 106–7, 108–10, 141, 170

Robinson, John Beverley, 144, 181, 233, 238, 249, 254

Robinson, Peter, 183

Rocky River, 293

Rolette, Lt. Frederic, 118–19, 226–27, 293, 294

Rottenburg, Baron Francis de, 134

Roundhead, 127, 182, 296, 297

Rouse's Point, N.Y., 263

Royal George, 222

Royal Navy, 25, 36–37

Ruddell, Stephen, 60

Rupes, Capt., 127, 147

Russia, 309

Ryerson, Lt. George, 184

Sackets Harbor, 202, 211, 221, 223, 307, 308

St. Clair, Gen. Arthur, 48, 191

St. George, Lt.-Col. Thomas Bligh, 121, 124, 125–26, 127–28, 137, 144, 292

St. Joseph's Island, 13, 85, 106

St. Lucia, 132

St. Stephen, N.B., 23

Salina, 141

Sandwich, 23, 24, 124, 125–26, 128

Sandy Creek, 302

Sauk Indians, 63, 76, 122

Scott, Gov. Charles, 267–68, 270, 273

Scott, Dr. John M., 268

Scott, Lt.-Col. Winfield, 218, 225,

Lewis Cass

Stephen Van Rensselaer

James Winchester

Robert Lucas

William Henry Harrison